S P R I N G B O K
RUGBY
AN ILLUSTRATED HISTORY

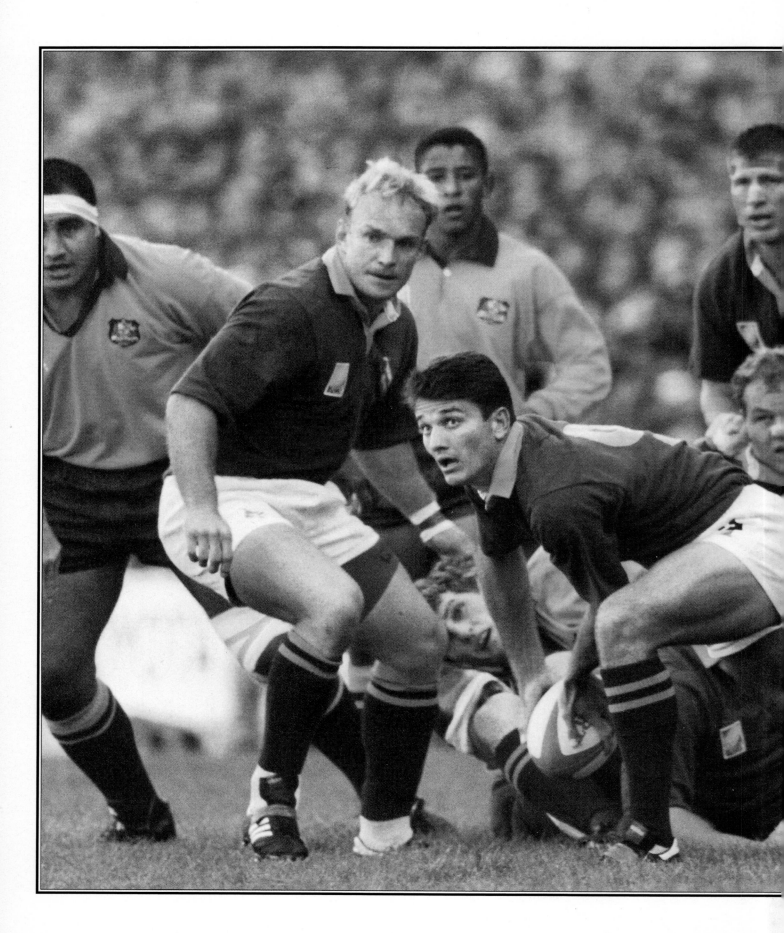

SPRINGBOK
RUGBY
AN ILLUSTRATED HISTORY

*The Proud Story of South African
Rugby from 1891 to the
1995 World Cup*

CHRIS GREYVENSTEIN

New Holland (Publishers) Ltd
London. Cape Town. Sydney. Singapore.

ISBN: 1-85368-749-9

First published by Sable Media (Pty) Ltd 1995
This edition published by
New Holland (Publishers) Ltd
24 Nutford Place, London W1H 6DQ

Editors: Chris Greyvenstein, Hilda Hermann
DTP design: Mandy Moss
Editorial management: Tracey Hawthorne
Production: Ingeborg Jones
Editorial consultants: Paul Dobson, Ian Gault
Statistics: Paul Dobson
Proofreader: Inge du Plessis
Picture research: Inge du Plessis, Tracey Derrick,
Neil Hayward, Duncan Cruickshank
Cover design: Rob House/Arden House Associates

Reproduction: Hirt & Carter (Pty) Ltd, Cape Town
Printed and bound by CTP Book Printers (Pty) Ltd
PO Box 6060 Parow East 7501

DEDICATION

▲▲▲

To Chris Greyvenstein and to all the players who have
represented South Africa in the international arena.

ACKNOWLEDGEMENTS

There are many people who, out of respect for Chris Greyvenstein,
willingly contributed their time and expertise in creating *Springbok Rugby*.
I would like to express my sincere appreciation to everyone concerned.
However, special mention must be made of Paul Dobson, whose wealth of
knowledge was tapped as a consultant and copy writer, and who undertook the
comprehensive task of revising the statistics. Your support was invaluable.
A vital role was played by designer Mandy Moss, whose talents, expertise
and professionalism were pivotal in bringing this book to fruition.
There can be no greater tribute to Chris Greyvenstein than the
Springboks winning the 1995 World Cup and the people of
South Africa being united through rugby.

HILDA HERMANN

FOREWORD

▲▲▲

No words are more appropriate here than those of Dr DH Craven in his foreword to *Springbok Saga* (1992) ...

Two expressions often used are 'His heart is in the right place' or 'He spoke from his heart'. Both convey a world of wisdom and when I think of Chris Greyvenstein these expressions definitely come to mind. Here is a quiet, frequently withdrawn man who indeed 'writes from the heart'. And his heart is the heart of a sportsman and it has revealed itself in the numerous articles and books he has written ...

[This] is a book that proves that this small country of ours has produced a greatness which has impressed the whole world of sport. No matter in which game or sport the true sportsman chooses to express himself; the spirit of sport remains the same and always speaks from the heart.

We do not belong to any particular era; all eras combine to form history and it is history which has the final say. It sifts the events and the people and eventually completes the jigsaw puzzle.

Chris Greyvenstein has kept pace with history and he has left us with a legacy that will live long after him.

How lucky we are in this country that our history has singled out so many personalities and events, giving them greatness and giving the rest of us pride in what is ours.

This history Chris has dug out of the past and presented here ... provides all the youth of our land with the strongest of all foundations on which to build the future.

CONTENTS

▲▲▲

CHAPTER 1

1891

BRITISH ISLES TOUR SOUTH AFRICA

▲▲▲

WE (Bill) Maclagan, captain of the 'rugby missionaries' who came to South Africa in 1891. He predicted a great future for rugby in the country.

The first week of July 1891. President Paul Kruger had a severe cold and decided not to address the *Volksraad*, although he later found it possible to attend a successful test of the new Grusonwerk machine gun in Pretoria. There was an earthquake in San Francisco, so powerful it was reported to have altered the course of the Colorado River, and part of Prussia was hit by a tornado. Civil war raged in Chile, press censorship was instituted in India and a financial crisis caused consternation in Lisbon. But the people of Cape Town had more important things to think about that first week of July 1891. They were busy preparing for the arrival of the first international rugby team ever to tour southern Africa.

▲▲▲

Rugby football had been played in South Africa from at least as early as the 1860s and, with its various offshoots soon withering, the game was firmly established by 1889 when the South African Rugby Board was constituted as the governing body. TB Herold, then honorary secretary of the Western Province Rugby Union, was the first to suggest that a touring team from Britain be invited, and with the

'Playing football on Camp Ground' is the title Otto Landsberg gave this painting he did of a match between Diocesan College (Bishops) and Victoria College in 1888. It is regarded as one of the earliest graphic works depicting rugby in South Africa.

strong support of WV Simkins, his president, contact was made with the England Rugby Football Union. After lengthy negotiations the project was approved. Cecil John Rhodes, then Prime Minister of the Cape Colony, offered to pay any possible financial loss, and in April 1891 it was duly announced that WE (Bill) Maclagan would visit South Africa with a team of 20 players.

A few days before the touring party was to arrive the Western Province Rugby Union organized a trial match to test their strength for the forthcoming games against the visitors. It was a disastrous affair with many of the invited players not showing up because, as the *Cape Times* reported, 'the doubtful aspect of the weather and the arrival of the mail mitigated against a strong muster'.

The game nevertheless helped to establish that Ben Duff and Alf Richards were in fine form, while HH Castens kicked well and, according to the report, 'put in a decent dribble'. A second trial match also failed to satisfy the critics who did not like the 'ill-formed scrums and loose footwork' and much fun was poked at an accidental collision between Japie Louw and Castens.

The *Dunottar Castle* docked in Cape Town after a 16-day trip, a new record for the journey at the time, and a large contingent of officials and supporters were there to welcome Maclagan, Edwin (Daddy) Ash, the manager, and the 20 players who were, incidentally, all from England or Scotland. An entire procession followed the team to the Royal Hotel which was festooned with flowers, ferns and a large 'Welcome to South Africa' sign. Eight members of the side had played international rugby before, while four had represented the South of England and two had played for Oxford. The remaining six were all Cambridge 'Blues'. WG Mitchell, reputed to be the best fullback in Britain at the time, Maclagan, RL Aston, Arthur Rotherham, Paul Clauss, W Wotherspoon, RG (Judy) Macmillan, WE Bromet and Froude Hancock were the best-known players and everybody clamoured to see them.

Shortly after their arrival, Maclagan took his men for a practice to loosen up after the long voyage and the large crowd of spectators was deeply impressed by what they saw. Of Maclagan the *Cape Times* critic wrote: 'He has acquired the acme of perfection as a tackler, can punt with considerable ability and with either foot, and can cover the ground at a splendid pace...'

The big centre from Cambridge, Aston, excited him as much. 'He is the best passing man in England and can take a ball when proffered, from almost any difficult position.' His summing-up was accurate, Aston was to be one of the biggest successes of the tour and for many years was regarded as the best centre to have been seen in South Africa.

The visitors were overwhelmed with hospitality – smoking concerts, dinners, a formal ball at Government House, picnics at Hout Bay and Constantia followed in quick succession – and no wonder that Maclagan was compelled to say in one of his after-dinner speeches: 'We have enjoyed ourselves, perhaps too thoroughly!'

In the meantime the two Cape Town newspapers were drumming up interest for the first match, Cape Town Clubs against the British team, and the *Cape Argus* predicted that the tour would put South African rugby on trial.

The Cape Government Railways advertised that first- and second-class return tickets between Cape Town and Newlands would cost 3/– with admission to the ground included in the price. Fans who wished to see the match in comfort could enter the ground in their landaus for 2/6 a carriage plus 2/– for each occupant. It was announced after the match that the gate takings amounted to £400 with the local Union officials declaring themselves well satisfied with the financial aspects.

ALF RICHARDS

Alfred Renfrew Richards was born in Grahamstown in 1868 and died at the age of only 36, but in his short life he made a valuable contribution to rugby and cricket in South Africa. He played in all three tests against Maclagan's men, captained South Africa in the first test ever to be played at Newlands, and in the 1895/96 season he earned international cricket colours against Lord Hawke's touring side. His brother, Dicky, played cricket for South Africa as early as the 1888/89 season.

THE VERSFELD BROTHERS

The Versfeld brothers played a major role in the early history of South African rugby. This photograph shows John and Charles standing and Marthinus and Loftus seated in front. Marthinus played in all three tests against the 1891 British team and Charles, known as 'Hasie', scored the only try to be notched against the tourists. Loftus Versfeld did much to establish rugby in the Transvaal and the game's headquarters in Pretoria carries his name.

Cape Town Clubs lost 15–1, but considering the touring team's eventual record of 224 points for (plus two more in the unofficial twentieth game against Stellenbosch which the British Isles won 2–0) with only one against, they did well.

According to contemporary reports, 'the play was a treat to watch' with 'the leather often in motion'. Duff, at fullback for the home team, played particularly well and his brave performance ensured his place in all three tests.

To Charles (Hasie) Versfeld belongs the honour of scoring the first-ever points by a South African against an international team. His unconverted try, which in those days counted for a single point, also happened to be the only score achieved against Maclagan's side throughout their 20-match tour of South Africa. His try came after a forward rush and this was how this historic moment in the history of South African rugby was described in the *Cape Times*: 'Versfeld found an opening, put in a grand sprint and scored a try for Cape Town amidst tremendous cheering. Duff took the kick, but failed to announce the major points'.

After the match it was back to another round of dinners and the smoking concerts so popular in those days. It was at one of these functions that Maclagan produced an elaborate gold trophy given to him by Donald Currie, the founder of the Castle Line and later to be knighted, for presentation to the team to give the best performance against them on the tour. Currie, incidentally, made it quite clear at the time that it was to be a floating trophy for annual internal competition and it is therefore incorrect to say that Griqualand West who, at the end of the tour, received the cup, had kindly donated it to the South African Rugby Board. The Kimberley rugby authorities simply carried out the donor's instructions. The cup, which was valued at the time at £40, was displayed at Burmester's shop in Adderley Street and caused a great deal of comment.

Two days after the opening match, Western Province did fairly well against the tourists. Led by Duff and with players like Richards, FH Guthrie, Barry Heatlie, and Castens, who had also refereed the Cape Town Clubs game, in the side, they only lost 0–6. This match took place on a Saturday and on the Monday the British team were in action again at Newlands, beating Cape Colony 14–0. Aston gave an outstanding performance. The youthful Heatlie, destined to become one of the first personalities of South African rugby, did a lot of good work on the defence, but he was criticized for 'being slow to get his head in to push'.

After the first three matches in Cape Town the team left for Kimberley and they soon discovered that the most strenuous part of their tour would be the travelling. The train trip to Kimberley took two nights and a day, and even the presence of the irrepressible Barney Barnato, on his way to fortune as a mining magnate, could not relieve the utter boredom and very real hardship to be endured. On arrival in Kimberley they were shocked to learn that they would be playing on a sun-baked ground with not a blade of grass on it – 'a wretched pavement', one of the players called it. The field was covered with red dust and once a game was in progress, sight of the ball was often lost in the miniature sand storms caused by 30 boots scuffling, kicking and pounding. And, as Clauss wrote later: 'The hard and gritty ground somewhat damped our ardour; it was no joke tackling or being tackled. The writer can testify to that, as a fall against Griqualand West injured his elbow to such an extent that he had to stand down for seven matches...'

Griqualand West gave the tourists a torrid time and lost only by a narrow margin. Maclagan scored a try (one point) and Rotherham a penalty (two points) for the British team to win 3–0. It was on the strength of this performance that Griquas were handed Currie's cup at the end of the tour.

After Kimberley the team trekked to Port Elizabeth where they welcomed the green grass and AA Surtees, who had come out from Cambridge to join them, with almost equal warmth. The tourists ran rampant on the soft turf and scored seven tries against Eastern Province; Aston, Wotherspoon and Thompson each scored two tries and Bromet got the seventh with Rotherham converting all of them to notch a 21–0 victory.

▲▲▲

South Africa entered the international rugby arena on the afternoon of Thursday, 30 July when their first representative side met the British team in Port Elizabeth.

Duff and 'Chubb' Vigne played well for South Africa and Richards was described as the best halfback on the field. Generally the British backs were far more sophisticated, and Aston and Whittaker 'planted tries' with Rotherham converting one to make the final score 4–0 to Britain. All the points were scored in the first half.

After easy wins at Grahamstown and King William's Town the tour nearly terminated in tragedy. The team had to be taken by tugboat from East London harbour to board the *Melrose* outside the breakwater for the trip to Natal. A strong wind blew the tug across the bows of the steamer, but fortunately it was struck only a glancing blow and the players made it on board the ship without further mishap.

In Pietermaritzburg they encountered the first of two opponents who, in the turbulent years to follow, were to gain fame as military leaders. Playing against them for Pietermaritzburg was WEC Tanner, who was to command the South African Forces in Flanders in World War I. A week later, in Johannesburg, Christiaan Beyers was a member of the Transvaal Country team who lost 22–0. Beyers was to become a general in President Kruger's forces in the Anglo-Boer War less than nine years later. While in Natal, incidentally, several members of the touring team made a pilgrimage to Majuba Hill where the British Army suffered devastating defeat against burghers of the Transvaal Republic in 1881.

The team travelled from Natal to the Transvaal in a coach drawn by ten horses, and after two successive wins in Johannesburg, played on a ground so bone-dry and in such a dust storm that 'it was difficult to discern what was going on', the team paid a brief courtesy visit to President Paul Kruger in Pretoria.

After that it was back into two coaches for the first leg of another body-shattering trip to Kimberley. The team, now thoroughly sick of travelling, managed to beat a Cape Colony side and followed it up with a 3–0 victory over South Africa, this time captained by RC (Bob) Snedden, in the second test of the series. It was customary in those days for the rugby

South African players met Maclagan's men for the second time in Kimberley. The South Africans were beaten 0–3.

authorities at the venue where the international was to be played, to make their own selection, and it is not surprising that only Duff, Vigne, Richards, Marthinus Versfeld and Louw played in all three tests. The South Africans did quite well in this match and they at least prevented Maclagan's men from crossing the line. The winning points came from a drop from the mark caught by Mitchell who, according to contemporary reports, 'made a fair catch a yard from the "25" flag and dropped a goal, the ball striking the bar and bouncing over'.

The British team won the third and final test at Newlands, with Castens this time as the referee, but again the South Africans showed further signs that they had blossoming talent. The visitors could only win 4–0, after tries by Aston and Maclagan, with Rotherham converting one, and for long spells they were forced on the defence by 'fast and furious play'.

Richards captained the side and, like Castens, he was also later to play cricket for South Africa. Richards was described as South Africa's 'mainstay' in the final test in 1891, 'working indefatigably, he spoiled the English chances of success time after time ... he had splendid dodgy runs and put in long punts'.

One more match remained for the tourists, a semi-official fixture against Stellenbosch. Their tour had been a tremendous success. They had scored 89 tries, 50 of them converted, four dropgoals, two goals dropped from a mark, one goal placed from a mark, six penalties and one goal dropped from a penalty for a total of 224 points. Against that formidable total South Africa could only offer the solitary point scored by Hasie Versfeld in the first match of the tour.

The South African tally would have looked a little better had it not been for the sheer physical strength of Maclagan. Jimmy Anderson, playing for Transvaal, was already over the line when Maclagan picked him up and carried him, ball and all, back into the field of play. Something similar happened to Marthinus Daneel, who also crossed for Stellenbosch only to be caught by Maclagan and dispossessed in what was then known as a 'maul in goal'. The laws of the time stipulated that other players of either side were not allowed to interfere in such a situation, which was considered a man-to-man clash.

Both Maclagan and his vice-captain Johnny Hammond predicted a glorious future for the game before they departed on the *Garth Castle* from Cape Town on 9 September 1891.

At least one member of the side was to anticipate the major problems touring teams of the future were to encounter in South Africa. 'Hard grounds and hospitality', Clauss, who played so brilliantly on the tour mused in an article written some years later. 'Too many dinners, dances, smokers? Certainly no modern team would dare to indulge in so many festivities, which often lasted far into the night.'

The second test in 1891 took place in Kimberley on a field described as a 'wretched pavement'. This photograph shows a general view of the match which the British team won.

VENUE	SOUTH AFRICA	RESULT	SOUTH AFRICA				BRITISH ISLES			
			T	C	P	D	T	C	P	D
PORT ELIZABETH	LOST	0–4	0	0	0	0	2	1	0	0
KIMBERLEY	LOST	0–3	0	0	0	0	0	0	0	1M
CAPE TOWN	LOST	0–4	0	0	0	0	2	1	0	0
		0–11	0	0	0	0	4	2	0	1M
SERIES: SOUTH AFRICA PLAYED 3; W0, L3, D0										
NB: IN 1891 THE VALUE OF A TRY WAS 1 POINT. M = DROP FROM A MARK: VALUE 3 POINTS.										

HH CASTENS

South Africa's first captain was HH Castens. Very little is known about Herbert Hayton Castens who also holds the unique distinction of being the country's first touring cricket captain, in charge of the 1894 team to visit England. According to *Wisden's* he was born on 23 November 1864 and died in London on 18 October 1929. He was, appropriately enough, educated at Rugby and later at Oxford where he gained his full 'Blue' by playing for his university in the traditional match against Cambridge in 1886 and 1887. He also represented Middlesex and the South of England. Soon after leaving Oxford he must have emigrated to South Africa where he did much to foster rugby in the Western Province. He played for Villagers, but also did a great deal of coaching.

Castens was described as 'a curious, but lovable character' in a letter from a friend to the editor of the *Cape Times* shortly after his brief death notice had appeared. No other details of his personal life could be found, although it is known that he was a good tennis player and 'extremely fond of billiards'.

He was also a fine wicket-keeper who captained his school in at least one of the annual matches against Marlborough, but the match was something of a personal disaster, Castens being dismissed with the first ball in each innings. He failed to get his cricket 'Blue' at Oxford, but did better in South Africa where he scored 165 for Western Province against Eastern Province in the 1890/91 season. Contemporary reports state that he was a good batsman, 'handicapped by nervousness'.

In 1894 Castens took the first South African cricket team to England and although they won 12 out of the 25 matches, including an 11-run victory over the MCC led by the legendary WG Grace, the tour was denied first-class ranking and was a financial flop.

The cost of the tour exceeded £3 000 with the gate receipts totalling only about one-tenth of that amount. The team was stranded in Ireland at one stage, penniless and unable to get back to London. Philanthropists came to their rescue, but generally the tour was 'unhappy', with Castens apparently unable to handle the British newspapermen and not making many friends. His own performances were poor and he averaged only 9,19 for 24 completed innings and twice not out.

Although the South Africans lost their first test, Castens did a lot better as a rugby captain than he did subsequently as skipper of the cricket team.

Herbert Hayton Castens has a special place in the annals of South African rugby. He led his country in the first-ever test to be played on South African soil. He also captained the first South African cricket team to tour the United Kingdom.

CHAPTER 2

1896

BRITISH ISLES TOUR SOUTH AFRICA

▲▲▲

The 'Thatched Tavern', just off Cape Town's Greenmarket Square, was a gathering place for distinguished citizens back in 1896 and it was there that members of the South African Rugby Board met to discuss final arrangements for the arrival of the second British touring team.

WV Simkins presided and announced that Johnny Hammond, vice-captain of the pioneering 1891 side, would be on the *Tartar*, due to dock on 8 July, with a team which would include players from England and Ireland only.

The ship steamed in too late that night for the passengers to disembark and a large group of enthusiasts and officials too eager to wait, promptly chartered the tug *Enterprise* and sailed out to meet the ocean liner. They boarded the ship and spent the night, enjoying breakfast with the ship's captain, his officers and the team before they all streamed down the gangplank to head a procession to the Royal Hotel where the British players were to be quartered.

Word of mouth had already notified the whole of Cape Town that the men to watch were Tommy Crean, a tall Irish forward who was the fastest player in the side, and Louis Magee, also Irish and a stocky halfback.

Hammond and 'Baby' Hancock were the only members of the side who had been here before, but Cuthbert Mullins, a South African studying at Oxford, was obviously also familiar with local conditions. The team was full of interesting players. Walter Carey, the Oxford forward, in later years became the Bishop of Bloemfontein and it was he who coined the Barbarians' motto that 'Rugby Football is a game for gentlemen in all classes, but never for a bad sportsman in any class'. Larry Q Bulger, the Irish wing, laboured under the odd nick-name of 'Fat Cupid', and two of the forwards, Crean and Robert Johnston, were both to be awarded the Victoria Cross, Britain's highest award for bravery in action, during the South African War only a few years after the tour.

The British players, picturesquely described by the *Cape Times* as 'all lengthy specimens of manhood', were taken in landaus to Newlands for the opening match of the tour against Cape Town Clubs, where more than 5 000 spectators had already paid about £600 to see the game.

Barnato was not to be disappointed. It was a thrilling game, the touring team winning 14–9 with most of the second half played in gathering dusk. Both teams scored two tries (worth three points each), but JF Byrne made the difference with two penalties and a conversion.

The newspapers were ecstatic over Crean's performance. They described at length his 'perfection of dribbling, such telling rushes combined with an honest share in the shoulder work and a great ability to keep his feet' but there was

WV Simkins was the second president of the South African Rugby Board (1893–1913). He was also president of the Western Province Cricket Union from 1902 to 1911.

general disappointment over the standard of backplay. It was felt that the tourists had good forwards, but that they could teach South Africans nothing new about halfback and threequarter play.

A team comprising players from Cape Town's suburban clubs gave the tourists a stubborn argument before losing 0–8 in a match marked by Heatlie's 'ponderous kicks' and Castens' controversial performance as referee. Several players were injured and the first signs were there that it was not going to be a tour quite as incident-free as the one of 1891.

The touring team's relaxed attitude to training took its toll when, in their third match in five days, they were held to a scoreless draw by a Western Province team in which JH (Biddy) Anderson gave an outstanding performance. The game was rough and the crowd once booed Carey for being too robust.

Considering the visitors' activities before the match, it is surprising that they were not beaten. At an official lunch at Groote Schuur, the Prime Minister's residence, Crean's only instruction was that no player should have 'more than four tumblers of champagne'! In a return match later in the tour the British team, steering clear of champagne for lunch, took full revenge.

The British forwards, realizing that their backs were not particularly good, perfected a technique of swinging the scrum after an initial heave as the ball was put in, and this manoeuvre gained them all the possession they required. They kept the ball mainly among the forwards and as they also had a way of pulling their opponents into their ranks and virtually holding them captive as the scrum swung, or 'screwed', their tactics proved to be very effective.

Once they left Cape Town the long journeys by train and coach and the 'gravel tracks' they had to play on in up-country centres like Kimberley and

In 1896 a British team toured South Africa and played four tests against the South Africans. The test held in Cape Town was the only one that they lost.

TOMMY CREAN

*Tommy Crean was far and away the star of
the 1896 team. He was described in several
reports as 'exceedingly handsome' and was
officially timed to have done the hundred
yards in just over ten seconds.
Reminiscing about the tour many years
later, Carey wrote about him: 'He was the
most Irish, the most inconsequent, the
most gallant, the most lovable personality
one could imagine, and he made the centre
of the whole tour. Tommy subsequently
won the Victoria Cross at Elandslaagte.
'The story told is that when with the First
Imperial Light Horse Brigade, whilst
attacking the Boer forces, something hit
him and bowled him over. Momentarily
dazed, he yelled: "By ... I'm kilt entoirely!"
However, he got up and found he was not
dead, though badly wounded. But the
insult had roused his Irish blood, and
with a wild yell he led the bayonet charge
and thus received the supreme award
for his bravery.'*

Johannesburg, caused injuries and problems. The trip between Grahamstown and
King William's Town took days by cart with the players doing more pushing than
riding because of the poor roads.

In Queenstown their arrival broke a drought that had threatened to ruin the
farming community, but there were staunch rugby fans who said that the rain
could have stayed away another day without causing much more damage.

Wherever they went the British team discovered that the opposition had
become strong and confident. In Cape Town they had encountered players like
Tommy Hepburn, Anderson, Percy Jones, 'Patats' Cloete and Heatlie. In
Kimberley they met the likes of TA (Theo) Samuels and AW (Bertie) Powell. In the
Transvaal Ferdie Aston, a brother of the England centre who was so brilliant on
the 1891 tour, George St. Leger Devenish and Alf Larard impressed them deeply.

Before their match against Transvaal, the visitors were warned that the Pirates
wing, Jack Orr, was a murderous tackler and had been primed to put a few of them
in hospital. Whether this rumour was true could never be proved because Orr was
so badly injured in the first minutes of the match that he had to be carried off.

▲▲▲

Forward power enabled the British team to beat South Africa 8–0 in the first international match in Port Elizabeth. Crean and his pack dominated the first half in
particular and only the superb defensive work of the halves FR Myburgh and
Guthrie saved South Africa on several occasions. Aston, who captained the local
team, Anderson and Jones counter-attacked well from the few opportunities to
come their way, but the critics roasted the South African forwards and Heatlie,
soon to be a national hero, was called 'worse than useless' by one irate scribe.

▲▲▲

The second test in Johannesburg on 22 August brought South Africa's rugby to
another milestone when, for the first time, points were scored in an international
match. South Africa lost the match 8–17, but the score was not a fair reflection of
the play. The British forwards did not have their usual complete control over
affairs and only Hancock and Crean really outshone their opponents. It was only
Byrne's place-kicking that gave the tourists their winning edge.

Ferdie Aston was the South African captain for the match and there had to be a
last-minute change when wing F Maxwell, from Transvaal, had to withdraw
because of injury. It was decided to replace him with Samuels, the Griqualand
West fullback. Such is fate; Maxwell today is forgotten while Samuels will always
have a special place in South African sport history.

The British team led 5–0 at half-time after Crean had sent Todd over for Byrne
to convert, and it was the irrepressible Crean again who made it 10–0 with a converted try shortly after the resumption. Hancock then used his great strength and
weight to bullock his way through for an unconverted try, but with the score 13–0,
the South Africans suddenly became inspired.

Toski Smith managed to kick the ball forward and Charles Devenish snapped it
up and passed to Aston. The captain ran hard for the line before passing to Forbes
who whipped the ball to Samuels who 'flashing up, received the pass and swerving through the threequarters, raced over grandly; tumultuous cheering, hats
and sticks flying, greeting this great success of the celebrated fullback'.

David (Davie) Cope, the Transvaal fullback destined to die only two years later in a tragic train crash at Mostert's Hoek, near Matjiesfontein, missed the conversion, but he was to get another chance at aiming for the posts not long afterwards.

It was certainly a great day for Samuels. The first man to score points for South Africa, he was also to get the second try ... 'Another brilliant passing movement initiated by George St. Leger Devenish and participated in by Aston, was ended by the latter, after drawing his opponents' threequarters, passing out to Samuels who received the leather at top speed and easily got over for his second try, the applause being deafening and renewed when Cope this time converted.'

And so Samuels got the first two tries ever to be scored by South Africa and Cope became the first player to succeed with a kick. With the score suddenly 13–8 South Africa seemed to have a chance to make more history, but Charles Devenish had to be helped off with a knee injury and the local forwards faded. With a minute to go, Mackie made it 17–8 with a marvellous dropgoal.

▲▲▲

A pigeon-shooting competition was held in Kimberley before the third international and Ireland's JT Magee took the honours, and the stakes, by not missing a single shot. The tourists would more than likely have preferred to settle the test with shotguns rather than on the rock-hard Kimberley field. Some of them had acquired a knack to tackle in such a way that they were likely to fall on top of their opponents, but it was an 'inexact science' at best and most of them nursed festering wounds long after they had said a farewell to Kimberley's dusty patch.

The test was played at a blistering pace with South Africa again making history by holding the lead at half-time in an international. It was Percy Twentyman-Jones, the Western Province centre who later became Judge President of the Cape, who sniped through for a try after AM Beswick and W Cotty had driven the breach. Jones took the conversion kick, but made a hash of it. During the second half, the British had slightly the better of the battle and Byrne converted a try by Mackie and then snapped over a swift drop in the final seconds of the match to give his team a 9–3 victory.

The South African team for the fourth test. Back: PA Scott, HD van Broekhuizen, PJ de Waal, HA Cloete, AM Beswick, TA Samuels. Middle: A Larard, PST Jones, BH Heatlie, CG van Renen, PJ Dormehl. Front: JH Anderson, TE Etlinger, TB Hepburn. Inset: FTD Aston.

▲▲▲

When Heatlie captained the South Africans for the final test in 1896, he decided to supply his team with jerseys from the Old Diocesan Club. It was a happy coincidence that the jerseys were green and that South Africa therefore won her first international wearing what were to become the national colours. Once again the South African team had to make a last-minute change. JJ Wessels was injured and Herman van Broekhuizen replaced him. There was a strong wind blowing across the field, favouring neither team, when Heatlie kicked off with the

sun in his face. From the first blast of referee Richards' whistle it was obvious that the South African forwards were not to be trifled with. Powerful dribbling rushes kept the British on the defence and Richards made them very unhappy by watching their scrummaging tactics closely.

Midway through the first half Larard, Aston, Anderson and Hepburn combined beautifully in a sweeping movement that took the South Africans deep into British territory. Byrne took the ball from the lineout, but was immediately brought down and Anderson took the ball from his hands and ran clear with only fullback Meares to beat. Like the intelligent player he was, Anderson allowed Meares to collar him before he passed to Larard who had an open field to score under the posts. Hepburn converted and South Africa led 5–0. The British team objected violently that it was illegal for Anderson to have taken the ball from Byrne, but Richards had made up his mind and the try was allowed.

Both teams attacked strongly in the second half and the posts at both ends of the field were peppered with abortive dropgoals and penalties. The crowd became more and more excited as the possibility of a South African victory loomed and the spectators were beside themselves with joy when the whistle went and South Africa had won an international match for the first time.

Controversy over Anderson's action which led to Larard's try unfortunately soured the taste of victory. Admitting that the British team had set the precedent with their 'violent dispossessing', the *Cape Times* rugby critic launched a bitter tirade against Anderson: 'It was a pity that the match should have been decided by what was after all a piece of sharp practice. A player less inclined than Anderson to take every advantage he can get whether lawful or unlawful, would have left Byrne in charge of the ball and allowed a scrum to be formed over the place where he was held'.

The writer added, however, that the South Africans had deserved to win. 'It was not a case of a well-whipped team snatching a lucky victory,' he wrote. 'It was apparent from the first ten minutes that the Englishmen had met their match.'

The controversy did not bother the wildly excited supporters who gathered in large numbers outside the dressingrooms, shouting for their heroes. When Heatlie and his team finally appeared he, Jones, Larard and Samuels were carried around the field in triumph.

The reporter who described the scene for the *Cape Times* readers added: 'It was some time before the exhausted players could make their way to the station'. From that it would appear as if Heatlie and his 14 heroes had to rely on public transport to get home after their historic triumph. One would prefer to believe that it was a special train, meant for them alone. They certainly deserved nothing less.

Percy Ross Frames was the first president of the South African Rugby Board (1889–93).

VENUE	SOUTH AFRICA	RESULT	SOUTH AFRICA				BRITISH ISLES			
			T	C	P	D	T	C	P	D
PORT ELIZABETH	LOST	0–8	0	0	0	0	2	1	0	0
JOHANNESBURG	LOST	8–17	2	1	0	0	3	2	0	1
KIMBERLEY	LOST	3–9	1	0	0	0	1	1	0	0
CAPE TOWN	WON	5–0	1	1	0	0	0	0	0	0
		16–34	4	2	0	0	6	4	0	2
SERIES: SOUTH AFRICA PLAYED 4; W1, L3, D0										

BARRY HEATLIE

Barry Heatlie Heatlie was appointed captain of South Africa in the fourth and final test to be played at Newlands on 5 September 1896. And the gods had decreed that this broad-shouldered product of Diocesan College be the first man to lead South Africa to an international victory.

Heatlie was born at Glen Heatlie, in the district of Worcester, on 25 April 1872, one of nine brothers, all of whom were good athletes and sportsmen. And yet he did not play rugby at Diocesan College until he was 17 years old. He captained Bishops for four seasons and was still at the college when he was selected for Western Province at the age of 18, and for South Africa in his twentieth year. In 1894 when he first captained Western Province, he was still at Bishops and this is a record that will surely stand forever. He represented Western Province in 41 matches and was never on the losing side in 26 Currie Cup matches. After leaving college, he was associated with Gardens before joining Villagers, but in 1905 he ran into personal troubles and departed for the Argentine.

In South America, Heatlie joined a huge sugar company of which he was general manager by the time of his retirement in 1924. He had much to do with the establishment of rugby around Buenos Aires and was an active player until he broke three ribs at the age of 49. Heatlie returned to South Africa in 1925 and never lost his love for the game that made him famous. In April 1951, Heatlie was on his way to an Old Diocesan dinner when he was struck down by a car. He never fully recovered from his injuries and died on 19 August of the same year. He is buried in Plumstead cemetery. Known as 'Ox' and 'Fairy' to his contemporaries, Heatlie was a big, robust forward and an intelligent, inspiring leader.

CHAPTER 3

1903

BRITISH ISLES TOUR SOUTH AFRICA

'UNCLE' DOBBIN

*Frederick James Dobbin, nicknamed
'Uncle' for no reason that anyone ever
bothered to record, was born in Bethulie in
1879, but grew up in Kimberley. He was a
short, immensely powerful player in an era
when halfbacks still alternated between
what we now know as the specialized
positions of scrum- and flyhalf. He formed
a splendid partnership with his provincial
teammate Jackie Powell and between them
they evolved an economical, cautious style
which was described by a contemporary
critic as 'cramping threequarter play'.
On the 1906 tour of the United Kingdom,
Dobbin had as his fellow-link the tall,
well-built Dirk Cloete Jackson, a product
of Diocesan College in Cape Town, and
under his good influence he learnt to use
his backs more freely. The result of this
change of attitude was that Dobbin quickly
earned the reputation of being the best
halfback in the world. Jackson generally
adopted what we now know as the flyhalf
role more often than Dobbin, who
preferred to work closer to his forwards.
Both are described in newspaper reports
of the time as 'men of quiet and
unassuming demeanors'.*

Japie Krige and Bob Loubser were obvious choices for the South African teams against Mark Morrison's touring team from Britain in 1903 and they were duly invited to play in the first test in Johannesburg. Krige accepted, but Loubser, then in his twentieth year, declined on the advice of his future father-in-law.

Krige was far from happy with his first taste of international rugby. The South African halfbacks, 'Uncle' Dobbin and Jack Powell, were both from Griqualand West and used to a pattern that did not allow much scope for threequarters. One cannot dismiss Dobbin with undue haste as he was soon to prove himself to be one of the best halfbacks in the world.

The Dobbin of the first test against the third team from the UK to tour South Africa was too much of an individualist for Japie Krige's liking. The centre from Stellenbosch was given no attacking opportunities to speak of and the 10-all draw rather flattered South Africa, who faded badly in the second half. The game was distinguished by a superb try by RT Skrimshire, a centre from Newport, Wales, who received a pass, feinted to drop a goal and, noticing the South Africans hesitate, suddenly put on a burst of electrifying speed to score.

The highlight for South Africa came from Jimmy Sinclair, a Transvaal forward who was the first South African ever to score a century in a match against a touring cricket team (Lord Hawke's 1899 tourists) and who eventually totalled more that 1 000 runs and took 63 wickets in 25 tests. The tall Sinclair is still recognized as one of the greatest hitters cricket has known and in his one and only rugby test he also made his mark when he dribbled the ball for a full 40 yards through a maze of defenders. South Africa's tries were scored by Dobbin and Frew.

Krige bluntly refused to play in the second test at Kimberley because, as he explained to friends, 'Powell and Dobbin won't let me see the ball.' The veteran Springbok forward Barry Heatlie also had to withdraw, to be in Cape Town for the birth of his second son. Another 'casualty' was the Springbok captain, Dr Arthur Frew, a former Scottish international, who handed over the leadership to Jackie Powell. The result of the test was another draw and this time neither side could notch a point.

The third international match, at Newlands on 12 September 1903, stands out as one of the real mileposts in the history of South African rugby. Barry Heatlie was brought back to captain the side and the Western Province Rugby Union who, as the host province had the responsibility of nominating the players, promptly appointed him, Jones and Anderson as the selectors.

All three were from the same school, Bishops, and members of the same club, Villagers, which was a remarkable vote of confidence in the integrity of the three

The British team played against the Orange River Colony at the Rambler's Ground in Bloemfontein. The local side lost 17–16. Back: EE Hill, C Pritchard, J MacDonald, JH Kuhlman, F Smith, AW Barlow, B Holmes. Middle: H Ferguson, R Holmes, JH Mackinlay, RB Barlow, McGuiness. Front: Blyth, HRB Barlow, Buks Maree.

individuals concerned. They promptly replaced Dobbin and Powell with Tommy Hobson, from the Hamiltons club, and Hugh Ferris, a former Ireland international then playing for Transvaal, thereby making sure that Japie Krige would be happy. Loubser and Paddy Carolin joined Krige at centre. The first choice as Krige's partner was Sid Ashley, who had done well in the second test, but unfortunately he was injured a few days before the match and his international career came to an abrupt halt.

There is a story that three selectors were discussing the team in the Café Royal in Cape Town, wondering where they would find big forwards, when John Botha walked in, on holiday from the Transvaal. He played in that third test.

There were other changes at forward as Heatlie came in, as did Alex Reid of Hamiltons (whose brother took part in the 1906/7 tour), Saxon McEwan the former Scottish international, and Jock Anderson of Hamiltons.

Newlands was sodden when the teams took the field, and it was the forwards as much as the skilful backs that gave South Africa victory and a first-ever win in an international series.

There was no score at half-time, but in the second half Joe Barry and Alex Reid managed to score tries. Barry's came after McEwan charged away from a line-out while Tommy Hobson made the break that led to Reid's dashing try, which was converted by 'Fairy' Heatlie.

South Africa would not lose a series for over 50 years after this.

VENUE	SOUTH AFRICA	RESULT	SOUTH AFRICA				BRITISH ISLES			
			T	C	P	D	T	C	P	D
JOHANNESBURG	DRAW	10–10	2	2	0	0	2	2	0	0
KIMBERLEY	DRAW	0–0	0	0	0	0	0	0	0	0
CAPE TOWN	WON	8–0	2	1	0	0	0	0	0	0
		18–10	4	3	0	0	2	2	0	0
SERIES: SOUTH AFRICA PLAYED 3; W1, L0, D2										

The South African team for the third test.
Back: J Anderson, P Roos, W van Reenen,
PO Nel, HH Ferris, J Barry, A Reid,
J Krige. Middle: JA Loubser, WM McEwan,
BH Heatlie, J Botha, C Brown. Front:
T Hobson, HW Carolin. This was the first
South African team to win a test.

SOUTH AFRICAN COLOURS

From a historical point of view, 1903 was the year the game saw the adoption of green as the South African rugby colours. As in 1896 when Heatlie captained South Africa in her first-ever international rugby victory, he again opted for the Diocesan Old Boys jerseys. This club had by then ceased to exist, but the outfitters had some stock left and Heatlie presented his team with these green jerseys with white collars, and black shorts. There were no socks available, but Heatlie had no difficulty in obtaining the consent of the Villagers Club for the South African team to wear their scarlet stockings. Resplendent in these outfits, Heatlie's team played brilliant rugby in atrocious conditions to win the test 8–0, in the process giving South Africa an international 'rubber' for the first time.

Probably influenced by the fact that Heatlie's Bishops colours had been worn in South Africa's two biggest triumphs up till then, the South African Rugby Board, according to their minutes dated 12 September 1906, settled on them as the official national colours.

When Paul Roos led the first-ever Springboks to Britain shortly afterwards, his players wore green jerseys with white collars, a badge showing a jumping Springbok on the left breast, black shorts and dark blue stockings with two white stripes around the calf. Each player also received a green cap with gold trimmings and a Springbok badge.

This was to be the Springbok 'uniform' until 1937 when the shorts became white, the collar the colour of old gold and the socks green. Against the Lions in 1938, the South Africans briefly reverted to black shorts, but permanently settled for white in 1949.

JAPIE KRIGE

Japie Krige was the finest centre threequarter of his era and certainly the first South African rugby player to capture the national imagination. Extremely quick off the mark, Krige was extraordinarily agile and he could weave and dodge his way through the toughest defence. At the height of his powers, he was supremely individualistic and difficult to combine with, but Markötter, his coach at Stellenbosch, solved this problem by building the rest of the backline around the genius, instead of attempting to curb him into conformity.

Krige was an easy man to underestimate. He was quiet and somewhat introverted but on the field he was an autocrat who refused to suffer fools gladly, if at all. Even the feared Markötter could not intimidate him and on the few occasions that he gave him a tongue-lashing, Krige sulkily withdrew from the practice until the coach would show in some way or other that he was sorry about his outburst.

Markötter, who never did play for South Africa because of a knee injury sustained in a cricket match, discovered and forged too many Springboks during his long career for anyone to deny claims that he was possibly the greatest rugby authority of his time, nevertheless had a soft spot for the temperamental 'Witkoppie', as he called him. During Krige's early years at Stellenbosch it irked Markötter that he could not find a wing fast enough to keep up with the centre.

He tried out several partners for Krige, but no-one could quite manage to be on the spot when needed. Players brilliant in their own rights had to suffer the humiliation of having to take up their positions in front of Krige and even then they lacked the pace to be there for the final pass after he had ripped the defence apart.

Like Richard III offering his kingdom for a horse, Markötter would wander around the rugby fields of Stellenbosch looking for a suitable partner for Krige. One afternoon he was again bemoaning his fate when Dietlof Maré, himself later to become a member of the 1906 touring team to Britain, came within earshot.

'All I need is someone with real speed and courage. For the rest he can be the biggest fool in the world,' Markötter was grumbling in his usual gruff manner.

Maré remembered his room-mate, an athlete who only the previous year had beaten Krige at a track meeting. Considering Krige once came a close second to Reggie Walker, later to win an Olympic Gold Medal over 100 yards, this could not have been a mean feat. 'Mark, I think I've got the answer for you,' Maré chipped in. 'His name is Bob Loubser.'

Loubser, short and stocky, was summoned to the ground and from the moment Markötter saw him, he knew that his search was over. Not only was Loubser incredibly fast, but he was a 'born footballer', the highest accolade Markötter ever cared to bestow on anyone. He prepared Loubser himself for his role as Krige's shadow and the two students developed quickly into a superb centre-wing combination, soon to be the best in the world. Between them they scored dozens of brilliant tries and Loubser rapidly developed to the stage where he was every bit as dangerous on the attack as his quicksilver partner.

Anecdotes abound to illustrate Krige's magnificence during a career that spanned the decade 1896–1906. Some of the stories are no doubt apocryphal, but there is more than enough in the official records to understand why Japie Krige has not been forgotten. He was only 17 when he gained provincial colours and it is remarkable that he never played in a losing match for Western Province. More often than not it was only Krige's genius that stood between his team and defeat.

Japie Krige and Bob Loubser were to go down in history as one of the best centre-wing combinations to play for South Africa.

CHAPTER 4

1906/7

SOUTH AFRICA'S FIRST OVERSEAS TOUR

▲▲▲

Paul Roos was chosen in 1906 to lead the first South African rugby team to go overseas, to the United Kingdom. Roos did not take part in the Currie Cup tournament that year and since these matches doubled as trials, he never expected to make the side. National selectors JH Crosby, CV Becker, JD Heddon, A Solomon, CJ van Renen and C Waymouth included him in the team neverthe-less although they did not appoint him as captain – this was a choice left to the team. Roos became captain because the team voted for him and HW (Paddy) Carolin was honoured with the vice-captaincy in the same democratic manner.

John Cecil Carden was appointed team manager and there is no doubt that 'Daddy' (as he became known) made a very solid contribution to the success of the tour. He was a good sprinter who also once held the high-jump championship of the Cape Colony and as a rugby player represented Eastern Province. His 75-yard run against Transvaal in a Currie Cup match in 1899 must count among the great individual feats in the history of the competition. In a subsequent match against Griqualand West an extra back was played just to keep an eye on the dangerous Carden and there is evidence that this ploy eventually led to the four threequarter system in South Africa.

It is obvious from all sources that the 1906 South African team had extremely talented halfbacks. Apart from Carolin, there were also 'Uncle' Dobbin and the almost equally adept Dirk Cloete Jackson, known to all as 'Mary'.

The team was probably even better endowed with threequarters which in-cluded the legendary 'Thin Red Line' from Stellenbosch – Johannes Alexander (Bob) Loubser, Jacob Daniel (Japie) Krige, Henry Alexander (Boy) de Villiers and Antonie Christopher Stegmann. Unfortunately this combination, so devastating for Stellenbosch and Western Province in club and provincial rugby, had only one opportunity of playing together in an international match. Fate decreed this to be the disastrous test against Scotland, where the elements conspired to make slick threequarter attacks impossible.

Krige outplayed the legendary Welshman Gwyn Nicholls on the one and only occasion they were in opposition, and then and there eliminated all lingering doubts that he was indeed the best centre of his time.

Loubser, with 24 brilliant tries in 21 tour games (three in the four official tests), also confirmed his greatness, while Anton Stegmann, with 18 tries in only 16 matches, showed that he was not far behind his more illustrious teammates. 'Boy' de Villiers, later to earn the nickname 'Bekkies' as an auctioneer and the University of Cape Town rugby coach, was the perfect centre partner for the mer-curial Krige. And then, of course, there was Arthur Frederick W Marsberg, born

DIETLOF MARÉ

Dietlof Siegfriedt Maré was an often forgotten personality in the 1906 team. Selected as a halfback, he played in nine matches as a forward and only three times behind the scrum! In the end-of-tour match against France he scored 22 points on his own which, had this been an official test, would still have been a South African record, shared since 1975 by Gerald Bosch. Maré is also the first Afrikaans-speaking South African to write a book on rugby – Hints on Rugby Football.

in Sterkstroom in 1883, and destined to become one of the first in a long line of great players to fill the fullback position for South Africa. Marsberg was a natural athlete who played himself into the 1906 touring team as a wing and fullback understudy for Arthur Burmeister. On the tour Burmeister broke a rib and Marsberg took over. With his fearless defence and speed on the counter-attack he established himself as the best fullback in the world.

Ten members of the 1906 contingent were Maties and of them only Maré (then playing for Transvaal) was not a current member of the club. The other Maties in the side were Roos, Daniel

(Koei) Brink, Henry Daneel, Pietie le Roux and Stevie Joubert. Joubert was selected but could not accept because of his studies. Ironically enough, Burmeister was the man chosen to replace him. When Burmeister was injured, Joubert was prevailed upon to play after all.

Shortly before the touring party's departure, they were split into two sides and each had the opportunity to play the Rest of Western Province at Newlands. They were beaten both times!

Even back in 1906 touring rugby players were a mischievous lot and the SS *Gascon* must have developed a few extra creaks and squeaks with 30 lively young men aboard. One evening not long before the boat was due to arrive at Southampton, a couple of players celebrated a little more thoroughly than usual and in the process hurled all the deck chairs overboard. All but one, that is, and this one they placed in a conspicuous position and labelled it 'JC Carden'. The caper cost the tour management a fair amount, but 'Daddy' Carden's main objection was the obvious attempt to saddle him with the blame!

The team officially became 'Springboks' shortly after their arrival in England and the London newspapers wasted no time in assigning their most imaginative reporters to satisfy public curiosity in the little band of cheerful, handsome and healthy 'Colonials' from darkest Africa. The result was some of the most bizarre articles ever to be written about rugby players from any country.

The team battle cry of *Igamaliyo* was interpreted as something the Springboks shout back home at the exact moment they drive an assegai into a foe's heart. But the Springboks quickly learnt to poke fun at the gullible reporters and there is the story of Paddy Carolin telling the general manager of British Railways that he did not think Eerste River station was quite as big as Clapham Junction!

The Springboks liked using the innocent Afrikaans expletive *allemagtig* and, no doubt with the aid of a tongue-in-cheek South African, one newspaper solemnly interpreted this as 'a Zulu war cry frequently heard in the Karoo desert and other parts of Central Africa'!

On the actual field of play the first of the Springboks to really capture the popular fancy was Marsberg, who proved fearless in the face of the dribbling forward rushes which were such a feature of the game. The Australian AG Hales, a best-selling novelist at the time, really took the Springboks to his heart and covered

The first South African team to tour overseas left Cape Town for Southampton, England, in 1906.

South Africa played the test against Scotland on a waterlogged field. Good ball handling was near impossible and the South Africans eventually lost 6–0.

most of their games on the tour. This is what he told his readers after one of the matches:

'I have to get back to Marsberg, for he made himself pretty near football famous this day. Once, when his goal was in danger, he went for the ball in a lightning-like rush, snapped it up and was off like a wild steer into the bush. He fairly flew for a few yards and then they came at him. He put all his great strength into the task and went through them or over them like wind through a wheatfield ... One got the shoulder, another the outstretched arm and hand; round this one he dodged like a Johannesburg debtor doubling around corners; over the next he bounded, making straight for the English goal line as a wilful woman for the divorce court. "Stop him!" yelled the crowd again. They might as well have yelled to a politician to practice what he preaches or a lawyer not to lie. It was a splendid rush and stamped the player as a crackerjack in any company in any country'.

SOUTH AFRICA vs SCOTLAND

With a magnificent set of backs and lively, though smallish, forwards, the Springboks played excellent rugby leading up to the first of the four tests – against Scotland. They were considered favourites to beat the Scots, but heavy rain and bitterly cold weather gave the home team just the conditions they wanted.

Hampden Park, Glasgow, was already waterlogged on the morning of the match and another deluge a few hours before kick-off had the Scottish team rubbing their hands and saying 'Gran' weether for the drooning of the Boks'. And this is exactly what happened. The bigger home forwards knew all about playing with a heavy wet ball in mud and sludge. While the visitors were trying to handle the treacherous ball and in the process 'working hands and arms like deaf mutes signalling for a fire escape', as the ever-present Hales described it, the Scots launched one dribbling rush after the other.

Marsberg was badly injured after a typically brave effort to stop such a charge and was carried off unconscious. Dietlof Maré had two broken fingers and Brink a damaged ankle after other attempts to stem the tide and eventually it was nothing short of a miracle that South Africa did not lose by a bigger margin than 6–0.

SOUTH AFRICA vs IRELAND

The test against Ireland at Balmoral, Belfast, was played under much better conditions and must have been one of the most exciting international matches in rugby history. The Springboks led 12–3 at half-time and seemed set to score an easy victory, but then a splendid try by wing Basil Maclear led an Irish revival and in the end the tourists had to be content with a narrow 15–12 win.

The scoring began with a penalty by Joubert and then Loubser beat two forwards, as well as Maclear, his opposite number, and GJ Henebrey, the fullback, with a wonderful swerving run for a try to remember. Within minutes he went

Burmeister and Jackson look on as Le Roux prepares for a punt during a practice session on the 1906 tour.

over again after Krige had taken advantage of an Irish mistake. Krige himself scored the next try when he again grabbed a fumbled pass and cork-screwed his way through the defence.

In the second half it was all Ireland. First Parke scored a penalty goal and then came Maclear's amazing effort. He scooped up a ball deep in his own half, stumbled and, off-balance, somehow managed to flounder past several defenders. The only man who could stop the flying Maclear was Joubert, but a terrific hand-off left the Matie sprawling in his wake. Almost immediately afterwards, Ireland drew level when they wheeled the scrum and Sugars went over after an irresistible dribbling charge.

Amid heart-stopping excitement, the Springboks swept back into the attack and Stegmann sped all along the touchline for the winning points. There was some controversy over this as 'Klondike' Raaff, the South African touch-judge, in his delight had hurled his flag skywards and for a moment it looked as if Stegmann had stepped out. But those were the days when even spectators knew how to accept defeat and the Springbok victory was generously applauded.

SOUTH AFRICA vs WALES

Then came the big one, the test against Wales. To beat Wales on their own ground was and always will be one of the toughest jobs any team can tackle. And it was a good Welsh team, that year, with men like Percy Bush and Dicky Owen at halfback, the immortal Gwyn Nicholls, persuaded to wear the red jersey just once more, RT Gabe at centre, and Teddy Morgan and JL Williams on the wing. In front of them this talented array had a typical Welsh pack of forwards; strong, fiery and cunning. Extra spice was added by the prospect of a duel between Nicholls and Krige, both contenders for the title of the world's best centre.

The game took place at Swansea before more than 45 000 Welshmen and a small gathering of South Africans, mainly students from Edinburgh and London.

Stegmann and Le Roux were out because of injury and Marsberg was selected to play on the wing with Joubert at fullback. This was the original plan. In that age of individualism, it is on record that soon after the game started Marsberg took up the fullback position and Joubert had no choice but to go on the wing.

But the Springboks also had a secret weapon they were about to try out on the Welshmen. Earlier in the tour, against Glamorgan and Newport, they had been badly beaten in the scrums because Wales, before any other rugby-playing nation, had by then discovered the value of the loosehead. The Springboks were quick to learn and in the test for the first time, 'Mary' Jackson was to use his throw-in, thereby giving themselves the advantage, whatever happened!

With the Welsh forwards beaten at their own game, the Springbok backs had a good opportunity to emphasize their superiority. Krige outplayed Nicholls on the day. Dobbin, De Villiers, Marsberg, Loubser and Jackson all proved to be better than their illustrious opposite numbers and Raaff was the star of the pack.

Again it was AG Hales who gave the most colourful description of the match: 'He sent "Klondike" Raaff headlong to grass... He caught them in their stride and helped them onward a yard or two, until they thought they were flying machines whizzing around on the whiskers of the world ... when they charged him he filled his lungs with air and met the rush, and they bounced from the shock as a he-goat bounces when he butts at a kopje. They brought him to earth now and again, but when this happened he was always up and off in a moment, whilst the men who tackled him limped as if they had been stopping trains ...

PADDY CAROLIN

Harold W (Paddy) Carolin, vice-captain for the 1906/7 tour, was a magnificent all-round sportsman who won the Jameson Cup as victor ludorum for four years running while at Cape Town's Diocesan College. He captained his school in cricket as well as rugby and was often on the fringe of selection to the Springbok cricket teams of his time. From all accounts he was a good bowler and an attacking left-hand batsman. After leaving school he joined Villagers, a club he captained at the time of his selection for the touring party, and later in his career he and another great Springbok of a slightly later era, Fred Luyt, helped to establish Moorreesburg as a rugby force in the Boland. Carolin was selected as a halfback and here some explanation is called for. In those early days flyhalf and scrumhalf positions were interchangeable and covered by the overall definition of halfback. As with the forward positions it was very much a matter of who got there first when it came to fulfilling the various functions.

'The Welshmen were determined to feed their old champion Nicholls; but either De Villiers or Krige was eternally in the way. Krige was watching the champion as a brood hen watches a weasel and his speed was too great for the Welsh wonder ... then Morgan came into evidence. He made a bold and dashing run, beating first one man and then another until nothing lay between him and the coveted try – but Marsberg.

'The Celtic crowd shrieked out wild cheers as their man strode boldly onward. Marsberg did not appear to be the least bit disturbed as Morgan came sweeping down on him ... Fixing his eye on the man, the great African player strode steadily to meet him as he came. Marsberg looked wonderfully slow in comparison with the fine runner who was making a bee line for the spot that would give him the long looked-for try ... Suddenly Marsberg spread out his long, lean arms; he dropped his chin on his chest and shot forward like a South Sea Islander diving from a schooner's bows ... One long brown hand closed on Morgan's breast bone, the other on the point of his shoulder. And then with a mighty heave Morgan was sent headlong to earth, and with a cry that rang to the cloud-clapped skies, the Welshmen mourned their idol's fall ...

'A little later Dobbin made the Celts wonder who had told them that their men were the trickiest players alive. At this stage in fact Dobbin and Jackson were as full of tricks as a zoo full of monkeys with Caruso's pet thrown in ... Loubser sent to Krige; the latter threw out to De Villiers who in masterly fashion drew the defence, and whipping the ball to Joubert, gave that artist a clear field, and he was over the line like a nigger into a neighbour's mealie patch.

'Fired by this success, in spite of a failure to convert, the Springboks were down on the Celtic stronghold in a moment. Joubert especially put in some fine work. He went through the enemy's line like a rat through a drain pipe, and could not be captured. But it was Loubser who got over the Welsh line, scudding like a hunted hare. Half time showed two tries to nil, and Wales was beaten. They played pluckily in the second half, but their wonderful system that had carried them so often to victory had broken down badly ... The fight became hot and the tackling very hard, and then Raaff went over the Celts' line for the third time, Joubert converted and scoring for the day ceased. When the fateful whistle sounded 40 000 Celts walked away in gloomy silence, wondering what in the name of all the saints was going to happen to "The Land of Our Fathers". As a general rule they sing this and wonder what is going to happen to the other folk'.

Thus the description by the famous novelist of the Springboks' finest all-round performance of the tour. The Welshmen themselves said afterwards that Marsberg and Dobbin were the best players in their respective positions in the world. But Krige, De Villiers and Jackson were also consistently brilliant throughout the match. It was, incidentally, to be the legendary Krige's last test match. He had to undergo an appendicitis operation shortly afterwards and did not play in any of the remaining matches.

SOUTH AFRICA vs ENGLAND

The final test, against England at Crystal Palace, was played in appalling conditions and ended in a hard-fought but unspectacular draw. It was a game for forwards only, played in mud and slush and the threequarters 'shivered like stray dogs at a street corner', according to one of the after-match reports. Once Marsberg went down to stop a forward rush and when he rose, a reporter wrote, 'he looked like a garden plot up for auction'!

Springboks in action on foreign soil for the first time. Duggie Morkel has just taken the ball in a lineout against East Midlands at Northampton, the first match of the 1906/7 tour. Sommy Morkel is just behind Duggie and the two Springboks turning around to help are Brink and Roos.

The Springboks' try was scored by Billy Millar. 'It came out of a wild mix-up,' Hales wrote. 'First one man and then another got the ball, ran a yard and flopped face downwards, where each in turn was walked on, sat on, flopped on by friend and foe.'

After half-time England equalized through a grand individualistic try by Freddie Brooks, a Rhodesian who actually competed in the 1906 Currie Cup competition, but could not be selected for South Africa because of the residential rule. The Springboks were severely handicapped by an injury to 'Sommy' Morkel in the second half and it was generally agreed that, but for this, the touring team would have won.

▲▲▲

In the final match of the tour the Springboks were thrashed 17–0 by an inspired Cardiff team on a sopping wet field and in a howling gale. The South Africans just could not adjust themselves to the conditions and they were outplayed in all facets. Krige was not there to keep a watchful eye on Nicholls who shrewdly guided his team. The great adventure was over. Roos and his team had established South Africa in the international rugby arena. The foundations were laid for future generations of Springboks to build on.

▲▲▲

Paul Roos, holding the ball, leads his team in a practice during the tour. From left to right are Bill Neill, Klondike Raaff, Cocky Brooks and Bert Reid.

Before their departure for home, the Springboks asked the rugby authorities for permission to play one match in France. This turned out to be a strange affair. The Springboks beat a scratch side 55–6 (with Maré notching 22 on his own), and scoring 13 tries. The game offered more humour than excitement, with the Frenchmen often politely applauding their opponents.

At the banquet afterwards, Roos was at his best when he admonished the Frenchmen for not trying hard enough and giving them a motto in the process: 'Remember in rugby it is a matter of all for the team, not each one for himself.'

South African rugby owes Paul Roos a very big debt, but it would appear as if France should remember him too.

Venue	South Africa	Result	South Africa				British Isles			
			T	C	P	D	T	C	P	D
Scotland (Glasgow)	Lost	0–6	0	0	0	0	2	0	0	0
Ireland (Belfast)	Won	15–12	4	0	1	0	3	0	1	0
Wales (Swansea)	Won	11–0	3	1	0	0	0	0	0	0
England (Crystal Palace)	Draw	3–3	1	0	0	0	1	0	0	0

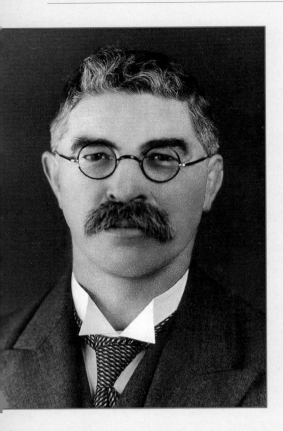

Paul Roos, captain of the first South African team to undertake an overseas tour. He told reporters to call his men 'Springbokken'.

PAUL ROOS

Standing on the touchline next to his father, ten-year-old Paul Roos saw Maclagan's rugby missionaries beat Stellenbosch in the final match of their 1891 tour. Until then Roos' sporting activities had been confined to watching his father on the cricket field, wearing the inevitable bowler and, as he would recall in later years, often dropping both hat and ball when going for a catch.

Now a new world opened for him – the world of rugby football. He was to excel as a player and later as an administrator and would become a source of inspiration to more that one generation of South Africans.

Above all, Roos held the unique distinction of having led the first South African rugby team on an overseas tour and it was he who told reporters that his players should be called 'De Springbokken' or 'Springboks'.

He was a forward, big and strong enough for his era, but rather small and light by today's standards. He had superb leadership qualities and his impeccable character and innate charm earned him the respect and affection of his players as well as his opponents. To the end of his days he maintained that a man's motto should be 'Let the stumbling blocks be your stepping stones', and in his own life he added to that utter devotion to duty and principles.

In those days all Currie Cup matches took place at a central tournament and in 1904 it was to be in East London. Roos felt that he could not spare so much time from his duties as a schoolmaster and declined the invitation to join the Western Province team.

When 'Fairy' Heatlie, captaining the Western Province team, realized the strength of the Griqualand West and Transvaal teams he urgently wired Jan Hofmeyr, the famous statesman and newspaper editor of the Cape Colony, to persuade Roos to change his mind. Hofmeyr, the well-loved 'Onze Jan', did not feel up to the task and passed the buck to the Stellenbosch University authorities. A Professor Malherbe called Roos into his study, showed him the telegram and asked him if he would reconsider.

'I cannot go because I have my duties here,' Roos informed him staunchly.

'It appears to me that your team also require you and that is also a duty,' the professor sparred back.

Checkmated and no doubt wanting to play anyway, Roos pointed out that his going to East London would entail travelling on no less than two Sundays and would therefore not really be in line with his strong religious beliefs.

'We can serve God on the train, too,' the professor countered and Roos, knowing when he was beaten, packed his bags. There is a happy ending to the story. Roos played a major role in beating both Griquas and Transvaal, and Western Province brought home the Currie Cup.

His reluctance to travel on a Sunday was genuine and he avoided it whenever he could. When he was a schoolmaster in Pietersburg for a brief period, he cycled 70 miles to Pretoria every Saturday to play rugby. Immediately after the game he would start the arduous journey home to make sure that he would not desecrate the Sabbath for the sake of personal enjoyment.

As a teacher he was a strict disciplinarian who never spared the rod, but those who knew him remember him for his fierce interest in the welfare – material and spiritual – present and future, of each and every pupil. He was appallingly absent-minded, invariably late for everything, and to have been a passenger in a car driven by him was, according to one who had the doubtful pleasure, 'tantamount to a peep into the Valley of Death'!

It was said that he held all records for speeding between Stellenbosch and surrounding towns. He never hesitated to lend his car to a student, but always with this advice: 'Now look, my boy, you have just as much a right to be on the road as any other driver, but just be careful of trains.'

He was constitutionally unable to arrive on time for any appointment and this used to drive his teammates to distraction. People and their problems mattered far more to him than clocks or watches. Once, when captain of Stellenbosch, his team had already gathered at the station for the trip to Cape Town where they were to play at Newlands and still there was no sign of 'Polla', as he was usually called. Finally it was time for the train to depart, but fortunately the station master was a keen rugby fan and he gave instructions to the machinist to wait. Another 15 minutes ticked by with everybody growing more frantic with every passing second. Just when it looked as if even the co-operative station master had run out of patience, Roos came cycling up at a furious pace. Hurling his bike against the waiting-room wall, he rushed into the compartment to join his team, sagged back into the seat and panted 'Wow! Just made it in time, eh!'

Near the end of his life Roos entered the political arena, but his one and only election campaign was conducted with so much sincerity, humanity and humour that his popularity never suffered and this during a period in our history when bitterness was rife and the political divisions sharp.

As a back-bencher in Parliament, he was a most impressive sight; big and powerful in his conservative suit with a stiff and formal wing collar, his hair thick and grey and his drooping soup-strainer moustache a bristling symbol of his individuality. At first the other Members delighted in teasing the old Springbok and headmaster, but he had too much natural dignity and common sense to rise to the obvious bait and soon he was listened to in silence.

It is rather indicative of the man's character that his last speech in Parliament dealt with helping the underprivileged. Political correspondents who knew him well wrote at the time that the speech was not delivered in his usual flamboyant style, that the big, dark eyes so startling under the bushy eyebrows were, as usual, in eloquent support of his words but that his emphasizing gesticulations were conspicuously missing. Only a few hours after completing his appeal for better housing for the poor, Paul Roos died.

Paul Roos (centre) and the Springboks in action against the Welsh. The game was held in Swansea and the South Africans emerged as victors by winning 11–0.

CHAPTER 5

1910

BRITISH ISLES TOUR SOUTH AFRICA

South Africa won the third test against the British side, held at Newlands. The final score was 21–5. Percy Allport (back row, second left) scored the first ever test try by a South African fullback.

Dr Smyth's British team was not a great side, but among its members were some outstanding individuals and from them further lessons were learnt to make the South Africans the unbeatable players they were soon to become. During this tour the duties of the forwards became more defined; especially that it must be their main function to obtain clean possession for the backs to exploit. It was also becoming more obvious that the two halfback positions should be filled by specialists and the traditional interchanging between the two became less frequent.

In JP (Ponty) Jones the British team had a brilliant centre and Stanley Williams was a fullback who could hold his own in any company. Harry Jarman, Phil Waller, (Billy) Tyrrell, R Stevenson and J Webb were outstanding forwards and in Charles Henry (Cherry) Pillman the tourists had a true rugby genius of the era.

Pillman was the game's first real loose-forward. He could handle the ball as surely as any threequarter, could kick brilliantly and to add to it all he was fast and had an instinctive flair for doing the right thing at the right time. In later years he became a distinguished and highly respectable member of the London Stock Exchange, but back in 1910 he was the scourge of the Springbok threequarters; the man who really laid the foundations for the roving forward style of play adopted eagerly by the South Africans. Phil Waller also had a lesson to teach the South Africans as he specialized in hooking the ball from the scrums, opening Springbok eyes to another valuable facet of the game.

A new generation of brilliant young players blended with a sprinkling of veterans to make Springbok rugby particularly strong at the time. WH (Boy) Morkel and DFT (Duggie) Morkel carried on the remarkable tradition started in 1903, when Andrew became the first of no less than ten members of this family to earn Springbok colours over the next 25 years.

Freddie and Richard Luyt also appeared on the scene and CHL Hahn had a brief spell of glory as a hard-running wing. Richard Luyt had a perfect centre partner in Dirkie de Villiers (a Cambridge 'Blue'), while Freddie Luyt was partnered at halfback in the first test by the experienced 'Uncle' Dobbin, but combined with his Western Province teammate Clive van Ryneveld (whose son many years later played rugby for England and captained South Africa at cricket) in the final two international matches of the tour.

Gideon Roos, younger brother of Paul, and PA Marsberg, younger brother of Arthur, gained their Springbok colours in 1910. The selection of Harry Walker for all three tests had added significance when his brother Alf played for South Africa in 1921 and 1924 and Alf's son Harry Newton gained his colours 43 years later.

Billy Millar would almost certainly have captained the Springboks in the first test in Johannesburg, but he could not obtain leave from his job, so the honour went to Duggie Morkel, who must be regarded as the first in a long line of superb Springbok placekickers.

Transvaal's Hahn made an outstanding international debut in the test and his powerful running and the incisiveness of Freddie Luyt, De Villiers' clever work at centre, and a real skipper's game by Duggie Morkel managed to tip the scales 14–10 in favour of the Springboks.

Millar took over the captaincy for the second test in Port Elizabeth and again the Springboks started off well with a try by wing Wally Mills, beautifully engineered between Dick Luyt, in Springbok colours for the first time, and De Villiers. But in the second half, Pillman, playing at flyhalf of all places, took over completely.

One report described Pillman as 'playing a game invented by himself'. Although officially down to play at halfback, Pillman actually bobbed up from centre to wing to fullback, wherever the need arose and he also led one forward rush after the other. His tackling demoralized the Springboks and he initiated both of his team's tries, one with a perfectly placed tactical kick, and he also put over a difficult conversion.

Duggie Morkel, a member of South African rugby's most famous family and the first great Springbok placekicker. From 1906 to 1913 he played in nine tests and must count among the most spectacular kickers ever to wear the Springbok jersey.

'Cherry' Pillman, the versatile English forward and one of the most outstanding personalities of the 1910 series.

As Billy Millar wrote years later: 'My memories of this game are all dwarfed by Pillman's brilliance. I confidently assert that if ever a man can have been said to have won an international match through his own unorthodox and lone-handed efforts it can be said of the inspired black-haired Pillman I played against on the Crusaders' ground on 27 August 1910 ...'

With the series poised at one win each, the third test, which was to be held at Newlands, created more public interest than any other rugby match up to then, and for the first time reports in the old newspapers refer to the 'perpetual Newlands roar'.

Smyth's team lost their star fullback Stanley Williams within the first ten minutes and they never really stood much of a chance after that set-back. Fred Luyt was in scintillating form and with Van Ryneveld and his forwards giving him more than enough possession, he launched one attack after the other. Here must have been a magnificent player with razor-sharp reflexes and a keen rugby brain. He opened up the defence for the first Springbok try, for instance, by feinting as if to pass to his backs and then suddenly streaking through a gap before switching direction again towards his forwards and sending Gideon Roos over for Duggie Morkel to convert with a beautiful kick from a difficult angle. This match saw the international debut of 'Boy' Morkel, regarded by many old-timers as the finest all-round forward the world has known.

The highlight of the match was undoubtedly a try scored by Percy Allport, the Springbok fullback in the last two tests of this series. Allport, who played centre as often as fullback for Villagers and Western Province, caught the ball from an abortive kick somewhere near the halfway line. He was about to boot for touch when he realized that he had half of the British pack on top of him. He dodged and swerved past them and suddenly saw that he had a clear field ahead. With a terrific burst of speed he just managed to beat the covering threequarters to fling himself over the line.

In reports of this test the first evidence can be found that tempers also flared in those days. This is how Millar described it:

'Then in the excitement of the moment, and when blood was rather heated from the virile nature of the play, a few of us lost our heads. Punishment had to be exacted, and a penalty goal was added to Britain's debit balance ...'

The kick failed, but Britain did get a consolation try by Jack Spoors, following a break by Jones, late in the second half. By that time the Springboks were already in an unassailable position, however, and the final score was 21–5. Spoors, incidentally, scored a try in each of the three tests, the only player so far to have notched a try in each test of a series against South Africa. No Springbok has yet achieved this feat.

Venue	South Africa	Result	South Africa				British Isles			
			T	C	P	D	T	C	P	D
Johannesburg	Won	14–10	4	1	0	0	2	0	0	1
Port Elizabeth	Lost	3–8	1	0	0	0	2	1	0	0
Cape Town	Won	21–5	4	3	1	0	1	1	0	0
		38–23	9	4	1	0	5	2	0	1
Series: South Africa played 3; W2, L1, D0										

BILLY MILLAR

South African rugby history is studded with examples of players conquering adversity and handicaps to play for their country. William Alexander (Billy) Millar is the only one, however, who had to overcome the effects of a serious war wound before he could even begin his rugby career.

Born at Bedford in the Eastern Cape on 6 November 1883, Millar was introduced to the game of rugby at the South African College School, but at the age of 17 his restless spirit made him exchange the rugby ball for the rifle when the South African War broke out late in 1899. He joined a cycle corps whose job it was presumably to deliver dispatches, but Billy was soon involved in heavy fighting. He received a severe wound in the left shoulder and after spending many months in hospital was discharged with a medical certificate declaring that he would probably never again have the full use of his left arm and could also be an invalid for the rest of his life.

He managed to obtain a job with the Railway Department, but found that he had such constant pain from his injury that he could hardly do the work required. A doctor advised him to get as much exercise as possible and on this recommendation he immediately took up long-distance walking, mountaineering and boxing with an almost fanatical dedication.

It must have been largely a case of the mind overruling the matter because in spite of almost instant success in every sport he tackled, Millar never really did recover fully from his wound.

A civil service job had little appeal for Millar, a man of action if ever there was one. He went on prospecting expeditions to Rhodesia and South West Africa before returning to Cape Town where he again concentrated on boxing.

Professional fighters like Jack Valentine and Jack Lalor coached him and according to the available records he never lost a bout in a fairly long and active career as an amateur heavyweight. As champion of Western Province, Billy sparred regularly against first-class visiting professionals in his weight division, but he never did consider fighting for anything more but fun.

Walking was a popular form of competitive athletics in those days and between 1903 and 1906 he won races over distances varying between two and 50 miles. In 1903 he began playing rugby once again, gaining his Western Province colours in 1906. In between he found time to play a range of sports, including tennis, golf and cricket. As a golfer he was quite outstanding, with a handicap of three, but on the tennis court and the cricket field he revealed more exuberance and enthusiasm than talent.

It was rugby that suited his temperament best and he was considered a certain selection for Paul Roos' 1906 touring team, particularly after a series of outstanding performances in that year's Currie Cup tournament.

Astonishingly, he was not selected, but got his place anyway when Bertie Mosenthal had to withdraw. Millar, one of the youngest players in the team, proved to be an unqualified success and it was he who scored a vital try in the drawn test against England.

Millar captained the invincible Western Province teams in the years following his return from the history-making tour with Paul Roos, and by the time Tom Smyth brought the fourth touring side over from England in 1910, he was an obvious choice to lead the Springboks.

William Alexander (Billy) Millar was so seriously wounded in the South African War that doctors thought that he would be an invalid for the rest of his life. But he recovered to lead the Springboks.

CHAPTER 6

1912/13

SOUTH AFRICA TOUR
BRITAIN AND FRANCE

▲▲▲

For some reason never disclosed the national selectors, whose job it was to pick the members of the second Springbok touring team to Britain and France in 1912, did not want Billy Millar as captain. They felt that he should be in the team, but strongly recommended that he not be appointed as captain. The South African Rugby Board disagreed and overruled the selectors, which proved to be a wise decision as Millar's team won all the tests and were beaten only thrice, by Newport, London Counties and Swansea. They thoroughly avenged the 1906 defeat against Scotland and beat Ireland 38–0, an international record which was to stand until 1951 when the Springboks scored a 44–0 victory over Scotland.

The 1912/13 Springboks were a very powerful combination. The forwards were heavier and better on the whole than their 1906 predecessors and the backs proved more competent than originally expected.

'Uncle' Dobbin, playing in his fourth successive test series, was as full of tricks as ever, and Jan Stegmann, EE (Boetie) McHardy, Wally Mills, Jackie Morkel, and Richard and Freddie Luyt were always consistent, often brilliant.

The team was almost a family affair. Richard, Freddie and John Luyt were brothers and so were Gerhard and Jackie Morkel. Boy Morkel was their first cousin and Duggie Morkel was also related. Jan Stegmann was a brother of the 1906 Springbok Anton, Willie Krige was a brother of the legendary Japie, and Wally Mills and Louis Louw were first cousins.

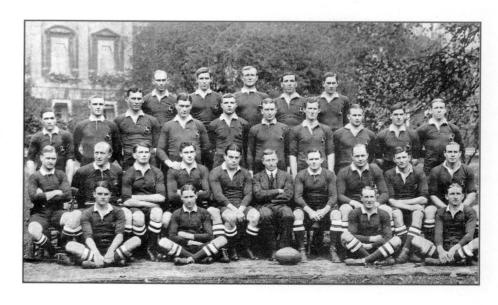

Left to right – Back row: JJ Meintjes, AS Knight, LH Louw, JD Luyt, PG Morkel; Middle row: FP Luyt, SH Ledger, TFJ van Vuuren, EH Shum, EE McHardy, JAJ Francis, JS Braine, WJ Mills, RR Luyt, ETA Delaney; Front row: WA Krige, G Thompson, SN Cronje, JA Stegmann, WA Millar, Max Honnet (manager), FJ Dobbin, DFT Morkel, WH Morkel, A de la R van der Hoff; On ground: GM Wrentmore, JH Immelmann, JD McCulloch, JWH Morkel.

Millar's team started their tour with six successive victories before they made the fatal mistake of underestimating Newport. For this match the Springboks should have selected their test side, but instead they ignored the well-meant warnings of their hosts – and paid the penalty. One Springbok who did come out of the defeat with an enhanced reputation was Richard Luyt, who beat the Newport defence with a scintillating break to send Duggie Morkel over for the South Africans' only score.

The Springboks only had themselves to blame for this defeat as they had already barely survived a match against Llanelly a week before, and should have recognized the enormous strength and vigour of all Welsh teams. Only the individual brilliance of Jackie Morkel enabled them to beat Llanelly. It was the big Somerset West centre who drew the defence in a tangle for Alex van der Hoff's early try which he also converted. Almost immediately afterwards Llanelly got an unconverted try and the Springboks could only draw further ahead after the interval when Morkel ripped through on his own for a try he failed to convert. This set-back stung the Llanelly forwards into furious action and the game became a real war of attrition.

Billy Millar described the match in his own inimitable way:

'I took the touch-flag on this occasion and believe me that wonderful Welsh crowd – probably the finest judges of football – gave me a roasting whenever I was on what is commonly known as the popular side. At length a rather hoarse voice shouted to me clearly above the din: "What do you think of Llanelly now?" Rather foolishly I shouted back: "Play the whole damn lot for Wales!" ... I now became the favourite of the crowd, instead of being barracked, I was applauded for everything I did. As a matter of fact, when Jackie Morkel, who really won the game for us off his own bat, scored the second try, the crowd encroached on to the field of play and I was forced to hit one fervent Welsh objector over the head with my flag stick. My drastic treatment immediately met with wholehearted approval, for now I could do nothing wrong!'

Millar never forgot the amazing scenes when Hiams, a Llanelly forward, dropped a goal a few minutes before the end to bring the Welsh team to within one point of the Springbok score. The Springboks held out to win 8–7 and Millar was subsequently formally presented with a saucepan, a hole punched in its bottom, which according to Welsh rugby tradition had been perched on the crossbar throughout the match.

After the Newport defeat, Millar and manager Max Honnet never again suffered from over-confidence. In fact they approached the next match, against a powerful London combination, as if it was a test and the team was only selected after hours of discussion. It was their first encounter with Adrian Stoop, the fly-half who was to English rugby then what Bennie Osler was to be for Springbok rugby a generation later. Stoop was an autocratic tactician, with a scientific approach well ahead of his time. The story is told of how he once tried to introduce a complicated system of signals based on numbers to be shouted by him at scrums and lineouts. One of his centres simply could not get the hang of it and on one occasion was not in position for the pass after Stoop had shouted: 'Three-four-five-seven!' or whatever it might have been. Stoop glared at the offender who shrugged and said: 'Sorry, Adrian, the number was engaged!'

The London match was played in a quagmire and it was Richard Luyt who once again guided the Springboks to victory, creating the openings for two wonderful tries by the Free State wing Boetie McHardy, one of which was converted by

Cardiff Arms Park was a sea of mud and water when Wales and the Springboks met in 1912. Here Duggie Morkel is pictured in the act of kicking the decisive penalty which gave his team victory.

The match against Swansea was played on a sopping St Helen's field and at half-time the Springboks took advantage of the many puddles to wash some of the mud off their hands and faces. The South Africans were beaten 0–3.

Duggie Morkel. Both teams were reduced to 14 men in the second half with the Springboks losing Wally Mills to a pulled leg muscle. The London forwards were on top after half-time and Stoop was a constant threat, but he was invariably let down by his three-quarters who, strangely enough, failed to adapt as well as the South Africans to the terrible weather conditions.

Nevertheless, it was often only Gerhard Morkel who stood between the Springboks and defeat. A reporter wrote afterwards that Morkel had 'gained for him a niche in the gallery of the world's greatest fullbacks' and Millar described his performance many years later as 'daring to the point of recklessness'.

After four consecutive breaks by Stoop had broken down in the face of great tackling, Duggie Morkel and Richard Luyt collided with a sickening thud and Morkel was so badly injured that he had to be carried off. With only 13 men left, the Springboks faltered and Stoop again drove an opening and this time 'Cherry' Pillman, the English hero of the 1910 series, scored.

Inspired by the example of Gerhard Morkel, Millar's men then staged a tremendous fight-back and as one critic put it, 'actually had the impudence to open the game'. From a scrum, that shrewd old campaigner Dobbin feinted towards the blind side and then hurled a long pass to Jackie Morkel on the open side who dropped a beautiful goal. Although London got another try before the final whistle after an all-out forward attack, they could not make up the leeway and the Springboks squeezed home 12–8.

Strangely enough, in a second encounter against London six matches later, the Springboks lost 8–10 on a fine, firm surface which should have suited the South Africans perfectly. This match was memorable for the fact that a penalty try was awarded against the Springboks. AO Jones, the referee and a former England cricket captain, took the drastic decision after a long kick-ahead had sent the ball rolling over the South African goalline. The London loose-forward WSD Craven was chasing after it when the referee ruled that Gerhard Morkel had obstructed him with his elbow.

It was generally a bad day for the Springboks. Mills and Millar were both injured and virtually passengers and the backs, even Richard Luyt, were right off form. Jan Stegmann, in spite of defending well, was particularly unhappy and did not look like the player who got four tries in the match against Glamorgan and who did so well in the tests later on the tour. Millett, the London fullback, was the hero of the match and his desperate tackles after breaks by Dobbin and Fred Luyt, saved certain tries. Playing for London was WJA (Dave) Davies, one of the greatest flyhalves in rugby history. Davies made his test debut against Millar's Springboks and went on to play for England for 11 years.

SOUTH AFRICA vs SCOTLAND

One of the major missions of Millar's team was to avenge the 1906 defeat by Scotland. Their chances of doing so were not regarded as being particularly good, mainly because their performances up to that stage of the tour were rather erratic.

Millar was injured and could not play in the test, so Dobbin, a survivor of the 1906 defeat in the mud, took over the captaincy. This time the raw Scottish elements did not come to the home team's aid; the weather was fine and the ground reasonably firm when the two teams trotted onto Inverleith in Edinburgh, accompanied by a band of pipers. In the vast crowd were about 200 South Africans who were studying at various universities in Britain and who had organized themselves into a small but very noisy task force of supporters.

The Springboks were in control from the first whistle to the last. The forwards were in particularly good form. Scotland, in those days, relied heavily on dribbling charges, but the Springboks countered this by falling on the ball and then quickly forming a loose scrum to regain possession. The plan was to beat Scotland up front before bringing the backs into the picture and it worked a lot quicker than the South Africans ever dared to hope for. Scotland obviously had the same strategy and when they suddenly found that their forwards could not take charge, they seemed too surprised to be able to think of an alternative.

The Springboks occasionally tried a backline movement, but with WM Dickson, a South African studying at Oxford, saving time and again they decided to hold the threequarters in reserve until their opponents had been thoroughly softened. It was a pattern foreign to Springbok teams of those days and it had Scotland really puzzled. In fact, the subdue-and-penetrate philosophy which was to become so ingrained in South African rugby was probably born that afternoon of 23 November 1912. It is a strategy that can only work if backed up by a powerful pack and Duggie Morkel that day was certainly leading an unstoppable line-up.

Just before half-time Jackie Morkel put a left-footed kick across the field towards the corner flag and right wing McHardy set off in hot pursuit. For once Dickson made a mistake. Instead of keeping his eye on the ball he glanced at the burly Free Stater steaming down on him and in an instant McHardy had whipped it away from him to crash over the line with 'his legs and arm flying'.

During the interval Dobbin gave instructions that the backs were now ready to do their share and the second half was to prove sheer hell for Scotland. Quick and smooth handling gave McHardy a chance to knock several opponents flying as he streaked to the corner flag. A desperate tackle not only stopped him from scoring, but, according to contemporary reports, hurled him into the lap of a lady spectator. McHardy was 6'2" tall and while the official records had him down for 180 lbs he always insisted that he actually weighed just over 200 lbs at the time of the tour. Minutes later the Springboks struck again and this time the move was so slick that not even the fiercest tackling could prevent a try. Freddie Luyt started it from the flyhalf position and the ball was handled twice by several players before Jan Stegmann scored in an easy position for Gerhard Morkel to convert. Another brilliant movement followed in which the passing between the backs and the forwards was so fast that by the time Richard Luyt got the ball at centre, the defence was already hopelessly outflanked and Stegmann galloped through a wide gap to notch his second try.

A brief fight-back by Scotland gave Gerhard Morkel a chance to bring friends and foes to their feet with a rivetting tackle on wing WR Sutherland, but it was just a dying effort on the part of the beaten but brave Scottish team.

JAN STEGMANN

Johannes Augustus (Jan) Stegmann, younger brother of the 1906 Springbok Anton Stegmann, was a big, exceptionally strong runner, who scored five tries in the five tests he played for South Africa. He was born at Bedford on 21 June 1887, the ninth child of a family of 13. Although he played most of his rugby for Stellenbosch and Western Province, Stegmann was actually a member of Johannesburg's Digger Club when he gained his Springbok colours in 1912. He retired from rugby after the tour to study dentistry at the University of Edinburgh, and subsequently represented Scotland as a hurdler against Wales, England and Ireland.

'BOETIE' McHARDY

Evelyn Edgar McHardy, known throughout the 70 years of his life as 'Boetie', was born on 11 June 1890 in Bloemfontein. He was an outstanding athlete at Grey College. Some of his track and field records stood for many years and while doing his matric in 1910, he won the Free State provincial championships over 100, 220 and 440 yards. A year later he represented Free State at the South African athletics championships in Cape Town and, in that same year, he also made his rugby debut for the province. It is interesting to note that McHardy somehow found the time to play first-division hockey and that he also took part in soccer when he was a teenager. McHardy holds another distinction in that he was the first Free Stater ever to score a try against Western Province and it is also a little-known fact that he represented his province from 1911 until 1924! In later years he served as a provincial coach and selector.

West of Scotland was humbled 38–3 only a few days later with McHardy scoring a hat-trick as a harbinger of what he and Jan Stegmann had in store for Ireland in the second test of the tour at Dublin on 30 November 1912.

SOUTH AFRICA vs IRELAND

The hopelessly outclassed Irishmen gave the Springboks the opportunity to establish records it took 40 years and longer to better or equal and the total of 10 tries is still the most ever to be scored by South Africa in an official test. Stegmann and McHardy both got hat-tricks and the feat of two Springboks getting three tries each in the same test has also not yet been equalled. Cold weather and frost had made the ground hard but firm, the conditions the mobile Springboks relished.

Apart from a few sporadic attempts early in the match it was just not a day for the Irish. Gerhard Morkel and Richard Luyt halted an early Irish rush with beautiful defensive work and from the next onslaught from the home team, who were in their traditional green after the Springboks had sportingly agreed to wear white jerseys, South Africa launched a counter-attack that just about broke the spirit of their opponents. The Irish forwards were dribbling furiously towards the Springbok line when Fred Luyt, with breathtaking timing, scooped the ball off an opponent's boot and whipped a lightning pass to Dobbin. The veteran Springbok halfback passed to Jackie Morkel deep in his own half, then it was on to Dick Luyt and finally safely into the hands of Stegmann.

Stegmann jerked himself past his opposite number, beat another defender and left the fullback standing to score after a magnificent 55-yard run. Not long after, McHardy received the ball three times in quick succession and scored on each occasion. The first of his three tries was a splendid effort as it came after a 50-yard sprint in which the fullback, who tried to tackle him, was sent cartwheeling as he bounced off the big Springbok's muscular body. The half-time score was 12–0.

The second half was a nightmare for the Irish supporters. Stegmann added two more tries to his tally to also notch a hat-trick, Jackie Morkel got two tries and forwards JAJ (Joe) Francis and Millar got one each. Freddie Luyt succeeded with one conversion and Gerhard Morkel with three.

David McDonigal, a well-known referee who settled in Cape Town, saw the Lansdowne slaughter as a boy and he gave a most amusing if not always strictly correct account:

'Ireland won the toss – it was the only thing we won that afternoon – and South Africa kicked off. The ball was fumbled and went into touch near our "25". From the lineout there was a scrum. I distinctly saw the ball heeled cleanly into the hands of the waiting half, and the next thing I saw was a gentleman called Stegmann taking long strides up to the touch-line and scoring behind the posts. He was a Springbok sprightly springing, or, as they say in Ireland, "Away he went, leppin' like a hare". That was only the beginning and I think it best to draw a veil over the rest of that awful day. I well remember a remark passed by a friend of mine from far-away Kerry. The Springboks had rattled up some 20 points and Ireland were kicking off for the umpteenth time. During that moment of waiting, my friend exclaimed: "Dearly beloved brethren, let us join in singing God Save Oireland, for it's destroyed we are, entoirely!"

'When we were walking away from the ground I happened to say, "Well, anyhow, it was a glorious exhibition of rugby."

'My friend replied: "Bedad, me bhoy, that wasn't rugby at all. At laste, if it was, heaven alone knows what we've been playing these past years!"'

SOUTH AFRICA vs WALES

Cardiff Arms Park was so waterlogged for the test against Wales that the Springboks fully expected to lose. But not even the Welshmen could come to terms with blinding rain and gale-strength wind which tortured players alike throughout the game. The imperturbable Duggie Morkel somehow steered a penalty over the crossbar early in the match and after that it was mainly a matter of, as Millar described, 'heavy tackling, battering, slashing – in fact a cheery mill'.

Gerhard Morkel and McHardy distinguished themselves with tremendous work on the defence, but with the players slithering and sliding all over the place, proper rugby was out of the question. Wales had a wonderful opportunity of levelling the score when they received a penalty virtually in front of the posts in the second half, but to the utter despair of thousands of drenched supporters, centre FW Birt, reputed to be the best placekicker in Wales at the time, sliced the ball so badly that Stegmann caught it on the corner flag!

It must have been a fantastic match for McHardy. Reports of the game describe at least three occasions where he saved the Springboks with his alert cover defence. McHardy used his exceptional speed and intuitive positioning to act as an extra fullback. In the final ten minutes of the match he very nearly crowned his remarkable performance with two tries. The first time he followed up his own punt only to lose the slippery ball as he dived over the line and on the second occasion he was stopped with literally inches to go. In the end it was Duggie Morkel's penalty that made all the difference.

▲▲▲

The match against Cardiff, who beat the 1906 Springboks, must have been the most exciting of the tour. It was a fine, sunny day and the South Africans should have won without too much trouble, but in RF Williams Cardiff had a fullback who could tackle a demon. He time and again tackled the dangerous Stegmann in full cry – a remarkable performance as Stegmann, in addition to his speed, had a

'Uncle' Dobbin is about to pass the ball to Freddie Luyt as Duggie Morkel looks on. This historic photograph was taken during the second match between the Springboks and London. The South Africans lost 8–10 but Luyt and Dobbin were in brilliant form.

On the 1912/13 tour, Newport took the head from the Springbok team. To this day, it can be seen in the museum at the Newport Club.

difficult high-kneed action. All the Springboks were unanimous that they had never seen a better tackler and for Stegmann, who rarely in his life failed to beat a fullback in a man-to-man situation, it must have been a most frustrating experience. McHardy also did not have a good day; with the line open in front of him he once slipped and fell for no apparent reason.

The Springboks eventually won 7–6 after a dropgoal by Jackie Morkel and a penalty by Duggie Morkel, who always seemed to kick best under pressure. The penalty given against Williams for obstruction should, under the advantage rule, not have been given as both Morkel and Stegmann were in position to score a try. Instead, it was up to Morkel to bang over a penalty from virtually the halfway line. This he did and another 1906 defeat was avenged.

SOUTH AFRICA vs ENGLAND

The test against England will always be remembered for the superb try by the England centre Ronnie Poulton. From an orthodox threequarter movement, Poulton suddenly cut sharply inside before swerving his way right through the Springbok team to score under the posts. Incredibly, the conversion kick was fluffed. Not long afterwards the great England player very nearly succeeded with a similar break, but McHardy's blistering speed on the cover defence stopped him a yard from the line. Typical work by Dick Luyt enabled Jackie Morkel to score the equalizing try, and two fine penalty goals from a long way out by Duggie Morkel sealed England's fate and gave the 1912/13 Springboks a clean sweep of the four tests. There is a tragic footnote to this match, however, as both Jackie Morkel and Poulton were killed during World War I.

SOUTH AFRICA vs FRANCE

The tour ended with a test against France at Bordeaux and although the Springboks won the game 38–5, veterans of the 1906 tour could note a marked improvement in French rugby.

The French pack turned in a lively performance, but their backs were woefully weak. McHardy scored two tries and Duggie Morkel tallied 13 points on his own, including a dropped penalty from near the half-way line and two tries.

The kick came after the referee had given the Springboks a penalty Billy Millar did not really want to accept as he thought the decision unfair. He instructed Morkel to give the French fullback a high up-and-under with plenty of time to gather and clear. Morkel, however, preferred to take a pot at goal and it is said that even the French players applauded when the ball sailed high over the crossbar.

And so Billy Millar's Springboks ended their tour on a triumphant note. They played exciting rugby, behaved impeccably and built further on the foundations laid so solidly by Paul Roos six years earlier.

VENUE	SOUTH AFRICA	RESULT	SOUTH AFRICA							
			T	C	P	D	T	C	P	D
SCOTLAND (EDINBURGH)	WON	16–0	4	2	0	0	0	0	0	0
IRELAND (DUBLIN)	WON	38–0	10	4	0	0	0	0	0	0
WALES (CARDIFF)	WON	3–0	0	0	1	0	0	0	0	0
ENGLAND (TWICKENHAM)	WON	9–3	1	0	2	0	1	0	0	0
FRANCE (BORDEAUX)	WON	38–5	9	4	1	0	1	1	0	0

THE LUYT BROTHERS

The three Luyt brothers in Millar's side deserve a special niche in Springbok rugby history. Freddie Luyt was a brilliant halfback, Richard as good at centre, while John who was not quite up to the standard of his brothers, was nevertheless a good forward.

Frederick Pieter Luyt was the youngest of the brothers. Born at Ceres on 26 February 1888, he was already an outstanding rugby player and cricketer when he went to Stellenbosch, where he concentrated on the fullback position. He was at Stellenbosch for only one season before transferring to the old South African College, now the University of Cape Town. While qualifying as an attorney he represented the university at both rugby and cricket and by 1910, when he played against Smyth's visiting British team in all three internationals, he was generally regarded as easily the best halfback in the country. He dovetailed particularly well with Clive van Ryneveld and his brother Richard, and it is recorded that these three formed the best match-winning combination of their day.

At the same time he was an extremely clever player who brought a new dimension to the functions of flyhalf, a position he preferred before the era of specialization, by designing various attacking ploys with his threequarters. Luyt's career was cut short by a knee injury and at the end of the tour to Britain he retired to practise law in partnership with Springbok Paddy Carolin in Moorreesburg, where the two did much to establish rugby in the Boland.

Freddie Luyt's older brother, Richard, was ranked by his contemporaries as a centre as good as Japie Krige and, surely, at that time there could not have been higher praise. He was nowhere near as spectacular as Krige, but he had the same uncanny ability to create openings for his teammates. Richard Robins Luyt was born on 16 April 1886. While at Stellenbosch he played mainly as a fullback, but it was as a halfback that he was distinctly unlucky not to make Paul Roos' team in 1906.

In that year, however, he finally switched to his proper position as a centre threequarter. Dick Luyt was an outstanding attacker, but it would seem as if he was also South Africa's first hard-tackling centre.

He was obviously also the best cricketer in the Luyt family and was described as a 'magnificent wicketkeeper, a splendid batsman and a dangerous googly bowler'. He narrowly missed selection as a Springbok cricketer. In later years he became a national cricket selector and at an advanced age continued to play club cricket, often completing a season with an average of 80 or higher.

The Luyt brothers, three of whom made a substantial contribution to the game of rugby in South Africa. From left to right are John and Freddie, GJ, who was a good all-round sportsman but who never attained international status, and Richard.

THE MORKEL FAMILY

Altogether ten members of the Morkel family from Somerset West gained Springbok colours between 1903 and 1928 – a feat unlikely ever to be beaten or even equalled.

The South African origin of the family dates back to 1691 when Philip Morkel arrived at the Cape as a gunner on board the *Oosterstyn*. He and his brother Wilhelm (Willem) had joined the Dutch East India Company after leaving Hamburg at the insistence of their father who did not want his sons to be conscripted into German military service.

Philip and Willem decided to settle in the Cape, then still little more than a halfway station for the Dutch merchant ships on their way to and from the East. Willem never married, but Philip's second marriage produced the four children from whom sprang rugby's most famous clan. For several generations the Morkels, who married mainly into the Myburgh family, remained clustered around Somerset West. Near the end of the 19th Century several members of the family moved to the then recently discovered gold fields of the Witwatersrand.

The intense interest in rugby seemed to have originated on the farm Rome, where the Morkel boys laid out their own field and played their bare-footed games against all comers.

The Somerset West Rugby Club almost certainly developed around this nucleus of enthusiasts, but for many years the only organized games were played after Cape cart journeys to the surrounding districts like Caledon, Stellenbosch and Strand. Nicolaas Morkel was the first captain when the club finally became affiliated to the Western Province Rugby Union in 1904. A year earlier, Andrew Morkel had already become the first Morkel to represent South Africa when he played in the first test against Morrison's touring team from Britain. He also gained his place in the first Springbok team to tour Britain and this time he was joined by brothers William Somerset (Sommy) and Douglas.

DFT (Duggie) Morkel was a match-winning kicker and altogether a splendid forward. Born in 1886, he learned the rudiments of the game in Kimberley, but soon moved to Johannesburg where, at the age of 17, he played for a Witwatersrand team against the 1903 British side. From 1906 until 1913, Duggie Morkel played in nine tests and he must count among the most spectacular kickers ever to wear the Springbok jersey.

In 1910 WH Morkel appeared on the scene. Better known as 'Boy', he was considered by internationally known authorities as the best all-round forward of his time. Boy was born in Somerset West in 1886, but he played for Diggers in Johannesburg at the start of his rugby career before returning to the Cape where he became captain of the Western Province side. In

Members of the renowned Morkel family included Gerhard – a remarkable fullback (back row, third from right); Jackie – a powerful threequarter (middle row, second from left); and WH 'Boy' – a magnificent forward (middle row, third from left).

later years he farmed in the district of Potchefstroom from where he was recalled to join Theo Pienaar's 1921 touring team to New Zealand. He was then 35 years old and yet he led the Springboks in all three tests.

In the 1912 team to tour Britain the Morkels were represented by Duggie, 'Boy', Jackie, a powerful centre, and his brother Gerhard who was to become the first player to be labelled 'the prince of fullbacks', a tag used so often since that it has become a rugby cliché.

Pieter Gerhard Morkel was born at Somerset West on 15 October 1888 and in spite of his instinctive talent, no player ever worked harder to perfect his game. As a youngster he was hardly ever without a tennis ball in his hands and this probably contributed much to the safe catching he was renowned for throughout his long career. Even as an established player, he regularly organized bands of schoolboys to pepper him with kicks during long hours on the practice field.

He also acquired the knack of screwing the ball off his boot to follow a curved route before swinging out, thereby ensuring that he gained the maximum ground even when he had to kick only a few feet in from touch. His dropkicks were legendary and here again it was the result of long practice. His positional play was perfect, making up for a definite lack of speed on the run and enabling him to play outstanding international rugby when already 33 years old.

Gerhard Morkel was also blessed with the perfect temperament for sport at the highest level and perhaps this was because there was no place on earth he would rather have been than on a rugby field.

He had the great player's intuitive ability to sum up a situation in a glance and he himself often claimed that he hardly ever looked at the posts when dropping for goal; he simply sensed where they were.

He first played for Somerset West at the age of 16, although it was by chance rather than design that he got into the senior team at such an early age. He happened to be at the railway station when the team, about to depart for a game in Caledon, discovered that they were one man short. A quick whip-around raised enough money for his train-fare and he turned in such a brilliant performance that he became a regular member of the team.

Henry, Royal and Harry Morkel only gained their Springbok colours after World War I, and all three were members of the 1921 team to New Zealand. There were altogether five Morkels in the touring party.

Royal Morkel, born on 22 March 1896, was massive for his era at 6'2" and more than 230 lbs. As a forward, Royal Morkel was a human steamroller, almost unstoppable when in sight of his opponents' goal-line.

The last of the Morkels to wear the Springbok jersey was 'PK' who played on the wing in the fourth test against Maurice Brownlie's All Blacks in 1928. All the Morkels were also interested in other sports and Royal was a particularly good swimmer and boxer while Denys, who did not reach international status as a rugby player, gained Springbok colours as a cricketer. All of them were good cricketers, in fact, and no slouches on the tennis court either.

Mention has only been made of those members of the family who represented South Africa, but their impact on our sport can probably be best underlined if it is pointed out that in the years just prior to World War I there were no less than 22 Morkels playing senior rugby in all parts of the country. This so impressed Sir Abe Bailey that he was actually in the process of arranging a tour to England for a rugby team comprising only Morkels when the war broke out and his plans. had to be abandoned.

Duggie Morkel played in nine tests for the Springboks between 1906 and 1913. He captained the national side for two tests.

CHAPTER 7

1921

SOUTH AFRICA TOUR NEW ZEALAND

ATTIE VAN HEERDEN

The tall, strongly-built wing, Attie van Heerden, was born on 10 March 1898, one of two sons of a Dutch Reformed Church minister. Both he and his brother Nico followed in their father's footsteps and played for the University of Stellenbosch. Attie was also an outstanding sprinter and represented South Africa at the Olympic Games in Antwerp in 1920 before he joined the exclusive brotherhood of double Springboks a year later. He scored the first-ever try between the Springboks and the All Blacks in the first test of the 1921 series. Rather surprisingly, he left for England after the tour to play rugby league for Wigan.

War, from 1914 to 1918, was the only reason why the first clash between world rugby's lustiest infants, New Zealand and South Africa, did not take place until 1921 – more than a decade and a half after both had made their first successful tours to Britain. South Africa did, however, gain some experience of All Black rugby when a team selected from New Zealand's Armed Forces visited in 1919. Winning 10 out of 14 matches with one drawn, caused serious pondering among the locals over how difficult it must be to take on a fully representative side.

The opportunity came in 1921, when New Zealand invited the Springboks for a full-scale tour. And since they would be in the vicinity, the South Africans were asked to play a few matches in Australia where the game was still in the fledgling stage and almost entirely confined to New South Wales.

National selectors Bill Schreiner, AF Markötter, James Leck (a gentleman almost as irritable as Mr Mark and who, as a referee, once gave Springbok and Western Province captain Billy Millar his marching orders in a Currie Cup match), SA Townsend and CV Becker, although they did their best, found there was general dissatisfaction with the team they selected to do battle with the All Blacks. In retrospect, this lack of confidence is inexplicable as the team was studded with players whose names are now bywords in the history of South African rugby.

Theodorus Barend Pienaar, already in his thirty-third year, was given the captaincy, although it was obvious to all that he was past his best and unlikely to earn a place in the test teams. But Pienaar had undoubted leadership qualities and the selectors' decision was certainly based on a desire to give HC Bennett, the tour manager, some mature assistance.

Pienaar was a good forward in his day and a member of 'Boy' Morkel's 1914 Western Province team, for many years considered to be the finest provincial combination ever to be assembled in the country. He later often captained Western Province and had an instinctive knack of handling a band of boisterous players.

'Boy' Morkel, long established as one of the mightiest forwards in the world, was appointed vice-captain and, at 35, he was even older than Pienaar. There were four other Morkels in the side: Gerhard, Henry, Harry and Royal. Gerhard, one of the heroes of the 1912/13 team in Britain and France, was then 33 years old, but such a master of positional play that his marked slowness was hardly a handicap.

The selection of 'Boy' Morkel was really an indication of how independently selectors could act in those days. Morkel was then farming in the Western Transvaal and playing only the occasional match. When the selectors called on him he, in the tradition of the Roman general Cincinnatus, left his plough because his country needed him more than his farm did.

The New Zealand tour also marked the appearance on the international scene of the young Phil Mostert, who was destined to become one of the finest South African forwards ever to wear the Springbok jersey.

▲▲▲

Pienaar and his men set out for the big adventure on the SS *Aeneas* and after 17 days at sea they docked in Adelaide harbour for the Australian part of the tour.

For the first match against the Springboks, an unofficial fixture, the small rugby community of Victoria had to actually advertise for players to raise a full team and it is hardly surprising that the South Africans romped home 51–0 without exactly over-exerting themselves. The three consecutive matches against New South Wales were also won, but the opposition was more fierce.

In the first match against New South Wales, Attie van Heerden's flashing speed carried him to five tries, a Springbok record until Roy Dryburgh notched six tries against Queensland in 1956. In one of the matches Gerhard Morkel's deadly crashtackling so annoyed a section of the crowd that he had to be smuggled back to his hotel with the aid of his Australian opponents. Although a veteran of 33, he was to play first-league club rugby for another ten years. Morkel was still a tremendous player; plain murder against opponents who did not know with what bullet-like force he could launch his tackles from the slight crouch he used to adopt as an attacker sped towards him.

Undefeated at the end of the Australian leg of the tour, the Springboks nevertheless were not in a happy mood when they boarded the SS *Mararoa* for New Zealand. No less than eight members of the team had been injured in the five matches in Australia, including LB (Jack) Siedle whose knee injury would spell the end of his playing days, Pienaar with severe concussion and Gerhard Morkel with a dislocated elbow.

Sas de Kock, the Springbok flyhalf, broke his ankle against Wangunui in the first game on New Zealand soil and was out for practically the rest of the tour. There was enough reserve strength in the touring party, however, for them not to worry unduly over the fact that their call for replacements had fallen on deaf ears and they managed to get through the tough provincial fixtures with only one defeat (4–6 to Canterbury) and one draw (0–0 against Taranaki).

▲▲▲

The first-ever test match between the Springboks and the All Blacks took place at Carisbrook, Dunedin, on 13 August 1921, beginning one of the keenest rivalries in sport. With Pienaar injured, the South Africans were led by 'Boy' Morkel while George Aitken was in charge of the All Blacks. Aitken was a centre threequarter described by contemporary newspaper reports as someone who 'understood the art of making gaps for his wings'. Morkel retained the captaincy for all three

'Baby' Michau turns away to avoid the attentions of Mark Nicholls in the second test of 1921. Left to right are Wallie Clarkson, Attie van Heerden, Nicholls, Michau, 'Moke' Belliss and 'Boy' Morkel. South Africa, having lost the first test, won the second by nine points to five.

tests, but Aitken took some of the blame for the defeat in the second test and had to make way for Teddy Roberts. In the words of Hugo (Tokkie) Scholtz, who played in that historic first test between the two countries, both teams were 'too scared to open up for the first 25 minutes'. Then the Springboks suddenly shook off their bad case of nerves and Van Heerden, showing the pace that made him an Olympic sprinter, slashed through for a try next to the posts. Gerhard Morkel converted and the half-time score was 5–0.

In the second half the All Blacks woke up with a vengeance and for the first time the Springboks got a taste of the fury of a thoroughly aroused New Zealand pack. With loose-forward 'Moke' Belliss playing like a man gone berserk, the All Blacks ran the South Africans off their feet to score three tries; two converted by Mark Nicholls who was to play a major role in one of the epic future battles between the two countries. One of the tries was notched by Belliss while wings Percy Storey and Jack Steel got one each to give New Zealand a convincing 13–5 victory.

Steel's try must have been something to see. New Zealand were pinned back deep in their own half when the ball was thrown haphazardly in Steel's direction. It went over his shoulder, but he flung up an arm and somehow managed to clamp it between his shoulder-blades. With the ball held in this extremely awkward position, he squeezed past the defence, was in the clear and running as hard as he could while frantically trying to get a more manageable grasp on it. A few yards from the Springbok goalline he at last had the ball in his hands to score what must have been a remarkable try.

▲▲▲

FRANK MELLISH

Frank Whitmore Mellish was a double international with a difference. In the European rugby season, just before he gained his Springbok colours, Mellish represented England against Scotland, Ireland, Wales and France. A tough bustling forward, he was born at Rondebosch in 1897 and learnt his rugby at Wynberg Boys High, Rondebosch Boys High and the South African College School. As a teenager he joined the Cape Town Highlanders and fought in what was then known as German South West Africa during World War I. He later joined the South African Heavy Artillery in France and won a commission and the Military Cross during the battles near the end of the war. Mellish, who attained the rank of Colonel in World War II, was to play for South Africa in six tests, but it would not be an injustice to say that his most lasting contribution to South African rugby was the magnificent job he did as manager of the Springbok touring team to Britain and France in 1951/52.

Over 40 000 people paid more than £4 000 to see the second test at Eden Park, Auckland. On a hard, dry surface the Springboks, the forwards in particular, played much better than in the first international. 'Tank' van Rooyen, a muscular Transvaler who hardly ever made his provincial team because he was considered 'too dumb', but whose latent talent was immediately spotted by the omniscient Markötter, was perhaps the best of a brilliant pack. Van Rooyen turned professional shortly after the tour to play rugby league for Wigan in England – a great loss to Springbok rugby.

It was he who initiated the South Africans' only try when he picked up the loose ball after a fine break by the balding Meyer, playing at flyhalf, although originally selected as a centre or wing. Van Rooyen passed to Mannetjies Michau who ran well before giving to Wally Clarkson whose perfectly-timed pass enabled Billy Sendin to go over in a good position for Gerhard Morkel to convert. The All Blacks equalized quickly enough when McLean scored after some good work between Roberts, Nicholls, Badeley, Aitken and Belliss. Nicholls converted with a rather lucky kick, the ball hitting the far upright and rebounding over the crossbar.

With the score level, the two teams really flew into the fray but according to contemporary reports the match stayed clean but 'rather untidy'. After half-time came the most memorable moment of the match. The All Black forwards started a dribbling rush, but the ball was kicked too far ahead and Gerhard Morkel picked it up near the halfway line and a few feet from touch. He ran infield a few steps and then 'he let go with the right foot, the ball sailing fairly and squarely between the goalposts and high up over the centre'.

The magnificent kick so thrilled the sporting crowd that, so the legend goes, a few uninhibited souls actually ran on to the field and offered the Springbok

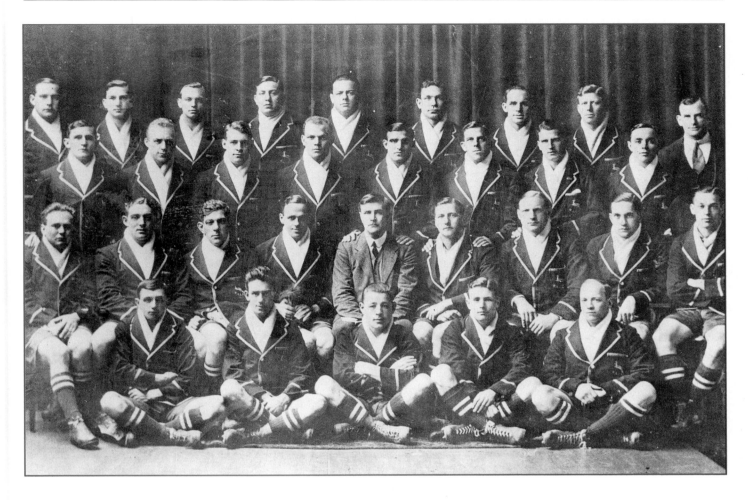

fullback a drink. Morkel solemnly lifted the glass in a toast to the crowd and took a few sips, again strictly according to unofficial reports. The huge crowd did, in fact, get rather out of hand in the tense second half. Springbok wing Bill Zeller was in the clear once after a strong run when he found himself surrounded by so many spectators that he mistakenly thought that he had run into touch. He duly stopped and gave the ball to an opponent for a lineout only to discover to his horror that he was still very much in the playing area!

And so the Springboks won 9–5 to keep the series in the balance, but for at least one of them there was a prize to take home. The Auckland rugby authorities presented Gerhard Morkel with a gold medal to commemorate his outstanding performance and, more particularly, the dropgoal that won the match for his team.

▲▲▲

The third and deciding test was played at Athletic Park, Wellington, in pouring rain and gale-strength wind which really made it impossible for either team to play constructive rugby. It is hardly surprising that neither side could score any points, but it was nevertheless a tense and exciting match.

Both fullbacks, CN Kingstone of New Zealand and Gerhard Morkel, were magnificent and the two packs 'laboured mightily in the mud'. Morkel, in the final test of his career, did not put a foot wrong and years later Phil Mostert recounted how he and his teammates would time and again hear the sound as the wet and heavy ball slapped into his hands followed by an even louder thud as his powerful boot

Theo Pienaar's 1921 Springboks: back row, from left to right: SSF Strauss, HW Morkel, A van Heerden, HJL Morkel, JM Michau, GW van Rooyen, AP Walker, HH Scholtz, Taffy Davies (baggage-master); standing: WA Clarkson, JS Olivier, FW Mellish, TL Kruger, PJ Mostert, NJ du Plessis, WC Zeller, LB Siedle; seated: JP Michau, IB de Villiers, JA Morkel, TB Pienaar, HC Bennet (manager), WH Morkel, MC Ellis, PG Morkel, JS Weepner; front : JS de Kock, WD Sendin, WH Townsend, JC Tindall, C du P Meyer.

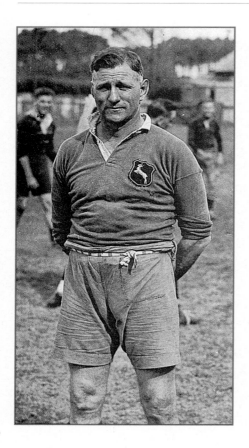

WH Morkel, better known as 'Boy', was recalled to duty from his Western Transvaal farm and captained the Springboks in all three tests against the All Blacks.

thumped it into touch a split-second later. 'It was raining so heavily that we could hardly see one another,' Mostert remembered. 'Gerhard was like a ghostly shadow somewhere at the back of us and he saved us from defeat, that's for sure'.

New Zealand came closest to scoring a try in the match when Keith Siddells, on the wing, dived on a loose ball behind the goalline, but AE Neilson, the referee, ruled that he did not get his hands to the ball. The Springboks also had their hard-luck story. Mostert, who played a storming game, once lost the slippery ball while diving over the New Zealand goalline.

The final whistle blew with no score on the board and the first test series between the Springboks and the All Blacks ended with honours even.

▲▲▲

Pienaar and his men were never given full credit for what they achieved on the first tour of New Zealand. Injuries hit the side so hard that they rarely had more than 24 players to draw from and why the request for two replacements was not only ignored by the rugby authorities, but actually ridiculed by some of the newspaper critics, is impossible to understand. Even after the return of the team, South Africans seemed reluctant to give them their due. No wonder Pienaar was compelled to write in an article published shortly afterwards:

'True, we may not have done much that was sensational, but let me stress this point, there is neither time nor place for the sensational in New Zealand football.' Over the years, a succession of Springbok teams have learnt through bitter experience that there was a world of wisdom in this statement.

The New Zealanders were kinder to their South African visitors. They labelled them the 'greatest defensive team' they had ever seen, pointing out that only 13 tries were scored against the Springboks in their 19 matches. What was praise in the land of the Kiwi was perverted into criticism in South Africa where, as Pienaar said even before the tour began, 'the public had a sad lack of loyalty to their own chosen gladiators'.

'The Springboks were sent to attack, not to defend', some critics claimed and for them Pienaar had an answer, the truth of which was to be recognized in the years to come:

'Go out there yourselves and fight a New Zealand team on its own soil,' he said. 'A team that is filled with consciousness of its own prowess and flushed with great achievements of the past. And if you do not eat humble pie on your return, well – I shall!'

Pienaar's words are still valid today. And what he said about New Zealand rugby, the All Blacks subsequently found to be as true of the game in South Africa.

VENUE	SOUTH AFRICA	RESULT	SOUTH AFRICA				NEW ZEALAND			
			T	C	P	D	T	C	P	D
DUNEDIN	LOST	5–13	1	1	0	0	3	2	0	0
AUCKLAND	WON	9–5	1	1	0	1	1	1	0	0
WELLINGTON	DRAW	0–0	0	0	0	0	0	0	0	0
		14–18	2	2	0	1	4	3	0	0
SERIES: SOUTH AFRICA PLAYED 3; W1, L1, D1										

PHIL MOSTERT

The greatest player to emerge from the 1921 tour was undoubtedly Phillipus Jacobus Mostert. He was born in Krugersdorp on 30 October 1898, but his widowed mother shortly afterwards moved to Somerset West where his instinctive rugby talent had the opportunity of blossoming in one of the strongest club sides in the country.

Mostert had the solid build of the ideal forward, but he was also remarkably fast, and could kick and handle with the aplomb of a top-class flyhalf. In fact, he is still the only Springbok ever to have dropped a goal from a mark in a test match (against Maurice Brownlie's All Blacks at Ellis Park in 1928) and he often did the most unpredictable things on the field. Bennie Osler, who always regarded Mostert as the best player he ever saw in any position, used to enjoy telling how Phil, in an interprovincial match, once refused to pass him the ball in an ideal situation for a pot at goal. Mostert, instead, took the kick himself and succeeded! As the ball sailed over the crossbar, he turned to the gaping Osler and grinned: 'You see, Bennie? You thought you're the only man who could do this sort of thing, eh?'

Superlatively fit, Mostert could maintain a cracking pace for the full duration of a match and at the start of his career his exuberance often tempted him into some aimless running around. Again it was the genius of Markötter who guided him on the right track. Mark knocked this particular habit out of Mostert with a single sarcastic remark. 'Mostert, you're a first-class player,' the Matie coach told him one day, 'but somebody should put a saddle and reins on you!' Mostert got the message. Very tough physically, Mostert believed in playing the game cleanly and his method of retaliation was to smile at his opponent, crack a joke, and then to squeeze the very life out of him with legitimately-used strength. He had a very nimble brain with a refined aptitude for all forms of gamesmanship.

Mostert always had a particularly high regard for his fellow forwards on the 1921 tour. He considered Kruger, Ellis, Van Rooyen, Du Plessis, Walker, Mellish and 'Boy' Morkel as players who would have more than held their own in any era of Springbok history.

The Springbok line-up, led by Theo Pienaar, before the start of the first-ever test against the All Blacks in Dunedin.

CHAPTER 8

1924

BRITISH ISLES TOUR SOUTH AFRICA

▲▲▲

Bad luck dogged Ronald Cove-Smith's 1924 British team almost from the moment the names of the touring party were announced. Several had to withdraw for various reasons and injuries presented a problem from the first practice when the one fullback, WF Gaisford, was eliminated for the rest of the tour and the other fullback, TE Holliday, suffered the same fate in the first match. Fortunately the first choice for this position, Dan Drysdale, survived. WA Cunningham, an Irish international then resident in Johannesburg, was invited to join the side and he actually played in the third test and also scored a try. Halfway through the tour HJ Davies, a Welsh centre, was sent over as a replacement and he also twice made appearances at fullback.

There had to be constant juggling throughout the tour to field a full team, and the versatile Tom Voyce, for instance, played a few matches as a wing or a fullback. Jamie Clinch and Stanley Harris, forward and wing respectively, also had to fill in whenever Drysdale needed a rest. Drysdale was one of the best players in the team although he did miss an easy penalty kick which could have given the Lions, as they were beginning to be called, their only test victory.

Jamie Clinch, whose father AD Clinch was a member of Hammond's 1896 team, was also outstanding and so was Voyce, who by accident or design was switched from centre to the pack during the England trials for the tour and nevertheless managed to earn his place.

The South African team selected to play the third test in 1924 against the British Lions in Port Elizabeth. Back row: SR Townsend, FJ Dobbin, NJ du Plessis, AF Markötter, JB la Grange, NJV van Druten, WA Millar, NJS Bosman, WF Schreiner, FW Mellish, MC Ellis, Middle row: D Devine, BL Osler, PK Albertyn, TL Krüger, AP Walker, BE Vanderplank. Front row: JT Slater, JS de Kock, KT Starke.

There were several interesting players in the touring team, with the selection of some gaining added significance in later years. Herbert Waddell, the Scottish fly-half, is the father of Gordon Waddell who also toured South Africa with the Lions many years later and became a member of parliament. AF Blakiston, the Blackheath and England forward, eventually became Sir Arthur Blakiston after inheriting his father's baronetcy and Stanley Harris was not only a good wing, but also a remarkable all-rounder. He was actually playing club rugby for Pirates, in Johannesburg, when he was chosen to join Cove-Smith's touring party.

In South African rugby history, 1924 must be remembered as the year in which Bennie Osler made his international debut. Albertyn led the Springbok team with calm confidence and as a centre he played with sound judgement, often creating gaps for his wings and scoring a try in the second test. Osler insisted that in spite of his bad knee, Albertyn played well enough in that series to be rated among the best centres he ever saw, and was deeply impressed by his leadership qualities. He remembered in particular how Albertyn patted him on the shoulder after he had stabbed over the first dropgoal of his test career, and said: 'Now I know why the Maties are so scared of you!' (Albertyn was overseas when Osler first made his name for the University of Cape Town, so often at the expense of Stellenbosch, and up till then he had only heard of the young matchwinner's deadly boot.)

▲▲▲

Highlights of the first test were Osler's dropgoal at a crucial stage of the game and a positively brilliant break by Albertyn's centre partner Wally Clarkson, which led to a try by Hans Aucamp on the wing. It also spelt tragedy for Clarkson because he tore a muscle so badly in making the try possible that he never again played for his country. The Springbok pack was outstanding because this was the era of men like Kruger, Mostert, Van Druten, Mellish, Du Plessis and Ellis, to name only a few, and it was rare for South Africa to have problems up front.

▲▲▲

For the second test the selectors gave Osler his favourite scrumhalf partner, Pally Truter, in the place of Myburgh who worked the scrum in the first international. This was probably the reason why the Springboks functioned so smoothly and won 17–0. The British team was plagued by every misfortune and even their best player, Drysdale, was badly injured in the final few minutes.

▲▲▲

The third test was a disaster for both teams. For some unaccountable reason the selectors dropped Truter in favour of Dauncey Devine, a Transvaal scrumhalf with whom Osler simply could not combine. Mostert was out of the game because of injury and the Springboks just could not find their feet. It was a windy, miserable day in Port Elizabeth and Cove-Smith's men were desperately unlucky not to have won. With the scores level at three-all, Drysdale missed a penalty from in front of the Springbok posts and the match ended in a draw everybody tried to forget as soon as possible.

▲▲▲

Kenny Starke, Springbok hero of the fourth test against the 1924 Lions. He scored two tries and dropped a goal for a personal tally of 10 points.

Action in the final test of the 1924 series at Newlands, Cape Town. A Lions defender is collared by Alf Walker as he is about to kick. The South Africans won the test by nine points, with a final score of 16–9.

Truter and Mostert were both back in the side for the final test at Newlands and, although played on a wet and muddy surface, this was an enterprising game which the Springboks won 16–9 after Kenny Starke, on the left wing, had scored ten of the points.

Starke, who had been quietly efficient in the first three tests, turned in an inspired performance. Early in the match he dropped a superb goal from an acute angle and later he cut through twice for tries the defence had no hope of preventing. The Springbok backs hardly put a foot wrong under Albertyn's shrewd guidance and Mostert led a pack of forwards that earned full marks from such authorities as Roos, Millar and Pienaar in after-match interviews. Mostert was particularly outstanding, but so too was Teuns Kruger until he was hurt midway through the first half. For the rest of the game the Springboks had to make do with only seven forwards – they not only survived, they stayed on top.

Springbok superiority was never seriously in doubt but Cove-Smith and his men earned everyone's respect for the cheerful way in which they stuck to their guns in the face of misfortune.

Albertyn continued to play on and off for several seasons and it is no secret that Markötter would have liked to have had him in the Springbok team against the All Blacks in 1928. He did play in the trials, but in an interview with AC Parker many years later, he said: 'On the Monday I played badly; on the Tuesday I was worse and on the Wednesday I was terrible!' Two years later he retired from the game, more than ten years after he had been told that he might be crippled for life.

VENUE	SOUTH AFRICA	RESULT	SOUTH AFRICA				BRITISH ISLES			
			T	C	P	D	T	C	P	D
DURBAN	WON	7–3	1	0	0	1	1	0	0	0
JOHANNESBURG	WON	17–0	4	1	1	0	0	0	0	0
PORT ELIZABETH	DRAW	3–3	1	0	0	0	1	0	0	0
CAPE TOWN	WON	16–9	4	0	0	1	2	0	1	0
		43–15	10	1	1	2	4	0	1	0
SERIES: SOUTH AFRICA PLAYED 4; W3, L0, D1										

PK ALBERTYN

Pieter Kuyper Albertyn, known throughout his life as Pierre or 'PK', would probably never have played for South Africa had it not been for a homeopath's treatment and the determination of Markötter that talent should not go to waste.

Albertyn was a brilliant left-wing at the University of Stellenbosch; so outstanding that Markötter ranked him with Krige and Loubser as one of the three greatest players he ever saw. Albertyn was tall and strong and he could hold his own with top athletes over the sprint distances, but he could also side-step with bewildering ease and guiding all that natural ability was a subtle rugby brain.

Early in the 1919 season, playing for Stellenbosch against Villagers at Newlands, he scored no less than six tries in the first 15 minutes of the match. Not long afterwards Albertyn was selected for Western Province Universities to play against a New Zealand Imperial Services team on a 14-match tour of South Africa. It was to be just another step up the ladder to Springbok colours, but it was in this game that he suffered the injury that should really have ended his career.

Slipping between two defenders, he was heavily tackled from both sides and one of the New Zealanders came down with his full weight on the wing's leg. The impact tore all the ligaments in his knee and there was so much internal bleeding that the leg turned black later that night. Doctors told him never to play rugby again, adding that he would be fortunate not to be crippled for life. Severn, one of the best-known nature-cure exponents in South Africa at the time, took a personal interest in the 22-year-old student's predicament. Albertyn was able to play again after only six weeks of treatment and he celebrated his return by scoring five tries against Somerset West, leaving Gerhard Morkel helpless on more than one occasion with a side-step the veteran Springbok fullback simply could not solve.

But Albertyn realized that he would never again be quite the player he used to be and with typical level-headedness he decided to adapt his game to his new handicap. He accepted that his days as a wing were over because he could not risk being tackled in full flight, and he also felt that he no longer had the speed so essential in this position. Albertyn played several matches as an extra back, but he found that he could no longer turn or change direction suddenly without feeling discomfort. At the end of that season, he left for Guy's Hospital to study dentistry.

The softer grounds in England did not put quite such a strain on his weak leg and he played some of the most enjoyable rugby of his life for this famous hospital. He represented the Barbarians, but refused an invitation to play in the England trials. When he returned to South Africa three years later, Albertyn regarded himself as virtually retired although he was then only 26 years old.

But Markötter had not forgotten him. His mind was made up that Albertyn would be one of the Springbok centres against Cove-Smith's 1924 British touring team. Albertyn was not selected for the first trials but, in the meantime, Markötter had asked somebody to take a look at Albertyn's form in club matches. He received an encouraging reply and acting in his usual unilateral way, he simply ordered Albertyn to report for a trial match to be played in Durban. This game was regarded by most as just a practice run for the probable Springbok side. When Albertyn arrived in Durban, Mr Mark gave him only one instruction: 'Don't go and make a bloody fool of yourself!' Albertyn proceeded to do nothing foolish and that night, to the astonishment of just about everybody, it was announced that he was to be South Africa's new rugby captain.

PK Albertyn, the 1924 Springbok captain. Four years before he gained international colours, doctors advised him to retire rather than risk further injury.

CHAPTER 9

1928

NEW ZEALAND TOUR SOUTH AFRICA

SP van Wyk was one of the few stars in the lethargic Springbok team who lost the second test to the All Blacks. Here he hands off RG McWilliams.

When the *Euripides* steamed into Durban harbour in mid-May 1928 and Maurice Brownlie led ashore the first fully-fledged team of All Blacks to come to South Africa, the large number of officials and supporters gathered to welcome them suddenly felt their hearts sinking.

'I have never seen men of such magnificent physique,' Devenish, one of the national selectors, remarked to a colleague.

In New Zealand, the experts were unanimous that an exceptionally fine team had been picked to be the first All Blacks to visit South Africa and some went so far as to claim that they were potentially a better combination than the 1924 'Invincibles' which had swept unbeaten through the United Kingdom and France.

For some inexplicable reason, South African rugby authorities and fans were in a state of nerves. There was a feeling that the general standard had dropped since the rather lacklustre series against Cove-Smith's team four years ago and reports of New Zealand's prowess certainly helped to create an air of apprehension.

The All Blacks lost their invincible tag very quickly, however, because their anti-quated scrummaging technique could not hold any well-drilled 3–4–1 South African formation. They took a long time to come to terms with the less-pointed ball and they blundered in not realizing until it was too late that in Nicholls, their vice-captain, they had one man who could have turned the tide in their favour.

Osler's influence had spread throughout South Africa by the time the All Blacks arrived in 1928 and almost invariably they encountered kicking flyhalves working with varying degrees of efficiency off a strong forward platform. Their biggest problem throughout the tour, however, was to try and cope with the South Africans' expert scrummaging methods.

It was an unfortunate coincidence that the 1928 All Blacks happened to be in Cape Town at the time of civil unrest. Their first two matches were to be at Newlands and after their arrival in Cape Town, where thousands thronged the station to welcome them, they were caught in riots which erupted with the hoisting of the newly adopted Union flag. In only the second match of the tour, the All Blacks suffered their first defeat when they met a powerful team selected from the various Cape Town clubs and which included players like Bennie and Stanley Osler, Jackie Tindall, Phil Mostert, JC van der Westhuizen, George Daneel and TG Osler – a side not far short of international strength.

There is a strong affinity between New Zealanders and South Africans and the 1928 All Blacks enjoyed their tour as much as their hosts loved having them here. They must have been a particularly nice bunch of fellows off the field because nowhere in all the thousands of words written about the tour can one find one line where they complained about the fact that they were given some of their toughest opponents within the first couple of weeks of the tour, with long zig-zagging train trips thrown in for good measure. Nine of the New Zealand players were out of commission through sickness or injury at various stages of the tour, six of them for five-week stretches, but these misfortunes were never used as excuses.

The tour produced a fair share of rough play but was free of the kind of 'blown-up incident' we have so much of in modern international rugby. The New Zealand forward Ian Finlayson was sent off the field for hitting an opponent in the match against Transvaal, but, as FM Howard (the later FM Honoré), reported:

'He was far from being the worst offender on the field. I had my field glasses focussed on the play at the time of the incident, which took place right in front of the grandstand, and I saw every detail of what occurred. It is only fair to state on behalf of Finlayson, not as an excuse, but to situate the facts quite clearly, that his blow was an act of retaliation ...'

According to the report, the referee, JG Finlay, was told by the All Black forward afterwards that he 'fully deserved his punishment' and that he knew from the moment he had hit his opponent that he was 'due to take a walk'.

The Transvaal player Finlayson punched was Manie Geere, a powerful forward who won his Springbok colours three years later. Geere, who with Teuns Kruger was the outstanding forward on the field when Transvaal beat the All Blacks 6–0 that day, received a stern warning from the referee later in the match and also came close to being sent off.

After losing two of their first four matches, the All Blacks scored four successive wins leading up to the first test at the old Kingsmead ground at Durban on 30 June 1928. There was tremendous interest in the game. The Springboks and the All Blacks were all-square after the 1921 series and subsequently the All Blacks had their undefeated tour of Britain. As far as the average rugby follower was concerned, the match was for the championship of the world.

▲▲▲

The historic first test between the Springboks and the All Blacks on South African soil was recorded in literally thousands of words published in every newspaper in the country. Overnight, Bennie Osler became a national hero.

This is how he described what became known as 'Osler's match' ...

'We were quite confident beforehand, mainly because we knew that the All Blacks could not hold us in the scrums with their outmoded 2–3–2 formation, but as usual the butterflies started fluttering inside me as the day of the match drew nearer. I was always terribly nervous before any big match and before my test debut against the British team in 1924, I just about drove Mr Mark to distraction when I virtually went into a state of shock on the morning of the match and could only make croaking sounds in reply to his questions!

'Kingsmead was packed with the biggest crowd ever to attend a sporting event in Durban up to that time. People came from all parts of South Africa and Rhodesia and by six-thirty on the morning of the match, the queues were already forming outside the ground.

'The weather was bad. Rain was threatening and a freezing, gusty wind whipped through the stadium when we arrived to sit through a curtain-raiser between Michaelhouse and Technical High School. I remember how I tried to calm my nerves by singing a popular song of the day under my breath.

Maurice Brownlie, captain of the 1928 All Blacks, met General JC Smuts shortly after the team arrived in Cape Town.

'Finally Phil Mostert, our captain, led us out onto the field where Maurice Brownlie and his All Blacks were already waiting. We stood in single file as the All Blacks danced the *Haka* and then we replied with our own war cry of bad Zulu and gibberish, if I remember correctly. The good thing about those war cries was that it allowed you to blow off a bit of steam.

'At last the referee, Boet Neser, could start the game and as usual my nervousness magically disappeared. The All Blacks had to defend the Umgeni end and as I glanced up at the sky I saw the clouds breaking and the sun coming through. We'll have the sun in our eyes this half, flashed through my mind and then Brownlie himself kicked off too deep and our fullback Jackie Tindall, one of the best and most versatile players of my era, caught it safely and banged it into touch.

'We were forced on the defensive at the start and for a while things looked bleak. The All Blacks missed three penalties in a row and then gradually our magnificent forwards began to assert themselves and I could drive our opponents back by using the touchline. I don't think I've ever seen a more relaxed and supremely confident Springbok pack than the one old Phil commanded that afternoon. I am not telling you a word of a lie, they kept chattering to each other throughout the match! Pierre de Villiers, my little scrumhalf partner from Paarl, was also in great form and he was getting his passes to me in spite of the attentions of his lively opposite number, Dalley.

'About 20 minutes into the first half we struck with a threequarter movement and Jack Slater, on the wing, had my brother Stanley unmarked next to him when he, for some reason, neglected to pass and ran slap into the arms of the All Blacks fullback, Lindsay. We were nicely on top and I, for one, quickly forgave Jack his lapse. Then disaster struck when Bernard Duffy, Stanley's fellow-centre, was badly concussed in a tackle and both Phil and I knew that he could never see out the game. From virtually the next scrum Pierre dodged Scrimshaw, who was acting as the All Blacks' so-called 'rover' that day, and passed the ball to me. I was

Flocks of photographers were already part of the rugby scene in 1928. Here they await the appearance of the two teams for the Newland's test. African Mirror's newsreel cameraman is on the right, ready to record the event for the cinema screen.

pretty hemmed in by the defence, but instead of smothering me as quickly as they could, the defence hesitated, the biggest crime you can commit in test rugby. I dropped for goal and we were leading 4–0 at half-time.

'We had to make do with 14 players throughout the second spell as poor Duffy simply could not be allowed to risk further injury. Phil decided at half-time to take Nick Pretorius out of the pack and we were still discussing our bad luck when Mr Mark walked up to us.

'"What are you going to do now, Osler?" he asked me in his usual manner.

'Startled, I stuttered: "I don't know, Mr Mark. I'm not the captain. Phil is."

'But Phil did not have an answer either and Mr Mark just glared at us. We simply had to think, which was Mr Mark's way of doing things.

'Finally I said, "From some of the scrums in the middle of the field I'll use Stanley on the blind side. But the rest of the time I feel I must use the touchline as long as Phil and the forwards can stay on top."

'Mr Mark nodded. "That's it", he said and walked away.

'Soon after the resumption I dropped my second goal and about three minutes later one of their forwards, Johnson, late-tackled me after I had punted ahead and Neser gave a penalty where the ball had landed, an uncommon thing for referees to do in those days. I was a bit shaken from the knock, but it was an easy kick and we were now leading 11–0. Pretorius was doing well among the backs and with such a useful lead, I began to use my threequarters more freely; Stanley, who was never again to play for South Africa because of injury, twice nearly went over and Phil also just failed to get a try after another break by my brother.

'In between I managed to add another penalty to our score and it was then that I again tried the plan to use Stanley on the blind side. He streaked right through and gave to Prinsloo on the wing, who dropped the ball as he went over the line! A few minutes later we tried again, except that this time I made the initial break myself. I slipped the ball to Jack Slater about ten yards from the goalline. Jack was

Selectors with the South African team for the first test. Back row: SA Townsend (selector), PJ Nel, AF Markötter (selector), HJ Potgieter, G St Leger Devenish (selector), GM Daneel, WFR Schreiner (selector), SP van Wyk, NF Pretorius; second row: JT Slater, JC Tindall, BL Osler, PJ Mostert (captain), TB Pienaar (manager and selector), TL Krüger, JP Prinsloo, Dr NJ van Druten; front row: P du P de Villiers, BA Duffy, SG Osler.

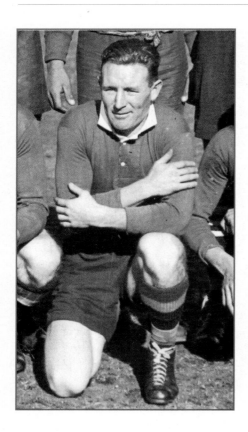

Jackie Tindall's talents featured in the 1928 tour to New Zealand. He was regarded by Bennie Osler as the best fullback of his era.

a burly and determined wing and he ploughed through to score. I gave the difficult conversion to Jackie Tindall, who could not get it over.

'It was only in the dressingroom later that I found out that my 14 points were a record individual contribution in a test, a record that was to stand for 21 years until Okey Geffin bettered it with five penalties against the 1949 All Blacks. Frankly, and this is not false modesty, the victory belonged to Phil Mostert and his forwards. I might have scored the points, but they did the work.'

The public and the press went hysterical over Osler's performance. Now the Springboks were the ones hailed as the supermen of rugby and the trouble was that some of them must have believed what they read in the newspapers.

▲▲▲

Less than a month after being beaten 17–0 in Durban, the All Blacks won the second test in Johannesburg 7–6 before what was then a record crowd of 38 000 which included such dignitaries as the Prime Minister, General JBM Hertzog. With the best tickets in the stadium priced at £2.2.0 (a huge sum in those days), it was hardly surprising that the gate receipts put the Transvaal Rugby Union well on its way to becoming the wealthiest amateur sporting body in the world.

The injured Stanley Osler and Bernard Duffy were replaced by JAR Dobie and JC van der Westhuizen, and Gerry Brand and NS (Jacko) Tod were the new wings. The selection of Brand, soon to become one of the most respected players in South Africa, caused quite an upset, of all places in the Western Province where he was not then highly regarded.

The selectors did make one blunder, though, by dropping De Villiers and giving Osler Transvaal's Devine as his scrumhalf. Devine had played well for Transvaal against the All Blacks and the selectors thought that he should get a chance.

The unwarranted tampering with a match-winning combination and an overdose of self-confidence proved the Springboks' undoing. Devine, whose passing was erratic, and Osler could not strike up an understanding and the centres could not find their feet. To add to all their problems, Tod, the one new Springbok wing, was badly injured after only a few minutes.

Yet the Springboks led in the scoring for most of the match after Phil Mostert had dropped a miraculous goal from a mark, caught after a drop-out, and Osler had succeeded with a penalty. Until later in the match the All Blacks had only a penalty by Lindsay to show for all their excellent efforts. Then WA Strang dropped a beautiful goal to give them a one-point lead and the Springboks, who played in a most desultory fashion, could not make up the leeway. In this period of desperate attack, Brand served notice of many wonderful efforts to come, when he hit the upright with a dropgoal described afterwards as one of the highlights of the match in spite of the fact that it failed.

As far as the Springboks were concerned the All Blacks' forwards were the real heroes of the day. They were learning to cope with the South African scrummaging technique and often pushed the Springboks clean off the ball.

'In the second half the Springbok forwards were smitten hip and thigh,' wrote New Zealand journalist Graham Beamish. 'They took command to display craft, pace and precision, which surprised the most fervent New Zealand followers and sent them into ecstasies of joy ...'

Mostert agreed. In an aftermatch interview he said bluntly: 'It was their forwards who carried the day.'

The selectors did a good job for the third and crucial test in Port Elizabeth on 18 August. De Villiers came back into the side and Manus de Jongh, on the wing, and Willie Rousseau, at centre, were new caps. Other newcomers were MM (Boy) Louw and the props John Olivier from Transvaal and AF du Toit from Western Province. Eleven members of the Springbok team were from Western Province, including the entire back line, three from Transvaal and one from Natal. It was also to be the first test in which the Springboks were to wear white shorts; the only reason being to make it easier for Neser who refereed all four tests. There was a record crowd in Port Elizabeth and to their great delight a far more purposeful South African team led 5–0 after only five minutes.

A bad pass under pressure had bounced off fullback Lindsay's shoulder and Phil Nel, the sole Natal representative, was over in a flash. Osler managed to convert from a difficult position.

It became a pretty robust struggle between the forwards after that, with Boy Louw showing that he was not to be intimidated. Fine work by Finlayson at a lineout, a few yards from the Springbok line, enabled Stewart to dive over for a try, but Lindsay's kick bounced away after hitting the post. De Jongh then had his nose broken and Pretorius had to substitute for him for a few minutes. On his return to the field, De Jongh, broken nose and all, scored a beautiful try after Van Druten, Osler, Rousseau and Van der Westhuizen had forced the gap.

Osler missed the conversion and with Grenside adding another unconverted try, the half-time score was 8–6 in favour of the Springboks. The second half was a titanic struggle with splendid touch-kicking the deciding factor. He nursed his pack carefully, but also never missed an opportunity to use his backs. It was the most exciting match of the series as first one team and then the other narrowly missed scoring chances until finally, after a concerted attack, Daneel went over for a try with Osler's kick just shaving the upright.

With the score 11–6 to the Springboks and time about up, Lilburne, Hazlett and Swain launched a terrific attack which stretched the Springbok defence to breaking point. A final pass gave Grenside a clear run to the goalline, but Brand and Van der Westhuizen caught up with the wing and crashtackled him on the corner flag. Neser blew the final whistle immediately afterwards.

Mostert summed it up when he told an interviewer in the dressingroom: 'This was one of the hardest games in which I have ever participated. Right up to the last minute no one could be sure of the result.'

▲▲▲

In the last match before the final test, Western Province, virtually a Springbok team, handed the All Blacks their fifth defeat of the tour after yet another brilliant display by De Villiers and Osler, in conjunction with a pack led by Mostert. PK Morkel scored a try with the double side-step which

Phil Mostert leads the Springboks in a rendition of their 'war cry' before the start of the first test in Durban.

The final test of the series against New Zealand was played at Newlands and became known as the Umbrella Test. The Springboks lost 5–13.

earned him Springbok colours for the last test and Osler added a dropgoal and a penalty against an unconverted try by Dalley for Western Province to win 10–3. Osler actually put over two drops, but referee Alec van der Horst ruled that in his first effort the ball had touched the All Black, Harvey, and refused to award the four points.

With the unlucky Jock van Niekerk, one of the great wings in our rugby history, selected for the one and only test of his career and PK Morkel having earned his place after his fine showing for Western Province, there were only two changes, both on the wing, in the Springbok team for the final test.

The All Blacks made a far more significant change for what was for them a do-or-die match. They brought in Mark Nicholls at flyhalf and it was due almost entirely to this gifted player, who scored 10 points with two penalties and a drop-goal, that New Zealand managed to win the test and draw the series.

Nicholls and the uninspired All Black forwards did to the Springboks almost exactly what Osler and his pack did to them in the first test. The match which took place before 23 000 drenched spectators at Newlands on 1 September 1928 was instantly named the 'Umbrella Test' as it rained almost continuously. The Springboks could not cope with the conditions, but it is doubtful whether any team could have beaten the All Blacks that afternoon.

South Africa did not concede their first defeat at Newlands for 37 years without an almighty struggle, but on the day the All Blacks deserved their victory. The game was often rough and at least two All Blacks received serious lectures from Neser, but the Springboks were no angels either.

The All Blacks had finally learnt to hold their own in the scrums and in all other facets of play they held the upper hand. Van der Westhuizen scored South Africa's try, converted by Osler, while Swain scored a try for the All Blacks with Nicholls adding two penalties and a superb dropgoal.

▲▲▲

Although there was an unofficial match against Combined Universities to follow, arranged only because of a delay in the departure of the *Ceramic*, the All Blacks tour of South Africa was over and once again the spoils were divided evenly.

It remained for skipper Maurice Brownlie to sum it all up when he said in his parting speech:

'In all our matches we have found South Africans most worthy foemen, and we shall carry away with us most pleasant recollections of the many and hard matches we have enjoyed.'

VENUE	SOUTH AFRICA	RESULT	SOUTH AFRICA				NEW ZEALAND			
			T	C	P	D	T	C	P	D
DURBAN	WON	17–0	1	0	2	2	0	0	0	0
JOHANNESBURG	LOST	6–7	0	0	1	1M	0	0	1	1
PORT ELIZABETH	WON	11–6	3	1	0	0	2	0	0	0
CAPE TOWN	LOST	5–13	1	1	0	0	1	0	2	1
		39–26	5	2	3	3M	3	0	3	2
SERIES: SOUTH AFRICA PLAYED 4; W2, L2, D0										

BENNIE OSLER

Bennie Osler played in 17 tests for South Africa between 1924 and 1933 and completely dominated the era with his controversial brilliance. Controversial he certainly was, because not everybody agreed with his heavy reliance on tactical kicking. Many thought that he was stifling the development of good threequarters, but even his severest critics had to admit he was a supreme matchwinner.

Benjamin Louwrens Osler was born at Aliwal North on 23 November 1901 and as a youngster at Western Province Preparatory School, later at Rondebosch Boys High and finally at Kingswood College, Grahamstown, he showed extraordinary potential as a rugby player and to a lesser extent, as a cricketer. He studied law at the University of Cape Town between 1920 and 1925 and it was in this period, so he always insisted, that he played the best rugby of his career.

This was before he became the most famous player in the country and therefore the automatic target for all his opponents. The newspaper reports of the time confirm that he was then a daring, attacking flyhalf who liked to run the ball. At the age of 20, Osler made his debut for Western Province as a centre threequarter, but he soon became his provincial team's flyhalf. In 1924 he played in the first of what was to be an unbroken run of 17 tests.

Osler's value as a player can perhaps best be proved by the fact that South Africa never lost an international series with him in the pivotal position, Western Province kept the Currie Cup throughout the period he regularly played for them, and University of Cape Town, Hamiltons and Villagers won the Grand Challenge competition in that order as he moved from one club to the other.

Of all the matches Osler won off his own bat, he remembered with the most enjoyment the one when he scored a last-minute dropgoal to snatch victory for Kingswood over Grey High School. He also always had a particular fondness and respect for the University of Stellenbosch and he preferred reminiscing about the keen intervarsity matches than talking about dour international battles. An intervarsity remembered with particular pleasure was his final one in 1925 when UCT fought back from a 0–7 deficit to win 14–7. It was in this match that Osler dropped two long-range goals and there was always the inevitable chuckle in his voice whenever he recounted how he heard Markötter shout at his players from the touchline: 'Don't wait, you fools! Run him down!' when they seemed to hesitate.

Osler was an autocrat on the field and he was quite capable of giving erring players, particularly scrumhalves, a tongue-lashing. Osler believed in using his threequarters only when the time was ripe and he was the sole judge of that. His immaculate touchkicking, invariably to the side nearest his forwards, was a boon to any hard-working pack and his tactical punting, cross-kicks and grubberkicks, could crack the most organized defence. In those days a dropgoal counted four points and Osler won many games by putting them over from the most acute angles and, more often than not, with only a split-second in which to do it. But this most talented of players could also break a line with devastating effect when he spotted a gap, and he handled and passed with swift precision. He preferred his University of Cape Town and 1924 Springbok partner, Pally Truter, to all the scrumhalves he played with, but also had the highest praise for De Villiers and Danie Craven. Craven, eventually to become the best-known personality in world rugby, often admitted that his respect for Osler bordered on awe and there is no doubt that he must have been a difficult man to combine with.

Bennie Osler perfected his skill through regular practice and insisted to his dying day that his younger brother Stanley was a more natural and better player than he ever was. Markötter agreed, but always qualified his statement by saying: 'If I wanted to play rugby, I would select Stanley. If I wanted to win, I would play Bennie'.

CHAPTER 10

1931/32

SOUTH AFRICA TOUR
THE BRITISH ISLES

▲▲▲

The third Springbok visit to Britain in the northern hemisphere rugby season of 1931/32 was South Africa's most successful overseas tour since entering the international arena in 1891. All four tests were won, the Springboks were defeated on only one occasion and twice held to a draw. And yet history has passed a rather harsh judgement on the team. Under the captaincy of Osler, then past his best and as he himself said with his usual frankness, playing the worst rugby of his career, the side received a reputation for being preoccupied with winning and having relied on stodgy and over-cautious methods to achieve their success.

'We played to our strength and we would have been foolish to adopt any other approach,' Osler explained. 'We had a magnificent pack of forwards, outstanding scrumhalves in Craven and De Villiers and a match-winning fullback in Gerry Brand. Our best wing, Jock van Niekerk, was injured right at the beginning of the

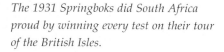

The 1931 Springboks did South Africa proud by winning every test on their tour of the British Isles.

tour, several of our other attacking threequarters were also handicapped by injury and our steadiest centre, my vice-captain JC van der Westhuizen, as well as the other senior players, were in general agreement with my tactics on the heavy grounds we invariably encountered in Britain.'

The Springboks played according to the same pattern they had employed against the 1928 All Blacks – one based on forward supremacy and Osler's tactical kicking. The 1931/32 team selected to tour Britain was a good blend of experience and youthful enthusiasm. Tindall and Mostert were the veterans, with the Somerset West forward embarking on his fourth international series and Tindall, like Osler, wearing Springbok colours for the third time. Brand, Van der Westhuizen, De Villiers, Boy Louw, Nel, Van Niekerk and Daneel had all been blooded against the 1928 All Blacks. At the age of 20 and without any experience of provincial rugby, Danie Craven was invited to the trials. Near the end of the week he did well enough to slip into the touring party as De Villiers' understudy.

The Springboks left for Britain on the *Windsor Castle* and team manager Theo Pienaar gave them a serious lecture on the responsibilities of representing their country on an overseas tour. Handling practices also came to an abrupt stop after three balls had been lost overboard and it was in a vain attempt to stop one that Jock van Niekerk, that most unfortunate of all Springboks, hurt the knee which was to ruin the tour for him and to end his career.

▲▲▲

The tour started off rather badly with the Springboks erratic in their first match and losing the Transvaal wing Floors Venter with a broken nose in the process. They failed to score a single try and dropgoals by Van der Westhuizen and Osler, and a penalty apiece from Osler and Brand, gave them their 14–3 win. Four tries in the next match, against powerful Newport, made their critics a bit more wary, but they were still regarded as well below the standard of previous Springboks.

Maurice Zimerman, the muscular Western Province wing, scored his first try against Newport and showed the hard-running, bullocking style which made him such a success on the tour. He was to go on to score many tries from kicks to the corner-flag by Osler.

The third match of the tour, against Swansea, must rate among the roughest and dirtiest a Springbok team has ever played. According to Craven, both teams were guilty of dirty tactics and at one stage Daneel, a Dutch Reformed minister, pulled his head out of a scrum and in exasperation said: 'Look, kick if you must, punch if you must, but please stop the swearing!'

The Springboks eventually won 10–3, but the spectators were in such an ugly mood that the players were kept behind a locked door in the dressingroom until things had cooled down. By the time the two teams met again at the official banquet the Welshmen were as hospitable as only these wonderful people can be, although several players on both sides were nursing the scars of battle.

Osler, who did not play that afternoon, and Pienaar were very upset, however, and in a team talk Pienaar threatened that the next Springbok to make himself guilty of dirty play would be summarily sent home.

In the next match, against Abertillery and Cross Keys, trouble flared again. At first the Springboks, mindful of their warning, did not retaliate, but they could endure only so much, and this game also deteriorated into a brawl. This time the Springboks were not to blame and Pienaar decided not to carry out his threat.

Gerry Brand's wonderful kicking made him the hero of Twickenham.

FOUR CAPTAINS

The captains of four Springbok touring teams photographed together just before the 1931 side's departure. Left to right: Paul Roos (1906), Billy Millar (1912), Theo Pienaar (1921 and also manager of the 1931 team) and Bennie Osler.

The match against Combined London, the team's first appearance at tradition-rich Twickenham, followed and for once everything clicked. Zimerman scored two typical storming tries, the burly Nic Bierman got two and Osler and Brand, playing on the left-wing, also went over. But Brand, nicknamed 'Firebrand' by an appreciative crowd, was the hero of the match. He converted all six tries. It was an excellent victory for the Springboks but they had to pay dearly for it as Geoff Gray suffered a cracked collarbone and Osler had a fractured rib.

In the next match, against Midland Counties, Jock van Niekerk made his first appearance of the tour and the first time he got the ball his weak knee packed up completely and he was never to play again.

With the injury list ominously long, Pienaar immediately cabled the South African Rugby Board, suggesting that DO Williams, an 18-year-old Villagers wing with outstanding potential, be sent over to help out. It was to be several weeks before Dai, South Africa's youngest international player, could arrive because there was no such thing as air travel for passengers in those days.

In the match against Cambridge, Craven finally learnt to relax and to combine smoothly with Osler, who had by then fully recovered from his injury. Craven, a much stronger man than De Villiers, was obviously a better bet on the heavy overseas fields and once he proved that he could dovetail with Osler, his place in the international matches was virtually assured.

The Springboks' only defeat of the tour came at Leicester against Midland Counties. They were hopelessly outplayed for most of the match and deep in the second half found themselves trailing 6–24. With Louw injured and off the field, the future looked dark for the South Africans, but they hit back with a series of marvellous attacks, including four tries by Zimerman.

With the score 21–24 the Counties got an easy penalty, however, and it knocked the stuffing out of the Springboks' come-back. They finally lost 21–30.

Barry Heatlie, one of the great pioneers of South African rugby who travelled with the team, had this to say about the match in an article written years later:

'Defeats are not national calamities. There is no need for a wave of depression to sweep the country if a team should suffer defeat, such as was evidently the case here. When the 1931 team was beaten at Leicester, I received on that occasion a cable from a certain town which shall be nameless, reading: "Send the team back home to come and plant potatoes"!

'A team may be greater in defeat than in victory. That defeat at Leicester meant more to the prestige and the sportsmanship of our team than all our victories. The way in which we took it made an indelible impression on all who saw it.'

Osler, giving one of his best performances, restored the team's self-confidence by guiding them to an excellent victory over Cardiff and Llanelly, and Neath and Aberavon also had to bow the knee before the big crunch came against Wales.

SOUTH AFRICA vs WALES

Tests between the Springboks and Wales are like the battles against the All Blacks – they have a special significance, an added spice.

Danie Craven, in his biography *Ek Speel vir Suid-Afrika* described better than anyone else what it was like before, during and after that famous match against Wales at St Helens, Swansea, on 5 December 1931...

'Uncle Theo had hardly finished reading out the names of the test team, when Pierre de Villiers came over to congratulate me. That there could be so much sportsmanship in any man, I could never forget.

'The Friday before the match it rained continuously. The many cables of congratulations made the tension even worse. You begin to wonder why you ever started to play rugby. There is a paralysis in your muscles and a slowness in your movements. Willpower seems to have disappeared. Your thoughts are centred around the game and there is fear that you might disappoint your team and your country. The night before the match you cannot sleep and nightmares interrupt what rest you do get.

'Breakfast tasted terrible and after the early lunch we slumped around the place... A traffic constable with his siren screaming led our bus through the rain and milling crowds towards the stadium and we arrived just in time to go to the dressingroom and to start changing.

'Bennie calls us together. "Boys", he starts, "we are all feeling a little scared. It is a feeling we all share. It is right that we feel like that, because the honour of our country is at stake."

At that moment the brass band blared out the first few notes of the Welsh anthem and the huge crowd began to sing.

'Then it is over and Bennie is speaking again. I have never heard such a speech before. Silently we listen to every word. Every word gives us more strength and courage. Each sentence brings back the will to win. Now we are ready. Come what may, we will live, we will die for South Africa. Bennie's last words are: "Remember, we will try to handle the ball. Let me have it. If we find that we can't handle the wet ball, I will tell you what to do."

'We threw everything into the game from the start, but missed two quick tries through our own mistakes. Once the ball got lost between Zimerman and I, and my desperate grab actually sent it right into the hands of Boon, their fast left-wing. At that moment my whole life passed before my eyes and I could see how we have lost the game, and all my fault. The next moment I could kiss Gerry Brand as he bundled Boon into touch. By now Bennie had decided on a change of tactics. It is now up to the two of us to kick, every conceivable kind of kick as long as it goes towards the Welsh half of the field. Our forwards are up to press ahead as Bennie and I launched one kick after another.

'Bennie Osler changed his tactics again at this stage. Instructing our loose-forwards George Daneel, André McDonald and Alfi van der Merwe to chase the ball with everything they've got, he ordered our forwards to actually give Wales the ball from the scrums and the lineouts. But a high punt from Boon presented Wales with first blood when Zimerman slipped and a second kick sent the ball past Brand for Davies to score an unconverted try. Midway through the second half another one of Powell's wild passes missed Ralph and this time Osler himself was on the spot. The ball bounced in his hands and he instantly placed a short kick ahead for his forwards. Ferdie Bergh dribbled it further and then George Daneel shot

A youthful Danie Craven is on his toes at scrumhalf as Phil Mostert and Fanie Louw battle for the ball in a lineout during the match against Midland Counties at Leicester in 1931. The Springbok behind Louw is Ferdie Bergh.

through like a bullet to score the equalizing try. Gerry's conversion missed and although we could feel that we were getting on top, we just could not get through for the winning points. With less than ten minutes to go, Phil Nel broke through from a lineout with the ball at his feet. He dribbled it through the sea of water as one defender after the other was beaten. Finally it was kicked past fullback Bassett and as Nel fell over him, Bergh tapped the ball over the line to score. Osler took the conversion himself and when he succeeded, we knew that we had won. Wales attacked furiously in the few remaining minutes, but our defence held.'

One of the epic victories in Springbok history – beating Wales in their own back-yard and under their own conditions will always be an achievement of pride.

The match against Lancashire and Cheshire immediately following the test was in many respects the most amazing of the tour. Although the Springboks won, no less than five of their players had to leave the field because of injury, leaving them with a scrum consisting of three forwards! At one point, one of the Lancashire players suggested to his captain that it would be a good idea to take lineouts instead of scrums only to get an answer so typical from rugby in England in those days: 'There are only three of them left. It would be unfair to capitalize on their misfortune. We don't play rugby only to win, you know.'

SOUTH AFRICA vs IRELAND
The test against Ireland was a lot easier than the one against Wales, but again the Springboks trailed at half-time. After the resumption, the forwards improved and Craven and Osler got more room in which to move. Zimerman scored a typical try after a high punt from Osler had caught the Irish fullback in two minds, and near the end of the match Osler broke around the blindside and gave the ball to Frankie Waring with Zimerman next to him, and only the fullback to beat. Waring, for a reason known only to himself, cut inside instead of drawing the fullback and passing to Zimerman. He ran right into the arms of loose-forward Jamie Clinch, a veteran of the 1924 tour to South Africa, but somehow he managed to wriggle past for the winning try which Osler converted to make the final score 8–3.

SOUTH AFRICA vs ENGLAND
The second match against London nearly brought tragedy when Tindall was seriously injured and his life was only saved after an emergency operation.

Then came the test against England, the most disappointing match of the tour. Bergh scored an unconverted try and in the last thirty seconds of the game, Brand caught a poor clearing kick on the halfway line and right on touch. From this spot he calmly kicked a dropgoal, still considered to be the best seen at Twickenham.

It is said that somebody afterwards went and measured the distance from where Brand kicked to the point where the ball landed after sailing between the uprights. The distance was 85 yards. No wonder 'Firebrand' was the toast of Twickenham. His miracle kick was one of only three highlights in a dull match, won 7–0 by the Springboks. The only other occasions the crowd had anything to shout over was when Bergh got his try after a fumble by Barr, and when Spong, the home team's flyhalf, slipped through the entire Springbok defence and had what he thought was a clear field ahead of him. He reckoned without the exceptional speed of Daneel, who flew across to cut him down with a magnificent tackle.

After the match, the Springboks were invited to Buckingham Palace to meet George V and this occasion led to the most familiar anecdote in our rugby history. Apparently the players were lined up for the traditional introduction and hand-

Bennie Osler, resplendent in the fashionable attire for men in 1931, goes out to inspect the pitch before the Springboks' match against Gloucester-Somerset at Bristol. His team won 16–5.

shake and, to their surprise, they discovered that the king had some sort of question or banter for each of them. When he got to Pierre de Villiers, looking smaller than ever as he was flanked by two huge forwards, he seemed amused and asked which position he filled on the field. The story goes that De Villiers who had quite a deep voice for his size, suddenly squeaked: 'Scrumhalf, Mr King!'

SOUTH AFRICA vs SCOTLAND

The only thing that bothered the Springboks at this late stage of their tour was the news that Tindall was still in a critical condition in a London hospital. Osler and Pienaar were at his bedside and kept the team informed with regular telegrams. They had already decided that should their teammate die, no further matches would be played.

Osler returned to the team just before the test against Scotland, the final match of the tour, with the news that there was improvement in Tindall's condition and that he had expressed the wish that they should not cancel the game.

There were more than 74 000 people packed around Murrayfield and once again the weather was appalling. During the first half the Springboks played against a strong wind which drove sleet with terrific force into their faces.

Scotland scored first when their flyhalf H Lind picked up and cut through after Osler had tried an interception, but the conversion was a total disaster. The home team nevertheless had the best of the first half and their dribbling rushes to the accompaniment of the chant 'Feet, Scotland, feet!' from the crowd, caused the Springboks one nightmare after the other.

In the second half, the Springboks had the advantage of the wind, but it was so powerful that it never really helped either side. The Springbok forwards were gradually getting on top, however, and a strong run by Venter took the touring team to within striking distance. Scotland hooked from the scrum, but they heeled too slowly and the pass between Logan and Lind went astray. Osler somehow managed to swoop down on it and before the defence could recover he was over the line. To try and convert was a waste of time and Brand's effort never looked like it would go in the right direction.

Scotland fought back with everything they had and managed to drive the Springboks back to their own goalline from where Craven used the gale effectively to find touch not many yards from the Scottish line!

From the next scrum McDonald fooled the defence by breaking away quickly, but without the ball. The Scottish loose-forwards charged down on him, leaving a gap which Craven took to score near the posts. Brand missed even this comparatively easy conversion as the wind blew the ball over in the fraction of a second before his boot hit it.

But it did not really matter. The Springboks had won 6–3 and the tour had ended on a triumphant note.

The Springboks attended a race meeting at Newbury and from their expressions it does not look as if they backed the winner of the Autumn Cup, the feature race of the day. From left, Bennie Osler, Theo Pienaar, Henry Forrest and Maurice Zimerman.

Phil Mostert is brought down by a tackle in the test against England at Twickenham. There is not a single Springbok up in support, but South Africa won 7–0.

VENUE	SOUTH AFRICA	RESULT	SOUTH AFRICA				BRITISH ISLES			
			T	C	P	D	T	C	P	D
WALES (SWANSEA)	WON	8–3	2	1	0	0	1	0	0	0
IRELAND (DUBLIN)	WON	8–3	2	1	0	0	0	0	1	0
ENGLAND (TWICKENHAM)	WON	7–0	1	0	0	1	0	0	0	0
SCOTLAND (EDINBURGH)	WON	6–3	2	0	0	0	1	0	0	0

Although Markötter never played for South Africa, he discovered and forged too many Springboks during his long career for anyone to deny claims that he was possibly the greatest rugby authority of his time.

MARKÖTTER'S CHOICE

The 1931/32 Springboks were selected following a week of gruelling trials at Newlands and Markötter's remarkable ability to spot hidden talent was much in evidence. André McDonald, for instance, was a centre in the Stellenbosch second team and a mediocre one at best, when Mr Mark at a practice one afternoon ordered him to buy a scrumcap. McDonald did as he was told, but when he turned up the next day with it he was horrified when the short-tempered coach told him to join the forwards as an eighthman. McDonald seemed to lack the physical qualities of a forward and after only a few minutes up front he had to be helped off the field. But Markötter was far from repentant. He forced McDonald to stay at number-eight and almost without knowing how it happened, the young theology student was outstanding in his new position – good enough to gain his place in the touring side. Daneel, who played scrumhalf in the lower teams while at university, was also plucked from obscurity by Mr Mark when he made him an eighthman at Stellenbosch. He also became a member of the 1931 touring team. And then there was Jimmy White, a product of Queens College, Queenstown, who played for Border as a centre, flyhalf and fullback, but impressed his own province so little that they did not even nominate him for the trials. Markötter had seen him in action and it was at his insistence that the national selectors invited White to Cape Town.

Ferdie Bergh was in the lower teams at Stellenbosch University when Markötter noticed his build and soon he was an outstanding forward in the first team and went on to play 17 tests for the Springboks and, with seven tries, was South Africa's leading try-scorer for more than 25 years. Bergh was already an established player by the time of the 1931 trials, but the tour was to be his first taste of international rugby.

Danie Craven was perhaps Markötter's 'masterpiece'. He came to Stellenbosch from the little Free State town of Lindley, and as an under-19 scrumhalf, ended his first season for the Maties by playing in the fourth team. The next year he was down to play in the second team in a practice against the senior side, when Markötter suddenly thundered: 'Craven, where are you? Go first team!'

His first senior club match was a disaster. Playing against a Hamiltons team studded with names like Osler, Brand, Tindall and Van Wyk, the Maties received a hiding and Craven was convinced that he would be dropped.

But it did not happen although Craven swears that he played match after match with the axe poised over his head. A few days before the intervarsity against University of Cape Town, the first four teams were addressed by Markötter. His first words were: 'Where's Craven?' And then he launched an absolute torrent of words at the squirming young scrumhalf. Craven was stunned at the tirade and then came the extra sentence that made everything bearable.'Remember, Craven', the coach added in a softer tone, 'I only shout at players whom I like'.

It was to be the first of many such harsh lectures and each one contained at least one pearl of rugby wisdom which helped Craven on the way to becoming one of the greatest players of all time and eventually to earn international recognition as an administrator. Oubaas Mark gave us many Springboks, but in giving us Craven he supplied us with perhaps the only man who could have steered South African rugby through the turbulent years of trouble and change the old coach could never have suspected were lying ahead for the game he loved so much.

GERRY BRAND

The 1931/32 tour was to establish Brand as one of the legendary figures in Springbok annals. Although Bennie Osler and other authorities often expressed the view that Brand was an even better wing than fullback it was for his performances in the last line of defence that he will always be remembered. He had a wonderful sense of anticipation and his fielding was immaculate, his tackling deadly. Although he was not particularly powerfully built, his timing was so perfect and his speed so great, that he was one of the most feared tacklers of his era. It was rare for him to miss his man, and veteran sportswriter Maxwell Price was once moved to write: 'On the field Brand was always a silent, mystic figure, whose presence on the opposing side always seemed to have an engulfing effect on the attackers. He would draw the player with the ball to his tackle like a human magnet...'

Brand had an instinctive flair for the game, but nevertheless perfected his kicking with hours and hours of practice. He was a left-footer, but could kick equally well with his right. His natural rhythm, such a vital factor for success at the highest level of sport, was a gift of nature, but it was sheer hard work that helped him to develop an exquisitely-timed screw-kick with which he could kick touches of enormous length and as a place- and drop-kicker he has had few equals.

Brand was painfully shy as a youngster and even at the height of his fame when he was the most-discussed player in South Africa since the heyday of Bennie Osler, he did not do much talking. Old-timers will tell you that Gerry Brand was always one of the neatest players on the field, his hair slicked back and everything clean from the collar of his jersey to the tips of his boots. After tackling an opponent he would 'trip back to position, quite unnecessarily dusting his white shorts which seldom were soiled in a game of rugby'.

South Africa has produced many world-class fullbacks over the years and only a fool would try and point to one player as being the best – it is, after all, impossible for anyone to have seen them all in action. It is sufficient to say that in his era Gerry Brand had no peers.

Gerry Brand, destined to become a legend in his own lifetime, entered the international arena in 1928. His kicking was outstanding in the test against England.

CHAPTER 11

1933

AUSTRALIA TOUR SOUTH AFRICA

▲▲▲

Danie Craven has the Australian defence in a tangle as he breaks powerfully in the third test at Ellis Park.

The year 1933 was one of the strangest in South African rugby history. Still flushed with the success of the tour to Britain and with a new crop of young Springboks backed up by a strong sprinkling of vastly experienced veterans, they should have been prepared to deal with any challenge. But in the second test of the series against Australia the Springboks suffered their biggest defeat up to that time and in the final international they were beaten again in a match that has often been described as the worst performance by a South African side.

It was Australia's first fully representative venture into the international rugby arena. Known until then as the Waratahs and with their players coming almost exclusively from New South Wales, the game had spread sufficiently to other states like Queensland and Victoria to acquire more of a national look about it. They were tabbed the Wallabies and under the captaincy of the New South Wales fullback Alec Ross, they came to South Africa for a full-length tour which was to include, for the first and last time, five test matches.

The Wallabies introduced a new concept of rugby to the South African public. Backed up by light and fast forwards, they played attacking rugby with an abandon we had never seen before. It was risky stuff, but the spectators loved it and the South African rugby authorities openly suggested that the Springboks follow suit. Although the Australians were beaten frequently in the matches leading up to the first international, the whole country was overcome with a fever of enthusiasm for the open game and there was insidious but powerful pressure on the Springboks to discard the subdue-probe-and-penetrate pattern they had so successfully evolved.

The Wallabies lost five of the nine matches played before the first test, but almost every team who met them left the field with a feeling that here was a team not to be dallied with. They were very quick to capitalize on mistakes and the best tactics against them would obviously be to dominate the tight phases, to nullify their loose-forwards and to be in complete control of possession.

Even with their captain Ross out because of an appendicitis operation and the vice-captain and best scrumhalf SJ Malcolm also injured, they were obviously in the process of perfecting their opportunistic style and the Springboks selected for the first test at Newlands were far from confident.

The team was selected after a week of trial matches played in the rain and the national selectors, Markötter, Schreiner, Devenish, Townsend and Kriek, decided to play it safe and included eleven members from Osler's 1931/32 touring party. The newcomers were Leon Barnard, a wing from South Western Districts, Jack Gage, a Free State wing who had already represented Ireland, George D'Alton and Innes Lyndon (Fronie) Froneman, really tight-forwards from Western Province and Border respectively but selected as flankers.

Shortly before the test, Barnard had to be replaced by Freddie Turner, then a youthful second-division player but destined to become one of the big stars of Springbok rugby in the 1930s because of his versatility. Turner was flown down from Port Elizabeth for the test, probably the first Springbok to make use of a form of transport then still in its infancy and, at just over 19 years of age, certainly the youngest to have actually played in a test to this day. Barnard, incidentally, never got another chance.

The selectors decided to include the veteran Osler in the team, but, rather harshly, took the captaincy from him and gave it to Phil Nel, the Natal lock forward. Many years later Nel told with what mixed feelings he accepted the honour:

'There was, for me, a tinge of regret that Bennie Osler had been deposed after our victorious tour of Britain. I felt, on hearing the news, that in some ways an injustice had been done to him. I was sitting in the lounge of a Cape Town hotel after Bill Schreiner had pinned the names of the selected players on the notice board and I was quite frankly shocked to hear that I had been nominated as captain. Just then I was called to the telephone. It was Bennie to wish me good luck, to add his congratulations on my appointment and to promise me his full support and loyalty. To me this was as fine a sporting gesture as I ever came across. Bennie and I always remained friends and I admired his strategic approach to the game tremendously.'

The reason for Osler's demotion could only have been that the selectors were unhappy with the winning, but sometimes unattractive, rugby the team had played in Britain. Battle-hardened veterans they might have been, but it seems as if even the national selectors were being influenced by the press and public to adopt the new Wallaby style.

The team refused to be influenced, however, and it was with typical forward domination that the Springboks won 17–3. A clever break by Craven brought the first try and at half-time the score was 6–0 after Brand had steered a penalty over the crossbar. After half-time Bergh went over for two unconverted tries and Osler, whose tactical kicking often bewildered the Wallabies, slipped through for a try, converted by Brand.

The final score indicated an easy victory as the Wallabies only had a penalty by flyhalf RR Biilmann to show for their efforts, but the Springboks, unlike the experts on the grandstand, knew only too well how often only a stroke of luck prevented the Wallabies from getting points.

They knew that to change their tactics and approach would only serve to accommodate the Australians.

Danie Craven, not yet 23 years old but already considered by many to be the best scrumhalf in the world, scores the first try of the 1933 series after a typical break early in the first test at Newlands.

The game was rough at times and even this seemed to worry the rugby authorities who had the strangest desire to lean over backwards in favour of the visitors. The Springboks got most of the blame for the incidents and nobody seemed to realize that in 'Wild Bill' Cerutti and Aubrey Hodgson the Wallabies had forwards who were certainly no angels.

Nel was injured in the first test and Osler took over the captaincy and was immediately subjected to a campaign from all sides to 'play open rugby'. The atmosphere for the test was all wrong; the Springboks were unmotivated and spent most of the time before the game enjoying themselves in the Durban surf. In addition, the selectors had made some inexplicable changes to the combination which won the Newlands international, switching Turner from wing to centre and Waring from centre to wing for reasons known only to themselves.

Osler, nearing the end of his illustrious career, was so sick and tired of the clamour for open rugby, which most people interpreted as a policy of never kicking, that he decided that just for once, he would allow himself to be dictated to. He knew only too well that the Springbok forwards, big and heavy men, needed nursing with judicious kicking and that they could never last the pace in eighty minutes of uninterrupted running, but, if that was what the public and the authorities wanted, then that was what they would get.

The result was a humiliating defeat with the Wallabies playing sensibly and kicking whenever necessary, winning 21–6. The Springboks were run ragged and except when Brand put over a penalty with a smooth dropkick and Waring scored a nice try, they seemed merely on the field for the sake of formality. Fullback JC Steggall, wing JD Kelaher, flyhalf Biilmann and forward Cerutti looked like world champions against the flat-footed Springboks.

The selectors did a far better job for the third test in Johannesburg bringing in Floors Venter on one wing and restoring Freddie Turner to the other, combining Jimmy White and Frankie Waring at centre and giving the forwards a little more pace with the inclusion of Fred Smollan and WH Clarke, both of whom had played well when Transvaal beat the Wallabies five days before the international. Nel, recovered from his injury, took over the captaincy again from Osler.

This time there were no shenanigans. The Springboks played it their way and with excellent tries by Boy Louw and Turner, one converted by Brand, and a dropgoal by Osler to an unconverted try by Cowper, won a good match 12–3. This, incidentally, was the fourth and final dropgoal of Osler's international career.

Craven became seriously ill after this test and, although he had practically recovered by the time of the fourth international in Port Elizabeth, he was not expected to play. On the Thursday before the match, however, both

Phil Nel, captain of the 1933 Springboks with referee Syd Malcolm and Alec Ross, captain of the first Australian team to visit South Africa.

Turner and Venter were injured and Craven had to fill one of the centre positions with Waring and with White and Brand in the wing positions while Border's Bunny Reid was brought in at fullback. De Villiers came back into the team as Osler's partner. It turned out to be a miserable match with the Wallabies concentrating so much on Osler that they forgot all about their 15-man pattern. The Springboks won 11–0 after tries by White and Fanie Louw, with Brand adding a penalty and Osler a conversion.

With victory in the series now assured, the selectors again made too many changes for the final international in Bloemfontein. The Wallabies had the services of their captain Ross for the first time in the tests and generally they were far better motivated.

It has been said that the level of discipline in the Springbok camp before this match was shocking. There were far too many social events and even a champagne party until the early hours of the morning. If the rumours were indeed true, then it is hardly surprising that they gave just about the worst performance in South African rugby history. The side appeared so ponderous and disinterested that it was rather a reflection on the Wallabies that they did not win by a much bigger score than 15–4.

In the second half, with both Nel and Fanie Louw injured and off the field, the Australians also seemed to lose interest in the affair and both teams, but particularly the Springboks, slunk back to their dressingrooms as thousands of disgruntled spectators trooped home. The only good thing to come out of this distressing match was that it brought home to the rugby authorities the fact that a test series should never consist of more than four tests.

It is a pity that the international career of the great Bennie Osler should have ended on such a dismal note. There was one consolation, though. A week later, in the final match of the tour, the Wallabies were beaten at Newlands by a team combined from Western Province Town and Country clubs. The score was 4–0 and it was Osler, with a typical dropgoal, who scored the points.

The 1933 selectors, from left to right: Charlie de Villiers, Piet Bayly, Phil Mostert, Bill Schreiner and AF Markötter.

VENUE	SOUTH AFRICA	RESULT	SOUTH AFRICA				AUSTRALIA			
			T	C	P	D	T	C	P	D
CAPE TOWN	WON	17–3	4	1	1	0	0	0	1	0
DURBAN	LOST	6–21	1	0	1	0	4	3	1	0
JOHANNESBURG	WON	12–3	2	1	0	1	1	0	0	0
PORT ELIZABETH	WON	11–0	2	1	1	0	0	0	0	0
BLOEMFONTEIN	LOST	4–15	0	0	0	1	3	1	0	1
		50–42	9	3	3	2	8	4	2	1
SERIES: SOUTH AFRICA PLAYED 5; W3, L2, D0										

Three great Springboks – Jimmy White, Pierre de Villiers and Bennie Osler.

CHAPTER 12

1937

SOUTH AFRICA TOUR AUSTRALIA AND NEW ZEALAND

▲▲▲

With Nel injured, Craven had to lead the Springboks in the first test of the series. Here he and Ron King are bringing their teams onto the field. The Springboks following Craven are Ferdie Bergh and Jan Lotz.

It was getting towards midnight on 10 April 1937, and inside the Metropole Hotel in Long Street, Cape Town, more than a hundred of South Africa's finest rugby players were waiting to hear who would be among the lucky 29 chosen to undertake the second tour of Australia and New Zealand in Springbok history.

A week of trial matches had ended at Newlands that afternoon and the national selectors were now deliberating in the Civil Service Club while the players were dining at the hotel. Bill Schreiner, chairman of the selectors, had promised to announce the names of the touring party at the hotel and hundreds of rugby fans had gathered in the street to wait for the big news.

For most of the players the dinner was a fiendish form of torture. Percy Twentyman-Jones, a former international player himself and then Judge President of the Cape Province, was in charge of the affair and he did his best to soothe raw nerves with a witty speech. Those were the days before smoking was regarded as an invitation to an early death and one newspaper reporter described the scene as one of players huddled in their chairs 'trimming their finger-nails with their teeth, gulping down stimulants to help to forget their anxiety, or strewing the carpets with cigarette ends as plentifully as autumn leaves ...'

Schreiner who became a national selector at the age of 26 while still an active player, was then in his sixteenth year as chairman. With him on the panel he had Markötter, a man of emphatic views, unorthodox methods and an unerring eye for talent, George St Leger Devenish who played for South Africa as far back as 1896, Frank Mellish who had the distinction of having represented both England and South Africa, and 'Gubby' Barlow, an outspoken man with years of experience.

Several players were obvious selections for the tour while Markötter with his usual supreme self-confidence had several places 'booked' for players in whom he had complete faith. Craven later revealed that Brand, Boy and Fanie Louw, Lochner and himself were notified well in advance that they would be making the tour. He also divulged for the first time that Mr Mark actually told him before the trials that he would be captain of the 1937 team. For once, something must have gone wrong with Markötter's plans because Philip Nel, and not Craven, eventually received the skipper's job. There is some evidence of disagreement between the selectors and the South African Rugby Board because it is a fact that Schreiner and his panel did not approve of the appointment of Percy Day as manager and Alec de Villiers as assistant manager of the side.

Reading about the trials now, it is rather startling to discover that Dauncey Devine, a 1924 Springbok scrumhalf and one of the originators of the dive-pass perfected by Craven, actually took part in them.

Ben du Toit, then regarded as the best loose-forward in South Africa, had been invited to the trials, but for some reason or other had decided to not make himself available for the tour. He came down from the Transvaal to watch the trials, however, and with the irascible 'help' of Mr Mark changed his mind and decided to play after all. The story is told that Du Toit was watching the trials from a seat in the stands when he felt a sudden urge to play. He then rushed to where the selectors were sitting and offered his services.

As they debated in the Civil Service Club, the selectors must have had their biggest headaches over the centre and flyhalf position. White, an experienced international player and the deadliest tackler of his day, was badly off-form, Louis Babrow and 'Koffie' Hofmeyr were also erratic and only the 19-year-old Johannes Lodewyk Augustinus Bester, known as 'Johnny', from Western Province had played consistently well throughout the week. The selectors decided to take the risk and to pick all four – a decision they were never to regret.

Outstanding flyhalves were even scarcer at the trials. The newcomers performed in the shadow of the retired Osler and their weaknesses were easier to spot than their strengths. Finally, Dirk van de Vyver and the virtually untried Tony Harris got the nod with the versatile Lochner selected as a utility back. Like the equally versatile Turner who was named as Gerry Brand's understudy at full-back, Lochner was destined to make his mark elsewhere among the threequarters.

Agreement reached at last, the selectors went to the Metropole Hotel where 'Uncle Bill' Schreiner, like a Roman senator of old, took up position on the first-floor balcony to read out the team to the players, at the same time giving the crowd in the street the opportunity to hear the names.

Boy Louw and so many other members of that mighty 1937 pack were at the peak of their careers at the time of the tour and an older generation of New Zealanders insist to this day that Phil Nel's forwards were the best ever to visit their country.

But when the team gathered in Durban in May that year to await departure on the *Ulysses* most South Africans were apprehensive about their prospects. Paul Roos travelled all the way from Cape Town to give them his blessing:

'We want the public and the men themselves to know that we are not sending the team over to become world champions. They must remember that they have been invited as guests rather than rivals. We hope that we shall learn mutually; you go over there as ambassadors of good sport and friendship. And my final words to you are that you keep yourselves in the pink of condition, because you have a duty to perform to your hosts who have invited you and secondly to your country which is sending you ...'

But Paul Roos was not the best-known headmaster of his day for nothing and he ended his speech with a ringing instruction:

'Let the spirit be the spirit of the Charge of the Light Brigade! Theirs not to reason why, theirs but to do or die! The message I bring to you from the South African Rugby Board is that you should go forth, my boys, and win your spurs!'

The 1937 team was run by the players for the players and perhaps there is a valuable lesson to be learnt in this. Percy Day, the manager, had no say in the training or selection of the side, which was entirely the responsibility of a committee consisting of Nel, Brand, Craven, Boy Louw and Strachan.

In fact, Percy Day's functions were so limited on the tour that when he, for reasons never officially explained, returned to South Africa before the end of the tour, it hardly caused any comment.

FRANKIE WARING

The trials must have been a period of anguish for Waring, who wore the Springbok jersey between 1931 and 1933. Business commitments had made it clear to Waring that he would not be able to go on the tour, but, although he informed the selectors of his predicament, he decided to play in the trials anyway. He performed brilliantly at centre throughout the week and it must have been heart-breaking for him when at the end of the final trial match, the selectors gave him exactly ten minutes in which to make up his mind finally. He decided to miss the tour.

One of the major problems on board the *Ulysses* was finding a method to keep fit. There was only one rugby ball on the ship and it was soon sent bobbing along the Indian Ocean waves by an unwise pass. The players then had to do the best they could with a medicine ball from the gymnasium which might have developed a few stronger wrists, but could not have helped much to promote swift handling.

Philip Nel's 1937 Springboks provided one of the most glorious chapters in South African rugby history. In fact, there is ample evidence to support the frequent claim that this was indeed the greatest team ever to wear the green-and-gold.

▲▲▲

On the tour of just under four months, they played 28 matches, including two unofficial fixtures, in Australia and New Zealand, were beaten only twice, and scored 855 points to 180. Both internationals in Australia were won and the series against the All Blacks went 2–1 to the Springboks – still the one and only time in the 56-year-old rivalry between the two countries that a rubber had been won by the touring side. To crown it all, the Springboks played the attractive, balanced rugby they had promised to produce.

SOUTH AFRICA vs AUSTRALIA

Australia and South Africa tackled each other once again when Phil Nel's mighty 1937 Springboks called around briefly before embarking on their triumphant tour of New Zealand.

In the first test on a soaking wet Oval Cricket Ground in Sydney, the Springboks played brilliantly although the final score was only 9–5. In many ways this was Jimmy White's match. White played opposite Cyril Towers, Australia's captain and star centre, and beforehand the Border Springbok was often told what a tough time he was in for. It was just the stuff to motivate him into giving a superb exhibition of crashtackling and Towers was drilled into the mud time and again.

An interesting sidelight was that a radio broadcaster brought a microphone on to the field at half-time and asked the Springboks if they had any messages for their teammate Ben du Toit, who had had a vertebra cracked in one of the early matches of the tour and was listening to the commentary from his hospital bed. The messages were in Afrikaans and unprintable!

▲▲▲

The second international, on the same ground, was a vicious affair, considered by some to have been the dirtiest test of all time. During the second half in particular, the referee, WFB Kilner of New South Wales, might as well have taken a seat on the stand for all the use he was.

The field was a sea of mud when New South Wales beat the Springboks in Sydney.

The Springboks were badly hit by injuries before the match and really only had seven fit forwards at their disposal. In addition, they were tipped off that the Wallabies had a scheme to give the South African flyhalf a deliberate inside gap and then, with the aid of their exceptionally fast loose-forwards, to cut him off from the backline they feared so much.

The Springboks decided to counter this by using the powerfully-built Craven at number eight with the idea that he would also act as extra flyhalf and so further confuse the Australians. This decision, incidentally, meant that Craven would hold the record for having played in a different position in each of four consecutive tests.

The plan worked well from the outset and the Springboks had 26 points on the board at half-time. The first half was rough enough, but in the second half the Wallabies must have decided that their only hope lay in provoking their opponents into losing their cool. They succeeded only too well.

From the moment De Villiers was crumpled into unconsciousness with a blatant kick and had to be carried off the field by Boy Louw, the game became a bar-room brawl. De Villiers returned after a while, but Van Reenen was hurt so badly that he could not resume. Fights broke out all over the place, with the Springboks so incensed that they virtually forgot all about the ball and allowed the Wallabies to notch 11 points without reply.

Harry (Kalfie) Martin and the Australian eighthman Aubrey Hodgson flew into each other on one occasion and stood exchanging punches like two boxers. More than 30 years later, Martin talked about that infamous incident.

'De Villiers was laid out completely. He was in a terrible state, his eyes were rolling and his tongue was hanging out. It really upset us and this is the only instance in my rugby career that I can recall being deliberately attacked and retaliating. Normally I never lost my temper on the field as I actually treated sport as an occasion for discipline.'

Even Craven lost his self-control as the match degenerated further. And again Hodgson was the central figure. It came after De Villiers had returned to the field and Boy Louw had told Craven to stop the Australian number eight from getting to the little scrumhalf. In the tussle that followed Craven was kicked on the shin and, very angry, the Springbok instructed Williams at the lineout to throw the ball directly at Hodgson. As Williams threw, Craven climbed into 'Awesome Aub' but unfortunately Dai's throw-in did not get to the right man and the referee caught Craven in the act, so to speak.

While the referee was lecturing Craven and actually threatening to send him off the field, Hodgson jumped off the deck and kicked the Springbok three times. The referee decided that Craven was the offender and the Wallabies got the penalty.

The next day the newspapers were full of photographs showing players kicking, punching and squaring up to each other. Both teams, but particularly the Springboks, were criticized and by the time they arrived in New Zealand they were sick of looking at pictures of the 'Battle of Sydney Oval'.

One picture showed Boy Louw in a boxing pose with his right hand cocked for a swing from way back. He had his own explanation. 'They're all wrong. I remember this incident very well. I didn't want to hit anyone. Somebody had jerked me out of a lineout and I was swinging my arms around to keep my balance!'

The 1937 Springboks learnt a lesson from the match after all. Realizing that they had scored 26 points before half-time but nothing after they had lost their tempers and, in fact, conceded 11 points, they never again lost their self-control on that wonderful tour of 1937.

Danie Craven, the Springbok scrumhalf, demonstrates his dive pass from the scrum in Sydney. His footwork in positioning himself for the pass is well illustrated.

Johnny Dick scores a try for the All Blacks in the first test played in Wellington.

VENUE	SOUTH AFRICA	RESULT	SOUTH AFRICA	AUSTRALIA
			T C P D	T C P D
SYDNEY	WON	9–5	2 0 1 0	1 1 0 0
SYDNEY	WON	26–17	6 4 0 0	3 1 2 0
		35–22	8 4 1 0	4 2 2 0
SERIES: SOUTH AFRICA PLAYED 2; W2, L0, D0				

SOUTH AFRICA vs NEW ZEALAND

The Springboks started the New Zealand leg of the tour after winning both tests against Australia, but losing 17–6 to New South Wales, in a match played in mud and rain. This defeat was given exaggerated importance by the New Zealand critics, who predicted that Auckland, Taranaki, Wellington, Canterbury, Southland, Otago and Hawke's Bay would be too strong for the tourists. As for the tests, there was no doubt in any New Zealander's mind that the All Blacks would win. They were adamant that the series would decide the rugby championship of the world and the Springboks were treated like visiting royalty.

Craven was a particular favourite of the crowds and the press. Reports of his revolutionary dive-pass preceded him and the photographers always on the look-out for an angle, singled him out for special attention. When it was discovered that the 26-year-old Master of Arts graduate was also most articulate, he was flooded with requests to address societies, schools and universities. And since he was once a theology student, he even had to deliver several sermons.

The Springboks beat Auckland 19–5 in the first match of the tour, but found their opponents strong and accomplished spoilers. From the lessons learnt in this match the Springboks evolved the tactics which were to prove so successful. It was mainly to concentrate on firm and solid scrummaging, thereby forcing the opposing forwards to stay in the scrum and leaving the Springbok backs free to cope with their opposite numbers on a man-for-man basis. Since there was the option between scrums and lineouts in those days, the plan worked like a charm.

The Springboks scored five tries in their magnificent 17–6 victory over the All Blacks in the third test, the match which clinched the series. Here Dai Williams is about to dot down just inside the corner flag. Flappie Lochner and Tony Harris are the Springboks nearest to Williams.

Waikato (combining with King Country and Thames Valley) were the next to fall, and in this match Brand finally struck the top form which had eluded him on the Australian part of the tour. Up till then, this legendary fullback was playing so badly that the tour selectors were beginning to look elsewhere for the approaching tests. But against the Waikato combination, in pelting rain and on a muddy field, Brand was flawless.

No one could stop the Springbok victory march and Taranaki was beaten 17–3, Manawatu 39–3 and Wellington 29–0 before the first test in Wellington.

▲▲▲

For days before the big match it rained steadily and the field was in a shocking state. The conditions moved the Springboks to decide on kicking tactics and for this purpose the tour committee decided to play Craven at flyhalf. Craven and Nel were against the switch, both preferring to give Harris a chance, but were outvoted. This was the match that led to a superstition most older Springboks believe in to this day – there must be no singing or facetiousness in the dressingroom before a big game. The victories over the strong provincial sides had given them a little too much confidence and in the dressingroom they sang and joked as if victory was already theirs. Brand was injured and so was Boy Louw, while skipper Nel was left out of the side, which meant that the Springboks were without three of their most experienced players.

The All Blacks, inspired by a wildly-cheering crowd, had the bit between their teeth from the start. The mud and rain proved too much for the Springboks, who were outplayed and never looked like a winning combination, even after a brilliant unconverted try by Williams had enabled them to catch up with the All Blacks who were off to a flying start with an early penalty by flyhalf Dave Trevathan. At half-time the All Blacks were in the lead again after another fine penalty kick by Trevathan, and after the resumption it was obvious that everything was over bar the shouting.

A brilliant back-line movement between Dalton, Hooper and Sullivan ripped the South African defence to shreds for winger Dick to score, and not long afterwards it was Trevathan again with a fine dropgoal. It was reported afterwards that even the referee LE Macassey, like Trevathan an Otago man, jumped with joy when the ball sailed over the crossbar.

This set-back finally seemed to jerk the Springboks out of their lethargy and White, feared mainly for his crashtackling, snapped over a dropgoal from nowhere. All other attempts to shake off the All Blacks' stranglehold failed, however, and the Boks were beaten 13–7.

It was a major triumph for the New Zealand forwards in particular, but selection blunders by the Springboks contributed heavily to their own downfall.

Nursing their wounds and taking stock of their mistakes, the Springboks went on from there to whip Nelson, Golden Bay-Motueka and Marlborough 22–0, and followed up with wins over Canterbury (23–8), West Coast Buller (31–6), and South Canterbury (43–6) before going off to Christchurch for the second and decisive test.

▲▲▲

For the second test there was no false confidence. The test players were only too aware of the task awaiting them. The New Zealand newspapers were freely predicting another convincing win for their team, and there was even a note of pity for the poor visitors in some of the reports.

Then followed the sort of sheer misfortune which would certainly have broken the spirit of a lesser team than the 1937 Springboks. They were on the attack when the All Blacks centre Jack Sullivan intercepted between Harris and Babrow and rushed through for an

Brand kicks while Craven watches, but the deciding test of 1937 had already been won by the Springboks.

The 1937 South African touring side. Left to right, back row: TA Harris, DF van de Vyver, SR Hofmeyr, J White, AD Lawton, L Babrow; third row: WE Bastard, JW Lotz, JLA Bester, GP Lochner, HJ Martin, DO Williams, JA Broodryk; second row: CB Jennings, SC Louw, MA van den Berg, FWFvRvO Bergh, GL van Reenen, AR Sherriff, BA du Toit, HH Watt; front row: PJ Turner, PJ Lyster, PW Day (manager), MM Louw, PJ Nel (captain), DH Craven (vice-captain), A de Villiers (assistant manager), GH Brand, LC Strachan; front: P du P de Villiers.

unconverted try. That was shock number one. Shock number two came only minutes later when he did exactly the same thing; but this time he kicked far over Brand's head to beat Williams in a desperate race for the ball to score his second unconverted try. The Springboks were reeling and from then until half-time it appeared to be only a matter of time before the All Blacks would add more points to their 6–0 lead.

Yet somehow, in those few short minutes of rest, the embattled South Africans found the inspiration for a second-half fight-back which must rank with the most glorious in South African rugby history.

Early in the second half Boy Louw, who was playing a magnificent game, was injured and for the rest of the match was unaware of what he was doing. A head injury can trigger the strangest reactions and in the mighty Boy's case it was a never-ending fit of the giggles. He ran around the field giggling and demanding to know from all and sundry what exactly was going on. In exasperation Craven told him to stop the All Blacks forward Dalton from breaking through the lineouts. At the very next lineout, Boy, still giggling, sidled up gleefully to Dalton and, although the ball was nowhere near the bewildered New Zealander, flew into him with all his strength. Dalton disappeared under flying fists and feet, but fortunately the referee was following the ball and did not see the semi-conscious Springbok's literal execution of his vice-captain's orders.

'Is that what you wanted me to do, Daantjie?' Louw panted as he finally caught up with Craven and for most of the rest of the match he continued his aimless running and more aimless laughing. Phil Nel had to pack in his place in the frontrow while Louw did the best he could in whatever position he could find.

Slowly but surely the Springbok machine accelerated into higher gear and the pressure grew stronger and stronger. Then, from a scrum in the All Blacks' twenty-five, Craven whipped the ball to White on the blind side who passed quickly to Turner on the left wing. Turner deftly side-stepped his way around one defender, handed off Dick and with a quick change of direction sped over the line for a try under the posts. Brand made no mistake with the conversion and the Springboks trailed by only one point.

But bad luck was still hounding the Springboks. With Boy Louw already dazed, they lost their second forward when the hard-working Ebbo Bastard was knocked into a state of semi-consciousness. He refused to go off the field but charged from scrum to loose scrum and back again, sobbing wildly and forcing Nel to make more emergency changes in his pack. It was at this point that Boy Louw had a rare moment of lucidity. He actually caught a crucial mark and put the Springboks on the attack with a magnificent touch-kick. Babrow almost got through after a quick heel, and from the ensuing scrum Craven was tackled illegally. The penalty was given on the halfway line and at a sharp angle.

'Well, it's up to you now, Gerry!' Nel remarked as he gave the Springbok fullback the ball for one of the most vital kicks of his career.

The crowd was silent as Brand, with tantalising care, placed the ball and prepared for the kick. A few seconds later they sat stunned as the ball rose and rose and then settled, like an arrow in flight, on its path to the crossbar. In the pavilion, the non-playing Springboks became almost hysterical with delight and Howard Watt jumped about so much in his glee that he sprained his ankle!

Two points ahead and with only a few minutes to go, the Springboks refused to sit on their slender lead. From the kick-off, Strachan jerked himself into a gap and kicked ahead for the ever-alert Turner, who jumped high off the ground to take it in full stride before passing to White. White forced a huge hole in the demoralised defence before passing inside towards Babrow, but it was the half-dazed Ebbo Bastard who bobbed up between them and instinctively held on to the ball to dive over the line. To make absolutely sure of the result the ice-cool Brand converted with yet another magnificent kick and the Springboks won the second test 13–6. As they left the field, Boy Louw collapsed and had to be helped off.

Back in the dressingroom, the South Africans and their few supporters were almost delirious with delight. The test players were embraced and kissed, and the story is told that Pat Lyster went even further in his ecstacy. Running up to Babrow, he shouted: 'Hit me, Louis! Hit me under the chin!' Babrow took him at his word and plonked him on the jaw with a blow which stretched him out unconscious!

A New Zealander watching all this came over and dared Babrow to try the same with him 'Why should I?' Babrow asked. 'Because I give you the right to try,' the New Zealander answered. Prompted by the other players, the powerfully built Springbok centre said: 'OK, are you ready?' and then let rip with his right. The New Zealander followed Lyster into the land of dreams.

This unfortunate fellow was not the only All Blacks supporter to be stunned after the match. They simply could not believe that their mighty team had been so decisively beaten after looking like winners all the way in the first half.

As for the triumphant Boks, they moved on to beat Southland (30–17), Otago (47–7), Hawke's Bay (21–12) and Poverty Bay – Bay of Plenty – East Coast (33–3) before it was time again to tackle the now deadly determined All Blacks in the third, final and decisive test of the tour. And if the All Blacks were determined, their loyal supporters were supremely confident.

Jennings' tackle sends All Black wing Cobden flying into the air in the hard-fought first test match.

The Springboks, while not quite as keyed-up as they were for the second test, were again in a perfect frame of mind to throw everything into the fray. They had several new plans ready, including one tactical move in which they hoped to use the exaggerated respect the All Blacks had developed for Craven's dive-pass.

There were 55 000 people packed around the Auckland rugby field, Eden Park, when Phil Nel and Ron King led their teams on to the field for the battle to decide the 'world rugby crown', as the newspapers labelled it. The Springboks were fielding the same side that won the second test except that the injured White was replaced by Lochner.

The Springboks had decided to pin a great deal of their hopes on their acknowledged scrummaging supremacy. They exercised their option to select scrums instead of lineouts at every opportunity and this, perhaps more than anything else, drove the nails into the All Blacks' coffin.

The first four scrums of the match all went to the Springboks and from the fifth they suddenly struck. Not a second was wasted between Craven and Harris and there was Lochner sailing through the gap between Hooper and Mitchell. He drew the fullback beautifully to send Babrow over for a try Brand could not convert, but which gave the Springboks an early 3–0 lead.

After both Brand and Trevathan had missed penalties with a ball both agreed had something wrong with it, Babrow, playing brilliantly, slipped through the defence with a devastating break and Bergh collected his perfect cross-kick to dive over near the posts. This one Brand could not miss and the Springboks led 8–0 as the crowd gaped in disbelief.

There was nothing wrong with New Zealand's fighting spirit, however, and after a good penalty goal by Trevathan, it was the local team who did all the attacking for the last 15 minutes before half-time.

Shortly after the resumption, Craven and Harris, both in tremendous form, decided to introduce some unorthodox tactics to the game. At a scrum, Craven, making sure that his opponents would notice, kept waving Harris further away

The 'Big Five' who controlled the destiny of the 1937 Springboks. From left, Danie Craven, Gerry Brand, Lucas Strachan, Boy Louw and Phil Nel.

Craven's dive-pass was a nightmare to the New Zealanders. Their exaggerated respect for it gave the Springboks a chance to use it as a tactical ploy.

from him. Harris eventually moved to a position virtually in the middle of the field and Trevathan, the All Blacks flyhalf, misled by the publicity about the distance Craven was supposed to be able to throw a ball with his dive-pass, moved into position directly opposite him. This opened a huge gap in the All Blacks' line.

Lotz hooked clean and fast, and when Craven picked up the ball Turner, who had streaked in from the blind side, virtually took it from his hands. Turner ran through the midfield gap and right up to Lochner who sent Babrow over in the corner for his second try. Brand failed to convert but there is no doubt that it was this magnificently executed try that knocked the wind out of the All Blacks.

From another scrum in the middle of the field, Williams was brought into the attack and there was no stopping him as he beat two defenders in a run to the corner flag. The conversion hit the upright, but it did not really matter any more with the score standing at 14–3 and the Springboks in full control. But the game was not over yet. Turner got another chance to run and he also went over in the corner for an unconverted try after Strachan had given him a long pass from a loose scrum.

Shortly afterwards the All Blacks got some consolation in the form of a penalty from Trevathan, but when the final whistle shrilled, the Springboks had won 17–6, five tries (one converted) to two penalties.

And so the 1937 Springboks returned to South Africa as champions of the rugby world – a title they were to hold for nearly twenty years.

On the boat returning home, Nel formally announced his retirement from rugby by throwing his boots into the sea. He had no further need for them because, like Alexander the Great, he had no more worlds left to conquer.

VENUE	SOUTH AFRICA	RESULT	SOUTH AFRICA				NEW ZEALAND			
			T	C	P	D	T	C	P	D
WELLINGTON	LOST	7–13	1	0	0	1	1	0	2	1
CHRISTCHURCH	WON	13–6	2	2	1	0	2	0	0	0
AUCKLAND	WON	17–6	5	1	0	0	0	0	2	0
		37–25	8	3	1	1	3	0	4	1
SERIES: SOUTH AFRICA PLAYED 3; W2, L1, D0										

Phil Nel played a total of 16 tests for South Africa between 1928 and 1937, when he was appointed captain.

PHILIP NEL

Philip Nel, a 34-year-old farmer from Greytown, Natal, who began his international rugby career against Maurice Brownlie's All Blacks, was a rather surprising selection as captain. Nel had virtually retired after leading the Springboks to victory over the 1933 Wallabies and was enjoying himself playing carefree rugby for Natal under the captaincy of Ebbo Bastard. A man of great strength of character, he was highly respected in South African rugby, however, and captained the A-team throughout the week of trials matches.

Nel, the eldest son in a family of five, was born on a farm in the district of Kranskop, Natal, in 1902 and he saw his first game of rugby when he was already 15 years old and had just enrolled as a pupil at Maritzburg College. His parents refused him permission to play because a relative had developed cancer after breaking a hip in a rugby match. Young Phil kept on pestering them, though, and they finally relented. Tall and heavy for his age, Nel was quickly promoted from the fourth to the first team and while still at school he gained his provincial colours for Natal under the captaincy of Herby Taylor.

After he left school Nel continued to play rugby although it meant getting up in the small hours of a Saturday morning, riding 30 miles on horseback from his farm to Greytown and then clubbing together with a few other players to hire a taxi go get to Pietermaritzburg for a club match. After the game the same tedious process would have to be repeated.

Philip and his younger brother Maritz were invited to the national trials in 1928 and in one of the matches the selector and former Springbok captain Theo Pienaar took the whistle. During the match Pienaar collided with Maritz Nel and had to be taken to hospital. The younger Nel never did make the Springbok team, but Phil played in all four tests. In 1931 he was included in Bennie Osler's touring side to Britain where he again played in all the tests. He replaced Osler as Springbok captain in four of the five tests against the touring Wallabies in 1933 and then, more or less accepting the fact that his international career was over and being heavily committed to his farming duties, Nel withdrew as Natal captain. He was playing such good rugby, though, that the selectors refused to discard him and so he was given the job of leading a side not many of the critics, professional or amateur, considered particularly strong.

Phil Nel, the farmer from Kranskop, in the district of Greytown, who became captain of the 1937 Springboks.

BOY LOUW

Matthys Michael (Boy) Louw, in particular, became a legend in his own life-time. A man of enormous physical strength, Louw also had an instinctive flair for the game and he understood the fundamentals down to the most minute details. Near the end of his career as a player, Louw became known as 'The Old Master' and there can be no more apt nickname for this phenomenal player. Boy Louw was a hard, relentless competitor who stood no nonsense from anyone, but it was his brain and not his brawn that earned him such a special place in our rugby history. Born on 2 February 1906 on a farm in the district of Wellington in the heart of the Boland, Boy was the fifth of ten brothers and four sisters. One of his brothers died while still very young, but the other nine all played senior rugby. Boy and Fanie became Springboks and four of the other brothers progressed to interprovincial level.

Boy Louw took his rugby seriously and not even Bennie Osler ever tried to overrule him in a match. Danie Craven tells the story of how Osler once called for the ball from a scrum during the wet and windswept test against Scotland in 1932.

'Hold, and play with the forwards!' Louw countermanded his captain's order from the frontrow. But Osler again commanded Craven to pass. This time Louw whipped his head from the forming scrum and snorted:

'Nonsense with you, Bennie! We're keeping it up front!' In fact he used a word much stronger than 'nonsense' and Osler saw no point in further argument.

On another occasion he told a captain: 'You make the speeches, I'll lead the pack!' and that is the way it was.

Louw has often fought a losing battle with tongue-twisters and his mal-apropisms have kept several generations of players amused. Some of the stories told about him are no doubt apochryphal, but it is a fact that he did sometimes produce a somewhat mixed-up version of what he really intended to say.

One of the most delightful anecdotes is the one Craven told of the time Boy and his pack were battling mightily in a match when Springbok centre Johnny Bester not only dropped hard-earned possession, but stood rooted on the spot and did not fall back to recover the situation. As Boy ran past Bester, he slapped him on the rump and reprimanded:

'Hey, do you think you have bought this ground of plot?'

Craven also vouches for the fact that it was indeed Boy who once looked at a sloppy lineout and said:

'Why you stand so crooked? Can't you stand in a straight stripe?'

Louw took his rugby seriously and throughout his long international career which included 18 tests, he was invariably the man the halfbacks and threequarters turned to whenever they were the victims of dirty tactics from the opposing for-wards. Boy's retribution was always swift and merciless. To quote Danie Craven:

'In one of the matches in New Zealand in 1937 there was a forward wearing a number-12 jersey who kept on climbing in on the wrong side of the loose scrums. I dealt with him twice, but he persisted and each time Mauritz van den Berg would ask me who it was and I would answer that it was number-12 again. Finally it was all too much for Boy. "What's wrong with you fellows today?" he asked and at the next opportunity the offending number-12 came flying out of the loose scrum to land at my feet, one eye already coming up like a balloon. Then I heard Boy's voice: "Mr Ref, you can blow your whistle now, number-12 is off!" '

Along with his brother, Fanie, Boy Louw was one of the greatest Springbok forwards of all time. He was also one of the 'Big Five' in the 1937 Springbok side.

CHAPTER 13

1938

BRITISH ISLES TOUR SOUTH AFRICA

▲▲▲

The year: 1938. The scene: A packed Ellis Park, South Africa's biggest stadium. Not an inch of space left. Hours before the game the Transvaal rugby authorities decided to abandon the gates and thousands more streamed in, jamming themselves together on the ramps and spilling onto the field, right up to the touchline. Now the match is on.

For nearly 80 minutes there has been one continuous roar from the crowd as the Springboks and the Lions thrust and counter in the sort of rugby test most of us can only hope to see once or twice in a lifetime.

Dai Williams has slipped around his opponent to flash over near the corner flag. Now there is silence as Brand prepares to take the conversion. In those days the rules stipulated that a teammate had to place the ball for the kicker when a conversion was to be attempted. With the spot a foot in from the touchline there is simply no room for Craven to prostrate himself for the placing of the ball and there is also no way in which Brand can take his run-up for the kick.

The spectators do their best; they heave and struggle back until some space has been cleared. Craven is about to go down when he notices hundreds of burning cigarette stubs and these have to be cleared away before he can ease himself down

The British Lions toured South Africa in 1938 and lost two of the three tests played. The final test, held in Cape Town, was won by the Lions 21–16.

to hold the ball. He glances up and notices that Brand has had to cut his usual run-up by several steps, that he is standing as far back as he can between the legs of a woman spectator, trying vainly to maintain her modesty as well as give the Springbok fullback an extra inch in which to manoeuvre. Craven cannot help smiling. 'Gerry,' he remarks to his old teammate, 'I'll buy you a farm in Eloff Street if you get this one over.'

'Watch me,' Brand grins back and from that truncated run he slams his left boot into the ball to lift it high over the crossbar. The final whistle is blown and the Springboks have won the first test 26–12. We will return to this tremendous game, rated by Craven as second only to the Murrayfield Massacre of 1951 for Springbok brilliance.

▲▲▲

Let us start at the beginning of the 1938 tour by Sam Walker and his Lions, the last international rugby to be played by South Africa before World War II. Walker, a 26-year-old Belfast Irishman, brought out a most powerful combination with only six of the members not having played international rugby before, and it was only the second time that South Africa was visited by a team truly representative of the British Isles. It was also a happy incident-free tour with the Lions having as their South African manager, Richard Luyt.

After a hesitant start, they found their feet and played attractive winning rugby; as bright as the 1933 Wallabies, but more constructive and certainly a lot cleaner.

The Springboks, of course, were riding the crest of the wave after the glorious tour of New Zealand. The nucleus of that tremendous team was available and the national selectors were so confident that no national trials were even considered. A number of players were invited, however, to attend a one-day session at the Old Wanderers ground in Johannesburg.

Three weeks before the first test the Lions had beaten Northern Transvaal, a new-born union. Northerns had Springboks Ferdie Bergh, Roger Sherriff, Nic Bierman, Harry Martin and Lucas Strachan among their forwards and Danie Craven and JA Broodryk behind the scrum, and yet the tourists won 20–12. More ominous than the score was the fact that the visitors looked completely at home with the now established 3–4–1 scrum formation and their threequarters out-classed the Northern Transvaal line.

Craven who had moved to Pretoria after resigning as a teacher at St Andrews, Grahamstown, to become director of physical education for the South African Defence Force, suffered a bad cut over the eye in this match. He turned up at the Wanderers with the rest of the players, but did not get a place in any of the trials teams. Mr Markötter only reluctantly allowed him to change. A disconsolate Craven was sitting on the touchline among some spectators and they kept on shouting for him to get onto the field and finally Markötter relented.

'Go on, pass the ball a few times, but don't allow yourself to be kicked to pieces,' Markötter instructed the man who was to remain his particular protégé no matter how far he wandered from Stellenbosch.

Within minutes Craven stopped a forward rush by falling on the ball and the terrible-tempered Mr Mark almost exploded with anger. Hurling abuse at all and sundry, but particularly at Craven, he rushed him off the field with an order to go for a run on a nearby ground. Craven now knew that he was a certainty for the first test team and all possible doubts about this disappeared when Brand, Du Toit

Carrying the team mascot and followed by the massive Boy Louw, Danie Craven leads the Springboks onto the field for the third test at Newlands.

and Harris joined him a little later after all three had first earned the 'Oubaas" wrath for taking risks. When the team was announced it was obvious that the selectors had wisely opted for the men who had done so well in Australia and New Zealand the previous season. The only newcomer to the side was Piet de Wet, the Western Province centre, who filled the place of Louis Babrow who was then furthering his medical career. The selectors certainly did strange things in those days and newspapers were a lot less inquisitive and adamant than they are now. In the published statement giving the names of the Springboks no mention was made about the captaincy! On the Friday before the test Craven bought a newspaper and to his astonishment saw that he had been appointed captain with Boy Louw as understudy.

The only preparation the team had was a long get-together on the night before the test where Craven and Louw outlined a few plans. The players knew each other so well that nothing more was really needed. That night they also received a telegram from the South African Rugby Board which can only be regarded as a most thoughtless gesture. The telegram warned the Springboks that dirty play would not be tolerated and that any player who ignored this warning would never again represent South Africa. It was absolutely uncalled for and these men who had done so much for their country's sports prestige, were justifiably upset. There was also a decision that the Springboks would again be wearing black shorts, and not the white they wore against the All Blacks.

The match was played at a terrific pace with one movement following the other and both sides opening up from all angles. The Lions led for a few minutes after a penalty right in front of the Springbok posts, but Brand soon equalized when the referee, At Horak, spotted an infringement and presented the South Africans with almost as easy a penalty. Not long afterwards the Springboks erred again just inside the Lions' half and the crowd laughed derisively when Vivian Jenkins, their Welsh fullback, indicated that he was going to kick for goal. But Jenkins, in later years probably one of the world's best-known rugby writers, knew exactly what he was doing and there was a split-second of stunned silence before a burst of cheering hailed the first of the many astonishing kicks which were to make this match such a memorable one.

The set-back did not bother the Springboks in the slightest and they sailed into the attack to drive the Lions deep into their own territory. Craven, realizing that it was time to do something out of the ordinary, decided to repeat the ruse that worked so well in the final test against the All Blacks in 1937.

He waved Harris further and further away from the scrum and the Lion's fly-half Jeff Reynolds saw it as a plan to break through on the blindside. He ran up to his forwards and warned them to be on the alert for such a move. Nothing could have suited the Springboks better. When Lotz hooked, Turner cut in from the blindside wing to take the ball from Craven's pass. Once Turner had driven the breach he sent a perfect pass to Lochner who waited for the right moment before giving to Williams for a beautiful try, converted by Brand.

The Springboks led 8–6, but only briefly as Jenkins again kicked a penalty from near the halfway line. The lead switched hands minutes later when Fanie Louw barged over after clever work between Craven and Du Toit. Brand made the half-time score 13–9 in favour of the Springboks.

The stadium was packed for the first test between the Springboks and the Lions, held in Johannesburg.

After the resumption the Springboks gave their delighted supporters a chance to see the sort of rugby which won them the world championship the year before. The inspiration came from Brand who kicked a penalty dropgoal from a distance and an angle even he thought impossible. The Springboks were given a penalty a few yards from touch and several yards into the South African half of the field. When Craven threw him the ball, Brand looked at him inquiringly. Craven pointed to the posts, but Brand shook his head and said: 'No ways, Daantjie. I can never get the distance.' But Craven had remembered seeing Brand succeed with two kicks from even further out in a club match at coast level and he was adamant that the fullback could do it in the rarefied Rand atmosphere.

Brand shrugged his shoulders, flipped the ball around once or twice, glanced at the posts, and then swung his left foot with perfect timing and power. The ball cleared the crossbar with room to spare. It was not the most vital kick Brand had ever put over for the Springboks, but with the possible exception of the one at Twickenham six years earlier, certainly the most spectacular and the crowd roared their approval.

The kick broke the spirit of the opposition and Harris, an attacking flyhalf of the highest class, attempted his only break of the match and sniped through without a finger being laid on him. Brand, the man with iced water for blood, place the conversion without any problems and although Jenkins helped his side with another penalty, the match had been won and lost. The Springboks used their threequarters time and again and in what was to be the final movement of the day, Dai Williams scored again in the corner for Brand to convert under the remarkable conditions described at the beginning of this chapter.

Nobody could have known it then, but this was to be Brand's last test. He was injured before the next test and could not play in the final two internationals. World War II then intervened and by the time it was over and top-level sport could be resumed, the serious playing days of Brand were over.

The first test against the Lions at Ellis Park in 1938 produced some of the best play in rugby history. The final score was 26–12 in favour of the Springboks.

▲▲▲

With Brand out, the selectors sensibly made only a slight reshuffle for the second test in Port Elizabeth. Turner went to fullback and Johnny Bester replaced him on the wing. Up front John Apsey, of Western Province, took over from Ebbo Bastard.

The temperature was in the nineties and it is a miracle that the players survived what must have been an ordeal. There was a great deal of furious activity at the start, but long before half-time both sets of forwards were dragging themselves around the field. At half-time most of the players simply dropped where they were and could not raise the energy to walk to the touchline for some refreshment. Du Toit and Lochner scored outstanding tries in the first half and Turner converted both. Early in the second half Craven broke on the blindside and Bester went over for an unconverted try to push the Springbok lead to 13–0. By that time the two weary teams were almost taking turns to rest and the backs, more often than the gasping forwards, were doing most of the work. Two successive penalties by Turner made it 19–0 with very little left for play. Strangely enough, the Lions seemed to endure the heat better than the South Africans and they then came back strongly with Reynolds, who later settled in South Africa, breaking brilliantly to send Laurie Duff through for an unconverted try. The Springbok forwards were stumbling around in a heat-induced daze when the final whistle blew and most of them hardly cared that they had won the match.

▲▲▲

The last test, at Newlands, once again produced sparkling rugby with the Lions showing the remarkable resilience for which they are justly famous. On the boat trip from Port Elizabeth to Cape Town, Mr Markötter was asked to select the Lions team he would like to see in the last test. He wrote the names on a piece of paper and handed it to Sam Walker. According to legend, the Lions followed Mr Mark's advice to the letter and it is, of course, history how they won the Newlands international against all odds.

Actually the team was something of a scratch affair because injury had depleted their ranks to the point where they had to make do with whoever happened to be fit and available. Jimmy Giles, a scrumhalf, was at centre and Bob Graves, a hooker, had to pack in the frontrow. Duff, an outstanding lock, was switched to flank and Charlie Grieve was at fullback, a position he had also filled in the second test as Jenkins had been injured.

Knowing that the rubber was safe, the Springboks found it difficult to get themselves in a proper frame of mind for a test match. They were put up in a quiet out-of-town hotel, but complained so bitterly about this that Craven had to ask the Rugby Board for them to be moved to one nearer the city. At first the Rugby Board refused and there was actually talk of the players refusing to play, unless their demand was met! Craven and Boy Louw did their best, but they could not motivate the team which with Bastard back again, consisted almost entirely of very experienced test players.

A strong wind was blowing on the day of the match, but Craven was assured by Johnny Robeck, who had been the caretaker at Newlands for many years, that it was bound to drop completely by half-time.

So, when the Springbok captain won the toss for the third time running with the 'lucky' gold 10/– coin given to him before the series by the then Mayor of Johannesburg, he decided to play with the wind in the first half, something he would normally not have done. When the wind did not drop at half-time the Springboks had to face it for the entire second half.

The Lions got an early unconverted try by Jones but the Springboks replied soon enough when Turner went over after a pin-point crosskick by Dai Williams. Turner injured his ankle in the movement, but managed to convert. Incidentally, Turner's try brought South Africa's points total to 500 in exactly 50 tests. A lightning interception by Bester gave the South Africans another unexpected bonus

The Springbok side for the first test.
Back: SC Louw, BA du Toit, AR Sheriff,
FWFvRvO Bergh, LC Strachan, JW Lotz,
WE Bastard. Middle: FG Turner,
GH Brand, DH Craven, JA Durie jnr (man-
ager), MM Louw, P de Wet, DO Williams.
Front: TA Harris, GP Lochner.

and they were leading 10–3 after Turner succeeded with the kick. Lotz made it 13–3 before half-time and at this stage it looked as if Craven and Louw's premonitions of doom were wrong.

But after half-time, with the stronger-than-ever wind helping, the Lions came back with tremendous fury. The Springboks by now also had a lot of problems with injuries: fullback Georgie Smith had a bad finger, Turner was limping and so was Piet de Wet.

The Lions forwards were getting on top gradually and a converted try by Dancer, followed by a penalty by McKibbin, brought them to within two points of the Springboks' score. Then Bob Alexander managed to add another try and the Lions were in the lead by just one point. A penalty from Turner nosed the Springboks ahead again, but Grieve forced the lead to change hands once more with a dropkick which might not have been allowed had the Springboks not sportingly indicated to the referee, Nick Pretorius, that it was over, the last four-point drop to have been scored in South Africa. Duff then came hammering through for his team's fourth try and with the score 16–21, the South Africans were reeling to certain defeat.

A scrum, and the referee informed the two teams that it would be the last of the match. The Springboks hooked, Craven broke around the blindside and passed to Bester. The young centre drew fullback Grieve beautifully and DO Williams was in full stride as he took the ball. He was over the line and behind the posts for what everybody, including the Lions, thought was the goal that would draw the match. But it was not to be. The referee ruled that the pass between Bester and Williams had been forward and he blew the whistle to end the match.

A brief moment of disappointment and then the Springboks carried Sam Walker off the field. Jenkins wrote years later that seeing Walker on the shoulders of his defeated opponents, was perhaps the real highlight of a series to remember.

▲▲▲

It was to be the end of all international rugby for a whole generation of Springboks. World War II broke out within a year after Walker and his team had returned home and by the time it was over and organized sport could be resumed, players who were youngsters in 1938, had lost the best years of their lives.

It meant that Tony Harris had his career end at the age of 22, Freddie Turner at 24, Flappie Lochner at 24, DO Williams at 24, Danie Craven at 27, Ebbo Bastard at 26, Ben du Toit at 25 and Jan Lotz at 27. Fanie Louw, in the prime of his life, collapsed and died a year later after captaining Transvaal in a match against Western Province at Ellis Park.

Freddie Turner played in 11 tests for South Africa between 1933 and 1938. He played at wing, centre and fullback, and was rated a splendid place-kicker.

Venue	South Africa	Result	South Africa				British Isles			
			T	C	P	D	T	C	P	D
Johannesburg	WON	26–12	4	4	2	0	0	0	4	0
Port Elizabeth	WON	19–3	3	2	2	0	1	0	0	0
Cape Town	LOST	16–21	3	2	1	0	4	1	1	1
		61–36	10	8	5	0	5	1	5	1
Series: South Africa played 3; W2, L1, D0										

CHAPTER 14

1949

NEW ZEALAND TOUR SOUTH AFRICA

▲▲▲

HENNIE MULLER

Nicknamed Windhond, Hennie Muller was the fastest forward ever to wear the Springbok jersey. He could tackle with ferocity and was a master of the basics of the game. Craven turned him into a one-man demolition squad to seek and destroy the All Blacks. The instant the ball left the scrum or the lineout, Muller would swoop on the flyhalf and if he should manage to get the ball to the centres, Muller's exceptional pace would enable him to arrive virtually simultaneously with the ball.

His defensive-offensive function soon expanded as it became clear that the All Blacks were developing a complex about him. He was often used as a decoy and once Ryk van Schoor had been added to the line-up, Muller had the additional pleasure of picking up a loose ball dropped from the limp fingers of an All Blacks centre who had just been flattened.

Originally the All Blacks were to visit South Africa in 1947, but kept requesting postponements, and it was not until May 1949 that the *Tamaroa* finally delivered Fred Allen and his long-awaited team. They had made sure that they were well prepared to avenge the rubber defeat in 1937. Several members of the side had had some experience of international rugby, a rare and invaluable asset.

It was a team with an immensely powerful pack of forwards. Johnny Simpson, Has Catley and Kevin Skinner formed one of the best frontrows in rugby history. Simpson was as solid as the proverbial rock, but he added to this a smouldering truculence on the field that made him one of the most fearsome forwards of his day. Catley, who knew more tricks than a circus clown and was not called 'the problem child of New Zealand rugby' for nothing, believed that the end always justified the means when it came to either hooking the ball or preventing his opponents from getting it. Skinner, then only 20 years old, was almost as strong and rough as Simpson, and more mobile. A newsreel of Hansie Brewis' try in the second test at Ellis Park bears striking testimony to the speed this New Zealand tighthead prop could generate in an emergency. When Brewis flashed over the line, Skinner was the only New Zealand forward anywhere near the scene.

Lauchie Grant was a magnificent lineout forward and CC (Charlie) Willocks and Lester Harvey were also outstanding locks. PJB (Pat) Crowley, Peter Johnstone and JR (Jack) McNab were fiery loose-forwards. In spite of an injury to Morrie Goddard and KE (Keith) Gudsell, the All Blacks also had excellent three-quarters. Fred Allen had a dazzling side-step, Ron Elvidge was a strong, courageous centre, Graham (Red) Delamore was a master of the inside break and Bill Meates, Eric Boggs and Peter (Sammy) Henderson, an Empire Games sprinter, was particularly dangerous and also splendid as a cover defender.

In Bob Scott, the All Blacks had the world's best fullback of his time. His place-kicking on the tour was abysmal, but as a player it is doubtful whether he made a single mistake in the 17 matches he played in South Africa.

The team's weakness was at scrumhalf where both Bill Conrad and Larry Savage were split-seconds too slow in serving a flyhalf like Jim Kearney, who was not particularly fast off the mark. This opened the way for the Springboks, guided by coach and national selector, Danie Craven, to use Hennie Muller to nullify all their opponent's efforts to mount constructive attacks. Brewis was the third trumpcard in Craven's hand. He was as near as could be the perfect flyhalf for modern international rugby. He had the ability to sum up a situation in the wink of an eye and his value to the Springbok team can be best underlined by pointing to the fact that they won every one of the ten tests he played in during his career.

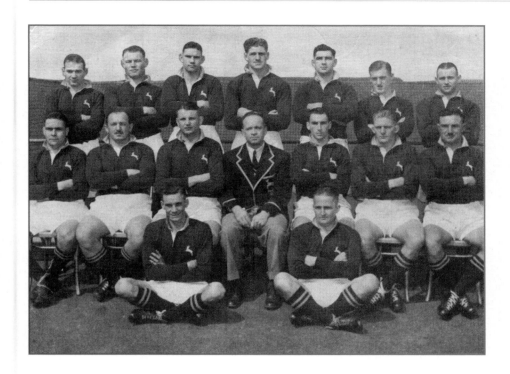

The team selected for the second test against the All Blacks at Ellis Park. Back row: F Marais, AC Koch, J van der Schyff, J du Rand, H Koch, MT Lategan, RAM van Schoor; middle row: RP Jordaan, A Geffin, F du Plessis (captain), Dr D Craven (manager), C Moss, H Muller, L Strydom; front row: H Brewis, PA du Toit.

The Springboks' biggest handicap for the series was their total lack of international experience while the All Blacks, again, made the mistake of over-preparing for the tour. Selected the season before their departure, they spent two weeks training at Hermanus before the tour started and it seemed at times as if many of the players went stale far too early in the tour.

The South African selectors – Craven, Schreiner, Mellish, Zeller and Kipling – organized a week of trial matches in Pretoria shortly after the tourists' arrival.

At the end of the trials the selectors named 32 players as being 'possibles' for the first test and, ironically enough, the name of Brewis was not on the list. In the meantime the All Blacks had had mixed fortunes in the early half of their tour, but succeeded in ruining the reputations of several fancied candidates for the first Springbok test team in the process. When they beat Western Province on the Saturday before the first test they actually forced the national selectors to change a team they had already selected. Chum Ochse, Dennis Fry and Otto van Niekerk, three Western Province players who had been in the side, were dropped. Fry and Ochse later on did get their Springbok colours, but the unfortunate Van Niekerk, a truly great wing then in the veteran stage, never got his chance.

Felix du Plessis, a Transvaal lock-forward who had played for South African Forces against their New Zealand counterparts in Rome during the war, was finally appointed captain of a team of Springboks, all of whom had had no experience of international rugby. At the time of his selection, he was considered the best lineout specialist in the country.

In retrospect, the Springboks settled down remarkably quickly. Van der Schyff kicked some magnificent touches although he did fail with an early penalty, and Tjol Lategan, the quiet Matie student who was soon to become a national hero, was only just stopped after a typically subtle break past Allen. But in the fourteenth minute of the match Bob Scott placed a penalty for the All Blacks and after that the Springboks seemed to lose impetus. A poor clearance by Van der Schyff was charged down by Sammy Henderson and, with the try converted by Scott, the All Blacks led 8–0.

Captain Felix du Plessis led an untried team of Springboks onto the Newlands turf for the first test of the 1949 series.

Van der Schyff, Duvenage, Brewis and Geffin were the acknowledged place-kickers in the team. Van der Schyff got the first two chances, but fluffed them and when Savage was caught with his hands in the scrum about 30 yards from his own posts, the ball just happened to land virtually at Geffin's feet and Du Plessis nodded. Placing the ball in the oblong hole he had dug with his left boot, with the laces down and a little mound of earth and grass to cushion the front, he stepped back five or six yards, his chin resting on his chest and his eyes always on the ball. Running up, he struck the ball just below the centre and the follow-through was so complete that his right boot ended up virtually in line with his head.

With the score 8–3, things looked a little rosier but just before half-time the All Blacks added another three points when Kearney lifted over an excellent dropgoal.

The second half belonged to Geffin as he methodically kicked the Springboks to victory with four successive penalties. The referee, Eddie Hofmeyr, was violently criticized afterwards for some of his decisions. In an article for the South African *Rugby News*, he gave his reasons for penalizing the All Blacks and giving Geffin the chance to kick himself into rugby immortality.

'In the first half I gave a penalty against Savage for hands in the scrum. In the second half the Springboks got another penalty for off-sides by Grant in the line-out. Then followed three penalties in the last 15 minutes for obstruction by Eric Boggs, Morrie Goddard and again by Boggs. In each case it followed diagonal kicks by Hansie Brewis, which were chased by Cecil Moss.

'In the first case Moss was prevented from getting to the ball when Boggs ran between him and the ball, and Scott fielded. The second one was almost identical, but it was Goddard who interfered.

'In the third case Boggs was again the culprit, but Moss nearly got to the ball before Scott, and I had to consider the possibility of a penalty try. However, I could see Peter Henderson, then the New Zealand sprint champion, coming across in cover defence and he would doubtless have prevented a try. After the match Boggs wanted to hit me, but other All Blacks stopped him. Dr Danie Craven, manager of the Springboks, and Mr Sport Pienaar, then president of the South African Rugby Board, were of the opinion that I should have awarded the Springboks a penalty try. Fred Allen, on the other hand, told me afterwards that if I had awarded a penalty try he would have taken the All Blacks off the field.'

Geffin's penalties not only brought the Springboks a rather lucky victory, but also enabled the burly frontranker to break the individual test scoring record of 14 points held by Bennie Osler since 1928 and equalled by Gerry Brand in 1938.

▲▲▲

It is not too much to say that South Africa's rugby honour was at stake when the Springboks trotted onto Ellis Park for the second test on 13 August 1949. More than 70 000 spectators circled the ground and most of them did not know what to hope for. There was little real confidence in Du Plessis' side, 12 of whom had been members of the team which looked so unconvincing at Newlands.

Although Scott again gave the All Blacks an early lead with a penalty, the Springboks were a lot more purposeful from the start. Du Toit and Brewis, Van Schoor and Lategan, two legendary combinations together for the first time in international rugby, began to run with a safe, sure rhythm, and Muller popped up here, there and everywhere. Two giants of South African rugby made their debuts that afternoon, Chris Koch and Salty du Rand.

Chris Koch, a legend in his lifetime, played eleven seasons of international rugby for the Springbok side.

Geffin soon levelled the scores with his sixth successive penalty goal against the All Blacks and then came one of the most marvellous tries in rugby history. There was a scrum near the grandstand touchline and deep into All Blacks territory. Jorrie Jordaan hooked and the ball flashed into Brewis' hands. For a split-second it looked as if he would drop for goal and the All Blacks thought so too. A battalion of defenders charged down on Brewis, but he changed his mind and streaked around the blindside with his opponents caught off balance and going the wrong way.

He was now very near the goalline, but again the way was blocked. He feinted as if to kick towards the corner flag; the All Blacks hesitated for a fatal instant and suddenly Brewis was off again like a rocket.

A few yards from the line he was threatened once more and this time Brewis dummied to the inside, fooled yet another defender, and then straightened out and went over with Scott too late to do more than just brush his shoulder. The more than 70 000 spectators went raving mad.

Geffin missed the conversion, the first time he had failed, but it did not really matter as the Springboks, with Muller criss-crossing the field on defence and attack, were playing inspired rugby. In the second half Koch and Du Rand, followed by Du Plessis, Jordaan and Strydom, charged through the All Blacks' ranks as if they did not exist. It was Du Rand who got the ball back to Du Toit and from him into the safe hands of Brewis. The flyhalf wasted no time before passing and with Muller taking the ball, the All Blacks centres were in a quandary. Lategan slipped through the gap as only he could.

Kearney halted the rampant South Africans briefly with a mighty left-footed dropgoal, but not long afterwards Brewis showed that he could do the same with the right boot. The All Blacks made a last desperate onslaught but Muller and Van der Schyff combined to stop the danger and shortly afterwards the referee, Ralph Burmeister, ended it all with the score 12–6 and the series safe for South Africa.

A lineout in the test in Port Elizabeth against the 1949 All Blacks. Referee Ralph Burmeister watches as Crowley, Willocks and Bubbles Koch jump for the ball.

▲▲▲

The third test in Durban, two weeks later, is best forgotten. Both teams played without fire and apart from three penalties by the infallible Geffin, the abiding memory of the test is one of collapsing scrums and leaden-footed forwards. Du Plessis, Koch and Du Rand were below form. After a good try by Morrie Goddard, the All Blacks seemed petrified by the spectre of Geffin and, although the match clinched the series for the Springboks, it was a miserable afternoon for both sides. But it did leave the Springboks poised to make a clean sweep in a home series for the first time in South African rugby history and with the All Blacks desperate to avoid being whitewashed, the final test in Port Elizabeth had a special significance.

Felix du Plessis leads the Springboks onto the field followed by Floris Duvenage, Hoppy van Jaarsveld, Okey Geffin and Jack van der Schyff.

Ryk van Schoor and Tjol Lategan joined forces in the second test of the 1949 series to form a legendary partnership as centres for the Springbok team.

With an eye to the future, the national selectors decided to replace Du Plessis with Willem Barnard and to hand the captaincy of the fourth test to Basil Kenyon, who had led Border so well against the touring team. Border beat the All Blacks 9–0, still New Zealand's biggest defeat against a provincial team in South Africa. In a second match between the two teams the result was a six-all draw. Transvaal flanker Piet Malan came in for the injured Du Rand and Geraghty got his only test cap. Kenyon replaced Koch on the flank, who moved to lock in place of Geel.

It was a match packed with thrills. Early in the first half Du Toit intercepted and, with a long way to go to an open line, was overhauled from behind by Henderson and Meates. On another occasion Brewis broke cleanly and flipped the ball to Muller who ran like the wind with Henderson coming across from the other side to cut him off. The two bodies collided in mid-air as Muller dived for the line and the referee, Burmeister, who was on the spot, ruled that he did not get the try. In the process Muller was badly concussed and he played the rest of the match without being able to focus properly. Tries by Johnstone and Elvidge and a conversion from Scott gave the All Blacks their eight points, but it was not good enough.

An inevitable penalty by Geffin, a try by Du Toit converted by Geffin and a soaring dropgoal by Brewis made the Springbok tally 11 and a sad bunch of All Blacks trooped off the Crusaders field.

In the dressingroom Bob Scott burst into tears, convinced that it was his poor placekicking which had let his team down. It was a black day in New Zealand rugby history, but fate had already decreed that revenge, almost as total as their humiliation was then, would be only a few short years away.

Venue	South Africa	Result	South Africa				New Zealand			
			T	C	P	D	T	C	P	D
Cape Town	won	15–11	0	0	5	0	1	1	1	1
Johannesburg	won	12–6	2	0	1	1	0	0	1	1
Durban	won	9–3	0	0	3	0	1	0	0	0
Port Elizabeth	won	11–8	1	1	1	1	2	1	0	0
		47–28	3	1	10	2	4	2	2	2
Series: South Africa played 4; W4, L0, D0										

'OKEY' GEFFIN

It was Adolph Hitler's birthday and as a special treat the commandant of the prisoner-of-war camp at Thorn, Poland, granted everybody an extra hour in bed. The Führer's birthday could not have been better timed as far as the South African and New Zealand inmates of the camp were concerned. They needed the extra rest because the first rugby trials were scheduled to be played later in the day. For some time the main topic of conversation had been a proposed 'test series' between the rugby world's two keenest rivals. Bill Payn, the 1924 Springbok forward, was the main organizer and he and Peter Pienaar, son of the 1921 Springbok captain Theo Pienaar, and Billy Millar jnr., son of the 1912 South African captain, very quickly discovered that there was more than enough talent among their fellow prisoners.

The senior medical officer in the camp had given permission for the games to be played, but he added a warning that he would soon put a stop to the activities if 'any player walks into hospital with a broken neck'. A field was marked off with yellow clay lines on the vast sandy parade ground and with army boots considered too lethal for the match, the players played with bare feet.

One of the most enthusiastic players among the South Africans was a burly Jewish boy born 22 years before, less than a good touch-kick's distance away from the Ellis Park rugby ground, the stadium where he once saw Gerry Brand in action and promptly acquired a healthy dose of hero worship. His fellow prisoners knew him as 'Ox' Geffin and his raw strength and accurate bare-footed kicking made him one of the stars in the many rough-and-ready matches to follow.

Geffin learnt a lot in those matches and it could well be, as has often been written, that he practised his placekicking on the mass grave in which thousands of Nazi-executed Poles were buried, but the truth is that he was already a promising member of Johannesburg Pirates by the time he donned the khaki uniform. It was at the Pirates club that Freddie Turner first spotted his potential and it was Turner who gave him his first practical lessons in the art of placekicking. Geffin was fortunate that he encountered a coach as intelligent as Turner, whose own style was completely different. Turner used to lift the ball very high while Geffin's kicks had a low trajectory. Instead of trying to change the boy's style, Turner merely helped him to make the most of it. As an under-19 player Geffin once succeeded with 12 out of 13 conversions and he was obviously already on his way to bigger things when the war intervened.

When the hostilities finally ceased 'Ox' became known as 'Okey' (nobody really knows how or why) and he was soon a regular frontranker in the powerful Transvaal pack under Jan Lotz in the late 1940s. Throughout his career Geffin never followed the flight of the ball until after his follow-through had brought his boot in line with his vision. He believed that this was the secret of timing and accuracy. Geffin must be the only Springbok never to have an official Christian name. Everybody accepted it to be Aaron but on his birth certificate there was nothing but a blank space until he had it rectified years later. Okey always had his own explanation for this. 'When my father went to register my birth and they asked him for my Christian names he must have said: "He's a Jewish boy! He's got no Christian names!" '

But whether he was 'Ox', 'Okey' or 'Aaron', this bull-necked Transvaler, with Muller and Brewis, filled the leading roles in the first post-war test series when the Springboks had to defend their rugby crown against the All Blacks.

Okey Geffin played in all the tests against New Zealand in 1949 and represented South Africa in 1951/52.

CHAPTER 15

1951/52

SOUTH AFRICA TOUR THE
BRITISH ISLES AND FRANCE

▲▲▲

The Springbok threequarters took some time to settle down on the heavier fields in Britain but once they discovered the inside gap, the machine broke down only once – when London Counties beat them. In a few other matches they faltered occasionally, but always recovered in time to win.

The main strengths of the team lay in their powerful but mobile pack, and outstanding halfbacks in Du Toit and Brewis. Second-string scrumhalf Oelofse was often bothered by injury, but Brewis throughout the tour had a deputy in Dennis Fry who probably in any other post-World War II era, would have been South Africa's number-one test flyhalf.

Van Schoor, famous for his murderous tackling, and Lategan, a subtle attacker, were the obvious centre-pair and Ochse, who, as Craven put it, was better at scoring difficult tries than easy ones, and the versatile Johnstone were brilliant wings. At full-back, the quiet, deeply religious and totally confident Buchler played as well as any one who ever wore the green-and-gold jersey in this position.

The Springbok frontrow trio of Bekker, Delport and Koch are still considered to be possibly the best in South African history and the loose-forward combination of Fry, Van Wyk and Muller might have been equalled but certainly never bettered. It was a tour of highlights; veritable Everests in South African rugby history.

One was the match against Cardiff on 20 October 1951. Glance at the statistics of this match and you marvel that the Springboks ever managed to win. They lost the scrums 18–26, the lineouts 15–18 and there were 15 penalties against them with nine in their favour.

With 12 minutes to go the Springboks were still trailing by one point and were only then beginning to master the Cardiff forwards and, more specifically, understand the interpretations of referee H Joynson. In the last minute of the match there was a lineout on the right-hand side of Cardiff Arms Park and the referee informed skipper Muller that it would probably be the last of the match. 'Get me the ball, whatever happens,' flyhalf Brewis told his leader.

The Boks duly won the ball and it went quickly to scrumhalf Hansie Oelofse who gave Brewis a perfect pass. Brewis, meanwhile, had signalled that he would kick for the left-hand corner flag and this he did with such accuracy that Ochse could beat Trott to the touchdown with about a metre to spare.

SOUTH AFRICA vs SCOTLAND

And then there was Scotland at Murrayfield on 24 November 1951. For once the weather was really kind; the field was firm and there was even a little sunshine. 'On a day like this we can beat any team by double figures,' Muller predicted

Roy John gets well up to take the ball in a lineout during the test between South Africa and Wales. South Africa won 6–3.

beforehand but not even he could have expected a winning margin of 44 points. The Springboks were in total control and with backs and forwards combining perfectly in one sweeping movement after the other, often from their own goalline, they scored nine tries, a dropgoal and seven conversions. Deep in the second half, Muller felt so sorry for his battered opponents that he actually told Angus Cameron, the young Scottish captain, to try and keep his forwards together a bit more effectively. It was the sort of sportsmanship you could have expected from that team and the Scots reciprocated by showing their admiration when they carried Muller off the field after the final whistle.

Before the match between the Springbok rugby team and Ireland at Lansdowne Road, the President of the Republic of Ireland was introduced to the South African team by Hennie Muller.

For the record, here are the scorers in that historic match: tries by Chris Koch (two), Salty du Rand, Willem Delport, Basie van Wyk, Hennie Muller, Ernst Dinkelmann, Ryk van Schoor and Tjol Lategan. Add to that a drop by Brewis and seven conversions by Geffin.

SOUTH AFRICA vs IRELAND

Seven minutes after the kick-off in the match against Ireland on 9 December 1951, Van Schoor was carried off the field, unconscious, after mis-timing a tackle on Browne. The Springbok machine was not working on all cylinders and at half-time the score was 3–5 in Ireland's favour.

Meanwhile there was even more drama in the dressingroom where three doctors decided that Van Schoor was too badly concussed to return to the field. Van Schoor insisted that he must and finally a worried Mellish, after asking a few questions to determine whether he had some idea of where he was, accepted the responsibility for the stocky Springbok's return to action. His courage seemed to inspire the Springboks. First Muller and Brewis combined to send Ochse over in the corner and then Brewis, ending once and for all the myth that Jackie Kyle was the world's best flyhalf of the era, stabbed over a superb dropgoal. Then followed a try by Basie van Wyk and with that Ireland's hopes of victory crumbled.

The final try of the match will be remembered as long as the game of rugby is played. An attack from the Boks was stopped and from the loose scrum the ball reached the dazed Van Schoor. Through instinct rather than intent he beat his man on the inside, stumbled, cut inside past several other defenders and then with an incredible final side-step again to the inside, he left the fullback grasping vainly to score the greatest try of his illustrious career.

SOUTH AFRICA vs WALES

The test against Wales was another titanic battle with Johnny Buchler in splendid form as Cliff Morgan wasted the hard-won possession gained for him by his forwards, particularly the mighty Roy John who completely outplayed Du Rand in the lineouts. In a vain attempt to foil the fast-breaking Springbok loose-forwards

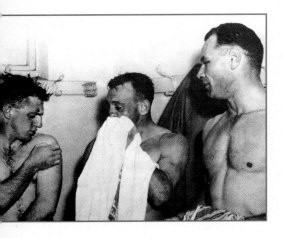

Tjol Lategan shows his wounds to an unimpressed Ryk van Schoor and Chris Koch. Three of the greatest Springboks of all time together in the dressingroom after a match on the 1951/52 tour.

and the ruthless defence of the centres, Morgan and his threequarters confined themselves to grubberkicks and Buchler easily dealt with these, driving the Welshmen back time and again.

Starved of possession, the Springbok backs had only two real opportunities to strike. The first time Brewis broke just far enough to draw Bleddyn Williams before passing to Lategan who flipped the ball high over Van Schoor and straight into the hands of Ochse. The wing went over in the corner with three defenders on his back, beating Olympic sprinter Ken Jones in the process. The second chance came when the Welsh loose-forwards hesitated ever so slightly to tackle Brewis. This was all the time he needed for his dropped goal to add three points to the Springbok total. The Boks won 6–3, but without Johnny Buchler, the cover defence of Van Wyk, Fry and Muller, and the attacking genius of Brewis and Ochse, they would have been defeated.

SOUTH AFRICA vs ENGLAND

England was beaten 8–3 through a typical try by Du Toit and a conversion and a penalty from Muller who proved his remarkable versatility by using himself as the placekicker. It was, from all aspects, the dullest of the tests played on the tour.

SOUTH AFRICA vs FRANCE

The test against France, won 25–3, produced a final try which was a fitting climax to a tour that will stand for all time to come as a testimonial to Springbok rugby at its best. According to Craven:

'There was a scrum near our twenty-five. We hooked and the ball flashed from Du Toit to Brewis, Lategan, Van Schoor and Ochse. Chum was halfway round his man when he passed inside to Van Schoor who gave to the forwards. With short, snappy passes they gained ground before passing to the backs, with everything happening so fast that Ochse was not yet back in position by the time it again came his way. But Johnstone had shot across to take the pass and he in turn fed the forwards on his inside.

'They carried on with another passing movement and then back again to the threequarters, all the way down the line to Ochse who lifted a short cross-kick for Basie van Wyk, to pick up and dive over.

'How often that ball was handled, nobody will ever know. But what we do know for sure is that Johnny Buchler is the only player who did not feature in the movement and that some players handled the ball five times and others three times!'

They were giants, those members of the 1951/52 Springbok touring side. South Africa can never forget them or the example they set on and off the field of play.

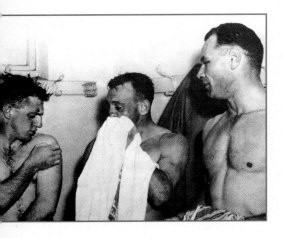

Koch nearly scores a try but is thrown off balance at the last moment by the English captain, NM Hall. South Africa beat England by eight points to three.

VENUE	SOUTH AFRICA	RESULT	SOUTH AFRICA							
			T	C	P	D	T	C	P	D
SCOTLAND (EDINBURGH)	WON	44–0	9	7	0	1	0	0	0	0
IRELAND (DUBLIN)	WON	17–5	4	1	0	1	1	1	0	0
WALES (CARDIFF)	WON	6–3	1	0	0	1	1	0	0	0
ENGLAND (TWICKENHAM)	WON	8–3	1	1	1	0	1	0	0	0
FRANCE (PARIS)	WON	25–3	6	2	1	0	0	0	0	1

OFF THE FIELD ...

The 1951/52 Springboks who toured the United Kingdom and France still epitomize all that is best in rugby, on and off the field. The bare statistics of their tour can be dismissed with a glance: 31 matches played in Britain and France, 30 victories, one defeat, 562 points for, 167 against. An on-the-field record that is only a fraction short of perfection, studded by magnificent performances they still talk about from Cardiff to Toulouse, Twickenham to Paris, and crowned by that incredible 44–0 massacre of Scotland at Murrayfield.

But the real triumph of this tour cannot be found in the record books and there is only a hint of it in what was written afterwards by the sportswriters who accompanied the Springboks. The nearest an outsider can get to the real truth is to be there when a few of the members of that team are together and sharing the memories not even the passage of time can dim.

Could there in all our sports history have been a more touching scene than the team's visit to Basil Kenyon in his hospital room in London on Christmas morning, 1951? The Springbok captain was recovering from an operation that saved his sight after an eye injury suffered at Pontypool early in the tour. But he knew, and his team knew, that he would never be able to play again. Team manager Mellish, coach Craven and 29 players filed into his room, ranged themselves around the bed and sang *Silent Night* to their captain. Basie Viviers who usually reserved his

Thirty South African rugby players arrived in London for the start of the 1951/52 tour of the British Isles and France

Chris Koch, Jakkals Keevy and Buks Marais try to look like Londoners as they doff their bowler hats.

rich baritone for more robust renditions, led the singing and when it was over, young Johnny Buchler read the prayers. This kind of warmth was a general characteristic of the team and not confined to their contact with each other. The Springboks mixed freely with their hosts, their camp followers, British rugby fans and even with their opponents.

The British public responded by going out of their way to be hospitable. The Springboks did everything they could not to disappoint their hosts: with men like Mellish, Craven, Kenyon and Muller in control it could not have been otherwise.

Craven could never forget how the Springboks returned to their hotel in Belfast one night after seeing Mario Lanza in *The Great Caruso* and then settled down for the usual cup of tea before bed. At that point an Irish international player walked in and told them that an advertisement had appeared in the newspapers saying that the Springboks would attend a certain dance, and that the people there were waiting for their arrival. The Springboks knew nothing about the affair, but, rather than disappoint, they wearily dragged themselves off to the dance. They arrived there at about midnight and such was the hospitality that they only left at half-past five in the morning!

Dave Lewis, an Englishman who was the official baggage master, learnt to love his protégés so much that when the time came to say goodbye, he disappeared quietly, sending a note to explain that he would have broken down and wept had he stayed to shake hands with every member of the team.

The loyalty between the players was amazingly strong and there is no better example than Ernst Dinklemann (a doctor by profession) nursing Salty du Rand before the test against Wales and then declaring him fit for the game although he knew that he would be the one to get Du Rand's place in the team should the then Rhodesian lock not be well enough to play. And after the Springboks had beaten Cardiff with a last-minute combination of the genius of Brewis and the alertness of Ochse, Basie Viviers, who was the touch-judge, actually burst out crying from sheer joy. Yes, this was a team with intense emotions, but they had the necessary maturity to balance it. In retrospect, they all seemed so 'grown-up' and each player fully aware of his responsibility to his team and his country.

This, in spite of (or perhaps because of) the fact that few touring sides from this country have ever had more players with a liking for mischief. Du Rand, Van Schoor, Muller, Myburgh, Viviers, Van Wyk and Sinclair were always alert to any opportunity to play a prank and Mellish and Craven were not exempt targets.

The team believed in singing and laughter. Apart from Gert Dannhauser and Basie Viviers, most of the others had to compensate with sheer volume and enthusiasm for a lack of a real musical talent. Geffin was always a big favourite with the team and the irrepressible Van Schoor had a remarkable repertoire of self-composed songs, which he fortunately only sang on special occasions.

Other players, by nature more quiet, also contributed to the general happiness that gave this team such an unique team spirit. A player, for example, like that enormously strong but always polite frontranker Jaap Bekker, had his own version of a threat he once heard a cowboy hero utter on the screen.

'I blows you up!' Jaap used to say darkly to all and sundry and eventually he bought some firecrackers to give his threat a little more effect.

Paul Johnstone, one of the outstanding successes of the tour, will always be remembered for his decision in the match against Munster that it was time somebody went to the assistance of Bekker who was receiving a pummelling from an opponent who was confusing boxing with rugby. Slenderly built Paul was all for climbing in when lock forward Willem Barnard gently pushed him away from the scrum saying: 'Wait a minute, Paultjie. This is a place for us big fellows'. But for the rest of the tour Johnstone was known as 'The Killer of Munster'.

The 1951/52 Springboks never started any rough stuff – all their opponents vouched for that – but heaven help any team who did not keep things clean. Their reputation as hard but fair players spread throughout the British Isles and even to France and they hardly ever had problems with punch- or boot-happy opponents.

It was never any secret that the team did have a small group of 'shock troops' who could, if necessary, take over, but their services were rarely needed.

One of the most enduring legends of the tour was the one of Basie van Wyk, the 'Witch Doctor'. It all started when he had trouble with a toe-nail that was injured and took an uncommonly long time to work itself off. The sight of the big, tough forward limping along in slippers was just too inviting for the rest of the team and while preparing at Porthcawl for the test against Wales, a gang of players over-powered him and ripped off the nail.

After that, Van Wyk used the nail and some pebbles he had picked off the beach to 'throw the bones' whenever the team had some minor problem – like who were the culprits who tied everybody's pyjamas into knots! He invariably found himself to be innocent.

There can be no doubt that the tour management, that included Muller, Kenyon and Du Toit, actively encouraged the light-hearted off-the-field approach to prevent the players from going stale on such a long assignment. But when it came to the actual playing side of things, few teams have ever approached their task with more dedication.

Whenever Craven felt it necessary, he gave them training sessions so tough that it sometimes left the fittest players in a state of collapse. One such practice, on the St Paul's school field in London, will never be forgotten. 'I swear some of us will turn pale whenever you suddenly whisper "St Paul's",' said Van Schoor.

Basil Kenyon, captain of the fourth Springbok team to tour the British Isles, enjoys the snow in Peebles, Scotland. After suffering an eye injury, he had to delegate on-the-field leadership to Hennie Muller.

Springboks and friends take a last look at Cape Town from the top of Table Mountain before their departure. Players in front are: Chum Ochse, Ernst Dinkelmann and Chris Koch. On the far left is Martin Saunders, Tjol Lategan and Willem Delport. Crouching at the back is Jaap Bekker.

CHAPTER 16

1953

AUSTRALIA TOUR SOUTH AFRICA

▲▲▲

Salty du Rand is stopped in his tracks by three Wallabies in the second test of the 1953 tour. Stephen Fry is to his left.

The strength of the 1953 Wallabies, like that of their predecessors twenty years earlier, was exceptional pace up front and behind the scrum. Their only hope lay in running the Springboks off their feet and capitalizing on every mistake. The odds were more in their favour whenever the Springboks forgot where their own strength lay.

Probably the best player in the side was Eddie Stapleton, a splendid runner who never panicked and always seemed to do the right thing. Garth Jones had blazing speed on the leftwing and his famous try in the Newlands test assured him of a special niche in South African rugby history.

John Solomon was by far the best centre in the touring party, quick-thinking and a sophisticated tactician. He was also an excellent captain who, like his team manager, Wylie Breckenridge, was always charming and tactful throughout the three months and six days of the tour. The Wallabies had great hopes for Jimmy Phipps as Solomon's partner, but after his first encounter with Ryk van Schoor he was never a threat to the Springboks. The Wallabies should have dropped him, and not Solomon, to make place for the solid Herb Barker in the final test.

Barker was bothered with injuries throughout the tour and his safe placekicking was often missed. Morrie Tate and Johnny Bosler were mediocre halves, but the slightly-built Cyril Burke and the veteran Spanner Brown formed a good combination. Keith Cross, Norman Hughes and Brian Johnson, three quick, intelligent loose-forwards, were the real king-pins of the team. They had a deep respect for Hennie Muller, the Springbok captain, and his style so intrigued them that they often cornered him at after-match functions and asked him for advice!

The tight forwards were adequate, no more than that, with Tony Miller and Alan Cameron easily the best. Nic Shehadie, Solomon's vice-captain, had the misfortune of having to pack against the mighty Jaap Becker and he took a merciless pounding in the third test in particular.

The Wallabies wore green jerseys that year and the South Africans, as a gesture of hospitality, settled for white jerseys in the tests.

Solomon's men opened their tour with a surprising defeat against Natal with Roy McLean, at flyhalf, dropping the winning goal. Leading up to the first test they were also beaten by Free State, Transvaal, Griquas and Northern Transvaal, and in one of three consecutive matches against Rhodesia they were held to a draw. Their best performance was a narrow win over Western Province who threw the game away with shocking mistakes. Whether they lost or won though, the Wallabies flung the ball around and soon there was a tremendous campaign for their opponents to follow suit.

Wylie Breckenridge was subtly putting across his message in after-match speeches, calling for less kicking and more passing movements, imploring the referees to be less whistle-happy and making everybody feel a little guilty because they were beating the Wallabies.

▲▲▲

The Springbok team for the first test at Ellis Park was selected entirely from members of the team who visited Britain and France in 1951/52 and Hennie Muller, after a struggle to regain something of his old form, was given the captaincy.

After eight successive and successful tests with Hansie Brewis, Fonnie du Toit, an outstanding scrumhalf who throughout his career regarded the serving and protection of his flyhalf as his main responsibility, had to make way for the more dynamic Hansie Oelofse. Injuries frequently interrupted Oelofse's career, but at his best he was a match-winner on his own; certainly there was no-one remotely approaching his all-round ability in 1953.

The first signs of the effects of the propaganda campaign could already be seen in this test. The game was often loose and without purpose, but in between there were flashes of brilliance from the Springboks. Practically in the first minute of the match, Van Schoor nailed Phipps on the halfway line with a tackle that made the chalk and dry grass fly, and the forwards and backs combined smoothly and often. From one such movement Marais went over for a try he converted himself. The Boland wing also put over a penalty just before half-time after Oelofse had worked beautifully with his forwards before Du Rand was sent over. Against all this the outclassed Wallabies could only show a penalty by Tom Sweeney.

In the second half Oelofse broke again and this time he needed no help. Then Buchler, as quietly efficient as ever, dropped a lovely penalty goal. Another crush-

Basie van Wyk scores a try in the second test at Newlands. This was the only test the Wallabies won on the tour with the final score a respectable 14–18.

ing tackle by Van Schoor gave the Springboks their next try. As the ball popped loose, Lategan was on the spot to snatch it up and weave his way through. Shortly before the end Van Schoor slipped through a gap with Fry, Van Wyk and Muller, who finally outstripped the shattered defence for a try near the posts.

The Springboks won a comfortable 25–3, having scored five excellent tries and kept the ball in play as much as possible. Brewis often passed when his sound rugby brain actually dictated that he should have kicked. But no-one is more fervent than a recent convert and the clamouring for 'open rugby' continued without challenge, with several former Springboks who should have known better, joining in the appeals for 'less kicking'.

▲▲▲

Brewis was axed for the Newlands international. He was well into his thirties and was worried by a jaw injury suffered in the match between Northern Transvaal and Australia. A year later Brewis was good enough to beat Western Province practically off his own bat, but he was never again to be considered for a Springbok team.

His place was taken by Ian Kirkpatrick, a lanky youngster who had played well for Griquas against the tourists and he was the only newcomer in the team. In later years Kirkpatrick became a regular Springbok centre, but his debut at flyhalf was a most unhappy one. He was jeered every time he kicked by a section of the crowd who did not know what they wanted and was saddled with much of the blame for South Africa's first defeat in eleven tests.

It cannot be denied that the Springboks were a little over confident for the second test. They had beaten the Wallabies without difficulty in the first encounter and on the Tuesday before the second international, Combined Southern Universities had made the Wallabies look like leaden-footed third-raters. The Springboks were well on top in the first half and there were ominous signs that they were rather too relaxed after the resumption.

John Solomon went off the field briefly after an injury and when he returned, he roved among his threequarters, looking sorry for himself and leaving Brian Johnson on the right wing and Eddie Stapelton at centre. This left Muller with the option whether to keep his pack intact and control possession completely or also to put a forward among the backs. He decided to keep his forwards together and was criticized for this later when Solomon came to life to help give Garth Jones the winning try. Muller's plan would have worked had the Springboks confined themselves to driving against the depleted and already beaten Australian pack. Instead Oelofse, renowned for his ability to play back to his forwards, kept on passing to his backs. Muller admitted often in later years that he knew that every member of his team wanted to 'show up' the crowd and the critics by keeping the ball in play as much as possible. But it would be churlish to make too many apologies and to degrade what was one of the finest fight-backs in modern rugby history.

Tries by Du Rand, Ochse and Koch, one converted by Marais, to an unconverted try by Stapelton, gave the Springboks a lead of 11–3 at half-time. Within minutes of the re-start Van Wyk made it 14–3 after a lightning break by

Hansie Oelofse about to gather a tumbling ball as Garth Jones pounds in pursuit during the fourth test against the 1953 Wallabies in Port Elizabeth.

Oelofse and it really looked as if the Wallabies might as well surrender. Instead they fought back. Cross was awarded a try after some untidy play which was converted by Colbert. Shortly afterwards Solomon and Phipps reverse-passed smoothly after a loose ball had been picked up. Brown took the movement further and as he was about to be tackled by Muller, he timed a perfect pass to Brian Johnson. It was a try right in the corner, but Stapelton converted with the kind of kick that wins matches.

With the lead whittled down to one point the Springboks launched a series of attacks. Koch and Van Wyk missed tries by losing the ball in diving for the line and Marais could not take full advantage of an overlap created by Lategan. To make matters worse, Marais and Buchler took turns to miss two fairly easy penalties.

In the first minute of injury time the Wallabies got their winning points from an unforgettable try. Once again it came from a loose ball, some ten yards from their own goal-line. Brown immediately started a movement and when Solomon came into the lineup to pass to Stapelton, the Springboks were in trouble. The big wing ran up to the 10-yard line before giving Jones a pass so perfect that the lanky Queenslander could take it without any slackening of pace. Johnny Buchler, the Springbok fullback, made the mistake of not trying to force Jones infield where Muller, in full chase, might have had a chance of getting him in his sights.

Instead Jones found himself with a long but clear run to the Springbok line, feeling, as he put it afterwards, 'Muller's breath on my neck every inch of the way!'

All along the railway-stand side of Newlands the two ran, Muller just too far behind to risk a desperate dive-tackle. Muller pounded after the flying Australian, the gap neither closing nor widening. Finally Jones crossed the line and collapsed behind the posts, completely exhausted. Muller pulled up a few feet behind him, shoulders hunched and knowing defeat for the first time in his test career.

The 14–18 disaster was just the medicine the Springboks, the selectors and a large section of the press and public needed.

RYK VAN SCHOOR

Ryk van Schoor's deadly tackling made him one of the most feared Springboks of all time but he was also one of the most inspiring members of the team. He was probably best known for his partnership with Tjol Lategan from 1949 to 1953. He ended his highly regarded test career against the 1953 Wallabies.

▲▲▲

Kock, Ochse, Marais, Dinkelmann and Kirkpatrick were left out for the third test. Jan Pickard got his first test 'cap' in place of his 1951/2 teammate Dinkelmann, while Koch was, as it soon proved to be, temporarily displaced by Harry Newton Walker. Steve Hoffman and Dolf Bekker, the younger brother of Jaap, were the new wings. Most significant was the selection of Transvaal's Natie Rens as flyhalf. Rens was built and played like Brewis. He did not have Brewis' superb judgement and quickness, but he was an outstanding kicker with both feet, had good hands and, above all, the perfect big-match temperament. Known to his Transvaal teammates as *Bokspeen*, this dairy farmer was one of the best place- and drop-kickers of his day.

A few days before the test Tjol Lategan, after ten successive internationals as Ryk van Schoor's partner, had to withdraw because of an injured shoulder. His place was taken by Daantjie Rossouw, a Matie who had done well for Southern Universities against the Wallabies.

The Springboks would no longer allow themselves to be influenced. The Kingsmead test would be played according to the traditional South African pattern.

With solid scrummaging, good line-out work and sensible use of possession, the Springboks won 18–8 and the Wallabies were never really in the picture. The spectators, probably chastened by what had happened at Newlands, cheered rather

Hansie Oelofse and Natie Rens formed a highly efficient half-back combination to help the Springboks save the series.

Jan Pickard, deep in thought with the 'Old Master' Boy Louw, added strength to the Springbok pack after the Newlands defeat.

than jeered Rens' long touchfinders and they understood and appreciated the tactics. Once the Wallabies had been properly softened, the Springboks scored some of the finest tries of the series, at least one the sort of effort the Wallabies would have been proud of. It came from a lineout with Dolf Bekker throwing to Pickard who, as quickly, whipped the ball back to the wing who went over in the corner before the Australians really knew what it was all about. Rens made the difficult conversion look easy and the half-time score was 10–0 including another converted try, scored by Rossouw who beat several defenders in a darting solo run after Muller had started a movement. Van Schoor's deadly tackles provided Fry, Van Wyk and Muller with plenty of loose balls from which to attack, and early in the second half Jaap Bekker steamrollered through for Rens to convert. Dolf and Jaap Bekker are still the only two Springbok brothers to each score a try in the same test.

A penalty dropgoal from Solomon followed, but then Oelofse slipped through again. Fry was up to give Van Wyk a try which Rens, for once, could not convert.

With the score 18–3 the match was won and lost and even the Springboks must have felt like cheering when the Wallabies, showing their typical never-say-die opportunism, got the final try. It came after Burke had picked up a careless pass before giving to Cross who ran practically the length of the field to score. Van Schoor, the only Springbok in a position to chase Cross, gave up after a few strides and smiled at Muller.

'Wow, that guy Jones can move, eh Hennie?' he remarked.

'What do you mean Jones?' Muller replied. 'That's Keith Cross!'

'What!' Van Schoor exclaimed. 'A forward too fast for me? I'm out of the next test, that's for sure!'

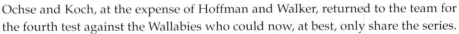

Ochse and Koch, at the expense of Hoffman and Walker, returned to the team for the fourth test against the Wallabies who could now, at best, only share the series.

The Port Elizabeth test was not much of a game. The Springbok forwards took over gradually but thoroughly and in the second half had complete control. The Wallabies, on the other hand, had decided on spoiling tactics this time. Their backs lined up very shallow and tried to counter Van Schoor's tackling by kicking grubbers with monotonous regularity. Buchler had no problems in coping with them. The Wallabies were still in there with a hope at half-time after Stapelton had scored an unconverted try and Herb Barker two penalty goals, but their efforts were nullified by Rens with two penalties and a dropgoal.

In the second half the Springboks battered their brave opponents who could do little more than defend – something they did very well. Kock got the first try after Oelofse had once again combined well with Van Wyk and Fry. Then Oelofse, brilliant in this match, punted ahead and scored from his own kick and Rens hit the target with both conversion kicks. In the last few minutes Buchler collected a poor clearance from one of the Australians and lifted over a dropgoal to make the final score 22–9. The series, in the balance while the Springboks flirted with a style that did not suit them, was well and truly won.

It was to be the final test for a host of Springboks. Van Schoor and Lategan, Ochse and Delport never again played for South Africa and injury was to virtually hound Oelofse into retirement. Why Rens, who made no mistakes and scored 19 points in only two tests, was never again considered by the national selectors nobody knows. He and the Western Province flyhalf Len Rodriques,

The two captains, Hennie Muller and John Solomon, shake hands after the Wallabies beat the Springboks in the second test.

who never did get his Springbok colours, would certainly have been worth their weight in gold to the embattled Springboks in New Zealand less than three years later. It was also the last test for Muller whose extreme exhaustion after each of the four internationals was known to be a source of worry to Craven. The 'greyhound of the veld', as his great opponent Bob Scott once described him, listened to the advice of the man who had been with him in triumph and defeat and one of the most illustrious Springboks in rugby history came to the end of the trail.

VENUE	SOUTH AFRICA	RESULT	SOUTH AFRICA				AUSTRALIA			
			T	C	P	D	T	C	P	D
JOHANNESBURG	WON	25–3	5	2	2	0	0	0	1	0
CAPE TOWN	LOST	14–18	4	1	0	0	4	3	0	0
DURBAN	WON	18–8	4	3	0	0	1	1	1	0
PORT ELIZABETH	WON	22–9	2	2	2	2	1	0	2	0
		79–38	15	8	4	2	6	4	4	0
SERIES: SOUTH AFRICA PLAYED 4; W3, L1, D0										

The Springboks win the third test and an exhausted Hennie Muller is warmly congratulated by John Solomon. Jaap Bekker moves up for a handshake and on the left, patting him on the shoulder, is Nic Shehadie. Muller's face is lined with fatigue and at the end of the series he announced his retirement from international rugby.

CHAPTER 17

1955

BRITISH ISLES TOUR SOUTH AFRICA

▲▲▲

Stephen Fry leads his team onto Newlands for one of the greatest matches the South Africans ever played.

Their mascot was an outsize toy lion called Elmer and bagpipes and a shillelagh formed part of the luggage, all solemnly marked 'team equipment' to save the individual owners any possible penalty for exceeding the weight limit imposed on each member of the first British team to travel to and in South Africa by air.

Robin Thompson's 1955 Lions were also the first team from the United Kingdom to show South Africa the new uniform they had adopted only five years before; the now-famous red jersey with the rose of England, the thistle of Scotland, the shamrock of Ireland and the three feathers of Wales combined in a shield-shaped badge on the left breast.

But the 1955 Lions had more than a new uniform to offer. Their tour record was the best of any team to visit South Africa since Johnny Hammond and his men, 59 years earlier. They radiated charm from the moment they stepped off the aircraft after the flight from London and gave the large number of fans and newspaper-

men waiting for them, a spontaneous 'concert'. Bathed in the floodlights of the newsreel cameramen, Cliff Morgan led the team in one song after the other and it must have been close to half-an-hour before the cheering crowd would let them leave for their hotel. This was to be the pattern for the tour. They always had time for their public, even near the end of what was a most strenuous tour, and they seemed to take a genuine delight in entertaining whoever was within earshot with impromptu 'acts' and singing.

The team was packed with talent, but there were five absolutely superb players in the side who added the touch of genius. They were the two England centres Phil Davies and Jeff Butterfield, Tony O'Reilly, the Irish right wing, Cliff Morgan, the flyhalf from Wales, and Bryn Meredith, also from Wales, who was a hooker of the highest class, but was also an extra loose-forward.

The Lions started off their tour by losing to Western Transvaal when, as in all of their defeats until they departed some three months later, their forwards failed to get enough clean possession to the backs.

Eastern Province, guided and driven by Amos du Plooy, capitalized on this weakness to tumble them 20–0 on the only other occasion they faltered in the 12 matches leading up to the first test in Johannesburg. By this time former Springboks like Harris and Turner were warning that the Springboks were up against a far from ordinary team and Craven, the Springbok coach and national selector, made no bones about the fact that he regarded the Lions as the most dangerous combination yet to visit South Africa.

When they massacred Transvaal 36–13, scoring seven tries in the process, the situation appeared to be desperate. Many people regarded it as a foregone conclusion that the Springboks would be beaten. The selectors decided to give Stephen Fry, the Western Province flanker and 1951/52 veteran, the formidable task of leading South Africa against the Lions. There must have been occasions during the series when he wondered whether it was all worthwhile as he became the target of a venomous campaign from an ill-bred section of the South African public. Fry immediately called on Craven to advise him and throughout that thrilling series these two suffered and rejoiced together. Both got more criticism than credit.

Cliff Morgan, the Welsh flyhalf in the 1955 Lions team, is collared by Springbok wing Theuns Briers in the exciting first test of the series at Ellis Park.

The team for the first test was selected after extensive trials and a Junior Springbok tour, and it marked the debut of several players who were to become household names. Men like Theunis Briers, the Paarl farmer who scored five tries in the series, a record for a Springbok on South African fields, and Karel Thomas (Tom) van Vollenhoven, Johan Claassen, a future captain and one of the finest lock-forwards in rugby history, and Daan Retief, former Northern Transvaal wing who was converted into an eighthman and was one of South Africa's best forwards of his era.

Jack van der Schyff returned to the team after not having been considered by the national selectors for nearly six years. The selection of Josias (Sias) Swart, on the left-wing, also established a new record as he was the first Springbok from South West Africa, while scrumhalf Tommy Gentles at 5'3" is still the shortest player to have represented South Africa.

The interest in this test was unbelievable. There was a flourishing black market; people paid the most ridiculous prices for tickets and eventually the biggest crowd ever to see a rugby international – estimates varied between 90 000 and 100 000 – crammed into Ellis Park for the match. The crowd, so huge that there was something frightening about it, saw a match to remember. Perhaps those who have called it the most thrilling test of all time are right. There was exhilarating rugby from both sides and the result was in the balance until the final few seconds.

Cecil Pedlow got the first points, but the try really belonged to Jeff Butterfield. The centre threequarter broke beautifully after his partner, Phil Davies, had nosed into a gap between Des Sinclair and Tom van Vollenhoven in the midfield. Davies threw a rather careless pass to Butterfield who scooped the ball towards him with one arm and then drew the defence before sending Pedlow over.

Two excellent penalties in succession by Van der Schyff took the Springboks into the lead; lovely kicks most people forgot in the wave of unfair recrimination which was to follow. An outstanding joint effort between Gentles and Fry then gave Briers a chance to pound away on a typical run, his inside swerve foxing Morgan. Van der Schyff converted, making the score 11–3.

In swift retaliation, Morgan drove a big gap in the Springbok defence and when Davies passed to Butterfield he had O'Reilly on his outside. The great England centre did not need the Irish wing's help; he simply kept going and Cameron had no difficulty in making the half-time tally 11–8.

After the resumption, the Lions lost Reg Higgins, who was playing an outstanding game, and it does say a lot for their character that the misfortune inspired rather than dispirited them. Perhaps it was the Morgan magic that did it because almost immediately after Higgins was helped off, he broke with tremendous speed, caught the defence in two minds, and flashed over with Basie van Wyk looking on in helpless frustration. Next, Van der Schyff was put under terrific pressure and the bounce of the ball deceived him cruelly twice in quick succession. There were tries by a rampant Greenwood and the long-legged O'Reilly. All three second-half tries were converted by Cameron.

Leading 23–11, the Lions suddenly appeared to have everything tied up in a nice, neat bundle, but back came the Springboks with an opportunistic try after a kick from Gentles had Cameron going the wrong way. Van der Schyff could not convert, but in the final minute of the match Koch showed what a tremendous forward he could be. He picked up some way back from the line and dodged, weaved and crashed through a swarming defence to score a try that made those heavily-weighted temporary pavilions sway as the massive crowd screamed their happiness. This time Van der Schyff converted and with what was about half-a-minute of injury time remaining, Fry picked up a loose ball and flipped it to Briers. He had two men to beat, Pedlow and Cameron, but with that amazing ability to swerve inside at top speed, he beat them both to flash over between the corner flag and the posts.

The conversion was not from a too difficult angle but the incredible tension of the moment had to be overcome. The huge scoreboard read 23–22 to the Lions and then the last numeral abruptly disappeared as the scorer, undoubtedly a Springbok supporter, prepared to make it read 23–24.

Gentles placed the ball for Van der Schyff with the referee, Ralph Burmeister, resting on his haunches a few paces behind and to the left of the kicker so that he would have a clear view to the centre of the crossbar.

The fullback took four steps back and then ran up for the kick that would decide the result. The instant his boot struck the ball everyone knew that it was going to swing outside the left-hand post and that the Springboks had lost. His head down in utter dejection, Van der Schyff turned away as the Lions, standing behind the goalline, jumped for joy.

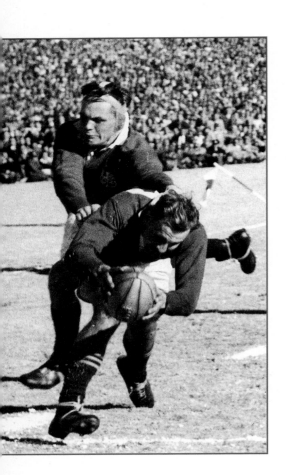

Theuns Briers scores at Ellis Park against the 1955 Lions. The final score was 22–23 in favour of the Lions.

Craven, Fry, Van der Schyff, Van Vollenhoven, the whole Springbok team were in disgrace all of a sudden with the rugby public. It should have been so easy to take a defeat like that with good grace, but instead there was a perverse desire to blame rather than to criticize constructively. It is a pity they were not present when Philip Nel came to Craven after the match and said: 'Danie, we came to within one point of beating them with players who have never been together in a team before. The foundations are there for the next test.' Nel's words were to prove prophetic.

▲▲▲

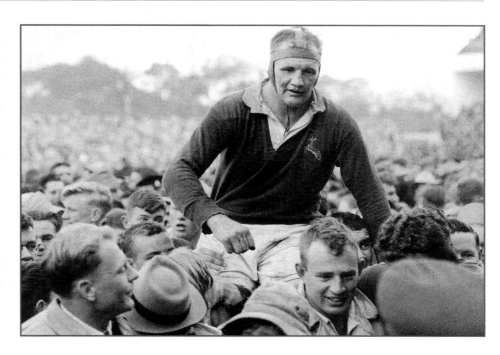

Happiness at the end of a job well done. Johan Claassen is carried off the field.

The embattled national selectors, Craven, Mellish, Zeller, Zimerman and Kenyon had only two further opportunities of seeing the Lions in action before they had to knuckle down to the unenviable task of selecting a team for the Newlands test.

The British team beat Boland 11–0 but did not play all that well and on the Tuesday before the test, had to give everything they had to score a 20–17 victory over the Western Province Universities. Brilliantly led by James Starke, they scored four tries to four and Pedlow's better placekicking saved the touring team. It is hardly surprising that 11 of the students eventually gained Springbok colours.

It took the selectors five hours of debate before they could reach consensus on the team for the second test. Roy Dryburgh took over from the hapless Van der Schyff at fullback, while Van Vollenhoven was switched from centre to left-wing and Sias Swart, who had done well in the first test, had to make way for him. Wilfred Rosenberg became Des Sinclair's new centre partner. Jaap Bekker took over from Amos du Plooy and Albertus Johannes (Bertus) van der Merwe replaced Colin Kroon to begin what was to be an illustrious career as Springbok hooker. Basie van Wyk lost his place to Matie, Dawie Ackermann.

The rugby public did not approve of the team at all and the selectors and the players were attacked bitterly from all quarters. The Springboks, managed by Boy Louw, prepared in virtual seclusion and outside telephone calls and visits from friends or fans were practically prohibited. There were many quiet team talks and a firm decision that the tactics would be traditional; a softening-up process by the forwards in the first half and then attacks from a sound foundation after half-time.

In this atmosphere the Springboks built up remarkable spirit and determination. Their critics had done them a favour; they were prepared to fight to the death.

In the dressingroom under the new Grand Stand pavilion at Newlands, Fry was too tense to address his team and asked Craven to do it for him. A few minutes later the two teams were on the field and Mike Slabber whistled them into action.

Cameron got an early penalty for the Lions, but it was soon clear that the Springboks were not going to allow any team to beat them that day. The forwards, with each man working with a fierce urgency, gave the Lions no mercy and they gradually established their superiority.

Near the end of the first half Gentles and Fry broke well and from the loose scrum that followed Sinclair cross-kicked towards the centre of the field. The ball travelled a bit too far for his forwards and three Lions, including the dangerous O'Reilly, were waiting for it with Van Vollenhoven alone facing them. The Springbok left-wing did the only thing he could. He swooped down on his three opponents and with a perfectly timed leap, plucked the ball out of the air, landed on his feet with cat-like agility and was streaking for the goalline before the Lions quite realized what was happening. Van Vollenhoven still had the fullback, Cameron, to beat, but this presented no problems to one of the fastest Springboks ever to wear the green-and-gold. The conversion failed, and poor placekicking was to be the only weakness revealed by the Springboks during the match.

Immediately after half-time it was obvious that Fry had decided that the time was ripe for attack and within nine minutes Van Vollenhoven had become the first Springbok since Boetie McHardy and Jan Stegmann against Ireland in 1912, to notch up a hat-trick in a test, and the first to achieve the feat in South Africa.

For his second try Van Vollenhoven ran fully 40 yards and for his third he beat O'Reilly hands-down with a feint and swerve, and again left Cameron standing with his bewildering ability to change direction at top speed.

Rosenberg was the next to score after Sinclair had flashed through a gap between Butterfield and Davies. Then more history was made when Dryburgh, after a perfectly executed scissors movement between Rosenberg and Sinclair, became the first Springbok fullback since Percy Alport in 1910 to score a try in a test. Dryburgh managed to convert his own try; the first successful kick from the Springboks in the match. A break by Ulyate gave Briers a chance to score his team's sixth try and then the Lions, at last, struck back when Morgan made an opening for an unconverted try by Butterfield.

Before the end Ackermann managed to celebrate his test debut with a try, converted by Dryburgh, to push the score to 25–6 and although Meredith added three points to his team's total with a brave try in the final minute, the much-maligned Springboks were the most convincing winners of one of the most crucial international matches of all time. Sports fans are fickle and suddenly the Springboks were heroes.

▲▲▲

The Springboks made only one change for the third test in Pretoria, replacing Gentles with Coenraad Strydom of Free State. Daan Retief had to withdraw because of injury, however, and his place was taken by George Phillip (Butch) Lochner, a young crashtackling eighthman from Stellenbosch. Injuries forced several changes in the Lions' line-up and Morgan led the side when Thompson also dropped out because of injury.

The agony of defeat. Daan Retief, the brilliant Springbok eighthman, seeks solace from a pondering Danie Craven on the touchline at Loftus Versfeld. It had just become clear to both Craven and Retief that the Lions were heading for victory.

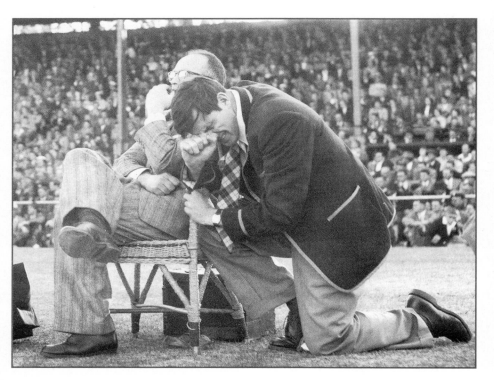

The Springboks played a slovenly game while the Lions, guided by Morgan who kicked more often than he passed, made few mistakes and deserved their 9–6 victory. Fry's men were sluggish, for some reason or other, and the best example of this came midway in the first half when Rosenberg, whose tackling was a highlight of the series, flattened Davies. The ball rolled loose, creating a perfect opportunity for the South African looseforwards. Instead it was the ever-alert Butterfield who snapped it up and dropped a beautiful goal. Many people thought that Davies had actually passed the ball off the ground and that a penalty should have gone to the Springboks but it was not a match South Africa deserved to win.

The Lions followed dull and effective tactics while the Springboks completely failed to find their feet. Butterfield also scored the only try of the match with Baker adding a penalty. Dryburgh scored all of South Africa's points with two penalties, one of them a magnificent dropped goal.

Apart from the return of Gentles and Retief, the selectors did not tamper with the team for the final test. The Lions made a fatal error by dropping Phil Davies and compounded the error by switching O'Reilly to the midfield.

For most of the first half it looked as if the visitors had to win. They launched one attack after the other and only desperate defence and a fair amount of luck kept them out. Finally Greenwood did go over after a clever kick by Griffiths which Pedlow converted. But it was Pedlow's inability to judge the high ball properly that enabled the Springboks to make it 5–3 at half-time.

In the second half, Ulyate tried the same kick and Briers made no mistake for his fifth try in four tests; a record on South African grounds. A break by Gentles, with Fry and Claassen in brilliant support, then gave Ulyate a try converted by Dryburgh and the Lions' hopes of making history were dashed. Van Vollenhoven was next to score after a short, sharp burst for the corner flag and a dropped goal from Ulyate made it 17–5.

There was a brief fight-back from the Lions and O'Reilly scored, but was so injured in the process that he had to leave the field. Then the Springbok forwards took complete command. Only desperate defence and the bounce of the ball kept the South Africans from scoring. With only a minute or so to go Retief got his try under the crossbar after an interception by Van Vollenhoven and strong running from Ackermann. Dryburgh converted to make the final score 22–8. The South Africans scored a record 16 tries in the series while the Lions notched 10. The total of 26 is the highest number of tries scored in a series involving the Springboks.

Stephen Fry attempts to charge down Jeeps' kick to touch in the third test at Pretoria

VENUE	SOUTH AFRICA	RESULT	SOUTH AFRICA				BRITISH ISLES			
			T	C	P	D	T	C	P	D
JOHANNESBURG	LOST	22–23	4	2	2	0	5	4	0	0
CAPE TOWN	WON	25–9	7	2	0	0	2	0	1	0
PRETORIA	LOST	6–9	0	0	2	0	1	0	1	1
PORT ELIZABETH	WON	22–8	5	2	0	1	2	1	0	0
		75–49	16	6	4	1	10	5	2	1
SERIES: SOUTH AFRICA PLAYED 4; W3, L1, D0										

CHAPTER 18

1956

SOUTH AFRICA TOUR AUSTRALIA AND NEW ZEALAND

▲▲▲

Springbok wing Tom van Vollenhoven catching his opposite number, Barry Roberts, in possession and effectively blocking his progress in the second test between South Africa and Australia. Van Vollenhoven was responsible for three surprise points for the Springboks when he put over a drop kick in the closing minutes of the game.

If 1949 was known to disgruntled New Zealanders as the year of Geffin's boot then 1956 is remembered by many South Africans for the merciless efficiency with which Kevin Skinner used his fists.

Geffin's kicking and Skinner's punching have become part of rugby folklore and have obscured the many other factors that influenced the outcome of the two series.

New Zealand's pride was badly bruised by their four test defeats in South Africa in 1949 and their rugby administrators spent the next few years calling for the demolition of the Springboks to wipe out the disgrace. It was to be nearly seven years before they got the opportunity and by that time the All Blacks were more than ready to take revenge for what Geffin, Muller and, as many of them firmly believed, the referees had done to Fred Allen and his 'forty-niners'.

All players with the remotest chance of wearing the black jersey were given special training schedules and diet charts and coaches went to great lengths to create a mental attitude which could best be described as one of relentless determination. The general public was as worked up about the tour as the players were and there was certainly too much tension in the air for the atmosphere to be healthy.

The Springboks' problems began when Salty du Rand, in a rash moment, punched Jan Pickard during the week of trial matches in Cape Town. Du Rand's indiscretion eliminated him as the tour captain and scrambled the cards for the national selectors. Basie Viviers, an affable veteran with admirable qualities but at that stage of his career no longer a player of international standard, was given the captaincy in what appeared to have been a compromise move.

Van der Schyff, whose powerful touch-kicking would have been so valuable on the tour, was sacrificed to make place for Viviers and, with the wisdom of hindsight, several other selection blunders were committed.

Some critics afterwards thought that too many players in the team were 'too soft' but, while it was true that there were a few who were rather frail, no one in his right mind could describe Springboks like Du Rand, Bekker, Koch, Walker, Retief, Lochner, Claassen, Van der Merwe or Pickard as 'softies'. It just so happened that the 1956 Springboks ran into a bunch of All Blacks who were prepared to be killed rather than to be beaten.

A rash of injuries had a lot to do with the Springboks' failures. For the first time a South African team had travelled by air and many thought that this was the reason for an epidemic of hamstring problems which bothered key players throughout the tour and caused two replacements, wing Theunis Briers and flanker James Starke, to be called for. The team also had its problems with refereeing decisions and the outspoken Craven got into hot water for commenting on the issue. It was the sort of thing all touring teams have to contend with, however, and, in retrospect, it is probably fair to say that the 1956 Springboks lost the series because they were playing inspired opponents in their own backyard.

SOUTH AFRICA vs AUSTRALIA

The traditional visit to Australia was unhappy, although the Springboks were undefeated and won both tests. Bertus van der Merwe, who was to be one of the stars of the tour, heard the news that his son had died back in the Boland and not long afterwards Ian Kirkpatrick was told of the death of his father. Then Basie van Wyk broke his leg at a practice, an accident which ended the career of this mar-vellous player, and a long line-up of other Springboks suffered injuries of varying degrees of seriousness. The only real highlight of the Australian part of the tour was Roy Dryburgh's feat of scoring six tries against Queensland.

The Springboks were hailed in Australia as the 'Mighty Springboks', the world champions. They themselves gave the pledge that they would play running rugby. They failed to live up to their promise or their billing, disappointing their hosts who had hoped that Springbok sparkle would help to promote the game in Australia, which suffered by comparison with the high profile of rugby league.

The first match started well enough when they beat Australian Capital Territory 41–6, seven tries to one.

They took New South Wales seriously, for they had beaten the 1937 Springboks. The state side, whose major reason for coming together in those days before the rise of Queensland and the introduction of various provincial competitions around the world, was to face touring teams, and they had been practising for the match. The Springboks lost Ian Kirkpatrick (and there were no replacements in those days) early on and led only 8–6 at half-time, but won 29–9 eventually in a great display, thanks largely to the brilliance of Tom van Vollenhoven.

Things looked good for the Springboks but then they stumbeld to a 15–8 victory over New South Wales Country.

The Springboks, suffering more injuries, won a drab test 9–0. It was not a con-vincing result. Queensland were annihilated, and then came the test, with the expectation that this time the Springboks would run. They did not. The test turned out to be one of the drabbest of drab tests. Basie Viviers played flyhalf and kicked and kicked. Again the Springboks won 9–0. The only notable occurrence in the match was Tom van Vollenhoven's dropped goal.

When the Springboks returned to Queensland in 1965, they were told that they had a lot to put right as after the 1956 visit back play had died in Queensland and the state decided that the Springbok's kicking game was the way successful rugby had to go. That was it in Australia, and on the Springboks went to New Zealand, where vengeance was waiting for them.

Ian Kirkpatrick is led from the field with a broken shoulder sustained in the match against New South Wales.

Alan Cameron, the Australian captain (wearing the noseguard), struggles for possession in the first test.

VENUE	SOUTH AFRICA	RESULT	SOUTH AFRICA				AUSTRALIA			
			T	C	P	D	T	C	P	D
SYDNEY	WON	9–0	2	0	1	0	0	0	0	0
BRISBANE	WON	9–0	2	0	0	1	0	0	0	0
		18–0	4	0	1	1	0	0	0	0
SERIES: SOUTH AFRICA PLAYED 2; W2, L0, D0										

SOUTH AFRICA vs NEW ZEALAND

On their arrival in New Zealand the Springboks were stunned by the fanatical interest in the game and even more startled when Waikato clobbered them in a brawling match on a rain-soaked field. It was in this game that they made the acquaintance of massive Donald Barrie Clarke, whose boot notched eight of his side's 14 points and which even defied the strong wind which blew throughout the match. They were to see a lot more of Clarke, who as a fullback and place-kicker played such a dominating role in world rugby for the next eight years.

▲▲▲

The Springboks won all their other fixtures up to the first test in Dunedin when Ron Jarden, one of the best wings in rugby history, virtually beat South Africa on his own in an injury-plagued match. Jan du Preez and Dawie Ackermann failed to see out the game for the Springboks while New Zealand lost prop Mark Irwin. Clive Ulyate, at flyhalf for South Africa, kicked away almost every ball he received from his over-worked and depleted pack, and Jeremy Nel, the Matie centre whom the All Blacks eyed uneasily throughout the tour, never had an opportunity to test the defence.

Dryburgh, playing at fullback as both Viviers and Buchler were injured, scored a penalty for the Springboks and centre Bennett (Peewee) Howe a try, after brilliant work by Popeye Strydom and the veteran Paul Johnstone. The All Blacks' points came from a try by Tiny White, a gaunt but great forward, which Jarden converted and it was the wing who also swooped onto a pass between Ackermann and Johnstone and outstripped the cover defence with majestic grace to score under the posts and give himself an easy conversion.

▲▲▲

Conforming to an ancient Maori custom, Dr Craven picks up a 'challenge stick'. This signified that he and his party had come in friendship and peace.

In between the first and second tests the Springboks also lost to Canterbury and their prospects suddenly looked very bleak indeed. Nevertheless, they won the second test at Wellington in spite of going into the battle with Viviers nursing an injury and with the arctic conditions all in favour of the home side.

The Springbok forwards, with Pickard giving solidarity and weight at number-eight and leaving Lochner free to rattle the opposing backs with his crushing tackles, played magnificently. Koch, Van der Merwe, Du Toit and Bekker dominated the scrums, Claassen earned praise as the finest lock-forward ever to visit New Zealand and Du Rand, Pickard and Retief kept it tight and hard. It was once again a bruising affair with Du Rand

Tommy Gentles, the smallest Springbok ever, gets good ball and protection from his forwards.

and Bekker looking like the victims of a road accident by the time the final whistle blew. In fact, Bekker was so badly concussed that he had to spend 24 hours in hospital under observation. In the dressingroom after the match, he had no idea what he was doing and frequently had to be restrained as he lashed out blindly at well-wishers. Not only the forwards played it hard; Johnstone, the South African wing, and his counterpart, Morrie Dixon, had several sharp arguments.

The Springboks' points came from tries by Retief (converted with a miraculous kick by Viviers) and Du Rand, while Ross Brown gave the All Blacks an unconverted try. The South African victory rocked New Zealand rugby; the thought that the 1949 disasters might go unavenged after all, horrified them. They decided that the Springbok frontrankers, Bekker and Koch, would have to be tamed if the All Blacks were to win the series. The New Zealanders were convinced that Bekker and Koch, by using what they called 'bullocking tactics, heaving, hacking and wrestling' were splitting the All Blacks' frontrow. They pointed to the fact that Mark Irwin had received severe chest injuries in the first test and that Frank McAtamney was lucky to come out of the second test relatively unscathed.

More pertinent was probably the knowledge that Bekker and Koch were giving the Springboks a definite advantage with their strength and know-how and the New Zealand selectors were determined that something be done about this.

▲▲▲

Salty du Rand, the great Springbok forward whose moment of indiscretion cost him the captaincy in 1956.

For the third test, the New Zealand selectors decided to recall Kevin Skinner, a 28-year-old veteran from the 1949 side, who had prematurely retired. Skinner was also once the amateur heavyweight boxing champion of New Zealand and this gave an extra dimension to subsequent events in the controversial test held in Christchurch. South Africans are adamant to this day that Skinner came into the

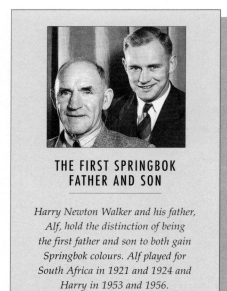

THE FIRST SPRINGBOK FATHER AND SON

Harry Newton Walker and his father, Alf, hold the distinction of being the first father and son to both gain Springbok colours. Alf played for South Africa in 1921 and 1924 and Harry in 1953 and 1956.

Bertus van der Merwe is under pressure from the All Blacks. In the background, Salty du Rand is visibly concerned.

New Zealand frontrow basically to punch Koch and Bekker into submission. As evidence they point to the fact that after Koch had been tamed, Skinner deliberately switched positions with Clarke to 'take care of Bekker'. There is no doubt that both Springbok frontrankers were hit, and hit often, but, in all fairness, the punching was not confined between Skinner, Koch and Bekker. Boots and fists flew indiscriminately in the first half and the referee, Bill Fright, a former policeman, could do little more than issue warnings and penalties.

The game was appallingly savage and within the first eight minutes, Don Clarke, playing in his first test, had scored six points from penalties, the first one given against Koch, who had been hit in the first lineout for aiming at Skinner. After 15 minutes the All Blacks led 11–0, when Dixon scored a try, with Clarke, who was successfully concealing a knee injury, converting. There was a lot of arguing about this kick afterwards as the Springboks were quite convinced that the ball had not gone over; a view supported by, among others, the well-known New Zealand sportswriter Terry McLean.

In the second half there was so much brawling that the referee spoke to Duff and Viviers and ordered them to control their men. Things then settled down to a grim but fairly legitimate battle of attrition and for a few glorious moments it looked as if the Springboks would pull it off after all.

Van Vollenhoven picked up a fly-kick from Jarden and darted through, switching direction as suddenly as only he could, to throw off the cover defence. A well-timed pass to Lochner left the All Blacks stranded and Viviers converted with a nicely-judged kick practically from touch. Only a few minutes later, Gentles broke brilliantly, passed to Ackermann, then on to Bekker and finally to Du Rand before the ball travelled to Rosenberg. The centre, hampered so often on the tour by injury, cut through to score after a spectacular dive for the line. Viviers again converted to bring the Springboks to within one point of their opponents' total.

It was then that Don Clarke showed that he was more than just a goalkicking robot. His touch-kicks swallowed large tracts of land from the Springboks and wore down the South African forwards. In the final few minutes the All Blacks were on top and Jarden, after an amazing exhibition of agility, and then Tiny White, scored unconverted tries to give New Zealand a convincing 17–10 victory.

The Springboks were very upset afterwards. Koch and Bekker looked as if they had been in the boxing ring and there were threats that Skinner could expect retribution in the fourth test. Later, Bekker's delightful sense of humour returned and in his book *The Battle for the Rugby Crown*, McLean recounts how the bull-necked Northern Transvaaler innocently asked someone whether Skinner intended going to the Olympic Games.

'No, he has long ago retired from boxing,' came the answer. 'Pity,' replied Bekker drily. 'He'd win his division.'

It also became a team joke among the Springboks that boxing classes would be arranged as part of the practices with Brian Pfaff, who was a schoolboy champion at Hilton College, doing the coaching.

▲▲▲

The final test at Eden Park, Auckland, was as bitterly fought as the epic third but, except when New Zealand's Tiny White was severely injured by what some considered a deliberate kick in the back, was comparatively free of the type of viciousness which marred the Lancaster Park battle. Both packs ploughed after

the ball with a furious intensity and Peter Jones played with such fierce dedication that he stood out even in such company. Clarke, once more, was the deciding factor with two long-range penalties and a conversion of a try by Jones, a remarkable individual effort in which he beat Viviers and then outpaced Nel and Retief.

The final minutes of the match were packed with tension and, at one stage, there was a brief but dangerous flare-up when White was injured and had to be helped off the field. Fright's stern warning to both teams prevented further trouble.

It was too late to really matter, but the Springboks did get some consolation by scoring the last try of the 1956 series. Briers ran strongly and Starke nearly got to the ball after the Paarl wing had cleverly chipped ahead. The All Black centre, Gray, snapped up the loose ball, but he was tackled hard and Howe picked up and flipped infield to Dryburgh, on the right wing, who scored. Viviers converted to make the final score 11–5.

The All Blacks had avenged the defeats of 1949 and now it was the turn of the Springboks to lick their wounds and to scheme for the next encounter.

Victory is fun. The Springboks celebrate in their changeroom after beating the All Blacks in the second test. From left: Clive Ulyate, Basie Viviers, Daan Retief, Bertus van der Merwe and Butch Lochner.

VENUE	SOUTH AFRICA	RESULT	SOUTH AFRICA				NEW ZEALAND			
			T	C	P	D	T	C	P	D
DUNEDIN	LOST	6–10	1	0	1	0	2	2	0	0
WELLINGTON	WON	8–3	2	1	0	0	1	0	0	0
CHRISTCHURCH	LOST	10–17	2	2	0	0	3	1	2	0
AUCKLAND	LOST	5–11	1	1	0	0	1	1	2	0
		29–41	6	4	1	0	7	4	4	0
SERIES: SOUTH AFRICA PLAYED 4; W1, L3, D0										

CHAPTER 19

1958

FRANCE TOUR SOUTH AFRICA

▲▲▲

I n 1952 Hennie Muller, leading what some consider the best Springbok combination in history, slammed France into abject defeat on their own ground,
but two years later the Tricolors, carrying the symbol of the rooster on their blue
jerseys, had beaten the All Blacks and were more than holding their own against
the four Home Countries – England, Scotland, Wales and Ireland.

In 1958, a French team visited South Africa for the first time and Denis Lalanne
of *L'Equipe* referred to it in his magnificently written book *Le Grand Combat du
Quinze de France* as the 'AD1 for French rugby', the true year of birth for the game
as far as he and his compatriots were concerned.

Michel Celaya was the tour captain but he was injured early on and it was
mainly Lucien Mias who led the team to five wins, two draws and three defeats.
Much more important to them was the fact that they drew one of the test
matches and won the other, thereby becoming the first visiting side to beat the
Springboks in a series in South Africa in over 60 years.

The language barrier presented some problems but, generally speaking, the
South African public was fascinated by the darting unorthodoxy of the visitors in
blue. The pugnacity and toughness of forwards shook the South Africans, and
backs like Pierre Danos, Roger Martine, Pierre Lacaze, Jean Dupuy and Henri
Rancoule delighted the spectators with the most impudent moves.

Rugby writers who had never seen French rugby players before were quite
stunned at the basic differences between them and the Springboks. Mias always
seemed to be arguing endlessly and loudly with his players. He then wandered
around the corridors of the Langham Hotel until the early hours and yet he
turned in a superlative performance against the Springboks. With Barthe,
Mommejat and Roques, he was one of the best forwards on the field, and they had
the South African pack slowed down to a trot by the time the referee, Chris
Ackermann, ended the match.

It was a team packed with courageous players, no one more so than Pierre (The
Butterfly) Lacaze who substituted for the injured Michel Vannier in both tests, and
who played at Ellis Park with several novocaine injections in his ankle. This did
not prevent him from scoring a penalty and a dropgoal.

▲▲▲

The first test, at Newlands, was frankly dull with the Springboks being barracked
by their own supporters as Kirkpatrick, at flyhalf, adopted kick-first, think-later
tactics. Pierre Danos once summed up his rugby philosophy by saying: 'There are

*Dawie Ackerman, an effective flanker
against the Lions in 1955 and the All Blacks
in 1956, tries vainly to barge past a French
defender. In the background is Alan Skene.*

two kinds of players; those who play pianos and those who shift them'. His performances on the tour left no doubt to which school he belonged; France's only points at Newlands came from a perfectly executed dropgoal by the scrumhalf. Danos often said that he never kicked for goal unless he was sure of success and he did not fail on the three occasions he attempted drop-kicks on the tour. The Springboks' only points came from a try by Lochner, one of the few South African players of distinction that season, and the Newlands match ended in a three-all draw.

▲▲▲

The second test, at Ellis Park, was more exciting. The Frenchmen had suffered a crushing defeat against a combined Western Province–Boland–South Western Districts side at Wellington shortly before the international encounter, and the South Africans had been lulled into

Jeremy Nel, an outstanding centre in New Zealand in 1956, attempts a cross-kick in the first test against France in 1958. In the background is Ian Kirkpatrick.

a false sense of security. As was the case in the first test, they again erred by over-estimating their forwards. The Springbok pack failed to master the French forwards and they also lost the battle of tactics. A scintillating break by Nel, the centre who played so well on the 1956 tour of New Zealand but who had been shifted to the flyhalf position, led to the only South African score, a try by wing Lofty Fourie and converted by fullback Mickey Gerber. A penalty and a dropgoal by Lacaze and a drop from Roger Martine made the game safe for the Tricolors.

The French dressingroom afterwards was a sight to see. Several of the players were weeping with joy and Martine totally overcome by emotion. When Danie Craven and Louis Babrow, who had often helped the visitors with advice on the tour, walked in to congratulate them, the team gave them a touching ovation. Craven and Babrow made some staunch friends for South African sport with their gesture; friendships which were to bear fruit in the difficult years to follow when France so often stepped into the breach whenever tours from other countries failed to come off because of political pressure.

VENUE	SOUTH AFRICA	RESULT	SOUTH AFRICA				FRANCE			
			T	C	P	D	T	C	P	D
CAPE TOWN	DRAW	3–3	1	0	0	0	0	0	0	1
JOHANNESBURG	LOST	5–9	1	1	0	0	0	0	1	2
		8–12	2	1	0	0	0	0	1	3
SERIES: SOUTH AFRICA PLAYED 2; W0, L1, D1										

CHAPTER 20

1960/61

THE EFFICIENT SPRINGBOKS

▲▲▲

NEW ZEALAND vs SOUTH AFRICA

The 1960 tour was very nearly called off as there were strong protests against the exclusion of Maori players. It was to be the last tour by New Zealand to South Africa for ten years, by which time the embarrassing situation had changed, with Maoris as welcome as anyone else.

Wilson Whineray commanded an extremely strong combination which in Don Clarke, Ian Nev MacEwan, Colin Meads, Kelvin Tremain and Peter Jones had players who simply must be rated among the best from any country, in any era.

Whineray, himself, was a born leader; firm but tactful. He had a deceptively soft appearance for an international prop-forward. His tussles with Piet (Spiere) du Toit, the immensely powerful Springbok frontranker whose pushing method the All Blacks regarded as illegal, proved, however, that the New Zealander was perfectly capable of looking after himself.

The star of the team, the player everyone in South Africa wanted to see in action, was Donald Barrie Clarke, the fullback who had made his international

The 1960 touring Springboks gather in Cape Town. Back row: Frik du Preez, Hugo van Zyl, Attie Baard, Piet van Zyl, Hennie van Zyl, Stompie van der Merwe, Dave Stewart, Martin Pelser, Michel Antelme. Third row: Ronnie Hill, Abe Malan, John Gainsford, Jannie Engelbrecht, Hannes Botha, Mof Myburgh, Doug Hopwood, Lionel Wilson, Doug Holton, Fanie Kuhn. Second row: Johan Claassen, Ian Kirkpatrick, Avril Malan, Ferdie Bergh (manager), Dick Lockyear, Boy Louw (coach), Piet du Toit. Front row: Charlie Nimb, Piet Uys, Mannetjies Roux, Bennie van Niekerk, Keith Oxlee, Giepie Wentzel.

debut against the Springboks four years earlier, and had since developed into the deadliest placekicker of his time. Meads and Tremain were then poised on the edge of greatness but already formidable men.

A nagging groin injury prevented Peter Jones, whom the 1956 Springboks had rated so highly, from being the force he should have been during this tour. Altogether, he could only play in 11 of the tour matches. Jones, whose blunt description of the fourth test against the Springboks in 1956 expressed over a public broadcasting system will remain a classic in the annals of pungent comment, was Clarke's unofficial bodyguard.

▲▲▲

The South Africans were well prepared for the tour, following a successful visit by the Junior Springboks to the Argentine and an early-season test against Scotland which served as an opportunity to blood several players who were to wear the green-and-gold Springbok jersey. The test, a so-so affair in Port Elizabeth, was won 18–10 with Des van Jaarsveldt becoming the first Rhodesian ever to skipper the Springboks.

The All Blacks, as usual, swept through the various provincial teams. Free State beat them 9–8, however, and Combined Service won 8–3 after brilliant performances by then relatively unknown players like Piet Uys, Mof Myburgh, Frik du Preez and Andrew Janson.

In several of the matches rough play was a feature and the whole thing reached boiling point in the match against Eastern Province, a game which came to be known as the 'Battle of Boet Erasmus'. The Eastern Province Rugby Union, renowned as one of the most hospitable in South Africa, had gone out of their way to be nice to the tourists, but on the field it was a different story. The props, Hambley Parker and Doug Holton, were both extraordinarily strong and their opposite numbers, Eric Anderson and Ian Clarke, objected to their methods.

Soon there was general fighting among the forwards and old-timers afterwards described it as one of the dirtiest matches to have been played in South Africa with players on both sides suffering unnecessary injuries.

Looking back on the tour, the All Blacks probably produced their best form outside the tests when they battered Transvaal into a 19–3 defeat. The Transvaal team were strong, with 12 members of the side either Springboks or Junior Springboks and a thirteenth, centre Eddie Barlow, destined for cricket fame. Transvaal were outclassed by the All Blacks, however, with Conway, MacEwan, Meads, Tremain, Horsley and the halfback pair of Briscoe and Nesbit in superb form.

An aerial view of Ellis Park during the first test between South Africa and New Zealand. South Africa won the match 13–0.

▲▲▲

Martin Pelser is too late to prevent Kevin Briscoe from getting his pass away. These two players had a private vendetta during the 1960 tour.

Roy Dryburgh was selected to lead the Springboks in the first test and he, Koch and Claassen were the most experienced players in a side which included six newcomers and six who had limited test experience.

The first test, before more than 75 000 spectators at Ellis Park, established the reputations of several Springboks. Among them were Hennie van Zyl, a wing who, at his peak, was almost impossible to stop; Michel Antelme, on the other wing; and two outstanding combinations – Kirkpatrick and Gainsford at centre, and Oxlee and Lockyear at halfback. Van Zyl and Pelser proved to be flankers of the highest class and Avril Malan, making his test debut at the age of 23, looked and acted the part of a future Springbok captain.

Oxlee, Gainsford and Malan played dominating roles in world rugby for the next few years but, although his career was relatively short, the man the All Blacks would have liked most to have had in a black jersey with a silver fern on his breast, was Pelser. This 26-year-old Transvaal flanker, who had lost an eye in a boyhood accident, and was withdrawn to the point of shyness, has probably never had an equal for sheer tenacity, toughness and aggression.

Pelser's feud with Briscoe was one of the interesting sidelights of the tour. It was more or less a draw until the fourth test when Pelser laid him out with a left-hook so perfectly timed that even the New Zealanders expressed admiration for the punch. Van Zyl packed on the other side of the scrum and with his unobtrusive efficiency he formed a tremendous partnership with the more dynamic Pelser. When they were joined by the equally skilled and talented Doug Hopwood at eighthman, South Africa again had a loose-forward trio comparable to the legendary Van Wyk-Fry-Muller combination.

The Springboks, as is invariably the case when the All Blacks are on a tour of South Africa, went into the first test as underdogs but long before half-time it was obvious that they would win. A brilliant try by Hennie van Zyl, very early in the match, seemed to shatter their self-assurance and Whineray's men could not get back into the game. The try was the result of a much-practiced version of the old ruse whereby the blindside wing is brought in to take the ball from the scrumhalf to breach the first line of defence. The Springboks used it from a scrum given to them just inside New Zealand territory. Malan duly hooked and Antelme, who was hanging slightly behind Oxlee, rocketed in, between the flyhalf and Gainsford, to take the pass at full speed. By the time Antelme had linked up with Kirkpatrick at outside centre, only Clarke was left to beat. Kirkpatrick drew Clarke in masterly fashion and then passed to Hennie van Zyl, who galloped over for a try which Dryburgh converted. Whineray then made one of the few tactical errors of his career. Instead of trying to regain the initiative he went on the defensive and delegated Conway to help the backs.

The Springbok pack, with virtually only seven forwards in opposition, took complete command and the All Blacks should really have lost by a bigger margin than 13–0. In the second half they were fooled again by Antelme cutting into the line and swift passing gave Hennie van Zyl a slight start on his opposite number Russell Watt. The left-wing shook off Watt's challenge and with an amazing

Keith Oxlee is surrounded by admirers keen to get the Springbok's autograph.

display of determination, fought his way through Clarke, Conway and Briscoe to score his second try. Lockyear converted with the first of the several vital kicks he was to put over in the series and, not long afterwards, he added three more points with an equally difficult penalty kick.

▲▲▲

Clarke towered over everybody else in the second test at Newlands; not only did he score eight of his team's winning total of 11 points but it was his fantastic touchkicking that enabled the New Zealand forwards to turn the table on the Springboks. He scored a penalty, a perfectly executed left-footed dropgoal, and converted a try by Meads, but it was his touchkicking that was unforgettable. South Africa's only points came from Oxlee, who scored a typically clever try. When Clarke converted Meads' try he reached his hundredth point on the tour and he eventually ended up with a total of 175, the most by any player on a tour of South Africa. The conversion also brought the total of points scored against South Africa to 500.

▲▲▲

The Springbok selectors made drastic changes for the third test. Dryburgh, who had been playing on borrowed time after a two-year battle with injuries, lost his place to Lionel Wilson, of Western Province, and the captaincy went to Avril Malan who, at the age of 23, became the youngest man ever to lead South Africa.

Koch finally faded from the scene after 11 seasons of international rugby. Fanie Kuhn took his place and filled it admirably for several years while Abie Malan went back to the middle of the frontrow after the magnificent veteran, Bertus van der Merwe, had been given a last chance in the Newlands test. Lofty Nel, tall, tough and always hard-working, made way for Doug Hopwood.

The choice of Wilson at fullback was severely criticized. He was virtually unknown and had detractors even in his own province. But his unflinching courage under any kind of pressure soon made him one of the most widely respected of all Springboks and he went on to play in 27 tests for South Africa, more than any other fullback to wear the South African colours.

The third test was an amazing affair. There were six minutes to go, South Africa was leading 11–3, and the huge Bloemfontein crowd was getting ready to celebrate. Then the All Blacks staged a fantastic comeback.

Until that moment all the New Zealanders had to show for themselves were three points from a penalty by Clarke. The Springbok score came from a try by Oxlee, and a conversion and

South Africa's longest serving centre partners – Springboks John Gainsford and Ian Kirkpatrick.

Keith Oxlee scores against the All Blacks at Newlands and referee Mike Slabbert is pleased to award the try.

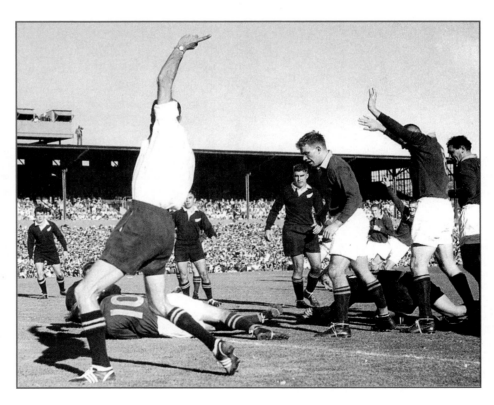

RICHARD JAMES CONWAY

Richard James Conway is not remembered in South Africa as one of the great All Blacks; even the few among us who recall his name will never mention it with the awe and admiration reserved for a Kevin Skinner, a Colin Meads, a Bob Scott, a Don Clarke or a Bryan Williams. And yet, what 'Red' Conway did to ensure his place in Wilson Whineray's touring team to South Africa in 1960, illustrates the unbelievable intensity of the rugby rivalry between the Springboks and the All Blacks. During the New Zealand trials one of Conway's fingers turned septic after an injury and his doctor told him that it would not heal in time for him to make the tour. A specialist suggested, probably in jest, that an amputation would mean quicker mending. Without hesitation Conway had the finger amputated and he played in three of the four tests of the series.

two penalty goals by Lockyear. Then the Springboks were penalized not far from the New Zealand quarter of the field. Whineray, noticing that the Springboks were slow in falling back, quickly took a tap kick and the referee duly gave them an extra ten yards. It was still an enormous distance from the Springbok posts, but Clarke was told to have a go. The All Blacks fullback admitted afterwards that for once he had doubts about his ability as he lined up the ball.

'That feeling of uncertainty stayed with me even after my boot hit the ball,' he said. 'The impact was not true and my doubts mounted in the split-second it took for the ball to begin its flight. Yet something happened, something beyond my doing, for when it was about 20 yards on its flight, the ball seemed to change direction, seemingly drawn to the goalposts so far away. On and on it flew until, almost unbelievably, the flags went up.'

The Springboks were still leading by five points but in the final minute Lineen snapped up a bad pass from Briscoe and gave to Laidlaw who kicked ahead for McMullen to chase. The ball bounced high but perfectly for the All Blacks wing who took it in full stride and crashed over the corner. The result then depended on the conversion and Clarke calmly placed it from an acute angle with what coach Jack Sullivan afterwards described as the greatest kick of his career.

By snatching a dramatic draw when all had seemed lost, the All Blacks managed to level the series.

▲▲▲

The fourth test in Port Elizabeth became the vital crunch. Jan Pieter Engelbrecht, a tall Matie wing who could run with such consummate grace and whose all-round ability was to earn him 33 test caps, eight test tries and 44 tries altogether in the green-and-gold, was selected to replace Antelme for the test. Engelbrecht, who had made his international debut against Scotland earlier in the season, developed tonsillitis however, and Antelme was brought back.

The only other change was an enforced one. Johan Claassen after playing in 16 successive tests, was injured and Northern Transvaal's Hendrik Stefanus van der Merwe, known to all and sundry as 'Stompie', had the unenviable task of substituting for one of the giants of South African rugby. Van der Merwe gave a superb performance and Claassen's absence was not really felt.

It was one of those tense, merciless tests, played in a nasty wind and it was won for the Springboks by their mighty forwards and the superb kicking of Lockyear. Oxlee saved a certain try within minutes of the beginning when he just managed to ankle-tap McMullen who was flying towards the goalline for what appeared to be a certain try. The All Blacks wing was knocked off balance and he fell short before reaching out and planting the ball behind the line. Referee Ralph Burmeister was on the spot and instead of giving the All Blacks a try, he awarded a penalty against them. There was to be a brief storm of controversy over this but Whineray's men were, generally speaking, not the squealing kind and the incident was not used as an excuse for defeat.

The Springbok forwards were invincible that afternoon at Boet Erasmus Stadium, as they drove forward with tremendous will and Pelser and Van Zyl rattled the All Blacks halfbacks into mistakes. Clarke gave them an early lead with a penalty but Lockyear levelled the score with a penalty of his own.

Early in the second half the Springboks clinched the series. There was a scrum near the All Blacks' posts and a hurried few words between Lockyear and Pelser before the South African scrumhalf let the ball in. The Springboks heeled, half wheeled, Lockyear ran wide and it was Pelser who picked up and threw everything he had into making those two precious strides to the tryline. He was tackled, sure enough, but it was not enough to hold his hurtling body and he scored his try, next to the upright. Lockyear converted and this time the Springboks were not going to fritter away the lead. There were a few narrow escapes as Clarke came close with huge kicks into the wind but when the final whistle ended the match and the series, the Springboks had won 8–3.

The 1960 All Blacks were a mighty side. South Africa was fortunate that she had the Springboks to match, and beat them.

The flying Springboks. Wings Hennie van Zyl and Mike Antelme prepare to meet the All Blacks.

Venue	South Africa	Result	South Africa				New Zealand			
			T	C	P	D	T	C	P	D
Johannesburg	WON	13–0	2	2	1	0	0	0	0	0
Cape Town	LOST	3–11	1	0	0	0	1	1	1	1
Bloemfontein	DRAW	11–11	1	1	2	0	1	1	2	0
Port Elizabeth	WON	8–3	1	1	1	0	0	0	1	0
		35–25	5	4	4	0	2	2	4	1
SERIES: SOUTH AFRICA PLAYED 4; W2, L1, D1										

Although the 1960/61 touring team to Britain and France had several members who deserve to be rated with the best Springboks of all time, the side as a whole was efficient more often than brilliant. Generally speaking, they were not a popular team. The British public and press criticized them frequently for playing stodgy, unattractive rugby and even for not being particularly friendly off the field.

The side had the misfortune of striking one of the worst British winters in living memory and often conditions simply did not allow sweeping threequarter attacks, especially since so many of the opponents encountered, relied heavily on spoiling tactics. With an abundance of forward talent available, the tour management consisting of Avril Malan, Dick Lockyear, Ferdie Bergh and Boy Louw, consequently preferred building their pattern around the pack and the threequarters were, in the conventional sense, forced to play second fiddle.

Doug Hopwood played the best rugby of his great career on the tour and Hugo van Zyl and Martin Pelser were nearly up to his standard. Fanie Kuhn, Piet (Spiere) du Toit, Ronnie Hill, Abie Malan, Mof Myburgh, Frik du Preez, Avril Malan, Johan Claassen, Stompie van der Merwe, to name only a few, were brilliant players either at the height of their powers, or beginning to approach it. Among the backs,

Avril Malan's Springboks have their photograph taken on board ship before their departure for the United Kingdom, Ireland and France.

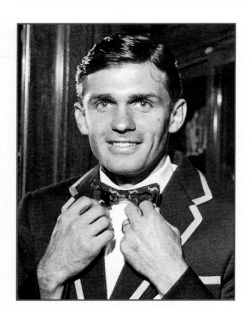

Posh Bok! Keith Oxlee appears to be well pleased with life.

scrumhalf Dick Lockyear was past his best and his placekicking was rather disappointing, but he had an outstanding deputy in Piet Uys. Keith Oxlee, Dave Stewart, Ian Kirkpatrick, John Gainsford, Mannetjies Roux, Jannie Engelbrecht, Michel Antelme, Hennie van Zyl and Lionel Wilson were invariably steady and often brilliant. Bennie van Niekerk, Giepie Wentzel and Charlie Nimb were too injury-ridden to hit their best form and with forward Doug Holton unable to complete the tour, Bobby Johns and Ben-Piet van Zyl were sent over as replacements.

No one can deny that their playing pattern was successful. Malan and his men stayed undefeated until the last match of the tour of Britain. Even then, had they been at full strength, it is virtually certain that they would have beaten an out-of-character Barbarians team who, for the occasion it seemed, approached the game as if it was a test match. The Springboks' record of one defeat and two draws in 34 matches over nearly four months in Britain and France, is ample testimony of their ability.

SOUTH AFRICA vs WALES

Cardiff was indescribably wet and bitterly cold on the morning of 3 December 1960. The field looked like a soaked green blanket with the chocolate-coloured water of the River Taff lapping at the edges. One wondered whether it would be necessary for the South Africans to leave the Seabank Hotel in Porthcawl about 30 miles away. A test match could surely not be played under such conditions?

But the Welsh laughed at the gloomy predictions and some 53 000 people, with only a little more than one-fifth of them under cover, packed around the ground.

The two teams, the Springboks still wearing their green tracksuits for last-minute protection against the weather, walked onto the field for the anthems. The band members did their honest best with *Die Stem* and *God Save the Queen* but after the first few strains one could hardly hear them as the huge crowd took over the anthem and affirmed their claim to a special identity.

The next eighty minutes were to prove the greatness of Avril Malan's 1960/61 Springbok team because more than just speed, strength and skill were needed to win. The deciding factor was an uncompromising refusal to be beaten.

By the time the game was under way for five minutes, the ground could hardly be seen. There was water everywhere, with two brave packs of mud-covered forwards straining and heaving to gain a few inches at a time, the steam rising from their bodies.

Wales had won the toss and Terry Davies had decided to give the Springboks the advantage of playing with the wind in the first half. There was controversy over this in Welsh rugby circles afterwards but Avril Malan would almost certainly have made the same decision; there was no doubt that the weather was likely to get worse rather than better. The Springboks adopted the obvious tactics and Wales were often driven into desperate situations with the wind carrying any kind of kick deep into their territory and, too often, into the dead-ball area.

The ball quickly became shapeless and slippery and handling was impossible. Placekicking was even more difficult and the Springboks missed several opportunities as Jock Taylor, the referee, spotted irregularities committed by the Welshmen as they kept the South Africans at bay. Hopwood, Engelbrecht, Roux and Kirkpatrick, in turn, came close to scoring after somehow managing to control the cake of black soap masquerading as a ball. For a long time it did not look as if the Springboks would be able to establish a lead to draw on when it would be their turn to play into the wind.

But, in the twenty-first minute, the Welsh scrumhalf O'Connor infringed at a scrum practically in front of his posts and Malan handed the ball to Oxlee. The flyhalf, who was so outstanding against the All Blacks a few months earlier, had not yet gained the international renown as a placekicker and the few Springbok supporters hardly dared to hope that the kick would succeed. Oxlee slammed his right boot into the soggy ball and lifted it high enough for the wind to send it tumbling over the crossbar for the first successful kick of his test career – it was probably the least graceful, but certainly one of the most valuable.

Only three points up at half-time and with Claassen handicapped by an ankle injury, the Springboks faced the grim prospect of playing against the elements as well as the inspired Welshmen in the second half.

The first fifteen minutes after the resumption Wales, past-masters of the art of rugby in the rain, laid siege to the Springbok line. Making expert use of the wind with kicks of every description, they had the South Africans reeling and it seemed only a matter of time before they would take

Nothing brings popularity like defeat. Avril Malan is chaired from the field by the Barbarians after they became the only side to beat the Springboks in 1961.

the lead. Then, suddenly and almost miraculously, the Springbok forwards pulled themselves together. From Kuhn, Hill and Du Toit in the frontrow, to Hopwood at eighthman, the pack seemed to realize that it was up to them to win the test.

Whenever Hill heeled, Hopwood would either pick up himself or take the ball from scrumhalf Piet Uys, playing in his first test. The seven other forwards would immediately rally around Hopwood as he bullocked ahead, making as much ground as possible. Possession was vital and yet to have used it in the normal way would have been to tempt fate. To have kicked would have been useless; the wind would simply have blown the ball towards their own tryline. The only answer was to keep the ball among the forwards or under control on the ground, where it would skid crazily over the puddles as the players slid and slithered in pursuit. All the forwards were covered in mud and the referee often had to stop play so that players could have their eyes attended to.

The backs on both sides were drenched and bedraggled; for once they were playing in the supporting role only. It was so cold that some of them had to hammer their thighs with their fists to keep the circulation going. Roux climbed into a loose scrum just to get a little action, and whenever there was an interruption in play, some of the backs would scurry towards the forwards to use their bigger teammates as temporary protection against the cold. Wilson once found that he

Cardiff Arms Park was under water the day after the Welsh test in 1960 – the one that was nearly stopped for bad weather.

was too frozen to get his arms into position to catch the ball and he had to allow it to bump off his chest into touch. Through it all, the Welsh crowd continued to sing and to encourage their team.

Hopwood endured terrific punishment but in the process he made it possible for the Springboks to win. Time and again he took the ball from the scrum and then drove into the Welsh pack, keeping possession, gaining ground and leaving no room for error. He was the centre of the whirling mass of mud-smeared, steaming bodies and it was hardly surprising that the spinal weakness which had plagued him since he had lifted a heavy weight as a teenager, began to give him severe pain in the last few minutes and forced him into a hospital bed for several weeks after the match. At one stage Taylor, noticing that the touchlines and goallines had disappeared under water, asked Davies whether he was prepared to abandon the game. Davies, who by then must have known that his forwards were in a vice-grip they could never have shaken off, refused, and the battle ran its full course.

It was a triumph for the Springbok forwards but the 3–0 victory proved something even more important. It showed that Avril Malan's touring team had character and courage in the true tradition of Springbok rugby.

SOUTH AFRICA vs ENGLAND

The test against Wales was the highlight of the tour in spite of the fact that it was hardly spectacular and had drama rather than thrills. The match against England was the most disappointing: dull, lacking in spirit generally and played in a rather unpleasant atmosphere. Vivian Jenkins, the 1938 Lions fullback, pictur-esquely but accurately described it as 'about as exciting as a couple of hippo-potami sawing logs, and not as novel ...'

Both teams seemed committed to the same monotonous kicking tactics and neither looked prepared to risk anything. Hopwood won the match for the Springboks with a typically clever try, two minutes before half-time, when he received from Claassen after a wheeled scrum, dummied, and then broke inside to catch the England defence in a hopeless tangle. Frik du Preez, playing in his first test on the flank in the place of the injured Pelser, converted with a magnificent kick.

The jeering of a section of the crowd at Twickenham made this the least memorable match. Once, when Du Preez was taking a placekick, he was given a slow hand-clap that visibly unnerved him and the *London Times* called it 'worse than a lack of sportsmanship; it is rank bad manners'. It was a mild forerunner of the smoke bombs, slogans and worse the Springboks were to face in the future.

SOUTH AFRICA vs SCOTLAND

The game against Scotland at Murrayfield was by far the best of the series as a spectacle and also for the type of rugby played. It marked Johan Claassen's twentieth test appearance and he suitably celebrated the occasion with his first try in an international match. The Springboks' other points in a 12–5 victory came from yet another try by Hopwood, who throughout the tour had the talent scouts for the professional clubs rushing about waving cheque books, and two penalties by Du Preez, whose remarkable natural talents were already obvious.

SOUTH AFRICA vs IRELAND

Ronnie Dawson's inspired Irish team put up the most exciting battle of the series in the test at Lansdowne Road, Dublin, with the Springboks winning after a push-over try by Hugo van Zyl during injury time. The South Africans made this a

Jannie Engelbrecht takes an awkward ball from Piet Uys in the test against Scotland.

tough one for themselves, with the backs missing several scoring opportunities. Eventually, after lying level throughout the match with a try by Gainsford against a penalty by Kiernan, the Springbok pack, from a five-yard scrum, put all their weight, muscle, sinew and will-to-win into one irresistible shove that pushed the Irish forwards well over their tryline. All the Paarl flanker had to do was to fall on the ball. Lockyear managed to convert the try, with the ball glancing off the upright and over the crossbar.

SOUTH AFRICA vs FRANCE

The Springboks played France at Colombes Stadium, a few miles from Paris. In the first scrum Hugo van Zyl was kicked, Martin Pelser had his cheek split by a punch and Piet du Toit received a blow against the head. Walters immediately penalized Moncla for having kicked Van Zyl but the Springboks were incensed and for a few minutes there was bedlam on the field.

Dick Lockyear hoists a kick while Jannie Engelbrecht prepares to chase in the test against France, held at Colombes Stadium.

Avril Malan tried to stop his team from retaliating but they were in too ugly a mood to listen to a captain for whom they normally had the greatest respect. Fortunately the referee took a firm stand at this point and he told both captains that he would have no hesitation in abandoning the game should the fighting continue.

The rest of the match was a superb struggle between two extremely powerful teams and, in retrospect, a scoreless draw was about the fairest reflection of the proceedings. Claassen and Malan dominated the lineouts but in the tight scrums and in the loose the Frenchmen gave as good as they got. The French forwards, in fact, won several vital tight head heels against the powerful Springbok frontrow of Kuhn, Malan and Du Toit. Stewart, at flyhalf, was off-form and even Wilson often failed to find touch. The biggest surprise of the match was the way in which Jacques Bouquet nailed Gainsford every time he touched the ball. The big Springbok was already then being described as the best centre in the world but Bouquet was quite unconcerned about the South African's fame. Gainsford gave Bouquet credit as the most difficult opponent he had in the 33 tests of his career.

VENUE	SOUTH AFRICA	RESULT	SOUTH AFRICA								
			T	C	P	D		T	C	P	D
WALES (CARDIFF)	WON	3–0	0	0	1	0		0	0	0	0
ENGLAND (TWICKENHAM)	WON	5–0	1	1	0	0		0	0	0	0
SCOTLAND (EDINBURGH)	WON	12–5	2	0	2	0		1	1	0	0
IRELAND (DUBLIN)	WON	8–3	2	1	0	0		0	0	1	0
FRANCE (PARIS)	DRAW	0–0	0	0	0	0		0	0	0	0

CHAPTER 21

1961

BRIEF VISITS IN EMERALD AND GOLD

▲▲▲

IRELAND vs SOUTH AFRICA

Mini-skirts were still to be discovered but mini-tours were much in vogue in 1961. Ireland and Australia paid brief visits to South Africa and just for once, test rugby was played in a more or less relaxed manner.

Even the trial match the selectors organized before the one and only test against Ronnie Dawson's Irishmen at Newlands, was marked by good humour rather than the usual unavoidable tension. More than thirty of the trialists had just returned from a tour of Britain and France, and the test side obviously had to be built around them. Gainsford and Engelbrecht were injured and out of contention but there were any number of outstanding candidates for the vacancies.

The tour veterans, finding themselves suddenly in opposition to each other, had to devise new signals and one, designed by the A-team to confuse their old team-mates, led to probably the only occasion in history where a Springbok trial match was interrupted because all 16 forwards had burst out laughing.

Piet Uys, at scrumhalf, was supposed to call out the name of an animal whenever he wanted the ball thrown in deep at a lineout and a bird when it was to be a short throw-in. 'Ostrich!' Uys instructed.

Two captains – South Africa's Johan Claassen and Australia's Ken Catchpole. South Africa won both tests against the Australians in 1961.

The South African team which met Ireland in the first test at Newlands Back: CF Nimb, RA Hill, LG Wilson, CM Greenwood, PdeW Uys. Middle: BP van Zyl, DJ Hopwood, SP Kuhn. Front: GH van Zyl, JT Claassen (captain), H Muller (manager), DA Stewart, PS du Toit.

'Ostrich?' Antelme asked, looking puzzled and as vague as only he could be. 'Hey, what's that, an animal or a bird?'

With Avril Malan also out because of injury, Claassen was given the captaincy against Ireland and the only new Springbok was Colin Greenwood, a fleet-footed Western Province centre. All the other players selected were members of the team which had toured Britain and France, although it was to be a first test appearance for Charlie Nimb, Ben-Piet van Zyl and Piet van Zyl.

The Irishmen, who foolishly insisted that the international be the first match on the itinerary, were outclassed and they were fortunate that the final score was only 24–8. Dave Stewart, who had previously played flyhalf and fullback for South Africa, was smoothly effective at centre and both Greenwood and Ben-Piet van Zyl were given every opportunity. Each scored two tries and Nimb not only kicked immaculately but dovetailed enterprisingly with Stewart and Piet Uys.

Wilson injured his shoulder in the second half and Stewart had to take over from him, with Ben-Piet van Zyl moving to centre and Hopwood, who had been outstanding at number-eight, going to the wing position. The enforced reshuffle saved Ireland from being massacred as the Springboks, who had led 13–0 at half-time, could add only 11 more points – two tries by Ben-Piet van Zyl, one after a devastating break by Uys, and a penalty goal from inside his own half by Nimb, who also converted one of the tries.

All Ireland's points were scored in the second half and all by Kiernan, their full-back, with a penalty, a try and a conversion.

There were, incidentally, no less than four Van Zyls in the Springbok team, Hennie, Ben-Piet, Piet and Hugo, which must have been a record and certainly a nightmare for radio commentators.

VENUE	SOUTH AFRICA	RESULT	SOUTH AFRICA				IRELAND			
			T	C	P	D	T	C	P	D
CAPE TOWN	WON	24–8	5	3	1	0	1	1	1	0

AUSTRALIA vs SOUTH AFRICA

John Edward Thornett wore the Australian colours on 118 occasions and between waterpolo, surfing and acquiring several scientific and engineering degrees, he also squeezed in nearly 200 other matches which qualify for inclusion in the category of first-class rugby. Only once, in all those games, did the Sydney forward pray to hear the final whistle and that was in the first of the two tests between the Wallabies and the Springboks, at Ellis Park, Johannesburg, in 1961.

This is how Thornett described what happened that afternoon in his book *This World of Rugby*:

'We went into this match a little cockier than we should have been after a couple of good wins against the provincial sides and we were absolutely overwhelmed. I have never had such a feeling of helplessness on a football field as when wave after wave of Springbok players poured through our defences. It was my first test as a frontranker and I remember that we were pushed back so fast in some scrums that even when we won the ball, Ken Catchpole had to dive to escape being trampled on by our own scrum which seemed to be almost running back.

'We had expected a dour struggle against opponents who would play tight, safe football, but the landslide started ten minutes after the start when one of the South Africans threw a long Fijian-style one-handed pass to a teammate standing unmarked on the opposite side of the field. Our backs were non-plussed and the Springboks scored.

'From then on they scored try after try, with Keith Oxlee at five-eighth, the centres Mannetjies Roux and John Gainsford, and Jannie Engelbrecht and Hennie van Zyl on the wings, forming the most devastating attacking combination.

'The Springboks' forward power and the altitude of Johannesburg soon absorbed all our energy. All we could do was to try and keep down the scoring against us; but whatever we attempted seemed to end with the Springboks breaking through again. The scrums were like South African charges and near the end, with my shoulder red raw from the pounding my opposite number had given me, I kept telling myself there couldn't be many more scrums. But in the last minute or two there must have been six. I had a tremendous feeling of relief as the whistle went to end the game because it meant South Africa couldn't score any more – the only time I have ever felt quite like that. They scored eight tries that day, a remarkable feat in a test.'

Thornett and his fellow Wallabies on that short two-test tour of 1961 were unfortunate to meet a Springbok team, the nucleus of which had been forged in a full year of continuous international competition, including a series against the All Blacks and a tour of the United Kingdom and France. Just about every Springbok who played against Catchpole's team was not only superlatively fit and confident, but had the added advantage of being test-hardened in spite of comparative youth. In 1961, at least, the Springboks

Wallaby captain, Ken Catchpole, is about to feed his line with Springboks Hugo van Zyl and Frik du Preez obviously too late to stop him. Australian forward Dick Thornett is in the background.

had as much right to call themselves the world champions as their illustrious pre-decessors of the late 1930s and the early 1950s. The Springboks established a record for a home test by scoring eight tries, of which only two were converted, and Hennie van Zyl joined the select band of Boetie McHardy, Jan Stegmann and Tom van Vollenhoven by accomplishing a hat-trick.

The South Africans gave an absolutely exhilarating performance of sound but uninhibited rugby, and the Wallabies could only manage to scrape up a solitary penalty in reply. Even during the brief spell when Keith Oxlee, who had been playing superbly in his position as flyhalf, had to go off the field to have a head wound attended to, the splendid machine never spluttered as Mannetjies Roux substituted with aplomb.

The Springboks were not nearly as efficient – or as motivated – for the second test in Port Elizabeth and they could only total three tries in their 23–11 victory. It would have been miraculous had they been able to maintain the standard they had set at Ellis Park; it was a peak of perfection seldom reached.

The Springbok team for the test against Australia, held in Port Elizabeth. Back: R Hill, JP Engelbrecht, FCH du Preez, HJ van Zyl, DJ Hopwood, JL Gainsford, LG Wilson. Middle: HJM Pelser, PS du Toit, JT Claassen (captain), M Louw (manager), K Oxlee, GH van Zyl, SP Kuhn. Front: PdeW Uys, FduT Roux.

Venue	South Africa	Result	South Africa				Australia			
			T	C	P	D	T	C	P	D
Johannesburg	WON	28–3	8	2	0	0	0	0	1	0
Port Elizabeth	WON	23–11	3	1	3	1	1	1	2	0
		51–14	11	3	3	1	1	1	3	0
Series: South Africa played 2; W2, L0, D0										

CHAPTER 22

1962

LIONS TOUR SOUTH AFRICA

▲▲▲

Lionel Wilson is tackled in one of the tests played between South Africa and the British Lions. After drawing the first test the South Africans won the following three.

Arthur Robert Smith, long-jump champion, veteran international wing-threequarter and known at Caius College, Cambridge, as a mathematician of exceptional ability, was selected to lead the 1962 Lions' challenge in South Africa. He had been to South Africa before, as a member of the famous 1955 side, but injury had sidelined him for most of the tour. Smith was a member of the 1958 Barbarians team to tour South Africa and he also came out with the Scottish side in 1960. His 60-yard run for a try for the 'Baa-baas' against Transvaal at Ellis Park in 1958 alone stamped him as a wing of the highest class.

He was given a pack of huge forwards – men like the indefatigable Bryn Meredith and Syd Millar, Michael Campbell-Lamerton, Keith Rowlands, Willie-John McBride, Bill Mulcahy, Kingsley Jones, Budge Rogers, Haydn Morgan and Alun Pask. Dickie Jeeps was first choice for scrumhalf, and he and Richard Sharp, a flyhalf from Oxford University, were expected to make the maximum use of the abundance of possession the forwards were certain to get.

Part of the prediction came true. Unlike most British teams of the past who had to make the most of a less than fair share of the ball, the 1962 Lions had no such problems. Their inside backs lacked sparkle, however, and they never came near to matching their predecessors of 1955 or 1938 for attacking ideas. David Hewitt, a centre who did well against New Zealand in 1959, was bothered by injury, Ken Jones invariably tried to do too much on his own, and Mike Weston and Gordon Waddell were steady rather than brilliant.

Sharp played exceptionally well at the start of the tour and it could be that the injury he suffered against Northern Transvaal just before the first test had meant the elimination of the one player who could have lifted the backline from comparative mediocrity to something more in the tradition of Lions of the past.

Sharp's injury caused a violent row as the British press representatives and some members of the team thought that he had been deliberately put out of action by Mannetjies Roux. Sharp was on the field for less than five minutes. Receiving the ball, he tried to cut through with a typical dummy to the inside and, as he did so, Roux hit him with a flying tackle that fractured his cheekbone. Roux insisted that Sharp ducked into his tackle and that it was an unfortunate accident.

'I met Sharp some time afterwards and he told me right away that my tackle was fair,' Roux said later. 'He was on the point of kicking, but realized that I would charge down the ball and, instead, he tried to duck away from me. This brought his head in line with my tackle.'

The injury sidelined Sharp for five weeks and meant that he had to miss the first two tests against South Africa, certainly a heavy blow to the tourists. Gordon

Waddell, whose father Herbert was a member of Cove-Smith's 1924 side, took over. A clever and sturdy flyhalf, he lacked speed and preferred to use his boot, and did not present many problems on the attack.

Engelbrecht and Stewart, both obvious choices for the Springbok team, were injured and their places for the first test at Ellis Park were taken by Roux and a newcomer, Melville (Wang) Wyness, from Western Province. Ormond Taylor, a Natal wing, and Mof Myburgh also made their international debut in the match.

The two packs were so evenly matched that neither side could ever really get going. A few minutes before half-time, Jones kicked for touch, Roux fielded and, switching direction twice, gave to Gainsford who showed astonishing acceleration and cut through for a spectacular corner try. Late in the second half Jones made amends for his earlier indiscretion with a try of his own and the result of three-all was generally regarded as a fair reflection of the game.

Arthur Smith tussles with Mannetjies Roux, his opposite number, after Roux thought he had a chance to score.

The Springbok selectors made several changes for the second test in Durban. Wyness retained his place but Taylor and Myburgh were dropped. Avril Malan and Hugo van Zyl were also left out and Du Preez locked the scrum with Claassen. Chris Bezuidenhout went into the frontrow and Hannes Botha and Louis Schmidt were on the flanks. Engelbrecht, as expected, came back into the team and Roux, who always preferred the centre position, was shunted from the right- to the left-wing. The most interesting newcomer to the side was Dawie de Villiers, the Matie scrumhalf who had made a remarkable recovery from injury to earn Western Province, Junior Springbok and Springbok colours, all in the space of one month.

It turned out to be one of those grimly fought tests, clouded by controversy. At half-time there was still no score but late in the second half Oxlee, the Springbok flyhalf, put over a penalty kick after Rowlands had tackled Du Preez from an off-side position. There was no argument about this one but all hell broke loose over what happened in the last few seconds of the game. There was a scrum on the South African goalline and the Springboks were pushed back and over, for the two packs to collapse in a tangled mound. Rowlands and all of his teammates were convinced that he had scored a push-over try but the referee, Ken Carlson, ruled that since he had not seen the try being scored, he could not award it.

A determined John Gainsford is only a few seconds away from South Africa's first try in the first test against the 1962 Lions at Ellis Park in Johannesburg.

A fully recovered Richard Sharp returned to the Lions for the third test, at Newlands, but the less impetuous

Richard Sharp was an outstanding 1962 Lions flyhalf, but a tackle by Mannetjies Roux laid him low before the first test.

Experienced test players John Gainsford and Doug Hopwood flank Dawie de Villiers after the scrumhalf had spurted from club player to international in the space of four weeks.

Waddell might have been more useful to Arthur Smith and his competent pack. His appraisal of his threequarters was probably more realistic than Sharp's. The Springboks had made only one change this time, bringing back Hugo van Zyl and dropping Louis Schmidt.

There was tremendous interest in the match and at one stage riots threatened at the gates of Newlands. Scores of people were arrested and many of them were found to be carrying knives and other dangerous weapons; prompt police action certainly saved Newlands from what could have been dangerous crowd reaction. The official attendance was 54 843, still the largest crowd in the history of Newlands, and more than 4 000 people had to be turned away.

With Meredith proving once and for all why he was regarded as the best hooker of his era, the Lions forwards dominated the tight phases but in the loose Hannes Botha, playing the finest rugby of his career, Hugo van Zyl and Doug Hopwood gave the Springboks the edge.

At half-time the score was three-all, with Oxlee having succeeded with a penalty after Sharp had put over a dropgoal. Their excellent efforts were overshadowed, however, by an amazing run by Engelbrecht after Gainsford had given him the ball just outside the Springbok '25'. The Stellenbosch flyer left everybody standing with a burst of sustained speed worthy of an Olympic Games sprinter and Kiernan, coming across to take him on the corner-flag, never had a chance. The huge crowd's roar turned into a rumbling groan when the referee, Dr Bertie Strasheim, ruled that Gainsford's pass had been forward, and that Engelbrecht's effort had been in vain. Later on in the match Engelbrecht also used his exceptional pace to prevent a certain try when he flashed across the field to neutralize a ball that had been grubbered over the goalline. The man of the match was Oxlee who, for the second successive test, scored all of South Africa's points.

An ill-advised attempt by Sharp to start a move on his tryline gave the Springbok flyhalf his chance. Jones was flattened by Wyness and Oxlee grabbed the loose ball, dodged inside and then sped towards the touchline, beating a baffled cover defence by his quick changes of direction. He calmly converted his own try and the Lions never looked like getting back into the picture after this set-back. The final score was 8–3.

▲▲▲

Piet Uys replaced the injured Dawie de Villiers for the final test in Bloemfontein and Ronnie Hill took over from Abie Malan, who had been thoroughly outhooked by Meredith at Newlands. It was a hot afternoon with an unpleasant wind periodically driving miniature dust storms across the field, a ground hard and barren at the end of a harsh Free State winter.

Up to referee Toy Myburgh's half-time whistle, the Lions were holding their own, although the Springboks were leading 10–6. Roux had scored a good try after a break by Wyness while earlier on a thrust by Gainsford, in turn, had given Wyness a try. Oxlee had no problems with the conversions, while a penalty by John Willcox and an unconverted try by Ronnie Cowan made up the side's half-time score.

After the resumption Gainsford slashed through three defenders for the only try of the day that Oxlee could not convert. The Lions, still very much in the picture, replied promptly with a try by Rowlands, converted by Willcox. But, after a penalty by Oxlee, the Springboks suddenly looked as good an attacking side as any in the history of the game. It was Du Preez who sparked it off. Gathering a pass from Engelbrecht, he burst away on a run in which he swept aside six defenders. With superb timing, he ran into the final tackle before flipping the ball to his left for Hugo van Zyl to score. Oxlee converted and when he also converted a try by Claassen after good combining between Hugo van Zyl and Hopwood, the Springboks had added 13 points in six minutes. A penalty goal pushed the flyhalf's personal tally for the match to 14 points and left him in sight of Okey Geffin's long-standing record.

With only a few minutes to go, Roux received a long pass on the half-way line and with electrifying speed he shot past Cowan and then cut sharply in-field to leave several Lions floun-

dering in his wake. With only the fullback left to beat, Roux revealed his instinctive genius. Instead of going for the corner-flag and running the risk of Willcox bumping him into touch, he ran straight at the fullback and swerved past him with such bewildering ease that Willcox realized the futility of it all and did not even attempt a tackle. Roux rounded off his spectacular run with an exuberant dive over the line for what must surely rate with the best tries ever to have been scored in test rugby.

Oxlee placed the ball for the conversion, not knowing that he needed two points to become the Springbok who had scored the most points in a test. The wind kept blowing the ball over and eventually Hopwood had to hold it down for the flyhalf's kick. It was on target, from the moment the boot hit the ball.

A moment later Mike Campbell-Lamerton broke away from a lineout to score the final try before referee Myburgh's whistle sent more than 60 000 happy spectators flowing towards the exits. The Springboks had scored six tries in their 34–14 victory and Oxlee had succeeded with seven out of the eight kicks he had aimed at the posts. Jeeps, who captained the Lions in the final test as Smith was injured, had correctly predicted the Springboks' winning margin. In an interview before the test he said: 'We have already lost the series and there is no point in playing it safe. We'll either win by 10 points or lose by 20!'

There are plenty of players but no ball in this scene from the test match at Ellis Park. Players, from left to right, are Du Preez, Pask and Uys (on the ground), Millar, Abe Malan, Kingsley, Jones and Mulcahy.

Venue	South Africa	Result	South Africa				British Isles			
			T	C	P	D	T	C	P	D
Johannesburg	draw	3–3	1	0	0	0	1	0	0	0
Durban	won	3–0	0	0	1	0	0	0	0	0
Cape Town	won	8–3	1	1	1	0	0	0	0	1
Bloemfontein	won	34–14	6	5	2	0	3	1	1	0
		48–20	8	6	4	0	4	1	1	1
Series: South Africa played 4; W3, L0, D1										

Keith Oxlee, the match-winning flyhalf from Natal, dominated the 1962 series. In his 19-test career he was responsible for 88 points.

CHAPTER 23

1963

AUSTRALIA TOUR SOUTH AFRICA

▲▲▲

In agony with a dislocated shoulder, Piet Uys gets some rough help from his captain, Abie Malan, in the fourth test against Australia at Newlands.

Thornett led the 1963 Australian team to visit South Africa and his Wallabies became the first touring team to beat the Springboks in two consecutive tests since 1896. His was an Australian team with a difference. Gone was the unpredictability, and the flair which used to impress South Africans so much. In its place was a new approach. The 1963 Wallabies rarely took risks, their backs were defenders first and foremost, and unless they received the ball quickly and cleanly they did not attempt to attack.

Sturdy and intelligent forwards and a brilliant scrumhalf in Ken Catchpole were the pillars on which the team was built.

Catchpole was then 24 years old and on his performances during the 1963 tour, particularly in the second and third tests (he missed the first because of a hand injury), he must be ranked among the best scrumhalves of all time. He had both the physical and mental agility demanded by his position and his judgement rarely failed him. 'Catchy', as his teammates called him, gave his flyhalf an impeccable service, he could break or kick when the situation called for it and on the

Haas Schoeman and Tommy Bedford scramble for the ball at the Boet Erasmus Stadium in Port Elizabeth.

defence he was simply wonderful. Phil Hawthorne became a top-class international flyhalf overnight and it was obvious that whenever Hawthorne was partnered by Kenneth (Nipper) McMullen, he was often exposed as still having a lot to learn. In the tests, with Catchpole behind the scrum, Hawthorne hardly ever made a mistake, however, and his two dropgoals in the tests were lovely efforts.

The Australian forwards were well-drilled by coach Alan Roper, who knew and appreciated the value of a solid scrum but whose policy of 'take no risks, make no mistakes' was criticized by some members of the touring party.

Apart from Catchpole, the stars of the side were the trio of loose-forwards, Greg Davis, Jules Guerassimoff and John O'Gorman.

Davis was actually a New Zealander who had played in All Blacks trials as a centre before settling in Sydney. He had a Kiwi attitude to the game and never allowed himself to be pushed around. His quick raids from the side of the scrum and powerful tackling caused the Springboks a lot of headaches and in the second test at Newlands, in particular, he gave Oxlee a torrid time. The Springbok flyhalf was, in fact, dropped for the third test, a mistake the selectors rectified by restoring him to the fourth test team.

Guerassimoff, of Russian descent and known as 'Julie', was a Boland Coetzee-type of flanker. He played it tight and hard and though not nearly as spectacular as Davis, did a great amount of work. O'Gorman was somewhat similar in style, a defensive eighthman who covered well and always seemed to be on the spot to either smother an attack or to help a teammate.

Stewart Boyce was the most accomplished wing threequarter in the side although he lacked the pace of his partner, John Williams, who as a sprinter had been considered for the Australian track team for the 1962 Commonwealth Games. Ian Moutray and Beres Ellwood were fair centres. Moutray was a tackler in the Ryk van Schoor mould. In the match against Northern Transvaal he brought down Frik du Preez with such force that the Springbok lock tore the ligaments in his foot and could play in only one of the tests. Moutray, however, lacked in other

Avril Malan in relaxed conversation with Australian captain, John Thornett.

The line-outs were the Australians' trump cards in the 1963 tests. Pictured here are Fanie Kuhn, John Thornett, Frik du Preez, Peter Crittle and Dick Putter.

John Thornett runs with the ball as Frik du Preez topples a Wallaby in the background.

skills and he only played in the second test. John Thornett whose attractive appearance and unfailing courtesy charmed the South African rugby public, was a strong leader of a most well-behaved party and although the standard of play from both sides was seldom memorable, it was a pleasant tour unmarred by squabbles, squeals and deliberate fouling.

The South African selectors did more than their usual share of chopping and changing in the series. It was almost a game of musical chairs as outstanding players were dropped only to be brought back again. Abie Malan, who had led the Springboks in the first two tests, was axed for the third, and Avril Malan took over. When the Springboks lost, Malan was reinstated for the final test. Uncertainty about the all-important captaincy was not the sort of thing to promote confidence in the Springbok camp.

The Springboks nevertheless won the first test in Pretoria 14–3, a match which marked the international debut of Tommy Bedford, Gert Cilliers, Trix Truter, substituting for the injured Engelbrecht, and the veteran frontranker Dick Putter. Cilliers and Bedford (on the flank) celebrated their debut with a try each.

A groin injury kept Cilliers out of the second test at Newlands and Engelbrecht was brought back while Stompie van der Merwe came in for the injured Frik du Preez. Mannetjies Roux replaced Truter and Wyness took over from Stewart who had played well at Loftus Versfeld.

The Springboks were given a penalty try in the seventh minute of the match after Engelbrecht had sprinted nearly the length of the field before chipping the ball over the Australian goalline. Bedford, following up, was held without the ball by Ellwood, and the referee, Toy Myburgh, awarded the first and still the only penalty try ever to be given in a test in South Africa. A series of injuries, with scrumhalf Piet Uys' dislocated shoulder being the most serious, undoubtedly disrupted the Springbok rhythm, but the Wallabies nevertheless looked the better side on the day. Catchpole and Davis were magnificent and O'Gorman, Guerassimoff, Rob Heming and Thornett played their hearts out to score a well-deserved 9–5 victory. Catchpole's tactical kicking in the final ten minutes, when he kept the Springboks on their heels, was perfect.

Abie Malan, Hopwood, Oxlee, Roux, Uys (injured), Wyness, Nel and Putter were all dropped for the third test at Ellis Park. Ronnie Hill, Dave Stewart and Gert Cilliers were recalled and Norman Riley, at flyhalf, Nelie Smith, scrumhalf, Hannes Marais, tight-head prop, Johan (Haas) Schoeman, flank, and Josua (Poens) Prinsloo, eighthman, were given colours for the first time.

Avril Malan decided on keeping the game tight, hoping that the Springboks would gain control up front. The plan failed because the Australian forwards actually had the better of things throughout. His work on the defence was particularly good and he so inspired his teammates that the South Africans failed to get even one try – all nine points coming from penalties by Nelie Smith. Terry Casey, the Australian full-back, put over a dropped goal, a penalty and he also converted Williams' try to give his team a winning margin of two points.

With Smith and Riley committed to kicking, the Springbok threequarters were rarely asked to do anything except chase and defend. The spontaneous way in which the Springboks afterwards gathered in their opponents' dressingroom to congratulate them was, frankly, about the only thing they did right all afternoon.

With South Africa in danger of losing the series the selectors dropped no less than seven players for the final test. Avril Malan, Hill, Marais, Prinsloo and Fanie Kuhn (after wearing the Springbok jersey with distinction in 17 consecutive tests),

Engelbrecht and Riley were all axed. Oxlee, Hopwood, Abie Malan (back as captain), Putter, Mof Myburgh, Tiny Naude and Corra Dirksen were the replacements. Naude, a mobile lock-forward who had provided one of the highlights of the tour with a huge 69-yard penalty goal for Western Province against the visitors, and Dirksen, a powerful Northern Transvaal wing who only the previous season was a lowly regarded club centre, were the new 'caps'.

Abie Malan very sensibly decided not to repeat the Ellis Park mistake of trying to play ten-man rugby. He and Hennie Muller, who assisted with the coaching, stressed to the team that they must not allow themselves to be too inhibited. Malan's relaxed confidence had the desired effect and the Springboks generally played their best rugby of the series.

With only eight minutes to go, the score was still six-all, but then a penalty by Oxlee nosed the Springboks into the lead and the Wallabies appeared to panic. Malan, Naude and Gainsford added tries in quick succession. Rather against the run of play, the Springboks eventually won 22–6 to share the series. Oxlee scored ten points with two penalty goals and two conversions and Naude, whose boot was to play such a dramatic part in several tests to come, added a penalty.

VENUE	SOUTH AFRICA	RESULT	SOUTH AFRICA				AUSTRALIA			
			T	C	P	D	T	C	P	D
PRETORIA	WON	14–3	2	1	2	0	1	0	0	0
CAPE TOWN	LOST	5–9	1*	1	0	0	1	0	1	1
JOHANNESBURG	LOST	9–11	0	0	3	0	1	1	1	1
PORT ELIZABETH	WON	22–6	3	2	3	0	0	0	1	1
		50–29	6	4	8	0	3	1	3	3

SERIES: SOUTH AFRICA PLAYED 4; W2, L2, D0
* PENALTY TRY

CHAPTER 24

1964

UP AND DOWN

▲▲▲

WALES vs SOUTH AFRICA

Victory over the Springboks eluded Wales from the first time the two teams clashed in 1906, but the men from the valleys had high hopes when they visited South Africa in 1964. They had a very strong side and, equally important, the South African rugby season had just started and Wales were expected to have a vital fitness advantage.

In the first half of the only test, played in Durban, it looked as if the experts had, for once, predicted correctly. The Springboks were just not combining properly and with Brian Price outstanding in the lineouts and Clive Rowlands and Dave Watkins dovetailing slickly at halfback, the South Africans were distinctly lucky to be level at three-all at half-time. A penalty by Oxlee was cancelled out by a penalty for Wales from Keith Bradshaw.

With only 20 minutes to go Lionel Wilson, who had saved his team repeatedly in a match of many errors, caught a poor clearing kick from Grahame Hodgson near his halfway line and just in from touch. For once in his long test career, the normally conservative Wilson gambled. He put everything he had into a dropkick

Nelie Smith puts a left foot to the ball from the maul. From left: John Mantle (Wales), Bedford, Smith, Mof Myburgh, Avril Malan, Doug Hopwood and Alun Pask (Wales).

The French side that toured South Africa in 1964. Back: B Dauga, E Cester, M Lira, A Herrero, W Spanghero, J-J Rupert, J-C Berejnoi. Third row: A Gruarin, M Etcheverry, M Sitjar, Y Menthiller, C Darrouy, J-M Cabanier, R Halcaren, J-P Capdouze. Second row: J Piqué, P Albaladejo, J Prat (assistant manager), M Saulnier (manager), M Crauste (captain), J Dupuy, J-C Lasserre. Front row: J-C Hiquet, P Dedieu, J Gachassin, M Arnaudet, C Laborde.

and, from that acute angle and nearly half the length of the field away from the posts, he sent the ball sailing safely over the crossbar. It did more than add three points to the South African score – it inspired the Springboks and disheartened the Welsh. In the less than 20 minutes remaining, Hannes Marais, Doug Hopwood and Nelie Smith scored tries, all converted by Oxlee who also stabbed over a penalty and Wales were beaten 24–3, their biggest defeat ever against South Africa. Hopwood's try meant that he became the first and, to date, only Springbok to have notched a try against each of the four Home Countries.

VENUE	SOUTH AFRICA	RESULT	SOUTH AFRICA				WALES			
			T	C	P	D	T	C	P	D
DURBAN	WON	24–3	3	3	2	1	0	0	1	0

FRANCE vs SOUTH AFRICA

Michel Crauste brought out a French team to play South Africa in a single test at Springs, and they won 6–8 in what has frequently been described as the worst international match yet to have been seen in South Africa.

The Tricolors, at that stage, appeared to have the Springboks taped; whenever they met, the South Africans looked disorganized and leaden-footed. This was certainly the case at Springs in 1964 when wing Christian Darrouy scored a try and Pierre (Monsieur Le Drop) Albaladejo added a conversion and a penalty. Dave Stewart, with his usual unobtrusive efficiency, notched all the Springbok points with a try and a penalty.

VENUE	SOUTH AFRICA	RESULT	SOUTH AFRICA				FRANCE			
			T	C	P	D	T	C	P	D
SPRINGS	LOST	6–8	1	0	1	0	1	1	1	0

CHAPTER 25

1965

ANNUS MISERABILIS

▲▲▲

I t was the year South African rugby plumbed the depths. Eight tests were played in 1965 – against Scotland, Ireland, two against Australia and four against New Zealand – and the Springboks won only one of them. The first warning signals of a decline were already flashing the year before when France won at Springs.

SOUTH AFRICA TOURS SCOTLAND AND IRELAND

Early in 1965, Avril Malan took a Springbok team on a short tour of Ireland and Scotland and they returned without having scored a single victory. It was an unfortunate venture from the beginning, soured by haggling over the captaincy. The selectors' choice was Doug Hopwood who had led Western Province superbly in the Currie Cup tournament, but they were overruled by the South African Rugby Board and Malan was appointed. The Springboks departed in an atmosphere of acrimony and, although powerful enough on paper, the side floundered through the tour, an unhappy combination without aim or spirit.

Venue	South Africa	Result	South Africa				South Africa			
			T	C	P	D	T	C	P	D
Scotland	Lost	5–8	1	0	0	0	1	0	1	0
Ireland	Lost	6–9	1	0	1	0	1	0	2	0

Shortly after returning from Scotland and Ireland, the team to tour Australia and New Zealand had to be selected. A week of trials at Newlands produced nothing startling and, taking into account the usual toll exacted by injury and retirement, the selectors relied on the best available talent.

Nelie Smith, also a scrumhalf, was given the vice-captaincy and this was not a sound move. Not that Smith could not do the job, but because it left the forwards without an appointed leader. Hennie Muller, the scourge of the 1949 All Blacks, was appointed coach and it was to be a frustrating tour for the former *Windhond*. He vainly advocated a more definite playing pattern and felt that too many of the players were not dedicated enough.

The team's active social life and the happy-go-lucky attitude of more than just a few players horrified and disillusioned a man to whom a Springbok blazer meant so much. Among the backs there were the steady Wilson at fullback, Engelbrecht, Gainsford, who was generally regarded as the best centre in the

DAWIE DE VILLIERS

Dawie de Villiers, at 24, became the youngest Springbok captain since Avril Malan was given the honour in 1960 and no one could have seriously doubted his qualifications for the task. De Villiers was an outstanding scrumhalf whose speed and incisiveness compensated for the occasional lapses in his service. He had overcome a serious knee injury which had prompted his surgeon to advise him against playing. But courage, physical and moral, was to be his strongest attribute on and off the field. He commanded the respect of his team through a combination of natural charm and total sincerity. His tactical appreciation of the game was frequently criticized, but he was nevertheless an inspiring captain.

world, Mannetjies Roux, Brynard, Oxlee and Jannie Barnard, and new-comers like Syd Nomis and the late replacement, Eben Olivier, who both went on to gain international fame. Among the forwards there were indi-vidual stars like Du Preez, Abie Malan, Naude, Don Walton, Hopwood, Andrew Janson, Andy MacDonald, Sakkie van Zyl, Lofty Nel, Hannes Marais, Johan (Haas) Schoeman and youthful Jan Ellis.

The controversial but often brilliant Tommy Bedford was prevented by injury from taking any active role in the tests and Hopwood, the best eighthman of his time, was plagued even more than usual by the back injury he had to live with throughout his illustrious career.

Hannes Marais and John Gainsford watch as Mof Myburgh and Jan Ellis scramble for the ball.

SOUTH AFRICA vs AUSTRALIA

The Australian leg of the tour was an unmitigated disaster. The Springboks failed to understand some inexplicable refereeing decisions and they were more than once unhappy with their hotel accommodation. For the first time the Springboks lost a test match in Australia.

The Springboks started with the traditional romps against Western Australia and Victoria before running into New South Wales on the Queen's birthday. The state side harried the Springboks and won 12–3, scoring the only try of the match.

Fourteen of those New South Welshmen were in the test side five days later. They piled into the Springboks from the start and built up a 9–0 lead before Jannie Engelbrecht opened the scoring for the Springboks. Eventually the Australian side won the penalty count 18–7 and the match 18–11.

The Springboks moved up to Brisbane where they thrashed Queensland 50–5, scoring 11 tries. Then came the test with a change of referee as Kevin Crowe took over from Craig Ferguson. The change did not help. The Springboks scored two tries to nil but the Wallabies kicked four kicks and won 12–8.

After three successive defeats and a lot of bickering, the Springboks were pleased to head for New Zealand.

Impartial observers from New Zealand agreed that the refereeing in Australia left much to be desired. With this added handicap, the Springboks not only lost to New South Wales but also could not win either of the two tests against one of the strongest teams ever to be fielded by Australia.

VENUE	SOUTH AFRICA	RESULT	SOUTH AFRICA				AUSTRALIA			
			T	C	P	D	T	C	P	D
SYDNEY	LOST	11–18	2	1	1	0	2	0	4	0
BRISBANE	LOST	8–12	2	1	0	0	0	0	4	0
		19–30	4	2	1	0	2	0	8	0
SERIES: SOUTH AFRICA PLAYED 2; W0, L2, D0										

SOUTH AFRICA vs NEW ZEALAND

Colin Meads described the Springbok forwards of 1965 as 'loose and shiftless' and it is a fact that, in at least two of the four tests, the All Blacks forwards were in complete command and they held the edge throughout the series.

This often forced the Springbok backs to try and strike from an unsound platform. Mistakes simply had to be made under such circumstances and the All Blacks, absolute masters of second-phase attack, were always quick to capitalize.

The Springboks were unlucky not to have drawn the first test at Wellington in a wind approaching gale strength. The All Blacks had it in their favour in the first half, but the Springboks defence stood up well and the All Blacks led only 6–0 at half-time. New Zealand deserved the first-half try by wing Bill Birtwhistle, but there was doubt about Tremain's try a few seconds from half-time. Dawie de Villiers tackled Mick Williment and the ball popped out of his hands towards the Springbok line when Tremain snapped it up to dive over. A dropgoal by Oxlee halved the lead after half-time, but the All Blacks held on to win. The Springbok forwards could not get enough clean possession for the threequarters while New Zealand did not have backs talented enough to make full use of what they got.

▲▲▲

The second test was played in Dunedin, on a field turned into a swamp by rain, and the Springboks failed to adapt to the conditions. The All Blacks forwards were on top from the kick-off and the Springbok pack was given a thorough beating. Had it not been for Wilson, at fullback, the final score would have been higher than 13–0. Wilson so impressed the All Blacks that Wilson Whineray, their skipper, paid a special tribute to the Springbok in his after-match speech. Lionel Wilson and Frik du Preez were later named as two of the five Players of the Year by New Zealand critics.

▲▲▲

The 1965 Springboks leave for Ireland and Scotland. From left: Haas Schoeman, Dave Stewart, Jannie Engelbrecht, John Gainsford and the great Boy Louw.

Dawie de Villiers, who did not play in the second test because of injury, returned for the third international and several other overdue changes were made. Oxlee had to make way for Jannie Barnard, Naude replaced Piet Goosen, Don Walton took over from Abie Malan, Lofty Nel was switched to the side of the scrum in place of Haas Schoeman and Doug Hopwood was brought back as eighthman. It was never announced officially, but by common consent, Hopwood was also given the job of leading the pack. New Zealand's Alex Veysey described the third test in *Colin Meads, All Black*, a book he wrote with Meads:

'If ever a country needed a test victory to salve its hurt pride in itself it was South Africa. When the Springboks took the field on a sludgy surface at Lancaster Park, Christchurch, the country had lost seven matches on the

It's all heavy going in Dunedin in 1965 as Jan Ellis leads the Springbok chase against the All Blacks.

trot. Pride seemed doomed to dip to its nadir when at half-time New Zealand led 16–5, a launching pad, it seemed, for utter rout. It was a Springbok team which had more than enough problems during the tour. There was not a tight binding of thought and allegiance at senior player-coach level and this in itself was shockingly uncharacteristic of South African rugby. It was also one strong reason why it seemed that at 16–5 down at half-time, there was no psychological spring from which a new life could be drawn.

'Meads believes that quite a magnificent first spell try by John Gainsford sowed the seed of hope in at least one Springbok breast – and this was an all-important one because it belonged to the captain Dawie de Villiers. At half-time while De Villiers delivered his message to the players – Forwards, give us the ball to play with; the backs can win it – the New Zealanders quite unconsciously relaxed ...'

Meads took over the narrative:

'Even though you tell yourself the job is still to be done there is an automatic mental reaction to a position such as 16–5 at half-time in a test match. Had it been 6–3 we might have won the match. As it was, De Villiers was proved right and the South African backs cut us up. Every man did his piece; while De Villiers was steady and reliable, outside him, Jannie Barnard, John Gainsford, Mannetjies Roux, Gert Brynard were inspired. Suddenly, after Brynard had scored a try early in the second spell and then another nine minutes later, we were on the back foot and once you get into this sort of rut, it's damned hard to get out of it. By the time Gainsford had scored another try it was 16–16 and one of the great triumphs of rugby was in sight. But we hoisted ourselves back into it by controlling play till just two or three minutes from time. Then I got myself offside and watched in despair as Tiny Naude kicked the goal from out of the slush...'

The clock at Lancaster Park showed less than three minutes to go before the end of the third test between the 1965 Springboks and the All Blacks. Lionel Wilson was tackled from an off-side position and the Springboks were given a penalty,

Syd Nomis and Lofty Nel autograph for the boys of Central Primary School, Gisborne, where the first match of the tour was played.

not far from the All Blacks' posts, but near the touchline. Victory or defeat – it all depended on the kick. Tiny Naude prepared for a date with destiny. Wing three-quarter Gertjie Brynard was wiping the ball against his chest to remove some of the clay. He whispered urgently: 'Tiny, look at those guys sauntering back! They've had it. Make it a short one, I'm sure I can beat them to the line!'

Brynard, whose agility and speed had brought him two tries that afternoon, considered the odds against him catching the defence napping to be no higher than the odds against anyone succeeding with a kick. But Naude had made up his mind. The responsibility of ending a run of Springbok defeats was to be his. Head down, body balanced, the right leg swung firmly in the follow-through. Only then did he look up to follow the flight of the ball; low and straight and Naude knew that he had not failed his team. His pent-up feelings exploded in a great shout and Lofty Nel was there to grab him in a bear-hug of joy and triumph. This was a fitting climax to one afternoon the 1965 Springboks can remember with pride.

▲▲▲

Unfortunately for South Africa the revival was short-lived. Soon they were in a slump, worse than before, and when they lost the fourth test 3–20, it was the biggest defeat the Springboks had ever suffered against the All Blacks. Whineray was worried about the Springbok backs before the final test. He worked out an elaborate scheme with coaches Neil McPhail and Fred Allen to contain De Villiers and his threequarters, but it was never necessary to employ the plan. The forwards dominated the proceedings with such absolute authority that the Springboks were forced to attack from poor possession and dangerous positions near their own line. They made numerous mistakes and the All Blacks had a field day, scoring five tries to none and winning with almost contemptuous ease.

The comparative mediocrity of much of the Springbok play on the tour was surprising – it was so out of character with South African rugby.

▲▲▲

John Gainsford is given the slip by Chris Laidlaw. Gainsford played in 33 tests for South Africa between 1960 and 1967.

During the tour the political pressure on South African sport reached breaking point with a statement by Dr HF Verwoerd, then Prime Minister of the Republic, that Maoris would not be welcome in any New Zealand team to visit South Africa. The future was to prove different, but at that stage it looked as if the long and tradition-rich rivalry between the All Blacks and the Springboks had come to an end. The year 1965 was indeed a terrible one for South African rugby.

Venue	South Africa	Result	South Africa				New Zealand			
			T	C	P	D	T	C	P	D
Wellington	Lost	3–6	0	0	0	1	2	0	0	0
Dunedin	Lost	0–13	0	0	0	0	3	2	0	0
Christchurch	Won	19–16	4	2	1	0	3	2	1	0
Auckland	Lost	3–20	0	0	1	0	5	1	0	1
		25–55	4	2	2	1	13	5	1	1
Series: South Africa played 4; W1, L3, D0										

JANNIE ENGELBRECHT

This is nobility in South African rugby. Just look at his credentials – the elegant, blue-eyed, handsome wing, upright, long-striding, swerving down the field. With all the elegance there was all the heroism of a boy's hero – scoring two vital tries against Northern Transvaal with a broken collarbone.

Look at his education – Paul Roos Gymnasium; Stellenbosch University. Look at his family – the beautiful wife, the good-looking children. Look at his house – the aged Cape Dutch manor house of Rust en Vrede.

When he stopped playing rugby, he had played 33 tests for South Africa, 67 times in a Springbok jersey. He had played on the great grounds of the world and been respected for his performances. He was fast and practised hard. His defensive covering of the fullback and his throwing in at line-outs – as wings used to do in those days – were both meticulous.

Add to that his loyalty. He loved Stellenbosch and travelled around 70 000 km a year to practise and matches when he was farming at Koekenaap. Being loyal and loving Stellenbosch, he was loyal to Doc Craven and did much to bring honour to the great man after his death.

Being loyal, he loved Western Province and served on its executive committees with forthright thoughtfulness. Being loyal, he loved South Africa and became an excellent ambassador for the country as manager of the Springboks.

CHAPTER 26

1967

FRANCE TOUR SOUTH AFRICA

▲▲▲

Jan Ellis charges at France with eager support from team-mates Piet Greyling and Dawie de Villiers.

France undertook their first full-scale tour of South Africa in 1967 and it coincided with a critical stage in South African rugby history. Including the 1964 débâcle at Springs, the Springboks had lost eight out of nine test matches and their chances of regaining self-confidence against opponents they had been unable to fathom on four successive occasions over a period of nearly ten years looked slim.

France was riding the crest of a wave after having won the Five-Nations tournament, an achievement considered so highly that skipper Christian Darrouy sent an after-match message to General de Gaulle reading simply: 'Mission accomplished'. The championship became theirs through powerful forwards and the Camberabero brothers, Lilian and Guy, as the halfbacks.

Guy Camberabero, protected by his scrumhalf-brother and some of the toughest and best forwards in the game, scored the points, and as a general rule the threequarters were neglected. Lilian could not make the trip to South Africa but 'The Flea' was fully expected to do to South Africa what he did so efficiently in the Five-Nations tournament: stabbing over penalties and dropgoals whenever his pack could bring him within potting range.

Darrouy's team was particularly strong up front with players like Jean-Michel Cabanier, Benoit Dauga, Walter Spanghero, Jacques Fort, Alain Plantefol and Christian Carrere.

Fullbacks Claude Lacaze (like his older brother, Pierre, he was known as 'Butterfly') and Pierre Villepreux, with centres Claude Dourthe and Jean Trillo, were the most impressive backs, but the ten-man pattern employed by the French did not give their threequarters much scope.

As for the South Africans, a new panel of selectors under the chairmanship of Flappie Lochner, refused to accept the commonly-held view that the Springboks were doomed. They selected eight newcomers for the first test in Durban, and by the end of the series had used only 17 players. Such confidence, as much as any other factor, helped to rebuild South African rugby in the second half of the 1960s.

The four tests were played in less than a month and this probably accounts for the fact that the standard of play dipped sharply after the first two matches.

The Springboks made a brilliant start to the series in Durban. Led with verve and fire by Dawie de Villiers, they played with such assurance and enterprise that the French were run ragged and could scrape together only three points against 26 for South Africa.

In HO de Villiers, the Springboks proved to have a new fullback who was unpredictably dangerous. Henry Oswald de Villiers, who was to play in 14 tests before injury tragically ended his international career at the age of 25, was a trump card against a team like France. They never before had to contend with a Springbok fullback who believed in counter-attack rather than a safe kick to touch. In spite of what they said later, they never solved the problem he presented; unless it was to make sure not to kick in his direction the way they did in the first two tests. In addition to his instinctive aggression, HO had wonderfully safe hands, a quick brain, raw courage and the sheer physical strength to break tackles and to flatten forwards.

Eben Olivier, an extremely nimble centre with remarkable acceleration and a bobbing running style also came as a nasty shock to the French. And Corra Dirksen, the stocky, fearless Northern Transvaal wing was a downright nightmare to them. Gainsford and Engelbrecht, and to a lesser extent, Dawie de Villiers, gave the backline the guiding hand of experience, and Piet Visagie, De Villiers' new partner, made no mistakes and was an excellent kicker and a valuable defender. The flyhalf from Griqualand West had to endure criticism in the initial stages of his career because his approach was considered too negative, but he was to go on to play in 25 tests, to score 130 points, and to be accurately acclaimed as just about the perfect pivot in the world of international rugby.

The new hooker, Gys Pitzer, not only did his job superbly well but he also proved himself to be one of the toughest men ever to pull the green-and-gold jersey over his head. Boxing ability should hardly be a qualification for a rugby player but some members of the 1967 French team often confused the two sports for it to have been an advantage in that hotly contested series. The Durban test marked the debut of Piet Greyling, who immediately dovetailed perfectly with

Happiness is a try! Corra Dirksen scored the first points for South Africa, only three minutes into the first test held in Durban.

Jan Ellis on the other flank, and the partnership became one of the mainstays of Springbok rugby in a record number of 24 tests. Albie de Waal, the selectors' choice at number-eight had a good enough series before fading abruptly, but the tight-forwards – Neethling, Naude and Carelse (replaced by Frik du Preez in the fourth test) – made solid contributions.

The South African rugby public was so numbed by the long run of defeats that the Springbok team for the first test caused hardly any reaction.

▲▲▲

Within five minutes of the start of the first test, Dirksen steamed inside from the left-wing position to take the ball from Dawie de Villiers. Without even making a pretence at side-stepping or swerving past any opponent, he ploughed through and over next to the posts, with HO de Villiers making it five points. The Tricolors replied promptly with an unconverted try by Claude Dourthe but rough play gave HO the chance to make the score 8–3 with a penalty.

Less than 15 minutes before half-time, the Springboks ripped the heart out of the French resistance with a sudden try. HO de Villiers, running at full speed, snapped up a poor clearance a few yards from touch, dummied once, bumped off two defenders, and then ran just far enough to bring his forwards on-side before kicking ahead with unerring accuracy. The French fullback, Lacaze, and the cover defence had no chance of saving the situation. Jan Ellis over-ran the ball but Piet Greyling was just behind him to pick up and score. HO steered the difficult conversion kick high over the crossbar as he did again a few minutes later when Ellis carved through a demoralized defence.

After half-time, Greyling scored his second try to make his debut really memorable and HO, already the darling of Newlands, became a national hero as he added two more points. The game then deteriorated as sporadic fighting broke out among the forwards and Spanghero was briefly knocked out by a punch which was apparently not even intended for him. With fifteen minutes to go, Dirksen again treated the French defence with contempt to score an unconverted try and the game ended with the Springboks having scored a remarkably comfortable 26–3 victory over the European champions.

▲▲▲

The second test in Bloemfontein was not quite so easy and it was not until the second half that the Springbok forwards gained enough grip to drive through to victory. At half-time the Springboks had only a long-range penalty from Naude to show for all their hard work and on several occasions only HO de Villiers stood between France and a score. Once, with three opponents coming at him and no other defenders in sight, HO

Marcel Puget passes as Albie de Waal covers and Syd Nomis, playing at centre, charges up on defence. The fourth test at Newlands ended in a 6–6 draw.

risked life and limb by successfully diving into Dourthe's boot as he tried to grubber-kick the ball towards the goalline. The other bright star in the Springbok line-up was Olivier, who scored a brilliant individualistic try in the second half, and who had the defence groping blindly more than once. He handed Dirksen his third try of the series after one such break and not long afterwards Engelbrecht was sent on his way with only fullback Villepreux to beat. The Stellenbosch wing left him standing with a typical outside swerve and, with HO converting, the Springboks won 16–3.

△△△

Guy Camberabero, with ten points out of a total of 19, six of them from two smooth dropkicks, steered France to an upset victory in the third test at Ellis Park. It was Lacaze's remarkable dropped penalty goal from the halfway line, however, that stands out in memory as the highlight of a game in which nothing went right for the Springboks. Olivier once again scored a try with his bewildering ability to vary his pace, but the rest of the South African points came from two penalties from Naude and a try by Ellis, converted by Visagie to make the final score 19–14 in favour of France. It was, incidentally, the first time Visagie had scored in a test. Gainsford, after playing in 33 tests and scoring a record total of eight tries, lost his place for the fourth test at Newlands to make way for Syd Nomis.

△△△

The final test ended in a draw and the game, played in a whipping wind, had no flow or pattern. Referee Piet Robbertse dished out no less than 26 penalties to the two sides. Camberabero and HO succeeded with a penalty each and the other points came from a try by Spanghero and a fantastic dropgoal from a difficult angle and practically on the halfway line by Piet Visagie. Generally, the Springbok halfbacks did not play well, and Dawie de Villiers was given far too little protection by his forwards. The match, once again, had moments of bad temper and Frik du Preez and Alain Plantefol had an argument that resulted in the Frenchman receiving a black eye. The two players made their peace in the dressingroom afterwards and exchanged jerseys to prove their goodwill.

Although the Springboks could not sustain the brilliant form they showed in the first two tests, the series at least proved that South African rugby was pulling out of the nose-dive. Brilliant new players had come to the fore, and pride and self-confidence had returned after the disasters of 1965.

Albie de Waal looks down at a French try by Walter Spanghero, the only try of the Newlands test, while Christian Carrère raises his hand in delight.

Venue	South Africa	Result	South Africa				France			
			T	C	P	D	T	C	P	D
Durban	Won	26–3	5	4	1	0	1	0	0	0
Bloemfontein	Won	16–3	3	2	1	0	0	0	1	0
Johannesburg	Lost	14–19	2	1	2	0	2	2	1	2
Cape Town	Draw	6–6	0	0	1	1	1	0	1	0
		62–31	10	7	5	1	4	2	3	2
Series: South Africa played 4; W2, L1, D1										

CHAPTER 27

1968

THE SPRINGBOKS HOST THE LIONS
AND TOUR FRANCE

LIONS vs SOUTH AFRICA

Thomas Joseph Kiernan, the experienced Irish fullback, was placed in charge of a team which looked strong on paper. Injuries handicapped the Lions from the start, however, and the loss of Barry John, the Welsh flyhalf, midway through the first half of the first test must have had an incalculable effect on them. Gareth Edwards, the Welsh scrumhalf destined for future greatness, played in only eight matches because of hamstring problems. Edwards, strangely enough, was not all that highly regarded by the majority of his 1968 teammates, who considered him selfish and inclined to 'keep the good ball for himself'. Roger Young, the extremely capable other scrumhalf in the side, was also hampered by injury and their best centre, Gerald Davies, could only play in one test because of torn ankle ligaments.

With Barry John out, Mike Gibson, who was expected to give thrust in midfield, had to play flyhalf and this further disrupted the pattern. In fact, there were so many injuries that three replacements had to be flown over and any assessment of Kiernan's team must be done with all these misfortunes in mind. The final judgement has to be that this was a side which promised more than it delivered.

Their general record was excellent with Transvaal the only provincial side to beat them, but tours are judged on the results of test matches and in these they failed badly. They drew the second test but lost the other three and could score only one try against eight by the Springboks. Take away Tom Kiernan's unbelievable 35 out of the Lion's total of 38 points, and it is painfully obvious that this was a team with an almost total lack of thrust.

The tour was marred by controversy with the Lions' manager, David Brooks, expressing his dissatisfaction with South African referees in such intemperate terms that he harmed rather than enhanced the image of British rugby. Brooks failed to maintain proper discipline in the team and there were several incidents of vandalism and other puerile behaviour. On the credit side, there was little rough play and although John O'Shea, the Cardiff tighthead prop, was sent off the field by referee Bert Woolley in the match against Eastern Transvaal, there was nothing but sympathy for this most likeable player. O'Shea took his punishment with good grace and it was he who gave Woolley a ticket for the third test.

Ronnie Dawson, the Lions' coach and an intelligent, dedicated man, tried but failed to convince his players that there is usually a huge difference between a South African provincial side and the Springbok team. This hard fact of life the undefeated Lions had to discover for themselves in the first test at Loftus Versfeld.

Rodney Gould, the Natal fullback who had been chosen in the place of the injury-ridden, out-of-form HO de Villiers, was the only new 'cap' in the side led

Lions wing Keith Savage (left) aims to get the ball from a breaking scrum in the second test in Port Elizabeth.

by Dawie de Villiers. Dawie's own selection was severely criticized in some quarters but he silenced his critics with an outstanding display.

The Springboks proved to be far too good for the Lions and the final score of 25-20 was not a fair reflection. Tiny Naude, Dawie de Villiers and Frik du Preez scored tries and Visagie added two penalty goals and two conversions while Naude succeeded with two penalty goals. Willie-John McBride scored a try for the Lions and Kiernan, kicking like a machine, put over five penalty goals and the conversion.

Frik du Preez's try was the highlight of the match. Receiving from Myburgh at a lineout, Du Preez slipped round the front, brushing off several half-hearted tackles before bursting clear. Kiernan made an attempt to stop him but the Lions fullback was sent cartwheeling into touch as the great Springbok lock barged over for a try only a player of his unique gifts could possibly have scored.

Springbok flanker Thys Lourens comes round the scrum to follow the pass of Lions scrumhalf Gordon Connell (on ground). To the left is Dawie de Villiers and right is Lions pack leader Jim Telfer.

Barry John suffered a broken collar-bone after a tackle by Jan Ellis midway through the first half and when Mike Gibson replaced him, the Irishman became the first substitute in a test, the new law having just come into effect. Kiernan's 17 points established a record as the most to be scored by an individual in a test against South Africa and the conversion of his first penalty goal, in fact, gave him his hundredth point in internationals.

The second test, in Port Elizabeth, was an awful affair made worse by the haggling over Mr Hansie Schoeman's appointment as the referee. The Lions wanted Walter Lane, of Natal, instead of one of the officials on the panel – Piet Robbertse, Cas de Bruyn, Wynand Malan and Max Baise. The colourful Baise had done well in the first test but the tour management, aware of a ruling that no referee can officiate in more than two tests in a series, wanted to hold him in reserve, for a later occasion. The South African Rugby Board then stepped in and named Schoeman as a compromise appointment.

The Springboks, with Thys Lourens in the place of the injured Piet Greyling, held a territorial advantage throughout the match but one mistake after the other prevented them from scoring. The Lions defended well but their task was made easier by the Springbok threequarters who were slow, unenterprising and guilty of elementary errors. Piet Visagie and Tiny Naude collected a penalty each and Kiernan scored all of his side's points with two penalties.

Jannie Engelbrecht was injured in a friendly match just before the third test at Newlands and was replaced by Gertjie Brynard while Mannetjies Roux returned at centre and Syd Nomis replaced Corra Dirksen. It was Nomis' first test on the left wing but he was to retain this position for the next 22 tests in succession.

For once there was no argument either before or after the game. The Lions were satisfied with Max Baise's refereeing and their forwards with McBride and Peter Stagg particularly effective in the lineouts, held their own for the first time. There was some grumbling over the fact that Gys Pitzer had knocked out his opposite

Scrumhalf Gareth Edwards gets the ball away in a spectacular fashion in preparation for the Lions tour of South Africa in 1968.

All eyes are on the ball as Dawie de Villiers aims to gather from the lineout. From left: J Ellis, J Telfer, R Arneil, R Taylor, G Pitzer, JL Myburgh, P Larter, J Naude, J Pullen, A Horton, referee J Schoeman.

number John Pullin with a punch thrown in front of the grandstand, but Baise was unsighted. The Springboks insisted that Pullin had provoked Pitzer and the Lions' manager, considering the fact that he so readily complained about other matters, was remarkably unconcerned about the incident.

The Springboks clinched the series 11-6 through a good try by Thys Lourens, a penalty goal and a conversion by Visagie and a penalty by Tiny Naude. Kiernan did all the scoring for his team with two immaculately taken penalty goals.

Although the result of the match no longer held much significance, more than 60 000 spectators packed Ellis Park for the final test. They were rewarded by the best rugby of the series, all of it coming from the Springboks.

Visagie only just missed a first-minute try after a good break and Brynard was also called back after the referee, Dr Strasheim, had spotted a forward pass. Except for the lineouts where Delme Thomas, Willie McBride and Peter Stagg did well, the Springbok pack had matters in hand and the backs were given many opportunities. Mannetjies Roux ripped the defence to shreds with a run in which he left Gibson and Kiernan standing and the little Springbok saved a certain try a few minutes later when he tackled Maurice Richards on the line.

A penalty by Kiernan halted the Springbok onslaught for a while but Tommy Bedford, the Springbok eighthman who played one of the best matches of his long and controversial career, attacked from deep in his own half of the field, De Villiers and Brynard came to his aid, and under intense pressure, centre Bresnihan sent a poor kick straight into the hands of Gould who dropped a lovely goal.

After half-time Ellis and Eben Olivier, who for the first time approached the form he showed against France the season before, and Syd Nomis added tries with Visagie converting two of them. Kiernan, scoring all his team's points for the third successive time, replied with a penalty and an entertaining game, played in a fine spirit, ended with the Springboks winning 19-6.

It was hardly a memorable tour but Kiernan's splendid kicking, Frik du Preez's explosive run at Loftus Versfeld, a couple of Tiny Naude's enormous placekicks and the scintillating running of Mannetjies Roux in the final test did give it a few moments of distinction.

South Africa's Rodney Gould kicks for touch. The fullbacks played very well in the tests between the Lions and South Africa.

VENUE	SOUTH AFRICA	RESULT	SOUTH AFRICA				BRITISH ISLES			
			T	C	P	D	T	C	P	D
PRETORIA	WON	25–20	3	2	4	0	1	1	5	0
PORT ELIZABETH	DRAW	6–6	0	0	2	0	0	0	2	0
CAPE TOWN	WON	11–6	1	1	2	0	0	0	2	0
JOHANNESBURG	WON	19–6	4	2	0	1	0	0	2	0
		61–38	8	5	8	1	1	1	11	0
SERIES: SOUTH AFRICA PLAYED 4; W3, L0, D1										

SOUTH AFRICA vs FRANCE

South Africa and France did not have long to wait before they clashed again. Dawie de Villiers' team lost one of the matches against South-West France, South Africa's first-ever defeat on French soil. Jannie Engelbrecht scored five tries in his five matches on the tour, a Springbok record in France. Engelbrecht, South

Africa's best wing for nearly a decade, at the time already held the record for the most tries by a Springbok on a tour of New Zealand established when he notched 15 in 15 matches on the 1965 tour. Piet Visagie, at his match-winning best on this tour, scored 20 points (out of a South African total of 26) against Auvergne-Limousin which is still the highest individual score by a Springbok in France. It was his ice-cool temperament and deadly boot that won the first test at Bordeaux. Visagie placed four penalty kicks to score all of South Africa's points.

The second test, in Paris, was a thriller with the Springboks trailing after first Puget, and then Paries, had succeeded with dropgoals. The Springboks were playing against a cold wind and the French forwards were rampant in the first half. The fearlessness of HO de Villiers under an absolute barrage of up-an-unders and some desperate all-round defensive work, somehow kept the Springbok goalline intact and by the end of the first half some of France's fury seemed to be spent. It was then that Visagie put over a perfectly judged penalty. Just on half-time an incorrect decision by the referee, Paddy d'Arcy, robbed Syd Nomis of a try scored after a well-controlled grubber by the Springbok flyhalf.

Twenty minutes after the resumption, Mannetjies Roux snapped up a rolling ball and after Nomis and Olivier had done their share, Frik du Preez passed to Engelbrecht for one of the best of the eight test tries he was eventually to leave next to his name in the record books. Not long afterwards, Dawie de Villiers broke cleanly from a scrum and ran right through without a hand being laid on him. Visagie converted and then came a try which Syd Nomis must have relived in many a nightmare in the years to come. Eben Olivier tackled Claude Dourthe near the French line and Nomis flashed up to dribble it over the line for what should have been an easy try. Instead Nomis stumbled...fell...struggled up...and fell again as cramp suddenly paralyzed him. As the defence thundered up, Nomis continued his slow-motion progress towards the ball and collapsed on it only in the nick of time. Visagie again converted and the Springboks won 16-11 after a comeback by France had been rounded off with Ellie Cester going over next to the posts.

Marie Bonal falls to the ground but tries to put prop-forward Lassere in possession in the first test, which was eventually won 12–9 by the Springboks in Bordeaux. In the foreground are Frik du Preez, Marcel Puget and Gawie Carelse.

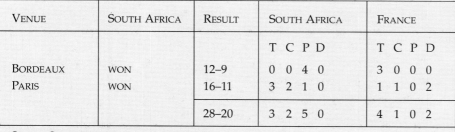

Venue	South Africa	Result	South Africa				France			
			T	C	P	D	T	C	P	D
Bordeaux	won	12–9	0	0	4	0	3	0	0	0
Paris	won	16–11	3	2	1	0	1	1	0	2
		28–20	3	2	5	0	4	1	0	2
Series: South Africa played 2; W2, L0, D0										

The great French lock, Elie Cester, comes away with the ball in the maul with Jean-Paul Baux in support. Springboks crowding in are Hannes Marais, Jan Ellis, Dawie de Villiers and Frik du Preez.

CHAPTER 28

1969

AUSTRALIA TOUR SOUTH AFRICA

▲▲▲

The 1969 Wallabies had problems dealing with the scrums. South Africa won all four tests of the series.

Greg Davis brought the Wallabies team to South Africa in 1969. This time the Springboks won all four tests and the visitors lost 11 out of 26 matches. It was probably the dullest series ever to be played in South Africa

'They came as middleweights to take on the heavyweights,' Maxwell Price wrote in his book *Wallabies Without Armour*, giving an account of the tour. 'They could not shove and batter through in the manner of the robust Springboks; they had no iron front, they lacked the reinforced steel and concrete of rugby where they needed it most. They sorely needed the heavy guns up front to pave the way for the excellent talent behind ...'

It was an accurate summing-up of the tour. The Springboks had simply too much all-round strength and with flyhalf Piet Visagie scoring a record 43 points in the series, the South Africans were never in any danger. Not only did the Wallabies lack the forward power they had in 1963 or, for that matter, when the Springboks met them on their own grounds in 1965, but they also did not have the services of a strategist of the calibre of Catchpole. Johnny Hipwell, their number-one scrumhalf, was a good player but he did not have the incisiveness of his predecessor and was handicapped by the fact that he seldom had the protective screen behind which Catchpole could cook his schemes.

The 1969 tour did produce some highlights, of course – Piet Visagie's marvellous kicking in the tests, for instance, and Rupert Rosenblooms's feat of scoring 11 dropped goals in 14 matches, a record that will take some beating. Altogether the Wallabies totalled 16 dropgoals in their 26 matches, more than any previous touring team in South Africa.

Visagie, Mannetjies Roux, Nomis, Ellis, Engelbrecht and Olivier each scored two tries in the series and it was rather fitting that Engelbrecht scored twice in the second international in Durban, the final test of his career. He scored eight tries in 33 tests, a South African record which he shares with John Gainsford who had played in the same number of tests. A nagging groin injury had handicapped him so much that the selectors had no option but to drop him in favour of Gert Muller for the third test at Newlands.

Frik du Preez was another giant dropped after the second test, but he soon proved the selectors wrong and carried on for another four international series before he decided that he had had enough.

With Dawie de Villiers able to play in only two of the tests, Tommy Bedford substituted capably on the other two occasions. The Wallabies had no counter to the loose-forward combination of Ellis, Greyling and Bedford or the solidity of Myburgh, Pitzer and Marais in the frontrow. With Visagie outstanding at flyhalf,

Olivier and Mannetjies Roux were steady centres and Muller and Nomis always looked better than their opponents. HO de Villiers, at fullback, was invariably in complete control of the situation, but for some inexplicable reason his flair for surprise attack was never exploited.

The Springboks played conventional rugby in the first three tests, with a slightly more adventurous approach in the fourth. They won 30–11, 16–9, 11–3 and 19–8, scoring 13 tries to two and 76 points to 31. It could hardly have been a more convincing triumph but the opposition was too dull and the Springboks too conservative for the public imagination to be gripped.

VENUE	SOUTH AFRICA	RESULT	SOUTH AFRICA				AUSTRALIA			
			T	C	P	D	T	C	P	D
JOHANNESBURG	WON	30–11	5	3	3	0	1	1	2	0
DURBAN	WON	16–9	3	2	1	0	0	0	3	0
CAPE TOWN	WON	11–3	2	1	1	0	0	0	1	0
BLOEMFONTEIN	WON	19–8	3	2	2	0	1	1	1	0
		76–31	13	8	7	0	2	2	7	0
SERIES: SOUTH AFRICA PLAYED 4; W4, L0, D0										

The 1969 Springboks. Back: HO de Villiers, Jan Ellis, Mof Myburgh, Gawie Carelse, Piet Greyling, Hannes Marais, Don Walton. Middle: Jannie Engelbrecht, Mannetjies Roux, Dawie de Villiers, Avril Malan, Tommy Bedford, Frik du Preez. Front: Eben Olivier, Syd Nomis, Piet Visagie. Inset: Piet Uys.

CHAPTER 29

1969/70
THE DEMO TOUR

▲▲▲

With demonstrators chanting messages of hate from the terraces and with tin-tacks and smoke bombs on the playing fields, Dawie de Villiers and his Springboks completed their tour of the United Kingdom in the winter of 1969/70 under conditions no South African team must ever be subjected to again.

The tour will be remembered for the Springboks' dignity and restraint under pressure and provocation, and for the moral courage and determination of their opponents and hosts who refused to be intimidated by the most violent campaign ever to be conducted against a group of sportsmen. It will be remembered, also, for the brave and patient British police-force who bore the brunt of abuse even more directly than the Springboks. Whatever convictions motivated the demonstrators were obscured by their uncouth behaviour; the slogans devalued by their spitting and cursing. Judged against a background of harassment on and off the field, the team's record of 15 wins out of 24 matches with four draws and five defeats is remarkably good. For the first time the Springboks failed to win any of the tests against the Home Countries.

Dawie de Villiers in action during the first match of the 1969/70 tour against Oxford University.

Apart from interference on the field of play which hampered their opponents as much as it did the South Africans, the Springboks had a multitude of other problems. For the sake of security, they had to spend much of their time practically locked up in heavily guarded hotels with bomb hoaxes, picketing and even the attempted hijacking of one of the team buses just before the test against England, disturbing their peace of mind and making proper preparations impossible.

Plain bad luck hounded the Springboks even more relentlessly than the demonstrators did. No less than four players were knocked out of the tour by injury and had to be replaced with substitutes, while several key men were incapacitated at one time or another. Ironically, left-wing Gert Muller, like Hennie van Zyl his predecessor in the same position in Britain in 1961, received news of his father's death while on the tour. He flew home to attend the funeral and then rejoined the side.

The loss of form of Piet Visagie, the team's first-choice placekicker and most experienced flyhalf, was a severe blow. It is conceivable that had Visagie been at his best the Springboks would have done better, as many points were missed through erratic placekicking. Dawie de Villiers, who early on in the tour had converted a penalty goal against Swansea, kicked extremely well against the Barbarians in the final match and he could have used himself more often in this capacity.

The tour management handled a difficult job well although Avril Malan's coaching methods were often criticized. He was pilloried in particular for assigning throw-ins at lineouts to the hookers instead of following the time-honoured practice of letting the wings do it.

Possibly such innovations should not have been imposed on a team already faced with so many difficulties, but Malan has since been vindicated and the throw-in is now automatically part of the hooker's function.

Dawie de Villiers' leadership under such abnormal conditions was faultless and he was admirably backed by Tommy Bedford. De Villiers' instinctive ability to combine tact with firmness contributed immeasurably to the fact that the team never cracked under the pressure and managed to remain dignified and courteous in the face of unbelievable provocation.

Bedford played some of the best rugby of his career and had injury not limited Ellis to only nine appearances, the Ellis–Bedford–Greyling combination might have been an even more decisive factor in the tests. Although Piet van Deventer, Albie Bates and Mike Jennings played consistently well throughout, they were never up to the same standard.

Among the tight-forwards, Hannes Marais further enhanced his reputation as one of the finest frontrankers in world rugby, but generally the Springbok packs found themselves up against teams who were rediscovering the value of solidity up front, a trend which was shortly to enable British rugby to dominate the international arena.

Visagie's poor form gave Mike Lawless the opportunity he had been denied since his unhappy debut against France in 1964, when he was unfairly saddled with all of the blame for an inept performance by most of his teammates. Lawless proved himself to be one of the steadiest players in the side, with an unruffled poise and total mastery of the basic skills of the game.

The Springbok midfield presented several problems throughout the tour. Tonie Roux, although more talented as a fullback, was the most reliable centre available, with JP van der Merwe showing glimpses of promise. Mannetjies Roux, who replaced the injured Johann van der Schyff, did not really have an opportunity to settle down and he played in only one test.

Ten minutes after the start of the London Counties match at Twickenham, a number of demonstrators invaded the field.

HO de Villiers, probably the best player on tour. His adventurous spirit contrasted with the team's uninspired performances.

The four wings, Gert Muller, Andrew van der Watt, Syd Nomis and Renier Grobler were outstanding. Muller, hit by injury and bereavement, played in only five matches, including two tests, but notched five tries with his rare blend of speed and raw power, while Andy van der Watt and Syd Nomis were always dangerous on the attack but even more valuable with their skill and tenacity on the defence. The comparatively inexperienced Grobler, destined to die when three SAAF jet aircraft were destroyed in a multiple crash against the slopes of Table Mountain shortly after the team's return, was not overshadowed by his more famous colleagues and it was a pity that such above-average players were so often starved of opportunities. Van der Watt and Nomis should certainly have been used more often and effectively than they were.

HO de Villiers, after being injured early on in the tour, nevertheless played in 16 out of the 24 matches and established himself, by consensus among opponents, critics and the British public, as the most brilliant player in the side. HO, Ellis, Nomis, Dawie de Villiers and Bedford were singled out by most British rugby writers as the stars of the team, but it was HO who was regarded as the only one without a challenger should a World XV have been selected at the time. HO's only weakness was his inconsistency as a placekicker; throughout his career he was as liable to miss the easiest kick as he was to succeed with the most difficult.

SOUTH AFRICA vs SCOTLAND

The 1969 test against Scotland was won and lost up front where Peter Stagg, at 6'8" probably the tallest man ever to play in international rugby, was virtually impossible to counter in the lineouts. And Frank Laidlaw, with the aid of master scrummager Ian McLauchlan, the future 'Mighty Mouse' of the 1974 Lions, made Charlie Cockrell's debut a miserable one by clearly winning the hooking duel.

It was a scrappy affair, generally, as Piet Visagie and Scottish fullback Ian Smith took turns at missing penalty kicks. Visagie succeeded with one while Smith also had a solitary success in the second half. Less than ten minutes from the end, the Scottish threequarters ripped the South African defence to shreds. Smith took a long pass which left the cover defence with no hope of stopping the long-striding fullback on his way to scoring the try that gave Scotland their 6–3 victory.

SOUTH AFRICA vs ENGLAND

Wallace Reyburn, a veteran New Zealand journalist, once wrote that the only time he had ever seen a referee acknowledging a score while three feet up in the air, was when Kevin Kelleher signalled the try scored against the Springboks at Twickenham on 20 December 1969.

The score came from a maul on the Springbok goalline late in the second half, with the South Africans clinging to an 8–6 lead. England hooker, John Pullin, hovered outside the ruck and when the ball rolled out to Dawie de Villiers, he dived for it. The Springboks vowed that their captain got the touchdown but Kelleher who was perfectly positioned, according to photographs of the incident, gave the decision in England's favour. Bob Hiller's conversion made it 8–11 and although the Springboks tried all they knew, they failed to prevent England from scoring their first-ever win over South Africa. Hiller's team had all the luck in the last few minutes. The ball shaved the upright from a dropkick by Visagie and only the bounce of the ball foiled Van der Watt after a perfect cross-kick by Dawie de Villiers. Bob Hiller, incidentally, made history in this match by scoring England's first-ever penalty against the Springboks in 63 years of playing against each other.

Scotland's full back, Ian Smith, on his way to scoring the decisive try in his side's 6–3 win over the Springboks.

SOUTH AFRICA vs IRELAND

The demonstrators were probably at their venomous worst in Ireland. To quote from *There Was Also Some Rugby*:

'The genuine anti-apartheid demonstrators were surrounded by as fine a rabble as you could wish to see, representing every breed of political and religious trouble-maker, trade union agitators, Sinn Fein, Young Socialists, communists, Britain-haters, Maoists, anarchists ... The switchboard at the Springboks' hotel was jammed by anonymous callers pouring out a flood of obscenities directed against the team, calls which the operators didn't put through, except to give samples to anyone in the hotel who wanted to know why it was so difficult to get the switchboard's attention ...'

Gert Muller scores one of his four tries against North and Midlands of Scotland. He rejoined the Springbok side after attending his father's funeral in South Africa.

Bomb scares were so frequent that the Springboks stopped worrying about such alarms and even after Dawie de Villiers had agreed to being interviewed by Bernadette Devlin, a member of the British parliament who had arrived in Dublin because, in her own (censored) words, 'These ... demonstrators aren't being tough enough with the ... Springboks', there was no relief for the beleaguered South African team.

The famous humorist Spike Milligan, a keen rugby fan, also attended the Springboks' match against Ireland. When the demonstrators recognized him they insisted that he join the parade. Grabbing a megaphone he marched along shouting, 'I'm a fascist bastard! I'm a fascist bastard!' His 'deceit' was eventually discovered, his megaphone confiscated and, as he put it: 'My career as a demonstrator came to an end.'

▲▲▲

The Springbok forwards gave one of their best performances in the test against Ireland, but Dawie de Villiers was off-form and Mike Lawless, Tonie Roux and Mannetjies Roux also made many mistakes. Had this not been the case, Ireland would surely have been beaten as Nomis and Van der Watt were in particularly good form while HO de Villiers, according to Reyburn, 'showed that he was ready to be upgraded from the category of one of the stars of the team to *the* star'.

A poor pass from Mannetjies Roux gave Mike Gibson the chance to send Alan Duggan through for a beautiful try, converted by the veteran Tom Kiernan. But HO cut the lead to only two points by putting over a long-range penalty kick before half-time. This was South Africa's one-hundredth penalty goal in all tests.

With Bedford, Greyling and Ellis working together smoothly and Frik du Preez showing something of the ability that made him one of the greatest forwards of his time, the Springboks seemed certain to clinch the affair in the second half. Greyling duly scored after half-an-hour of narrow escapes for Ireland and HO made it 8–5. This was still the score after the full forty minutes of the second half, but referee

Mof Myburgh tries to secure possession against Wales while HO de Villiers watches in the background.

Grierson allowed an extra eight minutes of injury time. In that last minute Alan Duggan intercepted a wild pass and, when cornered, cross-kicked towards the midfield. Ellis gathered the kick in front of his own posts and, surrounded by Irishmen and with no immediate support, Ellis, rather than concede a try under the posts, had no option but to hold on and to refuse to let the ball go after being tackled. He was penalized, of course, and Kiernan levelled the score, the whistle ending the match immediately afterwards.

SOUTH AFRICA vs WALES

Fortune seldom smiled on the 1969/70 Springboks. The test against Wales was also drawn, and again the equalizing score came in injury time. The Springbok forwards outplayed Wales. Ellis, Greyling and Bedford were superb on attack and defence. As usual in tests between the two teams at Cardiff Arms Park, it rained throughout the game, but there was no wind and both teams were enterprising.

Dawie de Villiers and Mike Lawless split the defence several times, both dovetailing well with Ellis to keep Wales pinned in their own half. A penalty goal by HO de Villiers opened the score, but Gareth Edwards made it three-all at half-time by somehow managing to lift the ball over the crossbar. After the resumption, Ellis broke away on three occasions and the third time Dawie de Villiers and Lawless rounded off the movement to send Nomis over for an unconverted try.

The Celts call it *hwyl* and the word describes that something only Welsh rugby players can draw on when they are fighting the odds. With five minutes to go and doomed to defeat, Edwards and his men launched a series of sustained attacks and it was the Springboks' turn to slither and slide in desperate defence.

In the second minute of injury time Barry John, the famous Welsh flyhalf, kicked deep into South African territory. When the ball came out of the ruck it popped safely into the hands of Gareth Edwards who sliced through a gap to score just in from the corner flag. With the tally at six-all, the final result depended on Edwards' conversion. The Springboks, stunned by the jinx that pursued them throughout the tour, stood with bowed heads and hunched shoulders, hardly daring to look as the Welsh scrumhalf lined up the ball. But the kick was missed and even the referee, Air Commodore GC Lamb, remarked afterwards that it would have been a travesty of justice had the conversion succeeded. The result, a draw, meant that the Springboks stayed unbeaten in encounters against Wales.

SOUTH AFRICA vs BARBARIANS

In the final match of the 1969/70 tour, against the Barbarians, the Springboks struck the form that had evaded them for so long. The two teams, playing in the finest spirit of the game, made sure that at least a few fond memories would remain of a tour that so often resembled a nightmare. David Duckham, Rodger Arneil, Keith Fairbrother and Alan Duggan scored magnificent tries for the BaaBaas while Ellis, who went over twice, and Van der Watt notched tries for the Springboks. Lawless dropped a goal and Dawie de Villiers was on target with

Gareth Edwards is delighted to have scored a try in the dying moments of the test held at Cardiff Arms Park. He missed the conversion, leaving the final score 6–6.

three conversions and a penalty. The second try by Ellis has been called one of the best ever to have been scored by a forward at Twickenham. Grabbing a loose-rolling ball, the flanker dummied twice, leaving several defenders confused and bewildered before he jinked past JPR Williams to cross the line without a finger having been laid on him.

▲▲▲

At a dinner that night, Brigadier Hugh Llewellyn Glyn Hughes, the president of the Barbarian Football Club, made Dawie de Villiers an honorary member, an honour traditionally bestowed on the captains of touring teams to visit Britain.

In two world wars, Brigadier Hughes had won the DSO with two Bars, the Military Cross and the *Croix de Guerre avec palme* among other awards for gallantry and he knew more about bravery than most. Perhaps that is why he took the unprecedented step of presenting each Springbok with a Barbarian monogram, including four extra for the players who had been injured and who had returned home before the end of the tour. It was an old soldier's way of paying homage to courage in adversity.

VENUE	SOUTH AFRICA	RESULT	SOUTH AFRICA							
			T	C	P	D	T	C	P	D
SCOTLAND (EDINBURGH)	LOST	3–6	0	0	1	0	1	0	1	0
ENGLAND (TWICKENHAM)	LOST	8–11	1	1	1	0	2	1	1	0
IRELAND (DUBLIN)	DRAW	8–8	1	1	1	0	1	1	1	0
WALES (CARDIFF)	DRAW	6–6	1	0	1	0	1	0	1	0

The 1969/70 Springboks watch as several demonstrators are cleared off the field at Twickenham in the London Counties match.

CHAPTER 30

1970

NEW ZEALAND TOUR SOUTH AFRICA

▲▲▲

If ever a side looked capable of beating the Springboks on their own fields, it was the one brought out to South Africa by Brian Lochore in 1970. They were the acknowledged world champions and the hard core of 'Unsmiling Giants' who had so convincingly conquered South Africa, Britain and France in the 1960s were still together although two remarkable forwards, Ken Gray and Kelvin Tremain, were missing in the line-up. They steamrollered over one provincial side after the other and players like Meads, Lochore, Strahan, McLeod, Kirkpatrick, Murdoch, Sutherland, Muller, Williams, Thorne, Going and McCormick looked every bit the great All Blacks they were.

Meads suffered a broken arm in a brawl-marred match against Eastern Transvaal and for a while it looked as if he would not play again on the tour. At the same time it seemed as if the All Blacks would hardly need his mighty services to be able to smash the national team with the same ease with which they crumpled the provincial opposition. As it turned out, Meads, with the aid of typical stoicism and an arm guard, did play in the final two tests, but not even he could save his team from the humiliation of losing three out of the four international matches.

Bloodied Piston van Wyk is led from Newlands during the second test between the Springboks and the All Blacks in 1970.

The tests between Lochore's 1970 All Blacks and the Springboks under Dawie de Villiers must, however, count among the most tense, gruelling and desperately fought in the history of rugby in South Africa.

The Springboks won the series, three matches to one. They scored 59 points to 35, seven tries against four. When somebody flips through the rugby record books some 50 years from now, these statistics will make it look as if it was all so easy to achieve. But, as is so often the case, looking at bare statistics can never convey the full story.

The All Blacks' magnificent performances against the provincial opposition and their unbeaten record stretching over five years, all helped to build them up into giants surrounded by an aura of almost mystical invincibility and hardly any hope was held out for the Springboks who had fared so poorly on the demo-plagued tour of Britain.

The Springboks had to prove quickly, to themselves as much as to their gloomy supporters, that the All Blacks were only human. Fittingly, it was skipper Dawie de Villiers himself who opened the first crack in a wall that had looked so impregnable. It happened in the fourth minute of the game. There was a scrum not far from the All Blacks' 25-yard line, the ball was held and Greyling kicked it through and over the try-line. Like a green-and-gold flash, Dawie streaked after it and the try was his. One wonders what the outcome of the series would have been had the All Blacks been the first to draw blood.

From that moment onwards there was confidence in the Springbok team and only three minutes later Joachim Scholtz (Joggie) Jansen, wearing the Springbok jersey for the first time, showed that he, already, was no longer awed by his opponents' reputation.

All-Blacks flyhalf Wayne Cottrell received from a set scrum and, moving to the blindside, he tried to probe for an opening. As he was about to pass, the big Free Stater hit him squarely with a shoulder-first tackle in the midriff and Cottrell was flattened as effectively as if he had been run over by a truck. Cottrell was never the same again and Jansen went on to terrorize the All Blacks midfield in the tradition of Jimmy White and Ryk van Schoor.

When Piet Visagie, who played with flawless efficiency in all four tests, snapped over a left-footed dropgoal on the run, reaching his century of test points in the process, the transformation of the Springboks from a collection of no-hopers into a team of winners, was complete.

Ian McCallum put over a magnificent penalty after Chris Laidlaw was trapped offside. McCallum was to score 35 points in the four tests, breaking Okey Geffin's 21-year-old record, and the All Blacks must have hated the sight of him and his immaculate left-footed placekicking by the time the series was over!

Then there was Bryan Williams' glorious try for the All Blacks when, with hardly any room to move, he beat three Springboks and ran himself right into the hearts of all rugby lovers in South Africa.

A lightning interception and a try by Syd Nomis, and Greyling refusing to show even the slightest sign of the excruciating pain he must have been suffering after a rib injury are other highlights that will always be remembered from the first test. It was the vital match of the entire series for the Springboks; the one they had to win to regain their much-needed self-confidence. And, in winning it, they laid the foundation for taking the rubber.

COLIN MEADS

After his retirement Colin Meads described his feelings on playing in South Africa: 'This is what it has all been about, this is South Africa and these are the players you most want to beat. That is the feeling inside you, as an All Black, when you play in South Africa,' he said. 'If you're ever going to play good rugby, you'll play it in South Africa. The atmosphere demands it of you ... To beat South Africa in South Africa! What a dream it was ...' Springboks, of course, feel the same way about the All Blacks and that is why tests between the two countries have such a special importance. Only once in 55 years of fierce competition have the Springboks been able to win a test series in New Zealand and for the All Blacks such an achievement in South Africa continues to be a dream to be realized some day.

Springboks and All Blacks lock horns again. Hannes Marais charges in and there is nothing All Blacks' wing Bryan Williams (Number 14) can do about it.

Mannetjies Roux is caught jumping on an All Black during one of the tests between the Springboks and New Zealand in 1970.

The second test at Newlands will probably be remembered for the rough play more than anything else. The forwards piled into one another as if they were on suicide missions and there were rucks so fierce that it sickened many in the crowd. From one such maul, Springbok hooker Piston van Wyk was led off the field with blood streaming down his face and onto his chest.

There was the notorious incident when Nomis was knocked unconscious by All Blacks fullback Fergi McCormick, and other ugly moments when the players swung savage punches and aimed brutal kicks at each other with complete contempt for the authority of the referee.

It was a dramatic, exciting match nevertheless, with the Springboks holding a narrow lead after a strong come-back in the second half. Then veteran centre Mannetjies Roux, who was in severe pain after a kick in the back, was judged to have tackled Bill Davis from an offside position and McCormick gave his team a one-point win with a penalty kicked from a comfortable angle.

▲▲▲

The Springboks had their easiest victory of the series in the third test at Port Elizabeth where the highlights were two magnificent tries by Gert Muller and, again, McCallum's kicking.

Muller's first try came after the Springboks had trapped Fergi McCormick with the ball. From the ruck Dawie de Villiers slipped away on a devastating break to send Muller over for his first test try. Later an All Blacks fumble gave Mannetjies Roux an opportunity to set Muller off on another powerful run for his second try. But the match was also unforgettable for the deadly tackle with which Greyling slammed McCormick into the ground with less than a minute gone.

It was a great series for Greyling and his partner on the other flank, Ellis. Their speed to the point of breakdown ruined the All Blacks efficiency in creating second-phase possession, and probably contributed as much to South Africa's triumph as did McCallum's kicking and Dawie de Villiers' inspiring leadership. The third test was a triumph also for Lofty Nel and Mof Myburgh, two veterans brought back by the selectors to a chorus of criticism from the experts and the collection of sportswriters.

The All Blacks had a lot to do with their own defeat. Their selection blunders cost them any advantage they had after their Newlands victory, and the omission of Alan Sutherland up front and the switching of Bryan Williams from wing to centre, were moves welcomed by the Springboks.

▲▲▲

The South Africans went into the final test as favourites to win for the first time in the series. Win they did, but only after more than 80 minutes of pulsating action that left the crowd limp and emotionally drained. Two players dominated the game, Ian McCallum for South Africa and Gerald Kember for New Zealand. Between them they scored 28 of the 37 points on the scoreboard.

When the All Blacks frontranker Jazz Muller incurred the disapproval of referee Bert Woolley and 65 000 Ellis Park spectators, Dawie de Villiers flipped the ball to his fullback with instructions to give his forwards a breather. McCallum decided he might as well give the All Blacks a fright in the process. He lined up for the target nearly 65 yards away – the longest penalty kick he had ever attempted.

The huge crowd was silent as McCallum's leg swung until the boot hit the ball. The follow-through was unfettered and complete. Then came the roar, first only from those sections where the unerring flight could be spotted and finally from all sides of the stadium as the flags shot skywards to salute one of the greatest placekicks in the history of the game.

In addition to McCallum's spectacular placekicking, one cannot forget Piet Visagie's clever break and try or Gert Muller's bulldozer run after Jansen had toppled Kember with a dive-bombing tackle – one that had a very definite bearing on the outcome of the match. The score was 17–14 and the All Blacks forwards, playing with frenzied fury, were in the ascendancy. Then Kember came into the line from full-back and the next instant Jansen hit him with such force that the ball jumped out of his hands. Mannetjies Roux, a supreme opportunist, was there to snap it up, make the defence hesitate and then pass to Muller. Muller, a compact bundle of muscle with the speed to match his power, beat two defenders on his way to score – a mortal blow to New Zealand's hopes of salvaging the series. Bryan Williams provided yet another memory to treasure when he picked up a pass from Sid Going and ran straight through with impudent ease for a try behind the posts.

And perhaps the most memorable scene of all ... The final whistle and captain Dawie de Villiers, his mission accomplished, had time for one little jump of joy before he was lifted high in triumph by his teammates. Seconds later hundreds of spectators poured onto the field and, swaying precariously but happily on many willing shoulders, the Springbok heroes were carried to the dressingroom.

As Nelson said after the battle of the Nile: 'Victory is not a name strong enough for such a scene.'

The veteran Mannetjies Roux displayed magnificent form against the 1970 All Blacks. He played in all four tests.

VENUE	SOUTH AFRICA	RESULT	SOUTH AFRICA				NEW ZEALAND			
			T	C	P	D	T	C	P	D
DURBAN	WON	16–7	2	1	1	1	1	0	1	0
BLOEMFONTEIN	LOST	9–15	0	0	3	0	1	1	2	1
CAPE TOWN	WON	15–10	1	1	2	1	1	0	2	0
JOHANNESBURG	WON	15–14	1	1	2	1	2	0	1	1
		55–46	4	3	8	3	5	1	6	2
SERIES: SOUTH AFRICA PLAYED 4; W3, L1, D0										

CHAPTER 31

1971

VICTORY UPON VICTORY

▲▲▲

The French side runs onto the field for one of the two test matches played against the Springboks. The first was won by South Africa and the second ended in a draw.

FRANCE vs SOUTH AFRICA

In 1971 France paid a short visit to South Africa when Christian Carrere brought out a strong side with one of its members, Roger Bourgarel, a nine-day wonder because he was the first black player to be seen in action against the Springboks on a South African field. The novelty soon wore off and the slightly built wing will be remembered not for the colour of his skin but for twice having stopped Frik du Preez in full cry for the line.

▲▲▲

The South Africans won the first test in Bloemfontein 22–9 with the immaculate left boot of Ian (Mighty Mac) McCallum contributing 13 points. It was the thirty-fourth test match for Frik du Preez, one of the most colourful and most idolized Springboks, and for a few dramatic seconds, it looked as if the big Northern Transvaal lock would score a try to celebrate the fact that he had become the most-capped South African up to that time.

It was Bourgarel who somehow knocked him off balance on the corner flag and the large Free State crowd expressed their absolute approval of his courage in no uncertain terms. To have tackled Frik du Preez under any circumstances took a very brave man indeed; to have stopped him at full speed in a test bordered on the foolhardy!

The best player on the field that day, however, was a member of the losing side. Benoit Dauga, the French eighthman, gave a magnificent performance but it was not enough to win the day for his country.

▲▲▲

The second test in Durban was spoilt by an ugly brawl midway through the first half. It erupted shortly after Jo Maso had to leave the field after being crash-tackled from behind by Joggie Jansen. His replacement, Dourthe, climbed into McCallum immediately after play resumed and he kicked the Springbok fullback who was nowhere near the ball. Greyling sped to McCallum's aid and a general free-for-all ensued with both teams equally guilty of disgraceful behaviour.

The fighting was eventually stopped but flared up again briefly, before good sense prevailed for the rest of the match which was bitterly contested but conducted more or less according to the rules. The result was an eight-all draw and Frik du Preez was foiled for a second time by the tenacious Bourgarel. This time the Springbok had actually shaken off three opponents and was pounding towards the tryline when Bourgarel got hold of his jersey and slowed him down long enough for the cover defence to bring him down.

Venue	South Africa	Result	South Africa				France			
			T	C	P	D	T	C	P	D
Bloemfontein	Won	22–9	2	2	3	1	1	0	2	0
Durban	Draw	8–8	1	1	0	1	1	1	0	1
		30–17	3	3	3	2	2	1	2	1
Series: South Africa played 2; W1, L0, D1										

SOUTH AFRICA vs AUSTRALIA

In 1971 a Springbok team boarded a Boeing 707 to tour Australia. For the first time the Wallabies would not just be fitted in during a stopover on the way to New Zealand. The 13-match itinerary provided for three tests and there was no doubt that Hannes Marais was given the best available team. Political demonstrators, backed by the Australian trade unions, made almost as much noise as they did on the 1969/70 tour of the United Kingdom, but a rather tougher reaction from the police prevented them from being a destructive force. The Springboks, many of whom were veterans of the campaign in Britain, learnt quickly enough to accept the situation with wry amusement and the demonstrations hardly affected them.

Ian McCallum kicks as Morné du Plessis watches in the 1971 test against Australia. Captain Hannes Marais' side won all three tests on the tour – the last for Frik du Preez before his retirement.

For the first time in history a Springbok team completed an overseas tour without a single defeat. They scored 76 tries, 42 conversions, 24 penalties and four dropped goals for a total of 396 points. Their opponents totalled 102 points with the Springbok goalline crossed on only 11 occasions.

Hannes Marais kept team morale at a high level, and Johan Claassen and Flappie Lochner, the coach and manager respectively, fitted well into the picture. Tommy Bedford and Gert Muller returned home after being injured early in the tour, but in both positions the reserve strength was more than adequate.

Hannes Viljoen, the Natal wing, notched five tries against Western Australia and ended up with a tour total of 16 in ten matches. Ian McCallum, Piet Visagie and Dawie Snyman scored 84, 55 and 54 points respectively.

The Springboks played attractive rugby, without undue frills. Attacks were launched from solid foundations, but there were plenty of opportunities and encouragement for individualism. One of the six tries scored against New South Wales, virtually an international combination, illustrates how Marais and his men managed to blend the correct with the bright. This is how Kim Shippey described it in his book *The Unbeatables*:

'Ian McCallum started it within his own "25", reaching out to retrieve an impossible ball as it floated towards the members' stand.

'He got it, cleverly kept his balance, and then, instead of belting the ball down the touchline, he opened up across field to his left. Hannes Viljoen took over and further unsettled an already shaken defence.

'Then Hannes Marais came inside Viljoen to take a pass to the right. The Springbok captain showed a turn of speed we didn't know he possessed. It was as though he had a smoke bomb in his pocket. Now the forwards were in command.

A demonstrator is 'encouraged' to leave the field during the match between South Africa and New South Wales in Sydney.

They swept infield with Marais shovelling the ball into the safe hands of Piet Greyling ... In support of him was the long-striding newcomer, Morné du Plessis. No one doubted for a moment that he would hold the pass. He took it with outstretched arms 15 yards from the line and dived for the far left corner. At the celebration dinner that evening Charles Blunt (president of the Australian Rugby Union) described it as the greatest try he had ever seen. "What's more," he said, "it was the most complete exhibition of rugby football I have ever experienced." '

With the exception of Theo (Sakkie) Sauermann who was replaced in the frontrow by Martiens Louw after the first test, South Africa kept the same combination for the series. They were: Ian McCallum, Hannes Viljoen, Joggie Jansen, Peter Cronje, Syd Nomis, Piet Visagie, Joggie Viljoen, Martiens Louw, Piston van Wyk, Hannes Marais (captain), Piet Greyling, Frik du Preez, John Williams, Jan Ellis and Morné du Plessis. There were strong challengers for several of the positions, of course, with Thys Lourens rather unlucky not to have been selected.

Joggie Jansen breaches the Australian defence in the third test in Sydney. His side completed a 13-match tour with 13 wins and won the test 18–6.

The Springboks won the first test with tries by the two Viljoens and Ellis, two conversions and a penalty by Ian McCallum and a dropped goal by Visagie (who also put over a penalty to give the Springboks an 18–6 victory in the final test).

Frik du Preez, that living legend of South African rugby, announced before the last test in Sydney that he intended retiring and Marais, with typical thoughtfulness, asked him to lead the Springboks onto the field for the game.

At a team function to celebrate the successful end to the tour, Flappie Lochner, Johan Claassen and Hannes Marais made moving speeches and then everybody turned to Frik du Preez. But after 38 tests and six overseas tours during which he earned almost as big a reputation for his ready wit as his amazing ability, the veteran could find nothing to say.

He leant against a wall, turning a beer can slowly between his fingers as his teammates waited in silence. And as Kim Shippey wrote:

'In silence they showed their respect for him, and in silence he acknowledged their adulation. It was the most eloquent non-speech I've ever heard ...'

VENUE	SOUTH AFRICA	RESULT	SOUTH AFRICA				AUSTRALIA			
			T	C	P	D	T	C	P	D
SYDNEY	WON	19–11	3	2	1	1	1	1	2	0
BRISBANE	WON	14–6	3	1	1	0	0	0	1	1
SYDNEY	WON	18–6	3	3	1	0	1	0	1	0
		51–23	9	6	3	1	2	1	4	1
SERIES: SOUTH AFRICA PLAYED 3; W3, L0, D0										

CHAPTER 32

1972

ENGLAND TOUR SOUTH AFRICA

▲▲▲

During the cold northern hemisphere winter of 1969 the Springboks toured Britain. The next contact with a team from the Home Countries in South Africa took place in 1972, when John Pullin brought an England side out on a short tour. The visitors were not highly regarded after poor performances in the Five Nations tournament of the previous season, but they remained undefeated throughout a seven-match tour and scored an 18–9 victory over South Africa at Ellis Park in the only test.

They also made history by meeting a team of coloured players from the South African Rugby Federation in Cape Town, and a black team in Port Elizabeth, setting a precedent for future touring teams to follow.

Piet Greyling led a combination of Springboks who seemed hopelessly unsure of themselves. Dawie Snyman collected all the South African points with three

John Williams, one of South Africa's superb lineout jumpers, bears the bloody badge of uncompromising test rugby.

penalties but several easy kicks were fluffed. England, with unspectacular competence, grabbed every scoring chance. Fullback Sam Doble converted a try by wing Alan Morley and booted four penalties to establish the highest points total by an individual player in tests between the two countries since Dougie Morkel scored six points for Billy Millar's Springboks in 1913.

The alarm bells were ringing for South African rugby but a loud chorus of excuses muffled the sound and precious few heard it.

England, who always had a grand record for fulfilling fixtures, however inconvenient it might be, then went on a tour of New Zealand the following year, lost all their matches before the test and won the test. This was a remarkable record, especially in the context of the later fate of Home Unions teams visiting the Southern Hemisphere.

The SAARB side selected to play England in Port Elizabeth. Back: N Singapi (manager), J Wani, D Njadu, M Ndzala, M Jacobs, J Doyi, W Xotyeni, P Danster (assistant manager). Middle: C Songogo, O Nkwandla, H Kethelo, W Diba, M Cushe, A Balintulo, L Ntshongwana, T Magxala. Front: B Mawni, S Cushe, N Mbiko (captain), C Sigwanda, J Dolomba.

VENUE	SOUTH AFRICA	RESULT	SOUTH AFRICA				ENGLAND			
			T	C	P	D	T	C	P	D
JOHANNESBURG	LOST	9–18	0	0	3	0	1	1	4	0

CHAPTER 33

1974

DESTRUCTION AND RECONSTRUCTION

▲▲▲

LIONS vs SOUTH AFRICA

Willie-John McBride's 1974 Lions became the first touring team to beat the Springboks in a four-match series in South Africa in 78 years. The final test was drawn but the Lions won the first three with convincing ease. McBride and his magnificently drilled team could well have been the best side ever to visit South Africa but they were made to look even better by Springboks who always seemed to be on their heels; demoralized and disorganized.

Georges Mazzocut, an impartial observer from France, commented in *L'Equipe*:

'The price of a Springbok skin, once so highly valued, is of very little value at this time ... who wants a goat's head above his mantlepiece?' – a harsh statement, perhaps not entirely fair to either the brilliant Lions or the embattled Springboks, but with enough truth in it to hurt.

The greatness of the 1974 Lions cannot be denied. It was a team without weakness from frontrow to fullback; led by an outstanding captain in McBride, coached by a dedicated man in Syd Millar, and guided by tour manager Alun Thomas.

They were a new breed of Lions. The sound fundamentals were no longer being sacrificed for flair and individualism but had instead been elevated to the point of prime importance. Millar believed in the old truism that tests are won in the

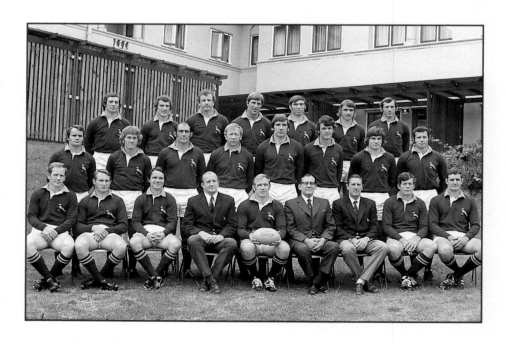

The South African team for the first test against the British Lions, played at Newlands. South Africa lost 3–12.

frontrow and that cohesion up front is essential. He had played in South Africa on three tours and, by his own admission, had acquired the Springbok approach to the game. He had noticed a defect in the South African philosophy but kept it to himself. Throughout the team's preparation in England and in South Africa before the tour actually started, he had stressed the difficulty of the task ahead. 'To beat the Springboks in their own country is more difficult than beating the All Blacks in New Zealand,' he had constantly warned. 'Conditions in New Zealand are similar to those we are used to. On South Africa's hard fields and under that bright sun, the ball will behave a lot more strangely.'

Millar's efforts ensured that no Lions team had ever been better prepared for a tour of South Africa.

In the third test against the British Lions at Boet Erasmus Stadium in Port Elizabeth, South Africa lost 9–26.

McBride provided the leadership that gave the team the character and dedication no amount of coaching could have brought. Millar and McBride came from the same club, Ballymena, and they shared the same attitude, the same desire to avenge the humiliating defeats they had endured together on previous tours.

British rugby had undergone a transformation since the lack-lustre days of 1968. It was better organized and officials, players and coaches had become more concerned with winning than ever before. The first fruits of the new approach were plucked when they beat the All Blacks on their own fields in 1971. McBride's men, in spite of undertaking the tour in the face of the official government disapproval and the vociferous criticism of anti-South African factions, were proud, almost arrogant, in their self-confidence.

John Gainsford, the great Springbok threequarter of the 1960s, summed them up best when he told sportswriter Neville Leck:

'They were mentally tougher, physically harder, superbly drilled and coached and disciplined and united. They were dedicated fellows who were trained to peak fitness, who were prepared like professionals and who were ready to die on the field for victory. They were rugged, even ruthless competitors who played their rugby to win and who were not squeamish about resorting to obstruction, gamesmanship and even the use of their fists and boots to achieve their end.'

The thorough preparation must have been one of the main reasons why the team suffered so few serious injuries on the tour. Alan Old, the England flyhalf was incapacitated by a late tackle against the Proteas, but not before he had scored 37 points against South Western Districts, a record for an individual player in a single match on a tour of South Africa.

Veteran Mike Gibson had to be flown over to join the team, and that was the only time the tour management had to call for aid. Gordon Brown, an outstanding lock, suffered a broken hand in the third test and had to be replaced by Chris Ralston for the final international, while Phil Bennett played in the third test with

The Lion meets the Leopard – Scotland's Andy Irvine, playing for the Lions, with Leopards' captain, Thompson Magxala.

Carel Fourie, a strong and aggressive wing, looks to pass as he is tackled in the match against France in 1974.

a foot so badly gashed that he had to leave the placekicking to Andy Irvine who had replaced Billy Steele on the wing. An indication of how seriously the Lions approached their task was the fact that they were all fitted out with special gum shields and knee guards and that they also took two 'slow sodium' tablets a day to counter salt loss in South Africa's hotter climate.

But all the preparation in the world cannot make world-beaters out of mediocrities and in the final analysis the 1974 Lions were successful because there was such an abundance of talent. Hannes Marais, who was brought from retirement to lead the Springboks, afterwards admitted that it took the Springboks until the final test before they could counter the Lions in the scrums where Ian McLauchlan proved to be the finest scrummaging technician ever to visit South Africa.

McLauchlan was regarded by the Springboks as the 'brains' of the Lions' pack and he, hooker Bobby Windsor and the massive Fran Cotton formed an invincible frontrow. Gordon Brown was the best lock on either side throughout the series and McBride, apart from his inspiring leadership, was nearly as solid. Fergus Slattery, Roger Uttley and Mervyn Davies made up a formidable loose-forward combination and used the sound springboard provided by their hardworking colleagues to wreak destruction among their opponents' halves and threequarters.

Behind that magnificent set of forwards the Lions enjoyed the services of the best scrumhalf in the world, Gareth Owen Edwards, an international player whose long and quick passing, speed and strength on the break and marvellous tactical kicking, had his opponents groping blindly throughout the series. Phil Bennett was nearly as brilliant at flyhalf where he always gave the impression of a man knowing what he intended to do and his place- and dropkicking made him one of the finest match-winning flyhalves to have visited South Africa.

Centres Dick Milliken and Ian McGeechan were reliable but John James Williams, 'JJ', was not a Commonwealth Games sprinter for nothing. His speed and intelligence on the field made him one of the most potent attacking weapons in McBride's armoury. His total of four tries is the most by any player in a series against South Africa, and is only one short of the record number scored by Theunis Briers in 1955. Andy Irvine, who took over from Billy Steele on the right-wing in the last two tests, was also a player of exceptional talent and his eclipse of Gert Muller underlined not only his skill but also his courage.

Edwards might have been the outstanding star of the team but JPR Williams, the tall Welsh fullback with the long, flowing hair and the distinctive white sweatband was not far behind. John Peter Rhys Williams spelt danger for the Springboks every time he touched the ball and with his weight and pace he sliced through defenders as if they didn't exist. Williams, like Edwards, was the best player in his position in the world in 1974. He played with supreme confidence and his aggression on at least one occasion led to a potentially explosive situation. The punches he rained on Tommy Bedford's face after a tackle in the match against Natal nearly caused a riot when some spectators invaded the field to avenge the attack.

The Lions never hesitated to use their fists or boots when they felt it necessary and at their captain's call of 'ninety-nine' just about every member of the team would select an opponent and start belabouring him. 'We will take no prisoners' and 'Let's get in our retaliation first' were phrases often used in team talks and one report in *L'Equipe* referred to the third test as *un combat de rue*, a fight in the street.

McBride and Millar, remembering previous visits to South Africa, had primed their men to expect the hardest games of their lives. It must have come as an anti-climax to these highly motivated competitors when the Springboks proved to be nowhere near as tough as expected.

After ten minutes of the first test, played at Newlands in muddy conditions, Millar predicted that his team would win the series. It took him only that long to realize that the South Africans, who had been masters of scrummaging for so long, had forgotten the art. Edwards could cook up all sorts of tricks behind his scrum while his forwards held the Springboks in the proverbial vice. In the light of subsequent events the Springboks actually fared reasonably well in the first encounter. Three penalty goals by Bennett and a drop by Edwards, against a drop by Dawie Snyman, made up a score of 12–3 in their favour.

South Africa have possession in the second test against the 1974 British Lions, held at Loftus Versfeld. South Africa lost 9–28.

The South African selectors became panicky and made the first of many mostly inexplicable changes which were to lead to 33 different players being used in the four tests; 21 of them gaining their colours for the first time. It was certainly not the best method of building a team with the hope of beating the Lions. The second test was lost 9–28, South Africa's biggest-ever defeat, and no less than 11 changes were made for the next international.

The selectors at this stage seemed to have lost control of the situation. There certainly was no reason to axe John Williams, the best lineout forward in South Africa, or to go into the third test without any mobility up front. With both scrumhalves, Roy McCallum and Paul Bayvel, injured the selectors, with an astonishing lack of logic, chose Gerrie Sonnekus in preference to experienced specialists like Barry Wolmarans or Gert Schutte. Sonnekus, an eighthman who played briefly as a scrumhalf and subsequently successfully returned to the scrum at provincial level, was literally thrown to the Lions. After doing reasonably well in the first half, the Springboks crumbled and were beaten 9–26, the second-biggest defeat in South African rugby history! It was the roughest test of the series with both sides dishing out and taking fearful punishment, and it was hardly surprising that the Springbok lock, Moaner van Heerden, who had a fiery first half, was so badly injured that he had to be replaced by Kevin de Klerk. In the second half the Lions more or less did as they pleased against a Springbok team who had run out of steam.

The selectors were more conservative when they chose their team for the final test and minimal changes were made. There was some continuity and pattern for the first time and the Springboks responded by holding the Lions to a 13-all draw. For once the Lions, who were beginning to lose their motivation, were not quite so slick, and by swinging the scrum the Springboks were occasionally able to put Edwards under pressure. It was a dramatic, controversial test and the 75 000 spectators who paid a record R500 000 were at least spared the sight of seeing the Springboks humiliated as they were in the second and third internationals.

The referee, Max Baise, had an afternoon of agonizing decisions and he left the field at the end of the match with Phil Bennett on his heels, hurling abuse at him.

Baise's disputed decisions affected both teams, however, and a draw was probably the best result. Uttley was awarded a try which the Springboks felt should not have been given. Chris Pope, the South African right-wing, was quite adamant that he had dotted down before the Lions flanker could get to the ball and a photograph published later supported his claim. It showed Pope putting the ball down with Uttley still in the process of diving for it.

In the final minute of the match, JPR Williams launched a fantastic run which split the Springbok defence before he passed inside to Slattery. As Slattery dived for the line, Peter Cronje slammed into him and it appeared as if the Lions flanker had pressed the ball on the Springbok centre's thigh instead of grounding it. The referee was unsighted and, according to the rules, he gave the Lions a five-yard scrum instead of a try. They were extremely upset about the decision and some outright insults were directed at Baise. Cronje, who had scored the Springboks' only try of the series earlier in the match, after a powerful burst by Pope, afterwards said that he had also thought that Slattery should have been given the score. Referees are only human and if Baise did indeed err on both counts, the one mistake cancelled out the other and the result remains a fair one.

The final test gave the Springboks some compensation but the Lions were emphatically the better side in the series and it was South Africa's most comprehensive defeat since Bill MacLagan's pioneers made a clean sweep back in 1891.

VENUE	SOUTH AFRICA	RESULT	SOUTH AFRICA				BRITISH ISLES			
			T	C	P	D	T	C	P	D
CAPE TOWN	LOST	3–12	0	0	0	1	0	0	3	1
PRETORIA	LOST	9–28	0	0	2	1	5	1	1	1
PORT ELIZABETH	LOST	9–26	0	0	3	0	3	1	2	2
JOHANNESBURG	DRAW	13–13	1	0	3	0	2	1	1	0
		34–79	1	0	8	2	10	3	7	4
SERIES: SOUTH AFRICA PLAYED 4; W0, L3, D1										

Moaner van Heerden watches out for developments as the French forwards fight for possession.

SOUTH AFRICA VS FRANCE

Hannes Marais took a rather subdued Springbok team to France. They won both tests, 13–4 and 10–8, and were beaten only once when West France defeated them on a muddy ground. Nevertheless, the Springboks were not entirely convincing. French rugby was also going through a crisis period as their defeats against Rumania, Ireland and Wales had proved.

The emergence of Morné du Plessis as a mature international player was one of the few benefits of the tour, and Robert Cockrell and Moaner van Heerden also showed signs of developing into test players of the highest class. The tour ended the career of Marais and had it not been for the solitary defeat at Angouleme, he would have gone into retirement with the unique distinction of being the only Springbok captain ever to have led undefeated teams on two overseas tours.

Among the backs Dawie Snyman was often brilliant, sometimes erratic. Willem Stapelberg was an unqualified success and Carel Fourie, on the other wing, did well enough and also proved to have a good boot for long-range penalties. Johan Oosthuizen and Ian Robertson showed glimpses of real class but Gerald Bosch, a match-winning kicker, too seldom revealed the other attributes expected of an international fly-half. His provincial scrumhalf Paul Bayvel had a good tour but he was certainly not a new Dawie de Villiers.

Stapelberg's try in the first test at Toulouse was the highlight of the tour. This is how Neville Leck described it in the *Cape Times* afterwards:

'In the nineteenth minute of the game Johan Oosthuizen kicks ahead. A French defender catches the ball but is promptly flattened by Marais. The Springbok forwards pour in over the ball, bunched together in a tight green knot. The ball spews back from the heaving Springbok machine and in a flash Paul Bayvel has spun the ball to Gerald Bosch and Bosch is flipping it

South African wing, Chris Pope, kicks the ball ahead during the Springboks' tour of France in 1974.

inside to Jan Ellis. It is a perfect pass. Ellis rips through the gap, hammers forward, 10, 15, 20 yards. He is stopped, but his trusty packmates roar in behind him, forming a perfect wedge. The ball shoots back again. This time Morné du Plessis, running at top speed, takes it and throws out a perfect pass to Ian Robertson. Robertson lets go immediately to Dawie Snyman who had slipped into the Boks backline like a shadow. Snyman waits just long enough to draw Roland Bertranne, then lets go. Next thing, Willem Stapelberg, given the overlap, has blazed the remaining 15 yards and dived into history ...'

There were minor political demonstrations against the visit of the Springboks and the team was frequently criticized for being 'anti-social'. Several of the matches were extremely rough and Carel Fourie was the man the spectators loved to hate, the role filled for so long on overseas tours by Mannetjies Roux. After a few of the tougher matches, the Springboks were described in several newspapers as 'buffaloes' and a 'savage horde', and one sportswriter claimed that they were a poor side who had to choose between 'finesse and force, and chose force'. Nobody took these charges very seriously as rugby in France is never a garden party.

VENUE	SOUTH AFRICA	RESULT	SOUTH AFRICA				FRANCE			
			T	C	P	D	T	C	P	D
TOULOUSE	WON	13–4	1	0	3	0	1	0	0	0
PARIS	WON	10–8	1	0	2	0	2	0	0	0
		23–12	2	0	5	0	3	0	0	0
SERIES: SOUTH AFRICA PLAYED 2; W2, L0, D0										

CHAPTER 34

1975

FRANCE TOUR SOUTH AFRICA

▲▲▲

Morné du Plessis watches as Klippies Kritzinger bursts away with the ball.

Five months after South Africa toured France, the two countries met again – this time in South Africa. It was to be a short but strenuous tour with eleven matches, including two tests, crammed into less than a month. Most of the top French players could not make the trip and their sportswriters, with their rather typical tendency to exaggerate, described the touring team as a gathering of lambs destined to be slaughtered. They *were* beaten, but it was no slaughter of the innocents, and 1975 became a particularly significant year in South African rugby history.

The simple announcement of the team established a record of some sort when not one, but two captains were appointed. Richard Astre and Jacques Fouroux were both given equal responsibility and authority, and although the touring party seemed to be definitely divided into two camps, the unprecedented set-up seemed to work. The team of largely untried youngsters adapted with remarkable ease and, probably because most French players are so well-schooled in the basics, they revealed astonishing versatility. Jean-Pierre Romeu scored 71 points on the

Kleintjie Grobler on the charge against France at the Free State Stadium in Bloemfontein. South Africa won 38–25.

tour, the highest individual total by a French player in South Africa, beating the aggregates of legendary match winners Pierre Albaladejo and Guy Camberabero.

Two mileposts in South African rugby history were reached during the tour. During the second test in Pretoria, Gerald Bosch, often criticized for his general performances at flyhalf but undoubtedly the most consistently accurate place-kicker of his era, scored 22 points to notch the highest individual total by a Springbok in an official international match.

And when Morné du Plessis, the Western Province eighthman, was given the Springbok leadership, it was the first time that the son of a Springbok captain had followed in his father's footsteps and earned the same honour. Morné s father, Felix, led South Africa in three winning tests against the All Blacks in 1949.

The two tests were both handled by Norman Sanson, a London-based Scot – the first time that a neutral referee officiated in South Africa.

The first test, in Bloemfontein, was a strange affair with the Springboks winning 38–25 for an amazing match aggregate of 63 points. It equalled the world record match aggregate established when Wales beat France 49–14 in 1910. At one stage the Springboks led 35–9 but then they inexplicably lost their grip and the French forwards came into their own. The South Africans were never in any danger of losing but their slump in the last 20 minutes cast a shadow over the brilliant first 60 minutes of the match when players like Dawie Snyman, Johan Oosthuizen, Peter Whipp, Gerald Bosch, Paul Bayvel, Kleintjie Grobler, Robert Cockrell, Moaner van Heerden, Kevin de Klerk and Morné du Plessis were outstanding.

▲▲▲

Brawling marred the second test, at Loftus Versfeld, and there was a fearsome toll of injuries. Moaner van Heerden was taken off the field in the sixty-ninth minute with his cheek flayed open and his hand fractured, while French forwards, Michel Palmie, Robert Paparemborde and Patrice Peron, all had to receive medical attention for chest and rib injuries.

The first 20 minutes after half-time were as torrid as any in the history of the game, but the Springboks kept their cool a little better than their opponents and deserved their 33–18 victory. Referee Sanson awarded no fewer than 34 penalties. Bosch succeeded with six and also converted tries by Fourie and Du Plessis. Carel Fourie also slammed over a massive penalty from the halfway line.

The turning point of the match came after Moaner van Heerden had left the field. Instead of trying to take violent revenge, the Springboks controlled themselves while the Frenchmen continued with their mad-dog tactics, conceding three successive penalties with futile fouling. Bosch converted the first two into points and Carel Fourie made sure of the third. It spelt the end of France's challenge.

FRANCE vs SA INVITATION XV

In 1975 the French team made history by, apart from playing against the Leopards and the Proteas (pictured), becoming the first team to play a South African Invitation XV selected from all races. The match took place at Newlands on 7 June 1975, when Morné du Plessis led a team, which included two players from the Proteas and two from the Leopards, to a thrilling 18–3 victory. These four pioneers will always have a special place of honour in rugby's hall of fame. They were Morgan Cushe, lively, if smallish, flanker, Toto Tsotsobe, driving wing, John Noble and Harold (Turkey) Shields, who could hold his own in most frontrows. South Africa's first-ever racially mixed team played well and a packed Newlands gave Noble a stirring ovation when he followed up a cleverly placed grubber by Dawie Snyman to score. It was South African rugby's first glimpse of a new dawn, heralding an era which could lead to achievements matching and perhaps even surpassing those of the past.

VENUE	SOUTH AFRICA	RESULT	SOUTH AFRICA				FRANCE			
			T	C	P	D	T	C	P	D
BLOEMFONTEIN	WON	38–25	5	3	4	0	4	3	1	0
PRETORIA	WON	33–18	2	2	7	0	1	1	3	1
		71–43	7	5	11	0	5	4	4	1
SERIES: SOUTH AFRICA PLAYED 2; W2, L0, D0										

Paul Bayvel kicks the ball over the scrum in a test against France in 1975. South Africa won both matches of the series.

CHAPTER 35

1976

NEW ZEALAND TOUR SOUTH AFRICA

▲▲▲

When Andy Leslie brought his All Blacks to South Africa in 1976, Morné du Plessis was the obvious choice for captain, with Thys Lourens his only serious challenger for the job. Lourens, Northern Transvaal's shrewd leader, a sterling player and a man of fine character whom fortune often treated unkindly, had his age counting against him and it is doubtful whether he or any of the others mentioned at the time were ever seriously in the race. The issue was settled once and for all when Du Plessis inspired his Western Province team to a thrilling win over the All Blacks at Newlands.

The Springboks won the series 3–1 but the All Blacks were distinctly unlucky in the final test and, instead of jubilation, South Africans were left with a vague feeling of unease. Not enough was accomplished, either against France the previous season or against New Zealand, to completely dispel the gloom caused by the appalling performances against the 1974 Lions.

The tests were hard and merciless in the accepted tradition of clashes between these two implacable rivals but, with rare exceptions, there was no enterprise from behind the scrum. Barry Glasspool, then sports editor of the *Sunday Times*, summed it up in *One in the Eye*, a book he wrote after the tour:

'Total commitment to the capabilities of a freakishly brilliant goalkicker (Gerald Bosch) whose form otherwise had slumped alarmingly, but who operated behind a screen of aggressive forward play, meant that the exciting talents of runners like Gerrie Germishuys, Peter Whipp and Johan Oosthuizen were largely exploited.

'With the exception of that breathtaking first test try by Germishuys which rounded off a backline thrust of sheer uncomplicated artistry, the Springboks hardly put together another worthwhile backline move for the rest of the series.'

The Springbok forwards did a sound enough job against the All Blacks. Moaner van Heerden, Jan (Boland) Coetzee, Kevin de Klerk and Morné du Plessis were always good, frequently outstanding, and the Transvaal frontranker Johan Strauss was of inestimable value in the crucial third test at Newlands. Threequarters like Whipp, who was dropped for the second test for no apparent reason, Oosthuizen, Germishuys and Pope were neglected. Bayvel had an erratic season while Bosch lacked the delicate judgement required of an international flyhalf.

Looking only at the records, there is no doubt that Bosch was the deciding factor in the 1976 series, played between two teams who were otherwise so evenly matched. He scored 33 out of the Springboks' total of 55 points and the lack of a goal-kicker of his stature was the All Blacks' biggest weakness. With 89 points scored in only nine tests, the important role he played in Springbok rugby in the mid-1970s cannot be minimized whatever criticism might be levelled at him.

Gerald Bosch, South Africa's prolific point-scoring flyhalf, kicks off against the 1976 All Blacks in the first test, in Durban.

The Springbok side for the third test against the All Blacks, held at Newlands. South Africa won the match 15–10.

Controversial refereeing decisions cast a shadow over the tour but the All Blacks had only themselves to blame. The South African Rugby Board offered them the services of neutral referees but their own authorities had declined, probably because acceptance would have created a precedent, with future touring teams to New Zealand expecting the same privilege.

The wrangle after the final test left a particularly sour taste. Throughout the match the All Blacks showed their annoyance with Gert Bezuidenhout, a referee whom they had praised after they had won the second test, had criticized after they had lost the third, and were prepared to draw and quarter long before his whistle ended the final test.

When Oosthuizen prevented Bruce Robertson from chasing a rolling ball he might well have reached in the in-goal area before the covering Bosch and Whipp, the All Blacks expected a penalty try. Bezuidenhout was not certain that Robertson would have got to the ball before the defence and, according to the rules, he gave New Zealand a penalty instead. It was the final straw as far as the All Blacks were concerned and Leslie, who had proved to be a most tactful tour captain until then, bluntly described the match as a 'hollow Springbok victory' in a television interview immediately after the game.

The anger was understandable as many judges agreed that a penalty try should have been awarded but the general dismissal of their defeats as being mainly due to refereeing decisions can never be accepted. The All Blacks also received their share of penalties which could have been converted into points, but both Sid Going and Bryan Williams were erratic and the tour management seemed to have no confidence in Laurie Mains, the only specialist kicker in the party.

Sid Going and Doug Bruce formed a most capable halfback combination while Peter (Pole) Whiting was the best lock-forward on either side. Ian Kirkpatrick was still an outstanding flanker in spite of his age and Joe Morgan, Duncan Robertson and loose-forward Kevin Eveleigh were consistently competent. Bryan Williams

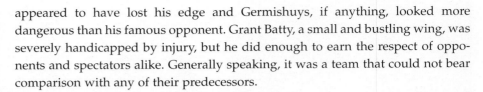

Paul Bayvel passes the ball from the scrum, while touch judge Piet Robbertse takes a breather in the background.

appeared to have lost his edge and Germishuys, if anything, looked more dangerous than his famous opponent. Grant Batty, a small and bustling wing, was severely handicapped by injury, but he did enough to earn the respect of opponents and spectators alike. Generally speaking, it was a team that could not bear comparison with any of their predecessors.

▲▲▲

The Springbok backs gave their best performance in the first test, held in Durban, when Germishuys scored a try to remember after everyone, from Bayvel to Roberstson (who had slipped into the line from fullback), had done his job with passes as swift and precise as could be found outside the pages of a text book.

A slashing break by Bayvel initiated the Springboks' other try of the match, scored by Edrich Krantz, after the young Free Stater, making his international debut, had kept his head as he snapped up a flicked-away ball on the try-line.

Ian Robertson, who substituted for the ailing Dawie Snyman at fullback, put over a dropped goal to crown a quite outstanding display and Bosch, who had been ill during the week preceding the test, added a penalty and a conversion to make the final score 16–7. The Springbok flyhalf, in fact, had to be replaced by substitute De Wet Ras a few minutes before the end.

Lyn Jaffray scored New Zealand's sole try after a superbly individualistic effort from Batty, while Bryan Williams contributed a penalty to his team's total. Although the score indicates a convincing victory for the Springboks there was actually little to choose between the two sides. Only tremendous work on the defence halted the powerful drives by the New Zealand forwards.

▲▲▲

Sid Going prepares to feed the ball to his backs. He is being watched by Boland Coetzee and Morné du Plessis.

The Springbok selectors wielded the axe with abandon when they selected the side for the second test in Bloemfontein. Whipp was dropped and Robertson, a success at fullback, was pushed into his place at centre to allow the out-of-form Snyman to return at fullback. Krantz, who had done well in his debut, was dropped for the more experienced Pope, while Jan Ellis had to make way for Martinus Stofberg, a 21-year-old Free State forward of immense, if raw, potential. Ellis had played in 38 tests and shared with Frik du Preez the distinction of being the most-capped Springbok ever.

The All Blacks never looked like losing the second test. Going was at his best and, apart from nursing the pack and backs, he scored two penalty goals and a conversion. He also harassed the life out of his opposite number, Paul Bayvel. Morgan broke through for an excellent try and Bruce, making good use of Going's impeccable service, dropped a goal. All the Springboks could produce were three penalty goals by Bosch.

It was an even more bruising, and far less enterprising, test than the first one and the Springboks lost their best lineout forward, John Williams, with a gruesome nose injury in the second half. He was replaced by Kevin de Klerk and the big Transvaal lock made sure of his place for the rest of the series with a furious display. The Springboks were generally subdued, however, and too many key players faltered and fumbled for them to be a serious threat at any stage of the match.

▲▲▲

South Africa won the vital third test at Newlands because of a truly great performance by Morné du Plessis who so inspired his team that they erased the bad memory of their groping incompetence at Bloemfontein. Play was rough to the point of being vicious and Du Plessis afterwards looked as if he had fought a losing battle for the world heavyweight championship. But, then, hardly a player came out of this match without scars of some sort or other. The Springbok frontrow of Rampie Stander, Piston van Wyk and Johan Strauss, as well as the second-row men, De Klerk and Van Heerden, were magnificent while Coetzee, with typical courage, skill and sheer doggedness, gave a rampaging Du Plessis all the support he needed. Even the young Stofberg, in company as rough as he could possibly encounter, showed that he was not a boy trying to do a man's job.

Oosthuizen, with a try after a perfectly timed interception, Bosch with two penalties and a conversion, and a dropgoal three minutes from the end by Snyman gave the Springboks their 15 points. Robertson, with an opportunistic try after Germishuys had got himself in a tangle near his own line, and Bryan Williams, with two penalties, made up the All Blacks' total of 10 points.

John Williams, Gerald Bosch (Number 10) and Boland Coetzee close in as the All Blacks fight to secure possession.

▲▲▲

John Reason, of the London *Daily Telegraph*, summarized the fourth test:

'The final test of this series was, sadly, a game which is all too typical of international rugby. It was a brutally hard, bludgeoning business, repeatedly interrupted by stoppages for deliberately inflicted injuries. It contained the minimum of movement and there were blood and bandages everywhere ...'

Prolonged complaining about the referee and some of his decisions overshadowed the Springboks' 15–14 victory and it was repeatedly claimed that the South Africans had been lucky to have won. It is true that the All Blacks scored two tries to one and that Bosch with two penalties, a dropgoal and a conversion, had made all the difference. Going and Kirkpatrick scored tries for the All Blacks while 'Klippies' Kritzinger went over for the Springboks' only try. But Morné du Plessis put it in perspective: 'Sure we were lucky, but I've also played in games where the opposition has been lucky. It's part of the game ...'

▲▲▲

It is a pity that the 1976 series could not have ended on a more positive note. After all, when the two teams disappeared into the tunnel under the grandstand at Ellis Park, the curtain closed on what will one day be known as only an era in our rugby.

VENUE	SOUTH AFRICA	RESULT	SOUTH AFRICA				NEW ZEALAND			
			T	C	P	D	T	C	P	D
DURBAN	WON	16–7	2	1	1	1	1	0	1	0
BLOEMFONTEIN	LOST	9–15	0	0	3	0	1	1	2	1
CAPE TOWN	WON	15–10	1	1	2	1	1	0	2	0
JOHANNESBURG	WON	15–14	1	1	2	1	2	0	1	1
		55–46	4	3	8	3	5	1	6	2
SERIES: SOUTH AFRICA PLAYED 4; W3, L1, D0										

Piston van Wyk, Morné du Plessis and Johan Oosthuizen move across to stop a New Zealand attack.

Manager of the South African side for World Cup 1995. Morné du Plessis guided the Springboks to victory in the final.

MORNÉ DU PLESSIS

They called him all sorts of things. The French called him the 'Windscreen Wiper'. Nasty people called him 'Maureen' because they believed he was a softy, but after an incident with Klippies Kritzinger at trials they called him 'Meanie', and northern dislike grew after he tackled a fair-haired boy called Naas in a vital Currie Cup match. And his team at the World Cup called him 'Ruggles' after the cartoon giraffe mascot of the 1995 World Cup.

The whole country knew him as Morné. There was no need to add the surname. He became a household name, a familiar brand standing for many good things. It is the greatest tribute possible to a hero - when his surname is redundant. In modern rugby it has been reserved for men like HO, Naas, Li and Chester.

Morné du Plessis stood for many good things at rugby. It was not surprising that he was a leader as he came from a family of sporting leaders. His father, Felix, captained South Africa at rugby in 1949 when they whitewashed the All Blacks, and Pat du Plessis, a Springbok hockey captain, sat in the stand heavy with the baby who would be christened Morné. Pat's brother, Horace Smethurst, in his time captained South Africa at soccer. Morné became the first son of an international captain to captain his country at rugby. It was just one of his achievements.

Schooling for Morné was at Grey College, the great factory of rugby players in Bloemfontein. There he shone more at cricket than rugby and eventually played

Morné du Plessis shakes off the attentions of Sid Going before passing to Western Province scrumhalf, Divan Serfontein. Du Plessis guided the side to a thrilling triumph over the 1976 All Blacks and then led South Africa to victory in the series.

The ball eludes Morné du Plessis in a test against the 1976 All Blacks. He led his team to a 3–1 series' victory.

cricket for Western Province. From Grey he went to Stellenbosch, making his educational credentials as a rugby player impeccable. There Dr Craven took a personal interest in him from the start, shifting him from lock to number-eight where he would achieve his greatest fame.

He played for Western Province Under-20, as a lock, then for Western Province at the age of 20, from 1970 to 1980. In 1971 he was chosen for the Springbok tour to Australia. When Tommy Bedford dropped out through injury, he was chosen at number-eight for the test team, playing with greats like Frik du Preez, Hannes Marais, Piet Greyling and Jan Ellis. That Springbok team did not lose a match on the tortured tour of many demonstrations against South Africa's apartheid.

Morné's career as a rugby player moved rapidly. He was an accepted leader of men, captaining Western Province 103 times in 112 matches and captaining South Africa 15 times in his 22 tests. He captained the Springboks to victory over the French in 1975 and 1980, the All Blacks of 1976 and the Lions of 1980. When he retired the nation was shocked – as if a great hero had died. MORNÉ RETIRES, the hoarding proclaimed. Dr Craven remained convinced that if Morné had stayed on the Springboks would have won the test series in New Zealand in 1981.

After his retirement he dabbled perfunctorily in rugby football, a man acceptable to all sections of rugby's community. Then came the World Cup in 1995 and Morné was appointed manager of the Springbok team - dignified, thoughtful, innovative and committed. His controlled ecstasy in victory was wonderful to behold, an example of a real sportsman.

Morné du Plessis has achieved greatly in rugby. And he could continue to do so, because he is a man of international stature.

CHAPTER 36

1977

THE WORLD'S CONSOLATION

▲▲▲

Louis Moolman, Robert Cockrell, Daan du Plessis and Piet Veldsmann watch Barry Wolmarans gather the ball. In the background is Willie-John McBride (wearing the white headband).

WORLD XV vs SOUTH AFRICA

To celebrate the opening of the reconstructed Loftus Versveld, Northern Transvaal invited a large number of outstanding players from all points of the compass to Pretoria in 1977. An afternoon of festival rugby was fittingly climaxed by a match between the Springboks and a World XV.

It was to be South Africa's sole and only too brief whiff of international rugby between the departure of the 1976 All Blacks and the amazing season of 1980 when doors which had appeared to be closed for ever suddenly swung open.

The match against the World XV has been accepted as an international encounter but for all the official recognition it enjoyed, it lacked the intense commitment which is such an integral part of rugby confrontation at the highest level.

The World team comprising magnificent individuals brought together for the occasion, understandably lacked cohesion. For the Springboks there was at least the knowledge that they were wearing the traditional green-and-gold to spur them to greater effort.

With so much talent on the field, it was hardly surprising that the game developed into a superb exhibition of skill and speed, with the motivation and the combination of the Springboks providing the winning edge. In the years to come the match will be remembered for the wonderful try scored by the Free State wing, Hermanus Potgieter, and the precise kicking of the Western Province flyhalf, Robbie Blair, who contributed five penalties and three conversions to the Springbok total of 45 points. Blair's 21 was only one point short of Gerald Bosch's record for a South African player in a test, established against France in 1975.

A final score of 45–24 in an international match can only indicate that defence and prudence were sacrificed for other considerations. It was nevertheless a worthy occasion in our rugby history – an afternoon in which old bonds were strengthened and new ones were fostered.

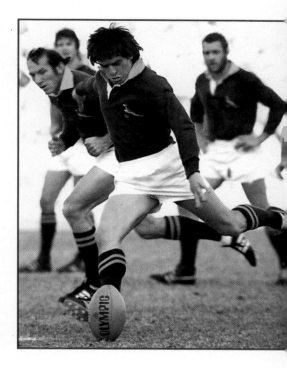

Robby Blair kicks at goal during the match against the World XV. He is being watched by Gerrie Germishuys, Morné du Plessis and Louis Moolman.

VENUE	SOUTH AFRICA	RESULT	SOUTH AFRICA				WORLD XV			
			T	C	P	D	T	C	P	D
PRETORIA	WON	45–24	6	3	5	0	4	4	0	0

The dark ages followed; more than two years of disappointment as the Springboks disappeared from the international calendar, years in which they became immune to snubs and accustomed to the moralizing of societies and systems reputedly more perfect than theirs. It should have been so easy to give up; to accept that there is no place for the Springboks among the righteous and to withdraw from the risk of further insult.

There is no knowing what would have happened had Dr Danie Craven not been at the helm of rugby in South Africa. His enormous stature in the rest of the rugby world ensured that the channels of communication remained open. Craven accepted the challenge of crisis and, drawing on all of his formidable intellect and seemingly limitless energy, he guided, prodded and often drove South African rugby along the course to re-acceptance.

Craven was often misunderstood; sometimes maliciously by those to whom his international fame is anathema and as frequently by the well-intentioned to whom the horizon is nevertheless not always immediately clear. He had that rare capacity of being a man of action as well as vision and such men have to break the eggs to make the omelette, leaving many snipers in their wake. Craven made mistakes, of course, but in the final analysis it was his voice in the international chambers and corridors of power which kept South African rugby going when it seemed as if all hope was lost.

In spite of squabbles and unnecessary controversy, great strides were made to eliminate racial discrimination in rugby in South Africa and the progress was genuine enough to impress members of the four Home Unions Committee who visited South Africa in 1977 and 1978. This led to several important club sides from Britain accepting invitations to tour the following year and their reports on the changing situation were extremely favourable.

The man behind the South African Barbarians was Chick Henderson, the Transvaaler who had played rugby for Scotland. Henderson had played for the British Barbarians and on his return to South Africa was brought onto the committee of the Quaggas, a group with the Barbarian spirit that had been founded by Cyril Biggs in 1957. In Natal, Basil Medway and Nick Labuschagne got the Barbarians going and approached the Quaggas, located in Transvaal, to take over the administration. This led to the formation of the Quagga Barbarians who became known simply as the South African Barbarians, an honourable team.

If it had not been for the 1979 tour by that team, the British Lions would not have come to South Africa in 1980. The Home Unions were considering aborting the tour for 1980.

It was at this point that the committee made the all-important decision to invite a South African Barbarians team to Britain and Ireland. The intention was obvious. They wanted to prove, to the British rugby public at least, that white and black do play together in South Africa and to make this point there was never any question of the side being selected on merit. There had to be equal representation for white, black and coloured: eight players from each group, regardless of ability. The clear wishes of their hosts presented no problems to the South African rugby authorities who shortly before had suffered a crushing disappointment when the French government had bluntly refused to allow a fully fledged tour by the Springboks.

Bombarded with protests from the anti-apartheid lobby, the British government reacted predictably. Dawie de Villiers, former Springbok scrumhalf and captain, who was then South Africa's ambassador at the Court of St James, was informed that there would be no official condoning of the proposed tour and Hector Munro, the Minister of Sport and, incidentally, an ex-president of the Scotland Rugby Union, officially asked his former colleagues to withdraw the invitation. It was a severe test of strength of the ties of loyalty between the four Home Unions and the South African Rugby Board which, in international terms, meant Danie Craven. The bonds held and in a remarkable display of resolution, the British rugby authorities ignored the official disapproval and arranged seven matches: three in England and two each in Scotland and Wales.

It was a low-key tour by largely untested players and yet a special place in South African rugby annals must be reserved for the 1979 Baa-baas. Their task was delicate and tough, with an overriding responsibility to their country and hosts which, in retrospect, must have been frightening at times to the team management.

Chick Henderson proved to be a perfect choice as manager, ably assisted by Alfred Dwesi, and with Dougie Dyers as coach. Henderson had all the

Daan du Plessis, Nick Bezuidenhout and Louis Moolman watch Jean-Pierre Rives collar Dirk Froneman.

qualifications for the job. A South African who had represented Scotland nine times as a loose-forward, he fitted easily into the British milieu and his comfortable affability was the perfect foil for the implacable aggression shown by anti-apartheid leaders. More than that, Henderson was never anything but completely frank. He did not gloss over the problems which still had to be overcome to remove racial discrimination in South African rugby but preferred to underline the quite dramatic progress which had been made, and his transparent honesty in this respect made a powerful impact on all those who were prepared to listen before they condemned.

The team gave their manager all the support he needed. There was absolutely no friction in the side and, more importantly, no patronizing either. The team played excellent but relaxed rugby against some of the strongest club sides, winning four, drawing one and losing two of their fixtures. Players such as Errol Tobias, Hennie Shields, Hannes Meyers, Solomon Mhlaba and Pompies Williams blossomed in good company while Rob Louw, Martiens le Roux, Divan Serfontein, Gawie Visagie, Tim Cocks and De Villiers Visser proved to be well up to international rugby standard.

Tobias, who first shone at 21 in the Proteas team which toured Britain in 1971, had moments of sheer brilliance at flyhalf and he laid the foundation for his future selection as the first black Springbok. Almost as good on occasion was the centre Hennie Shields, who developed into a most effective partner for the versatile Gawie Visagie.

In the match against Cornwall in Camborne, Morgan Cushe became the first black ever to captain a representative South African team, bringing a rare warmth to cold statistics.

The South Africans encountered none of the violent demonstrations which made the 1969/70 Springbok tour of the United Kingdom such a horrifying experience and Henderson had good reason for his optimistic statement that 'this (tour) has shown the progress made towards integration in South African rugby and it will open many doors'. So it did. Not long afterwards, a Lions tour of South Africa was announced and the inevitable outcry was just beginning to gain momentum when Russia invaded Afghanistan and protests against playing rugby in South Africa became politically unprofitable.

Made wary by so many sad disappointments, most South Africans still feared the worst and in spite of Craven's optimism for the future, few believed that 1980 would really see the end of a three-season drought. But Craven was right. The Springboks were about to return to the international arena.

Robbie Blair kicks against the World XV in the only game that he played for the Springbok side.

CHAPTER 37

1980

RECALLED TO LIFE

▲▲▲

From the moment it became clear that the Springboks were to return to international rugby in 1980, no one looked further than Morné du Plessis to lead the team. A captain was needed who could cope with pressure which went far beyond the game itself, and Du Plessis was obviously the man for the job.

In all other respects the strength of South African rugby was an unknown factor at the beginning of the 1980 season. There was a sprinkling of survivors from the 1974 and 1976 international series but most of the key positions would have to be filled by players who had no knowledge of real test rugby. Morné du Plessis with 14 caps was the most experienced international player in the country, followed by Moaner van Heerden with 11, Kevin de Klerk with eight and Peter Whipp and Gerrie Germishuys with six each.

The South African Rugby Board managed to squeeze in a short tour by a South American team to give Butch Lochner and his fellow selectors a chance to see the candidates handle themselves under fire.

Had it not been for the two tests against the Jaguars the Springboks might have lost the series against the Lions. The South Americans were ideal sparring partners to help the Springboks in their preparation. All but four of the touring party of 26 were Argentinian, but to avoid political implications they carried the banner of their continent rather than their country.

South African team for the first test in Cape Town. Back: Richard Prentis, Rob Louw, David Smith, Willie du Plessis. Middle: Divan Serfontein, Gysie Pienaar, Ray Mordt, Martiens le Roux, Willie Kahts, Naas Botha. Front: Moaner van Heerden, Theuns Stofberg, Butch Lochner (manager), Morné du Plessis (captain), Nelie Smith (coach), Gerrie Germishuys, Louis Moolman.

SOUTH AMERICA vs SOUTH AFRICA

By 1980 Argentina had earned their spurs in international rugby. Their recent record was impressive: they had drawn a series with Australia, drew internationals with England and France and lost a test against Wales by a single point. In addition they beat powerful club sides like Cardiff and Newport.

The Jaguars' tour was preceded by brief visits from San Isidro, Argentina's leading club team, and a combined side from the universities of Buenos Aires. They did not do all that well and there was a tendency in some circles to underrate the South Americans. This over-confidence soon evaporated when they averaged nearly five tries per match in their four outings leading up to the first test.

Porta's Jaguars were a lively lot and at their most dangerous just when it appeared as if they were fighting a lost cause. The records show that the Springboks won both tests by comfortable margins but the real facts tell a different story. There was never a moment at either Wanderers or King's Park when the South Africans could afford to relax.

Nelie Smith, who had done so much to make Free State the force it became in Currie Cup competition in the 1970s, received his due reward when he was appointed Springbok coach for what was to be one of the most strenuous seasons in rugby history.

The decision to give the job to Smith, the Rugby Board's national director of coaching, led to problems with the international authorities who argued that he was a professional. The point had to be conceded eventually but Smith (like Ian Kirkpatrick, a fellow selector who was full-time coach for Transvaal) was given dispensation for the season and, working closely with Butch Lochner and Morné du Plessis, proved to be invaluable to the Springboks.

The first test was allocated to Johannesburg but, with Ellis Park in the process of being rebuilt, the game had to be played on the Wanderers cricket ground. The national selectors relied heavily on the previous season's Currie Cup form and there were no shocks or even mild surprises in the first test team.

Six others were to make their international debut. Pierre Edwards was a fully justified choice at fullback although he was soon to make way for the most exciting player of the year. Edwards, whose wraith-like appearance on the field earned him the nickname 'The Pink Panther' had received the votes of 47 out of 51 rugby writers the previous season as the best fullback in the country and the subsequent scramble among the experts to claim discovery of Gysie Pienaar was amusing. Ray Mordt came in on the wing and selection of the Northern Transvaal halfback combination of Naas Botha and Tommy du Plessis presented itself as an obvious move.

It is rare for South Africans not to have at least one controversial player to squabble over. In 1980 the target for adulation and vilification was Hendrik Egnatius (Naas) Botha. From the time he made his debut for Northern Transvaal at the age of 19, the flyhalf attracted the attention of detractors, who, while conceding that his match-winning kicking was little short of miraculous, saw nothing but gaps in the rest of his make-up.

A war of words was to rage throughout the 1980 season although there could hardly have been any real doubt that Botha could not be left out of the test sides. By the end of the year and with a string of test victories behind him, Botha's judgement was beginning to match his natural skill. It made sense to give Botha his provincial partner, the strongly-built Tommy du Plessis, as scrumhalf in his first test. Du Plessis, in spite of being somewhat erratic, made a career out of protecting the 'golden boy'.

Rob Louw, Hempies du Toit and Robert Cockrell enjoy a drink on the 1980 tour to South America.

WILLIE DU PLESSIS

Willie du Plessis, a 24-year-old student at the University of Stellenbosch, became the 500th Springbok and, in the process, underlined the remarkable importance of his university as South Africa's rugby nursery by being the 110th Matie to earn the green-and-gold.

Richard Prentis, Transvaal's loosehead prop who never touched a rugby ball until after his school-days at Pietersburg, and the Western Province flanker Rob Louw were the only newcomers to international rugby in the scrum, although it must be added that Louis Moolman's experience was limited to the match against the World XV. The Northern Transvaal lock-forward was by far the best lineout specialist in the country.

▲▲▲

The first test was action-packed and although the Springboks won 24–9, their performance did not augur that well for the hurdles to follow. The Jaguars did well up front with the South Africans struggling in the lineouts and the scrums. The biggest shock of all came when eighthman Gabriel Travaglini scored his side's only try after the Springbok forwards had been pushed over the line. Although comparatively light, the Jaguars had an excellent scrumming technique, binding particularly well and timing their shove to a nicety.

Tommy du Plessis and Ray Mordt joined the select band of Springboks who could boast of a try in their first tests while Gerrie Germishuys also went over for a good start to what was to be a golden season for him. Naas Botha succeeded with three conversions, a penalty and a dropgoal to Porta's conversion and penalty.

Ken Rowlands, from Wales, took charge of both internationals against the Jaguars and, later in the season, Jean-Pierre Bonnet and Francis Palmade, of France, controlled the series against the Lions.

▲▲▲

Rob Louw, who must surely be one of the fastest forwards ever to play for South Africa, moves in on a Jaguar player in the two-match test series played in South Africa. On the right is Hugo Porta (Number 10).

The Springboks beat the Jaguars 18–9 in the second test, at King's Park, Durban, but had it not been for Botha's boot it might have been a different story altogether. Travaglini and Silva inspired the South American pack to unexpected heights and at times the heavier Springbok forwards were pushed off the ball at will. The defence on both sides was relentless and the only try of the day came when Morné du Plessis went over near the posts. The inclusion of Daan du Plessis, the Northern Transvaal tighthead at the expense of Johan Strauss meant that there were no fewer than four players named Du Plessis in the Springbok team for this test.

Juan Piccardo, playing at centre for the Jaguars, scored all of his team's points in the match by putting over three penalties.

Naas Botha was in devastating kicking form. He managed to convert his skipper's try, succeeded with a penalty, and, with almost casual ease, lifted over three dropgoals which must have driven his opponents to despair.

Shortly before the end of the match Edwards had to be carried off the field with severe concussion and his place at fullback was taken by Gysie Pienaar. Pienaar grabbed the unexpected opportunity and brought a noticeable sense of purpose into the Springbok team. Before the end of the 1980 season, he was to be the hero of the South African rugby fans and rated by his opponents as probably the best fullback in the world.

▲▲▲

Most of the critics and authorities were dissatisfied with the Springboks' performance in the second test and dire things were predicted for them against the Lions. Two men disagreed. Luis Gradin, the Jaguars' coach, claimed that it was the best performance by a South American team in fifty years and that the Springboks deserved praise for having won. Dr Danie Craven agreed and he repeated what he had said before the tour: 'If the Boks can beat the Jaguars, they'll beat the Lions.'

There is no doubt that the visit of the Jaguars provided the preparation the Springboks needed for the Lions. The tour brought back the feel of international rugby and at the end of it all there was just enough criticism and public doubt to promote determination and team spirit.

Springboks Theuns Stoffberg, Willie du Plessis, Rob Louw and Morné du Plessis pressurize the Jaguars.

Venue	South Africa	Result	South Africa				South America			
			T	C	P	D	T	C	P	D
Johannesburg	won	24–9	3	3	1	1	1	1	1	0
Durban	won	18–9	1	1	1	3	0	0	3	0
		42–18	4	4	2	4	1	1	4	0
Series: South Africa played 2; W2, L0, D0										

LIONS vs SOUTH AFRICA

Billy Beaumont, an amiable Lancastrian who had impressed the hard-bitten All Blacks when he went over to New Zealand as a replacement lock-forward in 1977, led England to winning the triple crown and the grand slam in 1980 and was duly rewarded with the captaincy of the Lions team to South Africa a few months later. Beaumont was a member of the North West Counties side which visited South Africa in 1979 and was a sound, if unspectacular, player and a captain who was to set a fine example with his unfailing courtesy and tact. Syd Millar and fellow-Irishman, Noel Murphy, did an excellent job as manager and coach respectively.

Theuns Stofberg watches as John Robbie clears the ball in the fourth test of the series. The Lions won 17–13.

British rugby has certainly changed since the glorious days of 1955 when the spirit of adventure dominated. In the 1970s emphasis switched to the forwards, and while they had the services of players like Gareth Edwards, Phil Bennett and JPR Williams behind their powerful forwards, teams from the United Kingdom became very difficult to beat. There was no one of that exceptional calibre in the 1980 team to take advantage of good work done up front, with the result that there was an over-dependence on the so-called rolling maul and forcing the second-phase, and a consequent predictability the Springboks frequently exploited.

The Lions seemed frightened to move the ball away from the set pieces, probably because their loose-forwards lacked pace for effective cover and their backs lacked incisiveness of thought or movement. On the defence, in particular, the Lions were downright clumsy on too many occasions. In mitigation it must be argued that no touring team had ever had such bad luck as Beaumont's Lions. Injuries forced them to ask for no fewer than eight replacements. In fact, they needed a replacement before the tour started when Andy Irvine failed to pass a fitness test! Irvine joined the side later but was erratic for such a brilliant player.

The loss of stars like Stuart Lane (within the first minute of the first tour match), Gareth Davies, Mike Slemen and Fran Cotton undoubtedly weakened them and must surely have forced a great deal of re-thinking of tactics and approach. The Lions won all 14 of the fixtures outside of the tests, several of them cliff-hangers which were only decided in the closing minutes. Amazingly though, they had no difficulty in beating Northern Transvaal and Western Province, the strongest provincial teams. Their 37–6 victory over Western Province was the biggest defeat suffered by South Africa's oldest union since John Hammond's team beat them 32–0 in 1896, but certainly the Lions' finest moment came in the closing minutes of the match against a South African Invitation XV at Ölen Park, Potchefstroom, on 21 May.

The home players were leading 19–16 when David Richards, at flyhalf, broke from his own 22-metre line to take play deep into the opposing half. He was stopped but the Lions won the ruck and continued the attack. They won four more rucks in succession and heaven knows how many players handled before Mike Slemen rounded off an incredible movement with a try under the posts.

With Peter Whipp, the most experienced and sophisticated centre in the country, troubled by injury, the South African selectors included David Smith as Willie du Plessis's partner in the midfield for the first test at Newlands on 31 May.

Pienaar was an obvious choice after his display as substitute for Edwards in the final minutes of the second test against the Jaguars. Tommy du Plessis was going through one of his bad patches and Divan Serfontein was drafted into the side to link with Naas Botha. Dave Fredrickson had conceded too many tightheads against the Jaguars, and he was predictably replaced by Willie Kahts, the Northern Transvaal hooker, while the frontrow was further strengthened by the inclusion of Martiens le Roux on the tight-head side. Moaner van Heerden took over from Kevin de Klerk, a see-saw situation these two lock-forward contemporaries became used to during their careers.

▲▲▲

The Newlands test turned out to be one of the most exciting internationals in the history of the tradition-rich arena. Minutes after the start, Derek Quinnell sent Morné du Plessis staggering with a foolish and totally unwarranted punch which

Bill Beaumont, one of the best captains England has had, led the British Lions on their 1980 tour to South Africa.

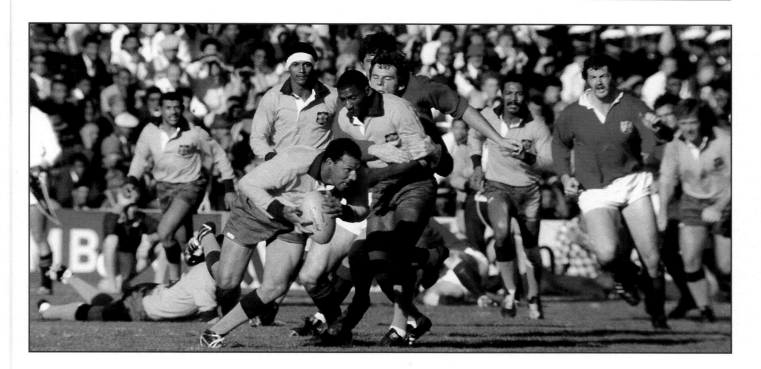

all but closed the Springbok captain's eye. With the level-headedness which marked the closing years of his career there was to be no retaliation and the tone was set for the most incident-free international tour in decades. Billy Beaumont must get his share of the credit for this. Throughout the series this most charming of men played his heart out without ever forgetting the true spirit of sport.

The match followed an amazing pattern. The Lions' forwards held the edge but the backs did not seem to know what to do with the ball. The Springboks, on the other hand, showed exceptional flair on the attack and they made the most of every opportunity, being particularly quick to counter their opponents' fumbles.

Rob Louw's speed and remarkable power for his build gave the Springboks their first try and from then on it was a question of whether the home team could score enough tries to stay ahead of Tony Ward's impeccable place-kicking. Ward, a rather ordinary flyhalf in other respects, succeeded with five penalties and a dropgoal for a personal tally of 18 points. Graham Price scored the Lions' only try.

Willie du Plessis and Van Heerden went over for tries while Germishuys stunned all those who had little faith in the sureness of his handling, by taking an awkward pass somewhere above his head at full speed and scoring a try to dream about. Throughout the 1980 season Germishuys was to play with wonderful self-confidence and at the end of it all he had earned the right to take his place among the best wings in history. In the meantime, Naas Botha added three conversions but, with hardly any playing time left, the score was 22-all. It would have been a crying shame had the Springboks failed to win this match and justice was to prevail. A thrilling Springbok drive brought play right up the goalline. Louw popped the ball to Serfontein and the scrumhalf dived over to make the final score 26–22.

▲▲▲

With the exception of De Klerk for Van Heerden, the same Springbok team tackled the Lions in the second test in Bloemfontein two weeks later. This was a match that will always be remembered for a superlative exhibition of attacking fullback

Maurice Colclough wins possession for the Lions in a lineout during the first test. Theuns Stofberg watches from behind.

The referee had to control heated tempers in the second test in Bloemfontein. Rob Louw and Theuns Stofberg are in the thick of things, while Naas Botha, Louis Moolman and Kevin de Klerk look on.

play by Gysie Pienaar. He made capital of every ill-conceived kick which came his way and it is hardly surprising that the Lions singled him out at the end of the tour as the man who caused them the most trouble.

Not far behind was the ever-alert Louw, who pounded around the field like a man possessed and who scored a try after initiating a move, being tackled, and then popping up again for the final pass. Louw was badly concussed just before the final whistle, giving the hard-working Thys Burger the opportunity to gain his Springbok colours. Germishuys was in top form again; probably the fastest man on the field and tirelessly looking for work. Like Louw, he was rewarded with his second try in successive tests.

With the score 16–15 in favour of the Springboks and the result in the balance, Pienaar scored a try which must have been heart-breaking for the Lions. They were strong on the attack when the ball went loose. With typical quick thinking, Morné du Plessis booted it far up-field and Pienaar followed up, grabbed the ball as the defence faltered, dummied and then accelerated to go over without a hand being laid on him.

Pienaar is not a man given to dramatic gestures but he allowed elation to get the better of him as he saluted the howling crowd with the ball held triumphantly above his head, a grin of sheer happiness splitting his face. It was, incidentally, only the fourth try to be scored in a test by a Springbok fullback.

The tries by Louw, Germishuys, Pienaar and Stofberg were supplemented by two conversions and two penalties from the boot of Botha, while O'Driscoll and Gravell notched tries for the Lions. Davies put over two penalties and a conversion, and Irvine also succeeding with a penalty. The final score of 26–19 in favour of the Springboks guaranteed that they could not lose the series.

Some of the British pressmen on the tour took great delight in sneering at Naas 'Botha's ability, probably because it was generally expected that his kicking would

play a bigger role than it actually did in the first two tests. One of them labelled the Northern Transvaal flyhalf 'Nasty Booter' and the nickname was used with puerile regularity in many dispatches published in the United Kingdom. In the third test they discovered just how nasty Botha's boot really could be.

▲▲▲

For the third test Van Heerden reappeared in the place of De Klerk, but otherwise the selectors wisely stuck to their winning combination. In pouring rain and with a howling wind blowing across Boet Erasmus Stadium, the Lions pack took the Springboks apart in virtually every facet of the game. At half-time, with the score 7–3 in favour of the tourists, including a try by Bruce Hay, it really looked as if they could not lose. A dropgoal and a penalty by Botha kept the Springboks in the hunt, however, and with less than ten minutes to go, the Lions were once again guilty of an unforgivable lapse in concentration. A cross-kick from Botha went into touch and Germishuys, with great presence of mind, gathered the ball as quickly as possible and threw it in to Theuns Stofberg. Stofberg ran a few paces to draw the defence towards him and then returned the ball beautifully to Germishuys, who streaked over in the corner to level the score, completely against the run of play.

Everything depended on Botha's conversion, a difficult assignment under any circumstance but made worse by the wind. Botha's right foot struck the ball beautifully and it defied the wind all the way over the crossbar. The Lions were beaten and with the defeat all their hopes of salvaging the series disappeared.

▲▲▲

Two weeks before the final test in Pretoria, the Lions met the Barbarians, in Durban, in what was probably the most spectacular match of the tour outside the first two internationals. The Barbarians fielded several guest players, including the peerless Hugo Porta, and the result was an exciting, carefree match won 25–14 by the Lions. Mark Loane, the Australian loose-forward who had been playing for Natal, gave a towering performance and the only off-key note was a serious injury suffered by Solomon Mhlaba, the Barbarians' fullback.

▲▲▲

An easy victory over Western Province, uncoordinated by the absence of the injured Morné du Plessis, and a narrow win over Griqualand West, prepared the Lions for the fourth test, in which they faced the disturbing prospect of becoming the first British Isles side ever to be whitewashed in South Africa. The vast major-ity of South Africans were quite happy that Beaumont's men managed to avoid this dubious distinction. Comparatively little heat was generated during the tour and with the series won, it was no great hardship for all but the most violently partisan to see the Lions win the final test. They thoroughly deserved their 17–13 victory, scoring three tries to one, a good effort by Willie du Plessis.

Naas Botha's placekicking skill seemed to desert him in this match and at a stage where he needed only one more point to better Keith Oxlee's record of 27 points against a Lions team, he had to hand over the kicking duties to Pienaar, who, with typical aplomb, succeeded with two kicks. The Lions' total was made

John Carlton cannot escape the Springbok defence in the second test played at the Free State Stadium in Bloemfontein.

Willie du Plessis chases the ball as Ollie Campbell moves in to contest possession for the Lions. The Springboks went on to lose 13–17 in the match played in Pretoria.

up from tries by Clive Williams, Irvine and O'Driscoll while Ollie Campbell added a penalty goal and a conversion.

The series had been played in the best of spirits. A good illustration of the absence of acrimony was the way in which the Springboks and their supporters accepted Andy Irvine's dubious try in the final test. There was a time when such an incident would have led to weeks of unseemly wrangling in the press; instead it was hardly referred to. Quinnell's ill-tempered punch in the first test was as summarily dismissed.

VENUE	SOUTH AFRICA	RESULT	SOUTH AFRICA				BRITISH ISLES			
			T	C	P	D	T	C	P	D
CAPE TOWN	WON	26–22	5	3	0	0	1	0	5	1
BLOEMFONTEIN	WON	26–19	4	2	2	0	2	1	3	0
PORT ELIZABETH	WON	12–10	1	1	1	1	1	0	2	0
PRETORIA	LOST	13–17	1	0	3	0	3	1	0	0
		77–68	11	6	6	1	7	2	11	1
SERIES: SOUTH AFRICA PLAYED 4; W3, L1, D0										

SOUTH AFRICA vs SOUTH AMERICA

The 1980 season was a severe test of the physical resilience and mental fortitude of South Africa's top players. After two international tours, including six tests, they still had to meet heavy Currie Cup commitments, to be followed by a tour to South America and a short visit from France.

After much mystery and speculation, Argentina was excluded from the South American itinerary and the tour was confined to Chile and Paraguay. The opposing teams in the two tests were staffed predominantly by Argentinians, however, and it was effectively a resumption of the series played against the Jaguars earlier in the season.

There were five other new 'caps' in the side. Fullback Tim Cocks, of Natal, a most talented player, had been making a strong bid since his good work on the 1979 Barbarians tour, and so had the promising Western Province lock-forward De Villiers Visser. Hempies du Toit, also of Western Province, was a prop who came prominently to the fore in 1980, while Eben Jansen, a Free State loose-forward and brother of the 1970 Springbok centre, Joggie Jansen, had a long-standing reputation for honest work.

Danie Gerber, a 22-year-old centre from Eastern Province, was one of the most exciting newcomers to the side. Fast, enterprising and aggressive, Gerber was an above-average investment for the future of South African rugby as he proved before the end of the 1980 season. Burger Geldenhuys, the hard-working Northern Transvaal loose-forward, was desperately unlucky not to make the side but otherwise the selectors could hardly be faulted. The captain-coach partnership of Morné du Plessis and Nelie Smith was retained while Hannes Pretorius, president of the Western Province Rugby Union and a vastly experienced official, was entrusted with the managership.

ERROL TOBIAS

History was made when the names of the touring party members were announced. Errol Tobias became the first black player to earn full Springbok colours. He and centre Charles Williams had already been awarded Junior Springbok blazers. An outstanding flyhalf and useful centre, Tobias was selected entirely on merit, as his subsequent performances proved. His selection was conclusive evidence that at the highest level of control in South African rugby, certainly, discrimination on the basis of colour had ceased to exist.

Only about 200 spectators were sprinkled around the San Jose College grounds in Asuncion, Paraguay, for the opening match of the tour. The Springboks galloped all over a South American invitation team, winning 84–6 in what was a peculiar game. The two halves were limited to 30 minutes each and yet the locals needed no fewer than ten replacements.

De Wet Ras scored 28 points in the match with 12 conversions and a try, bettering Piet Visagie's record of 25 established during a tour match in Australia in 1971.

The opposition fared slightly better in the second match, the Springboks winning 79–18 and Naas Botha notching 27 points on his own. This was to be the pattern for all four tour games outside the two internationals and the Springboks eventually averaged 62,66 points a match, scoring 66 tries in the process. They had no need to worry unduly about penalties and only bothered to turn two into points. On the other hand, they converted no fewer than 50 tries. In one match Tobias succeeded with ten successive conversions and Ras improved still further on Visagie's Australian performance by kicking 12 conversions and a penalty and scoring two tries, less than a week after first breaking the record.

The Springboks photographed on tour in South America at the end of 1980. The Andes range is visible in the background.

A shoulder injury sustained in a Currie Cup match against Eastern Province kept Morné du Plessis out of action and Theuns Stofberg led the Springboks in the first international, played on a rather under-sized field in Montevideo. Stofberg had steadily grown in stature since making his debut against the All Blacks in 1976 and he proved to be a worthy substitute for Du Plessis.

It was nevertheless not a particularly good victory for the Springboks, probably because the ease with which they had won the early tour matches had robbed them of the fine edge. They dominated the lineouts and scrums but lacked rhythm and made many mistakes.

Louw, Stofberg and Thys Burger hunted well together and Gerber, playing in his first test, scored a brilliant try when he took full advantage of a long pass from Botha to cut through a disorganized defence. The final score of 22–13 should have been much higher, however, as the forwards had things all their own way.

The Springboks worked much better in the second test in Santiago. Morné du Plessis, by now as vital to the Springbok team as he had been for Western Province for many years, was back at the helm and the South Americans did well to keep the score to 30–16 in the visitors' favour. The Springbok pack was in total command and the loose-forwards combined well with the backs. Pienaar was in sparkling form and the halfbacks, Botha and Serfontein, gave the threequarters all the scope they needed. Gerber was particularly active while the wings, Germishuys and Mordt, ran with splendid flair, grabbing a brace of tries each. Germishuys' two tries brought the Transvaal wing's test total to eight, level with the South African record held by Jannie Engelbrecht and John Gainsford.

VENUE	SOUTH AFRICA	RESULT	SOUTH AFRICA				SOUTH AMERICA			
			T	C	P	D	T	C	P	D
MONTEVIDEO	WON	22–13	3	2	1	1	2	1	0	1
SANTIAGO	WON	30–16	6	3	0	0	2	1	1	1
		52–29	9	5	1	1	4	2	1	2
SERIES: SOUTH AFRICA PLAYED 2; W2, L0, D0										

FRANCE vs SOUTH AFRICA

The Springboks had one more hurdle to negotiate to make the 1980 season one of the most successful in history. Jean-Pierre Rives' French team arrived for a mini-tour of four matches, including one international.

The Springboks were top-heavy favourites and the Frenchmen, in fact, left their country in gloomy despondency. A report in *France Soir* lamented, 'In a few days' time our players will face the greatest rugby war machine in the world. Let us just close our eyes and pray!' Frenchmen are great fighters, however, and the nastiness of their own supporters provided them with ample motivation. They beat Natal 27–16, giving a far more convincing display against Wynand Claassen's lively combination than the Lions did. The South African Invitation XV went down 27–32 in Bloemfontein, and although it was Errol Tobias who was chaired off afterwards by admiring spectators in recognition of his two thrilling tries, the band of men in blue deserved their success. Going into the solitary test of the tour, the Frenchmen had scored 12 tries in three matches and there was no room for complacency in the Springbok camp.

Morné du Plessis and Martiens le Roux watch Rob Louw being tackled in the so-called Christmas Test.

The ninth and final international match of the 1980 season was a suitable climax to a year in which South Africa made a triumphant return to world rugby. The Springboks were brilliant against a brave but eventually out-gunned French team. As a spectacle the game was as good as any seen

Springbok captain Morné du Plessis feeds the ball to his backs in the one-off test match played against France in Pretoria.

on the new Loftus Versfeld, but as important was the sound rugby played by Morné du Plessis and his team. Le Roux, Kahts and Prentis did everything and more than can reasonably be expected of a frontrow. Van Heerden was a veritable bulldozer and Moolman proved yet again what a superlative lineout specialist he had developed into. Stofberg, Louw and Morné du Plessis revived memories of the greatest of Springbok loose-forward combinations, being ruthlessly efficient but also innovative.

Behind such a pack Serfontein's immense talents could not but blossom and the scrumhalf gave a quite remarkable all-round performance. Botha played with complete assurance. With such confident halfbacks making the most of good possession, it is hardly surprising that the Springbok threequarters drove frequent gaps in the brave French defence.

Germishuys, rounding off a golden season, got his ninth and record-breaking try while Gerber, who frequently showed the dash of a Mannetjies Roux, revealed startling acceleration which led to an incredible try by Kahts. Pienaar became the first Springbok fullback to score more than one test try and his counter-attacks frequently bewildered the sorely stretched French team. Stofberg and Serfontein also scored tries while Botha contributed four conversions and three penalties to the South African score of 37 to France's 15. (A try by Dintrans, a conversion and three penalty goals by Viviés.)

Jean-Pierre Rives tried hard to stem the tide. With his long blond hair matted with blood from a head injury, Rives gave an exhibition of raw courage which alone ensured that France's honour was unsoiled in spite of the big defeat. When the Irish referee, John West, ended the match Springbok rugby had well and truly returned to the world arena. In one wonderful season they had accounted for South America, the British Isles and France.

VENUE	SOUTH AFRICA	RESULT	SOUTH AFRICA				FRANCE			
			T	C	P	D	T	C	P	D
PRETORIA	WON	37–15	5	4	3	0	1	1	3	0

CHAPTER 38

1981

RUGBY ON A WAR FOOTING

▲▲▲

WYNAND CLAASSEN

*A bespectacled architect who had played
61 times for Northern Transvaal before
moving to Durban, Claassen had also
briefly captained Northern Transvaal after
the retirement of Thys Lourens but a
serious eye injury had knocked him out for
a season. When he moved to Durban he
took over the captaincy of the Natal team,
ironically gaining national recognition of
his leadership qualities by guiding the
underdogs to victory over former Northern
Transvaal teammates. Claassen had been
a contender for Springbok colours from the
mid-1970s but with an exceptional player
like Morné du Plessis in possession, the
number-eight position was virtually
permanently booked.*

IRELAND vs SOUTH AFRICA

Fierce opposition from anti-apartheid groups failed to stop an Irish team from visiting South Africa in May 1981. Seven matches, including two tests, were scheduled over four weeks. Managed by Paddy Madigan, coached by Tom Kiernan and skippered by Fergus Slattery, a superb loose-forward, the visitors were not expected to provide particularly strong opposition.

Ireland had finished last in the Five Nations tournament before their departure for South Africa, but from a local viewpoint the two tests would provide good preparation for the tour of New Zealand later in the season. The retirement of Morné du Plessis meant that a new captain had to be selected. The selectors decided to give the job of leading the Springboks against Ireland to Wynand Claassen.

There was a rumour that the names of the Springbok team for the first test had been leaked, and some newspapers jumped the gun on the official announcement. It must have caused some pain to Eastern Transvaal centre Jannie Els, Northern Transvaal eighthman Thys Burger and Theuns Stofberg, who was thought to have been appointed captain, when the reports were exposed as inaccurate.

The omission of Els, who was fated never to gain Springbok colours, caused a minor stir, particularly as there was a school of thought who regarded Errol Tobias as a good flyhalf but not a suitable replacement for the injured Willie du Plessis as Danie Gerber's partner at centre.

With an average age of 28, the team for the first test had the dubious distinction of being the oldest ever to be selected to play for South Africa. Hooker Willie Kahts and prop Richard Prentis, both 34 years old, were the oldest men in the side with centre Gerber and flyhalf Naas Botha the youngest at 23.

Ireland lost against the Gazelles in the opening match of the tour but in subsequent outings it became obvious that despite injuries and the absence of several star players who had remained home for various reasons, they had the kind of aggressive and intelligent loose-forwards, particularly the brilliant Fergus Slattery on the flank and Willie Duggan at number-eight, who could cause problems for the Springboks. The local side were nevertheless odds-on favourites to win the first test at Newlands.

▲▲▲

Francis Palmade of France, in South Africa to control both tests, penalized Ireland early on in the first test and Botha placed the goal. But the Springboks lacked rhythm and, at scrumhalf, Robbie McGrath was distinctly quicker and more decisive than Serfontein. It was to be one of the worst performances of Serfontein's otherwise impressive career. He was not the only Springbok to perform below usual standard. Botha, trying to open up the game from his own half, passed to Gysie Pienaar and the fullback, normally relishing such adventurous tactics, made a hash of it before giving to Gerber, who was a sitting target for the Irish loose-forwards. He was robbed of the ball and McGrath scurried over for a splendid try which Ollie Campbell easily converted.

Two more penalties by Botha, against one from Campbell, kept the scores level and then Gerber scored the first of his two tries. He received the ball from a line-out about 40 metres from his opponents' line and cut inside, straight into a thicket of defenders. For a moment it looked as if, foolishly, Gerber had chosen the wrong option. But with one dazzling side-step after the other he weaved his way through a mesmerized defence to score under the posts. For sheer individual brilliance this try equals anything in the history of Springbok rugby and had Gerber's career ended then and there, he would still have been assured of a special niche in the annals.

Ireland quickly shook off the effects of this try and left-wing Freddie McLennan scored after fullback John Murphy engineered the opening. Campbell converted to make the half-time score 15-all.

The Springboks started the second half with Northern Transvaal prop Ockie Oosthuizen replacing the injured Martiens le Roux and for a while it looked as if Slattery and his men were beginning to crack. A slashing break by Tobias was smartly supported by winger Edrich Krantz and when he was stopped, Stofberg was up to make more ground before Louw rounded off the movement with an excellent try. Ireland fought back valiantly but could not prevent Gerber from getting his second try, his fourth in as many tests, and this time it required little more from the Springbok centre than a characteristic burst of speed after Pienaar and Germishuys had managed to pull the defence apart.

Claassen's men wore white jerseys in the tests as a courtesy gesture to the visitors, whose green tops would otherwise have been too easy to confuse with the traditional Springbok green-and-gold.

Wynand Claassen, second from the back in the line-out, watches developments in the test at Newlands.

With Campbell and Murphy injured, Ireland were in desperate trouble for most of the second half of the match but the Springboks, not quite firing on all cylinders, could not overpower their opponents and the final score of 23–15 reflects the competitiveness of an exciting match.

With Ireland forced to make changes because of injuries to key players, the Springboks retained tight-head front-rank replacement Oosthuizen, and brought back the strong and fast right-wing Ray Mordt in place of Krantz.

The second test, in Durban, gave the Springboks, who scraped home 12–10, even less reason to be complacent about the tour to New Zealand. This was the one-hundredth test match played in South Africa, and coincidentally it was also South Africa's one-hundredth victory in all test matches played. Flyhalf Botha, with three dropgoals and a penalty, gathered all of his side's points while Ireland's fullback Kevin O'Brien scored the only try of the match. Flyhalf Mickey Quinn placed two penalties to make up the rest of the visitors' total.

The short tour made a realistic evaluation of South African rugby possible and gave Wynand Claassen a chance to establish himself. It also enabled the Springboks to stretch their run to ten victories in 11 tests, played at the amazing rate of approximately one every five weeks.

VENUE	SOUTH AFRICA	RESULT	SOUTH AFRICA				IRELAND			
			T	C	P	D	T	C	P	D
CAPE TOWN	WON	23–15	3	1	3	0	2	2	1	0
DURBAN	WON	12–10	0	0	1	3	1	0	2	0

SOUTH AFRICA vs NEW ZEALAND

It took some time before the 1981 Springbok tour of New Zealand found a niche in rugby history. Over the years the off-the-field violence and the bizarre conditions in which the matches were played have faded. In happy contrast, memories of outstanding performances and a final test as dramatic and controversial as any in the history of Springbok and All Blacks rugby rivalry, have grown stronger and taken on a lustre at first obscured by flour bombs and barbed wire.

Uncertainty marked the months before the tour and near the end of the 1980 season Cec Blazey, chairman of the New Zealand Rugby Union, still stated that no decision had been taken on the proposed invitation to a Springbok team to play 12 matches in New Zealand in 1981. While the rugby officials were hesitant, however, the Maoris extended a hand of friendship. The Muldoon government removed the last major obstacle when, despite their declared disapproval of the tour, they refused to deny the Springbok team visas. In South Africa, Butch

Lochner and his fellow selectors began to prepare while in New Zealand, Halt All Racial Tours (HART) planned its strategy for disruption.

Graham Mourie, the reigning captain of the All Blacks, became the first well-known player to publicly adopt high moral ground by declaring himself unavailable to play against the Springboks.

On the playing front, New Zealand claimed to be far from confident in the face of the impending Springbok challenge. While the Springboks had looked generally competent and frequently brilliant during the 1980 season, New Zealand rugby circles had been stunned by a series of defeats suffered by their provincial teams against their Australian counterparts.

▲▲▲

There was a general feeling of satisfaction among the experts as well as the rank-and-file with the Springbok team. Wynand Claassen's stature had grown in the tests against Ireland and he was the obvious choice as captain. But behind the scenes, it became known later, there had been turmoil, manipulation and duplicity in the lead-up to the selection of the team and its leader.

A few years after the tour Claassen revealed in his biography that there had been strenuous efforts by two members of the selection committee, Butch Lochner and Nelie Smith, to block his selection. Claassen claimed that Smith had designed a blueprint to defeat the All Blacks, an accomplishment he believed would earn him the undying gratitude of the South African rugby establishment and, no doubt, the fringe benefits that would go with such a happy situation. Claassen, as person and player, did not fit into Smith's masterplan and only, so it was said, the firmness of the other members of the committee, Professor Daan Swiegers, Dougie Dyers and Brian Irvine, ensured that he made the team and retained the captaincy. Smith apparently even then did not abandon his scheme and on the tour he, it was claimed, tried to sideline all the players for whom he did not have a role in the script.

The disastrous first test, however, destroyed his influence among the players. They very much took over from that point and despite the most discouraging of circumstances made the tour a success. The appointment of Johan Claassen, one of the greatest

Louis Moolman wins lineout possession for the Springboks against the All Blacks, while Hennie Bekker looks on.

The 1981 tour to New Zealand split the country into antagonistic groups. Here, supporters of the anti-tour faction make their feelings known.

lock-forwards in rugby history, as manager of the touring party, did not receive general approval. Claassen, no relation to the team skipper, was considered by many to be unsuitable for a task calling for sophistication, diplomacy and a comfortable familiarity with English. His bleak personality and monosyllabic responses to media queries did not impress New Zealand and off-the-field public relations work on behalf of South Africa was done by the assistant manager, the eager and likeable Abe Williams. In the strict definition of his job Claassen was a success. He looked after his players and their needs with admirable devotion, advised them shrewdly from his vast store of experience of All Blacks rugby and New Zealand conditions, and sensibly steered clear of issues beyond his scope.

▲▲▲

Gerrie Germishuys, still extremely quick and a supreme opportunist, was the most experienced international in the team with 17 tests, although Willie Kahts, the Northern Transvaal hooker, at 34, was the oldest member of the side. Errol Tobias, who had played so well against Ireland, became the first coloured Springbok on a major tour on merit and the inevitable allegations that his selection was window dressing were politically inspired.

In retrospect, it was an exceptionally talented team. Theuns Stofberg, the vice-captain, a lock and loose-forward with splendid skills allied to his massive height and weight, must be considered whenever the Springbok forwards are discussed. So must Louis Moolman, a lineout specialist who had few peers during his long career. Then there was Rob Louw, a loose-forward whose exceptional pace and instinctive flair did so much to disrupt Billy Beaumont's Lions in 1980, and whose decision to turn to rugby league was a severe loss.

Burger Geldenhuys, the Northern Transvaal flanker and his provincial team-mate Thys Burger, skipper Claassen, Hempies du Toit, the Western Province front-ranker whose strength and technique reminded some of a famous namesake of the 1960s, De Villiers Visser, a lock of unlimited potential unfortunately not to be realized, Hennie Bekker, a superb handler and runner and a lineout specialist who matured late, front-rankers Henning van Aswegen, Ockie Oosthuizen, and Flippie van der Merwe, at 132 kilograms the heaviest Springbok of all time, Willie Kahts and Robert Cockrell, the hookers originally selected, and Shaun Povey who eventually joined as a replacement, as well as Eben Jansen and Johan Marais, two bustling loose-forwards, were all outstanding players, whether they made the test combinations or not.

Behind the scrum, the line-up was even more glittering, although some of the backs had difficulty in adapting to foreign conditions. Divan Serfontein was a scrumhalf about to hit the peak of his career. The number-two scrumhalf was Barry Wolmarans, who, despite injuries, remained a player of exceptional ability. During the tour, Gawie Visagie was called over as a replacement when there were doubts whether Wolmarans would recover from an injury. Naas Botha was backed up at flyhalf by Colin Beck, who was comfortably polished anywhere among the backs.

Errol Tobias was selected as a utility player but on the tour he was invariably pressed into service at flyhalf. He was never quite comfortable on the soft, muddy surfaces and the fact that he was not given an opportunity at centre did not help. The 21-year-old Carel du Plessis was included in the team as a centre, but within the next couple of seasons he was to mature into a magnificent left-wing. His

South African wing, Gerrie Germishuys, inspects security arrangements during the bizarre 1981 tour.

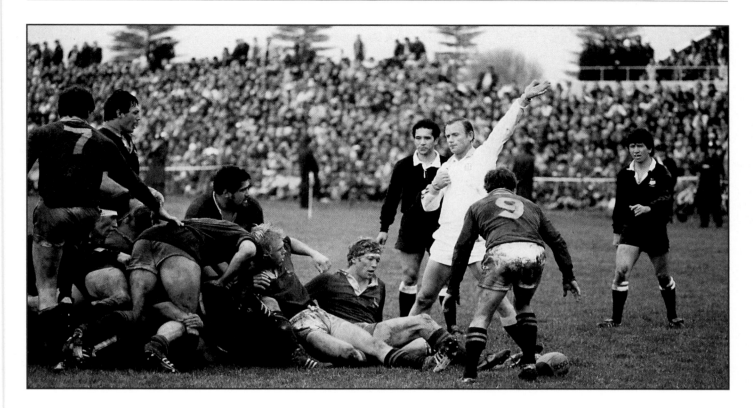

older brother, Willie, was bothered by injuries throughout the tour while Danie Gerber was seldom at his explosive best. In fact, most New Zealand critics singled out a lack of real penetration at centre as one of the weaknesses in the Springbok team. Darius Botha and Edrich Krantz also failed to find their form and although Germishuys had a sluggish start it was soon obvious that he and Ray Mordt had no serious challengers. Johan Heunis was well up to international standard as a wing, and he emerged from the tour as one of the most valuable players. Gysie Pienaar had a disappointing tour for someone so uniquely talented.

The 18 capped players shared a total of 134 tests between them. Eleven players received colours for the first time and four were members of the 1980 South American tour but had not played in any of the tests. Somewhat to the astonishment of the New Zealand writers who had been in South Africa to gather first-hand knowledge of local standards for their newspapers, Western Province, with 11, had the highest representation. The Kiwi scouts were much more impressed with Northern Transvaal players.

▲▲▲

The tour began in Gisborne and within a few hours of arriving, the team management suffered a severe mauling at a press conference with New Zealand and Australian journalists who had come well armed. Johan Claassen, Nelie Smith, Abe Williams and Wynand Claassen were not prepared for this type of intellectual free-for-all where a shrug and a 'We're not politicians; we're here for the rugby' would not be accepted as answers.

Anti-tour protesters showed from the start that they would stop at nothing when they smashed through the gates of Poverty Bay's rugby ground and then sprinkled broken glass on the playing field. This was to set the pattern for the rest of this traumatic tour. In the process, a nation was thrown into turmoil, individual

The South Africans were awarded a penalty against the New Zealand Maoris.
The Springboks eventually drew the match thanks to a controversial drop goal which was awarded by the referee, BW Duffy.

freedom was interfered with, large sums of money were wasted, and, at the end of it all, not a single South African black was better off than before. A hat-trick of tries by Krantz gave some lustre to the easy 24–6 victory the Springboks achieved against Poverty Bay in the opening match. Waikato, then the Ranfurly Shield champions and always remembered for their famous victory over the 1956 Springboks, were next in line.

A group of protesters estimated at 3 000 gathered at the Hamilton's Rugby Park and when a few hundred managed to smash through a fence and onto the playing area, the crowd of 26 000 spectators who had paid to see the match had to accept that there would be no rugby on that particular afternoon. A few were furious enough to launch individual counter-attacks and the police tried vainly to clear the field. The final straw came when a crazed fanatic, rumoured to be terminally ill, flying a light plane over the ground, threatened to crash into the main stand. Fearing the loss of life such a terrifying act would have caused, and with the situation out of control on all fronts, the Waikato officials surrendered.

The future of the tour was obviously in severe jeopardy and while the New Zealand rugby officials and the police met high-ranking government officials, the Springboks played golf, fraternized with the locals, and generally learnt to become philosophical about events over which they had no control.

Claassen led a potential test team against Taranaki in New Plymouth and with Louis Moolman dominating the lineouts and loose-forwards Burger Geldenhuys, Thys Burger and Claassen himself guaranteeing a steady flow of good possession from the loose, only a lack of match fitness prevented the final score of 34–9 from being even more impressive. Serfontein and Botha combined well at halfback and the flyhalf scored 18 points.

For security reasons the tourists had to be at the ground more than two hours before the scheduled kick-off and probably for the first time ever Springboks played snooker or read while waiting to go on the field.

Rob Louw watches as Theuns Stofberg tries to brush off an All Black tackle.

The Springboks continued to improve and their 31–19 victory over Manawatu, New Zealand's champion provincial side, at Palmerston North, so impressed Graham Hamer, the home team's coach, that he rather prematurely predicted that they would go through the tour undefeated. Botha scored 16 points and obviously found Serfontein's service to his liking. This match marked the beginning of an ongoing feud between Botha and Doug Rollerson, Manawatu's flyhalf. Gerber also starred among the backs but Pienaar was again disappointingly uncertain under pressure. Geldenhuys gave yet another superb performance and he was obviously the perfect loose-forward for New Zealand conditions. Wanganui gave the Springboks an unexpectedly tough time and the scores were level at half-time. But with Jansen and Oosthuizen shaping particularly well, they woke up after the resumption and notched up eight tries to win 45–9. Pienaar, who replaced the injured Heunis early in the match, failed on the defence and the fullback's lack of confidence was becoming a major headache.

A painful reminder that the battle against demonstrations was continuing to rage came at this point of the tour when it was announced that the fixture against South Canterbury had been cancelled. Timaru's Fraser Park was too exposed for the police to guarantee security.

Naas Botha pushed up his personal tally to 44 points in three matches when he guided the side to a 22–6 victory over Southland in the last game before the first international but, once again, the Springboks took a long time to find their rhythm. Rob Louw scored a vital try while Pienaar showed encouraging signs of a return to form. Darius Botha put in a couple of aggressive runs to challenge Germishuys for a test spot and Gerber removed all doubts, if there could have been any, that he was the team's best centre.

The forwards were again in total command against Otago but their sterling efforts were largely wasted by a backline which panicked against quick-to-spoil opponents. It was a hard, mauling match in which the Springboks made life difficult for themselves, eventually scraping home with a four-point margin. Tobias was out of touch at flyhalf and Naas Botha was sorely missed. So was his goal-kicking, with the Springboks placing only two out of 11 pots at the posts. Beck, substituting at fullback, was positively brilliant, however, and had it not been for him the tourists could well have lost this game despite the work of the forwards.

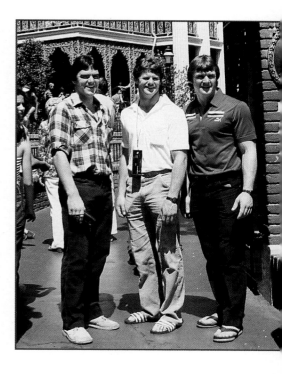

Danie Gerber, Willie du Plessis and Ray Mordt enjoy being tourists in New Zealand.

▲▲▲

More than 6 000 demonstrators, howling their determination and carrying banners espousing most of the popular causes of the time, virtually laid siege to Christchurch's Lancaster Park, kept at bay only by barbed wire and more than 2 000 policemen. It was one of the most remarkable and also one of the saddest days in the history of the game. For more than two hours the battle raged around the stadium but only about 100 protesters, all holding tickets, managed to get inside the ground. Some minutes before the kick-off, they made a run for the field to a frightening roar of anger from the 40 000 spectators. Some managed to scatter broken glass and tacks on the playing area before they were dragged off and thrown out and the game was eventually played without significant interference.

The Springbok brains trust had opted for a brawn-and-no-risk policy with their team selection and it backfired hopelessly. The massive South African pack, led by Theuns Stofberg, was outplayed by Andy Dalton and his more mobile, more fiery colleagues. They controlled the rucks and mauls, scrummed with more cohesion, and all but held their own in the lineouts against taller opponents. The Springbok forwards, except at the start and for a few minutes towards the end, played with a fumbling ineptness and lack of will which, in the words of the respected critic Terry McLean, would have caused the likes of Phil Mostert, Philip Nel and Boy Louw to cringe with shame.

Naas Botha compounded the problems by playing an ineffective game. He kicked poorly and used possession injudiciously. Bekker's try near the end of the match and some good running by Louw, Gerber and Mordt, proved that a more adventurous approach might have brought better results. Despite the lethargy of the tourists they managed to remain in contention throughout, losing only 9–14.

Andy Dalton, the All Blacks captain, said afterwards that they found that the Springbok forwards did not like going backwards on the heavy, muddy field and that they were surprisingly slow to get to critical breakdowns. The Springbok manager, Johan Claassen, with commendable frankness, felt that his team had been outplayed in every department and that the tactical approach had been all wrong. Coach Nelie Smith agreed in general, but did add that the Springbok cause was hardly helped by the fact that they spent the night sleeping on stretchers and being woken up by protesters in the early morning hours.

Dan Retief wrote in his book *Springboks Under Siege*:

'Could the Springboks really have been expected to produce their best form considering the demands made on them in the interests of safety? Instead of going straight to Christchurch following a hard midweek game against Otago in Dunedin, the Boks returned to Invercargill... because here at least they would be free to move about as they pleased and train in peace.

'On the Friday before the test the team were flown to Christchurch and the test players were smuggled into the Linwood Rugby Club of former All Black Fergie McCormack, where camp beds were erected in a squash court. The other 15 players were billeted in private homes, including tour skipper Wynand Claassen, who was thus separated from the test team.

'The test squad left for Lancaster Park at daybreak and got their first sight of the field on which they were to play when they arrived. After that they played pool and cards and some tried to sleep on mattresses strewn on the floor.

'By the time the players ran onto the pitch they were psychologically and mentally drained, and this may in some measure account for their lack lustre play and inability to change their tactics when they ran into trouble.'

And yet the Springboks got off to a good start when Botha dropped a neat goal after good work from Stofberg, the captain of the day following Claassen's axing.

More anti-tour demonstrators make their feelings known about the Springbok visit.

But after their early success the Springboks steadily deteriorated and first Doug Rollerson and then Stu Wilson scored excellent tries to take the half-time score to 10–3. New Zealand had lost fullback Allan Hewson early on after he had suffered a neck injury. His replacement, Brian McKechnie, and wings Bernie Fraser and Fred Woodman coped admirably, however, as Botha continued to pepper the touchline with poorly directed kicks instead of occasionally bringing such dangerous threequarters as Gerber, Willie du Plessis and Mordt into the attack. The score that decided the match came after ten minutes of the second half and underlined the weakness of the Springbok forwards. Bekker made an ill-judged hash of a lineout and Mark Shaw burst through, passed to Murray Mexted when tack-

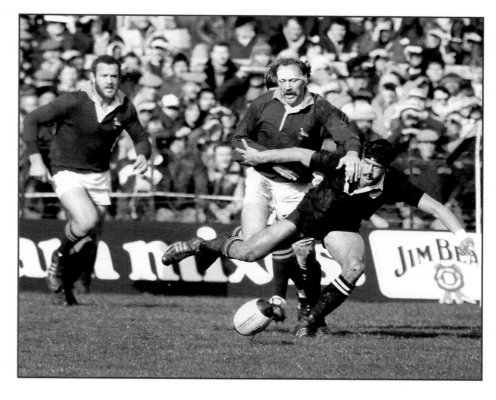

led, and was up again to go through after a maul on the Springbok line. In the final minutes of the game, the Springboks showed flair when Louw started a movement. Mordt took it further and Bekker galloped through for a try. Botha solved the wicked angle with a magnificent conversion from near touch.

Louis Moolman and captain Wynand Claassen move in to gain possession in the second test played at Wellington.

The dour and ultimately unproductive tactics of the Springboks were heavily criticized and it was obvious that the dropping of Claassen had been a mistake. The emphasis on sheer weight and size up front had also failed but Dalton was enough of a realist to be publicly concerned that such a disorganized Springbok team had managed to confine New Zealand's winning margin to only five points.

Laurie Prideaux, the England referee who handled the game, deserved special credit for the way in which he controlled the situation at one stage when tempers threatened to get out of hand. Prideaux showed sound judgement by pointing out to the players that brawls on the field would only serve to add even more acrimony to a situation. There were no further incidents.

▲▲▲

The tour selectors were again the targets for criticism from virtually all quarters when they announced the team for the second test. Six changes were made up front and one behind the scrum, where Germishuys, after showing a return to form, was the obvious choice on the left wing.

The return of Claassen to the side was generally hailed, but the dropping of Rob Louw, rumoured by some to be for disciplinary reasons, inspired damning headlines in the New Zealand and South African newspapers. Louw was said to have upset Johan Claassen and Nelie Smith by joining the All Blacks lock Andy Haden for a night on the tiles after the Christchurch disaster. This, it was argued, was hardly a serious enough offence to warrant the axing of the quickest loose-forward in the side.

Springbok fullback, Johan Heunis, tries to shake off an All Black tackle in Auckland, scene of the 'flour-bomb test'.

Springboks Naas Botha, Willie du Plessis, Theuns Stofberg, Wynand Claassen and Danie Gerber close in on an All Black player.

The retention of Stofberg was regarded as sheer folly, considering that tardiness to the loose ball was probably the biggest single factor in the first test defeat. Calmer observers pointed out that the selectors had opted for a pack dominated by Northern Transvaal forwards. This, some astute experts argued, would provide the solid protective shield Naas Botha had lacked. The inclusion of Geldenhuys also improved the likelihood of more controlled possession from the tight-loose.

The All Blacks also had their problems, the most severe being the absence of Gary Knight, one of the greatest of modern forwards, who had to withdraw because of difficulties on his new farm in Manawatu. He was replaced by Greg Burgess, and another last-minute replacement up front was veteran lock Frank Oliver for the unfortunate Graeme Higginson who had broken an ankle during warm-up exercises before training.

Among the backs Allan Hewson returned for Brian McKechnie, who had reason to feel hard-done-by after his fine showing in the first test. The All Blacks selectors were also obviously worried about their midfield defence against a centre of Gerber's quality and Lachie Cameron was brought in to replace Andy Jefferd.

The Friday before the match the Springbok test team slipped into Athletic Park and settled down for the night in a huge room in the bowels of the stadium. Beds, television sets, and pool and card tables were made available in the area which was normally used for social gatherings; meals were supplied by a local catering firm. The conditions were the best the Springboks had enjoyed up to then and it was the first time they had a chance to sleep late and without interruption.

A cold southerly wind nipped through the stadium and winning the toss was, as always in Wellington, an important factor. Andy Dalton, calling correctly, decided to let the Springboks have the advantage in the first half. The Welsh referee, Clive Norling, was no stranger to the players.

In all the annals of Springbok rugby it would be difficult to find a better performance than the one Wynand Claassen inspired from his players that day. The baying of the demonstrators outside the ground and even the smoke bombs that exploded behind the All Blacks' posts at one stage, did not have the slightest effect on the players and their concentration. From the moment Naas Botha kicked off, the Springboks took firm hold of the proceedings.

The forwards hunted the ball with single-minded ferocity but their drive was disciplined and planned. Divan Serfontein was alert and sure in anything he did, and outside of him Botha proved that he was one of the finest flyhalves in history. The threequarters Gerber and Willie du Plessis (replaced in the second half by Beck), Germishuys and Mordt responded superbly and fullback Gysie Pienaar gave the New Zealand fans an inkling of the phenomenal ability which made him one of the world's most exciting players.

The All Blacks seemed to lack control and at times they were downright rash. As Ian Gault wrote in *The 1981 Springboks in New Zealand*:

'The frighteningly accurate boot of Naas Botha drove much of the stuffing out of the All Blacks. He taunted them with touch kicks and he sickened them with his goal kicks. He made capital out of what Andy Dalton called the plain stupidity of the All Blacks, and wrote another chapter of South African rugby history.'

Less than ten minutes after the kick-off the Springboks led 6–0 as a result of two penalty goals placed by Botha after blatant infringements. Even the loss of Kahts who went off with a shoulder injury and was replaced by Robert Cockrell, did not affect them. Before the match was a dozen minutes old, the All Blacks were sent reeling with a try by Germishuys.

Gerber had forced Hewson to fly-kick the ball into touch and Visser won the ensuing lineout. Serfontein's quick pass barely reached Botha but the flyhalf picked it up off his bootlaces and in the same movement swung the ball to Gerber, who wasted no time before passing to Du Plessis. At this point, with lovely timing, Pienaar joined the line and gave Germishuys the suggestion of an edge he needed. Woodman was beaten with a swerve and Fraser brushed off before the wing scored and Botha converted with consummate ease.

Two more Botha penalties brought the score to 18–3 at half-time, Hewson having succeeded with a solitary kick for the All Blacks. After the resumption the Springboks had to cope with the wind, several injuries and three further penalty goals, but the brilliant first 40 minutes had given the home team too big a leeway to catch up. Botha, who never lost his composure in the face of increasingly vicious niggling from his opposite number, Doug Rollerson, added a fifth penalty and dropped a typical goal to give the Springboks a 24–12 victory. Germishuys had scored his tenth test try, pulling further away from the previous South African record of eight held jointly by John Gainsford and Jannie Engelbrecht.

While the records belonged to Naas, a sense of triumph must have been felt by Wynand Claassen. Discarded for the first test he had come back to lead his team to an unexpected but decisive victory.

▲▲▲

Strange interpretations by the referee, Bill Adlam, caused the Springboks some hassles in their next tour match, against the Bay of Plenty, but the 29–24 score made it look a lot closer than it was. In this match Johan Heunis, with some magnificent kicking, and De Villiers Visser were quite outstanding.

▲▲▲

The match against Auckland will mainly be remembered for the genius of Naas Botha and a skinny Anglican priest called Geoff Walpole, who managed to get onto the field of play by posing as a reserve referee. He proceeded to kick one of the balls into the stand and with that grand gesture presumably made his point.

Playing against a driving wind, the Springboks were lucky to lead 14–0 at half-time, but after the resumption Botha sparked the home team's collapse with two scintillating tries and South Africa ended up with a 39–12 win. Botha also scored a penalty and four conversions with tries by Geldenhuys, Gerber, Oosthuizen, Serfontein and Pienaar making up the rest of the total.

The first of Botha's efforts came after a penalty near the posts, when he picked up and dummied his way over, and the second was generally rated as the best try of the tour. Botha received on his own 22-metre line and accelerated through a gap, side-stepped a covering tackle and then fooled the last defender with a dummy before scoring.

A succession of injuries clouded the 19–10 win over North Auckland in the last provincial engagement before the final test and, in stark contrast to the splendid second half the South Africans played against Auckland, the match was dull and ill-tempered. It did, however, give the Springboks the satisfaction of an unbeaten run against all comers except the New Zealand national side in the first test. Bekker, Burger, Heunis, Beck and Shaun Povey, playing his first game, showed up well for the 'dirt-trackers'.

Hempies du Toit and Errol Tobias appear to be delighted to be leaving on tour.

The decisive final test of the series could not have been more exciting, controversial, dramatic and in some respects bizarre, had it been scripted for a rugby soap opera. Throughout the match two irresponsible people were making their anti-South African statements by swooping over the players and parts of the 50 000 spectators in a Cessna aircraft, dropping flour bombs. One such missile felled All Blacks forward Gary Knight and it was a miracle that the crazy afternoon ended without tragedy.

Injuries caused the withdrawal of Visser and Stofberg, to be replaced by Bekker and Louw respectively. To aggravate the situation, Willie du Plessis, Flippie van der Merwe and Bekker himself were suffering from a variety of injuries. The All Blacks also had their difficulties but the inclusion of two Maoris, Steve Pokere and Frank Shelford, undoubtedly strengthened the team.

The third change, newcomer Gary Whetton for veteran Frank Oliver, was rather surprising as he did not do that well against the Springboks when he played for Auckland. A couple of days before the game, Mark Shaw, the All Blacks flanker withdrew because of a bruised hip and was replaced by Geoff Old.

Once again the Springboks moved into temporary quarters in the bowels of a stadium, this time Eden Park, on the day before the match and, makeshift accommodation and all, the remarkably adaptable men were comparatively rested when the morning dawned, clear with, for once, a dry field and no rain expected.

Wynand Claassen won the toss and elected to play against the wind in the first half. Botha kicked off for what was to be a thrilling match, played at great pace.

This time the All Blacks took early control and although Botha levelled the scores with a kick into the wind after an early Hewson penalty, the New Zealand forwards plied their backs with a steady supply of good ball and the Springbok defence was stretched to breaking point. Cracks had to be found and right-wing Stu Wilson duly scored an unconverted try after taking a difficult pass from Hewson, who had opened the gap. Then Rollerson made it 10–3 with another penalty. The Springbok pack seemed beaten in all phases and only clumsiness on the part of the opposing backline saved the South Africans from a rout. Their prospects of winning the test seemed to evaporate when New Zealand struck again just before half-time.

Mexted picked up at the back of the lineout and when he was stopped he ensured possession for Knight who forced his way over. When Rollerson converted to make the half-time score 16–3, the game, for all intents and purposes, seemed in the bag for the home side.

At this point Pienaar, with a damaged shoulder, and Willie du Plessis, with a hamstring injury, made way for Heunis and Beck respectively. It was a grubber from Beck, not long after the resumption, that gave Mordt his first try. His quick follow-up beat Hewson to the rolling ball and Botha converted to make the score a slightly more respectable 16–9. But the All Blacks forwards were still driving furiously and after Heunis had saved what looked like a certain try, Hewson made no mistake with a penalty goal and New Zealand appeared safe with the score 19–9.

But it was Hewson's casual approach which gave the Springboks a try that abruptly changed the flow of the game. Mordt chipped the ball towards the corner and ran around the New Zealand defence. His quick arrival on the scene caught the All Blacks fullback a little offguard. He allowed the ball to bounce and the powerfully built Mordt grabbed it and notched his second try. Botha converted and all of a sudden the Springboks were only four points in arrears.

Flippie van der Merwe, Robert Cockrell and Ockie Oosthuizen made up the powerful Springbok front row to tour New Zealand.

The Springbok and Maori front rows prepare to go down for a scrum.

Another Botha kick from touch made the score 19–18 but after play was interrupted to revive Knight, who had been knocked out by a flour bomb dropped from an aircraft, the All Blacks pack seemed to regain their stranglehold and drove the Springboks deep into their own half. An ill-advised attempt by Gerber to break the line, gave Rollerson the easiest of dropgoals to increase New Zealand's lead to 22–18.

During injury time Botha's extraordinary skill gave the ever-alert Mordt his third try and a very special place in the record books. A hard tackle knocked the ball from Beck's hands and Botha snapped it up and ran hard at the defence. A perfect chip, which he collected himself, opened the gap and then, taking the tackle from the last remaining defender, he gave Mordt a perfect pass. Mordt's third try made him the first Springbok ever to score a hat-trick against the All Blacks and the fifth South African to achieve the distinction in 90 years of test rugby.

The try was scored in the forty-fourth minute and most thought that the final whistle would be blown after Botha's conversion kick; with the score 22-all the result depended on the kick. The Springbok flyhalf had to wait for the injured Dave Loveridge to be carried off and then followed a major scare as the plane swooped over an open stand, clearing the heads of the spectators by a few metres. Only after all this could Botha kick and, for once, he fluffed it.

Ideally, the match should have ended there and then because the drawn series would have been the perfect result. But referee Clive Norling allowed the second half a lot of extra time and it was in the forty-ninth minute that he awarded a controversial penalty that was to cost the Springboks the game. He explained afterwards that he gave a free kick against Cockrell for foot-up (it is a fact, however, that Serfontein had not yet put the ball in when Norling blew his whistle) and that the Springboks had tackled Rollerson before he had gone five metres, thereby incurring the penalty Hewson calmly placed to give the All Blacks a 25–22 victory. The excessive amount of extra time suggested that the South Africans had valid reason to be disgruntled.

Terry McLean wrote the next day:

'Above all it was a shame the Springboks lost. A draw would have been a fairy-tale ending to the most difficult tour in all New Zealand's experience.'

After 56 days of turmoil the tour had come to an end and as Dan Retief wrote in *Springboks Under Siege*:

'The abiding memory of Wynand Claassen and his men will be of their dignity and good humour. They always conducted themselves as gentlemen and all things considered, that was a significant achievement which speaks volumes for their character.'

VENUE	SOUTH AFRICA	RESULT	SOUTH AFRICA				NEW ZEALAND			
			T	C	P	D	T	C	P	D
CHRISTCHURCH	LOST	9–14	1	1	0	1	3	1	0	0
WELLINGTON	WON	24–12	1	1	5	1	0	0	4	0
AUCKLAND	LOST	22–25	3	2	2	0	2	1	4	1
		55–51	5	4	7	2	5	2	8	1
SERIES: SOUTH AFRICA PLAYED 3; W1, L2, D0										

SOUTH AFRICA vs UNITED STATES OF AMERICA

An International Rugby Board resolution dictated that on their journey home the Springboks would stop over in the United States for three matches, including an official test match, over two weeks. It proved to be, without exception, the strangest tour ever undertaken by a Springbok team.

The first encounter was scheduled for Chicago but politicians picked up the scent of publicity and the match had to be transferred to the remote Racine, on the shores of Lake Michigan, where the Springboks won 46–12 on a converted grid-iron field. The second match was to take place at Bleeker Stadium, Albany, up-state New York, but again political pressure threatened and it was called off. The average American does not take kindly to such interference, however, and Tom Selfridge, chairman of the Eastern Rugby Union, went all the way to the Supreme Court in Washington where Judge Thurgood Marshall gave him the nod and also reaffirmed his right to demand police protection from disruption. In appalling weather, the Springboks won 41–0 before not much more than 300 spectators, while outside the stadium more than a thousand demonstrators screamed insults. The rain had one good effect, it helped to prevent an expected pitched battle between the protesters and the state troopers. The test was expected also to take place in Bleeker Stadium but on the Friday

The United States Rugby Football Association president, David Chambers (right), was not informed of the change of date for the international between the USA and South Africa, and therefore didn't get to see the match.

The game between the Springboks and the Colonials held in Albany, New York State was an unusual affair. The game was played on an American football field where the goalposts are positioned behind the dead ball line! South Africa won the match 41–0.

before the set date, it became known that the game had, in fact, already been played. There was what appeared to be a spur of the moment decision to get it over with and the Springboks were ordered to get dressed and to leave for a polo ground at nearby Glenville. The non-playing Springboks remained behind in the hotel. The referee assigned to the match, Don Reardon, from Texas, was not in his room when the summons came and he was unceremoniously replaced by Dr D Morrison. Several members of the USA Rugby Football Association, including the president, David Chambers, were also not informed and they were as stunned as the media when they heard the news.

The polo ground had a distinct list and although the Springboks had to literally run uphill in the second half, Skip Niebauer, captain of the less fit US Eagles, correctly pointed out afterwards that theirs was the even less enviable job of chasing them up the slope.

Apart from Burger, other try-scorers in South Africa's 38–7 victory were Mordt with three, thereby becoming the first Springbok to notch hat-tricks in successive internationals, Germishuys with two, and one each from Beck and Geldenhuys. Botha succeeded with three conversions.

In the 1982 edition of the *SA Rugby Annual*, editor Quintus van Rooyen recorded that 35 spectators, 20 policemen, a television crew, one reporter and no demonstrators were present. These figures alone tell the story of one of the most pathetic chapters in South African sports history.

VENUE	SOUTH AFRICA	RESULT	SOUTH AFRICA				USA			
			T	C	P	D	T	C	P	D
NEW YORK	WON	38–7	8	3	0	0	1	0	1	0

CHAPTER 39

1982

SOUTH AMERICA TOUR
SOUTH AFRICA

▲▲▲

South America played two tests against South Africa in 1982. Naas Botha, Danie Gerber (Number 13) and Divan Serfontein (Number 9) look on as Hugo Porta retains possession after being tackled.

The international scene became bleak for South Africa in 1982. A Welsh tour was cancelled and for the first time semi-professional rugby was mentioned in respectable circles. Dr Danie Craven, while accepting the very real possibility that isolation might eventually force South Africa in that direction, frequently reiterated the view that as long as there was a hope of official tours, the International Rugby Board could count on his support and that of his board.

Smouldering dissatisfaction with some of the events of the previous season cost Butch Lochner and Nelie Smith their positions and Professor Daan Swiegers, a former Northern Transvaal loose-forward, became the new chairman of the national selection committee. Dr Cecil Moss, a 1949 Springbok wing and one of the best-liked and most respected men in the game, took over the coaching, assisted by Dr Hannes Marais, the great former frontranker and a captain whose fine reputation had suffered rather unfairly as a result of the 1974 debacle against the Lions.

South America, or more specifically Argentina, again came to the rescue to give the Springboks some international competition during 1982. Sailing under the banner of the Jaguars, the team was captained by Hugo Porta and included 30 Argentinians, five Uruguayans, five Chileans and two from Paraguay. The group of 42 players were to be divided into two teams, each playing seven matches, with two tests arranged between the Springboks and the A-team.

The composition of the two sides was to be based on performance during the tour and players could accordingly be promoted or demoted.

▲▲▲

The Springboks, captained by Wynand Claassen, gave an amazing exhibition of uninhibited rugby in the first test at Loftus Versfeld, scoring eight tries to one in a 50–18 victory, and at times playing as if they were being paid to

Theuns Stofberg (Number 7) joins the maul to help make the ball available to the fast-moving Danie Gerber.

show off the more flashy side of their skill. The forwards supplied the platform, Serfontein and Botha spun the ball time and again, and centre Danie Gerber and left-wing Carel du Plessis created and scored tries that were simply sensational.

Gerber scored three tries, one of them an incredible effort in which he received from Claassen in his own area and ran more than 80 metres along the touchline to dive over in the corner. Carel du Plessis, one of the most elusive runners ever to play for the Springboks, also produced an unforgettable long-range effort when he got the ball from Serfontein on the blindside touchline. He bamboozled two defenders with an outside swerve and then ran 70 metres before he was finally checked. Louw and Stofberg were up to take the movement further and the outstanding Oosthuizen, showing remarkable speed for a frontranker, was on the spot to take the final pass to score.

Du Plessis celebrated his international debut with a try of his own when Claassen sent him on his way just before half-time. He rounded his opposite number as if he was rooted in the turf and then easily outstripped the cover defence with his lazily-graceful, deceptively fast running style.

Mordt was somewhat overshadowed on the day by the spectacular feats of Gerber and Du Plessis but he did manage to get two tries, one of them a typical effort in which he simply crashed through the defence. Willie du Plessis unhampered by injury for a change, also got a try but impressed even more with the intelligent way in which he dovetailed with Gerber.

The 50 points scored by the Springboks was the highest total by any team in an official test and the combined aggregate of 68 points by the two sides was also a record. Gerber's hat-trick was the seventh by a Springbok and the first ever by a

Nick Mallett, the Springbok number eight, looks for a gap in the Jaguar defence. Michael du Plessis moves up in support.

South African centre. It is difficult to believe but it is a fact that when all four threequarters (Mordt, Carel du Plessis, Gerber and Willie du Plessis) scored tries in this match it was the first time it had happened in 163 tests played by South Africa to that date. Naas Botha reached a milestone of his own when he pushed his world record for dropgoals in tests to 12. At the end of the first test he had scored an impressive 296 points.

▲▲▲

The Jaguars strengthened their pack with the inclusion of their best lock-forward, Elisio Branca, who had suffered from 'homesickness' up till then, prop Serafin Dengra and loose forward Mario Negri, and they also made two changes among the backs to give themselves more solidity for the second test to be held a week later in Bloemfontein. The same Springbok team did duty again and there can be no doubt that despite a few warnings about complacency, over-confidence in the South African camp was one reason for their appalling performance.

The Springbok defeat in an often ill-tempered match is arguably the biggest upset in South African rugby history. Behind a vastly improved pack, Porta proved that, at 31, he was still a masterful flyhalf and he guided his band of no-hopers to a thoroughly deserved 21–12 victory. Porta scored all of his team's points with a try, conversion, four penalty goals and a dropgoal, against which the Springboks managed a try by Gerber, and a conversion and two penalties by an off-form, subdued Botha. The Argentinian's total of 21 was the highest ever scored by an individual against the Springboks.

The Springboks came in for a drubbing from the critics after their fall from grace. The forwards, who lost the powerful frontranker Hempies du Toit in the second half (he was replaced by Henning van Aswegen), were outplayed, and behind the scrum, Serfontein and Botha failed comprehensively in what was to be the final match of their partnership. Gerber and Willie du Plessis were equally bad in midfield and only Heunis at fullback and Carel du Plessis, on the left-wing, could feel remotely satisfied with themselves. Not since the disastrous season of 1974 had a Springbok team given a more dispirited performance.

VENUE	SOUTH AFRICA	RESULT	SOUTH AFRICA				SOUTH AMERICA			
			T	C	P	D	T	C	P	D
PRETORIA	WON	50–18	8	6	1	1	1	1	4	0
BLOEMFONTEIN	LOST	12–21	1	1	2	0	1	1	4	1
		62–39	9	7	3	1	2	2	8	1
SERIES: SOUTH AFRICA PLAYED 2; W1, L1, D0										

1982 – BITS AND PIECES

Late in the 1982 season an uninspired Five Nations combination played a South African President's XV to celebrate the inauguration of the new Ellis Park Stadium. It was to have been an official test but the four Home Unions threatened to withdraw unless the game was stripped of all representative flavour. The South Africans won 35–19 but, with the competitive angle obscured, the game had less impact than the average provincial match. A scheduled tour by France in the 1983 season was cancelled by their government and the nearest South Africa came to international competition was a visit from an overseas team who were invited as individuals by Western Province to share in their centenary celebrations.

The visitors, led by England's Peter Wheeler and consisting of players from Britain, France and New Zealand, played three matches on their brief tour, including one against a South African XV at Newlands. It was won 37–35 by the local side and produced 12 tries between the two teams. The overseas stars lost two of their tour matches but ended up with interesting statistics, scoring 82 points and 13 tries, and having conceded the same points and number of tries.

Danie Gerber, Hennie Bekker and Errol Tobias played for the British Barbarians against Scotland and Cardiff and gave outstanding performances. Gerber totalled six tries in the two matches and there is little doubt that, at the time, he and wings Carel du Plessis and Ray Mordt were among the best, if not the best, in their positions in the world.

Naas Botha left South Africa at the beginning of the 1983 season to establish himself as a specialist kicker for the Dallas Cowboys in the United States. Not yet 25, Botha had rewritten the record books during his brief career of only 17 tests and his defection to what was regarded as a form of professionalism, removed from the scene a flyhalf who was already being compared with the legends of the game. He was to be reinstated two years later, after the IRB accepted the principle that American football was not a form of professional rugby.

Ray Mordt, seen here scoring the third try of his hat-trick in the third test against New Zealand, was regarded as one of the finest wings in the world during the early 1980s.

CHAPTER 40

1984

ENGLAND AND THE JAGUARS REVISIT

▲▲▲

In 1984, Johan Heunis' name was added to the long list of magnificent Springbok fullbacks. He took over this position from Gysie Pienaar.

The Springboks returned to the international arena in 1984, remaining undefeated in two tests against England and two tests against another Argentinian-dominated, Porta-led South America and Spain combination.

They scored 122 points to 52 and 18 tries to three in the four tests played and although the strength of South African rugby was hardly tested to the limit by the opposition offered, there was at least some international contact.

ENGLAND vs SOUTH AFRICA

Injuries and work commitments forced more than 20 of England's best players to declare themselves unavailable and the England selectors had few options when they selected the team to tour South Africa during May and June 1984.

Their decision to appoint John Scott as captain received a lukewarm response. The general view was that the team was in for a hiding, and the more optimistic supporters relied heavily on an old adage that England players are prone to 'coming right' while on a tour. South Africans had not forgotten how England had beaten the Springboks a dozen years before, however, and the wailing of the British newspaper experts was taken with the proverbial pinch of salt. But for once they were proved correct. It was indeed a weak side. In fact, some authorities rated it the worst team to tour South Africa in living memory.

With three victories and a draw under the belt, England went into the first test at Port Elizabeth against a Springbok side, led by Theuns Stofberg, which was without matchwinning kicker Naas Botha for the first time since 1980. John Villet replaced Willie du Plessis as Danie Gerber's partner, and Avril Williams was brought in on the wing in the place of the injured Mordt. Errol Tobias was selected as flyhalf. Newcomers in the pack were Chris Rogers and locks Rudi (Vleis) Visagie and Schalk Burger. The selection of Gerrie Sonnekus provided a happy ending to one of the shabbier stories in Springbok history. Ten years before, Sonnekus was one of the victims of the great panic of 1974 when he was selected to play scrumhalf against the Lions. The experiment failed and Sonnekus seemed consigned to oblivion but he kept playing, and his perseverance and ultimate justification serves as a lesson for any player who has suffered disappointment.

The Springboks won the test 33–15, three tries to none, but the bulk of the points came from fullback Heunis who crowned an excellent all-round performance with 21 points (five penalties, three conversions). The South African tries came from Gerber, Du Plessis and Louw. For England, Dusty Hare, a ponderous full-back but a superb placekicker, scored four penalties for his side, and flyhalf John Horton managed to put over a drop to increase the score.

The Springbok forwards generally had the better of things and with the England backs fragile under pressure, more than three tries should have been notched. Gerber and Du Plessis, given plenty of opportunity by their pack and a good halfback pairing in Serfontein and Tobias, were dangerous every time they touched the ball but the act never quite got together. Gerber's speed and power ripped the England defence apart on several occasions and only a desperate late tackle prevented him from going over after a most sophisticated chip. The try he did get came after he collected a kick ahead from Serfontein and burst through.

Carel du Plessis gave a devastating performance. Serfontein received from a ruck about 20 metres from the England line. Heunis took his pass in the flyhalf position and from him the ball went to Tobias. Then came the unexpected. Villet threw an appalling pass which bobbed off the ground at least a metre in front of Gerber. The bounce hurled it into Du Plessis's hands, however, and fate could not have been more unkind to England because, of all the Springboks on the field that day, no one could have exploited such a situation better than he. A feint to the left and then a quick jink inside forced a defender into an off-balance tackle. He was brushed off without so much as causing the Springbok to falter in his stride. Du Plessis jinked twice more and each time a would-be defender was left talking to himself. Finally he was in the clear and accelerated to outpace the sole remaining defender for a try next to the left upright.

▲▲▲

The Springboks had such a dominant second half during the first test that the selectors wisely gave Stofberg an unchanged combination for the second test a week later at Ellis Park. Scott's embattled band, only too aware of their shortcomings, went into this match hoping for a miracle. They got, instead, a Springbok team which, except when they lost the edge towards the end of the second half, gave a quite outstanding performance.

The South African forwards, with Stofberg in phenomenal form in his fourth match as captain, plied their threequarters with quality possession and Gerber scored his second hat-trick in international rugby. With 12 tries in 13 appearances the Eastern Province centre, who had respiratory problems during the match, joined Gerrie Germishuys as the leading try-scorer in Springbok test history.

Gerber's hat-trick came between the sixteenth and thirty-third minute of the first half. The first followed a clean lineout won by Visagie. Villet, on Gerber's outside, drove a breach and then passed back inside to Gerber. He took the attack further midfield by jinking inside the panicking defence, before swerving outside again for a clear run to the line.

About ten minutes later Serfontein tried the blindside and Gerber flashed up to his pass at great speed. A despairing tackle barely brushed the Springbok's back and a dummy pass to his inside eliminated the remaining feeble obstacle on his way to his second try. A little more than five minutes later the Springboks won a quick heel from a ruck and Tobias, who shone on the attack behind such a dominant pack, drove home the advantage by feinting the defence into frustrated impotence before feeding Gerber, galloping up on his outside. No one so much as touched him as he rushed through to dot down behind the posts.

1985

As far as international competition was concerned, 1985 was a bad year for the Springboks. The scheduled All Blacks' tour was cancelled because of political pressure, no invitation was extended to South Africa to compete in the World Cup tournament planned for 1987, and late in 1985 and 1986, the Lions tour was aborted because it was felt that the climate overseas was not right for it. An unofficial 'Springbok' team, led by Theuns Stofberg, was selected for an internal tour of four matches against Barbarian combinations, and although it was a pale substitute for the real thing, the tour served to give a sound evaluation of the talent available.

Two outstanding Springboks of the 1980s, Rob Louw and Ray Mordt, joined Wigan, the prominent British Rugby League club in 1985 and there was a general feeling that many others would follow as isolation from international competition continued. The fear was to prove unfounded but there is no doubt that proper and even lucrative remuneration of players was encouraged by the orphan status South African rugby was given by its traditional playing partners.

The Springbok side that took on England in 1984. Gerrie Sonnekus (middle row, third from left) played eighthman, having played at scrumhalf against the 1974 Lions.

Tobias used his speed and a terrific hand-off of England centre Huw Davies to score a try of his own, and Stofberg and Sonnekus notched the other two in a total of six. Heunis placed three conversions plus a penalty and Tobias a conversion for a final tally of 35 to England's nine, made up of three penalties from Hare.

The Springboks, generally stronger, faster and with more flair than their opponents, had obviously been the better team and the Fleet Street press reports that Scott's men were beaten because they were too fond of parties and had actually been encouraged by the South African Rugby Board to drink excessively, said much about the state of British tabloid journalism.

VENUE	SOUTH AFRICA	RESULT	SOUTH AFRICA				ENGLAND			
			T	C	P	D	T	C	P	D
PORT ELIZABETH	WON	33–15	3	3	5	0	0	0	4	1
JOHANNESBURG	WON	35–9	6	4	1	0	0	0	3	0

SOUTH AMERICA AND SPAIN TOUR SOUTH AFRICA

The Springboks had learned to be wary of South American teams and the arrival of Hugo Porta's 1984 combination of players drawn from Argentina, Chile, Uruguay, Paraguay, Peru and Spain was awaited with trepidation. The tour started at the end of the South African season and by the time of the first test at Loftus Versfeld there was a real danger of staleness. Injuries and retirement had eliminated Stofberg, Hempies du Toit and Villet. The selectors replaced Villet with Michael du Plessis, who became the third member of the Somerset East family to earn Springbok colours. Michael, who had withdrawn from rugby for several seasons because of injury and dentistry studies, was a subtly-skilled player, with a personal preference for the flyhalf position, whose talent was overshadowed in his younger years by a tendency to be rash and ill-tempered on the field.

Anton Barnard and Attie Strauss were the new frontrankers, Kulu Ferreira replaced Stofberg on the flank, eighthman Nick Mallett took over from Sonnekus, and Schalk Burger had to make way for the fit-again Louis Moolman. Another player to return was Ray Mordt who took over from Avril Williams.

▲▲▲

DIVAN SERFONTEIN

Divan Serfontein, a veteran of 17 tests, became the eleventh Stellenbosch University product to captain the Springboks since Paul Roos in 1906, an appointment no one could quibble over. Serfontein was the thirty-ninth Springbok captain since South Africa entered the international arena in 1891.

The Springboks went into the first test without a reliable placekicker. Heunis, who had filled the role since the departure of Botha, was suffering from a groin injury and could not risk aggravating it with placekicking. Gerber, who was selected as Heunis's understudy, was erratic to say the least, and Tobias, whose record indicated that he was slightly more reliable, also had more than his share of off-days.

After a poor first half, at the end of which the Jaguars led 12–10, the Springboks came to life and eventually won 32–15, with tries by Louw, Heunis, Serfontein, Gerber and Mallett. Tobias, who had to be called up for duty by Serfontein after Gerber missed several kicks, succeeded with two penalties and two conversions.

Gerber's only successful kick of this particular afternoon was a most significant one, however. With it he converted his own first-half try, his thirteenth one in fourteen tests, and with it he became the Springbok who had notched the most tries at the highest level of rugby.

The South Americans had not done badly at all, however, with tries by Jose Palma and Ricardo de Vedia, and one penalty and two conversions by Porta.

▲▲▲

Recalling only too clearly how the Jaguars had turned the tables in the Bloemfontein test two years previously, the Springboks went into the second international without any illusions. The Springbok forwards played much better and only poor placekicking prevented a larger winning margin than 22–13.

The Springboks scored four tries to one, with Carel du Plessis, Ferreira, Mordt and Gerber going over, and

Powerful Springbok eighthman, Nick Mallet, stands up to the Jaguars' defence in the second test played at Newlands.

Tobias managing to put over two penalties. Porta placed three penalties and Martin Sansot scored an unconverted try. Gerber's try, his fourteenth in 15 tests, highlighted his extraordinary strength and determination. Lock-forward Visagie started the movement, and Louw took it further before passing to Michael du Plessis. The centre slipped the ball to his brother Carel who fed Tobias. The flyhalf almost lost control but the ball dropped backwards and into the hands of Gerber who had come roaring into the left-wing position. An opponent sailed into the muscular Springbok with a will but he bounced off and away as if he had collided with a runaway truck. A second defender made a much more half-hearted attempt and Gerber pulled free. A short distance from the corner flag he was hit squarely by another tackler and the impact momentarily caused him to falter, but he quickly regained his balance to score a try to remember with awe.

Carel du Plessis also scored a typical try. Serfontein had taken the ball from a ruck and, skipping Gerber, had passed directly to the left-wing. Du Plessis swerved outside fullback Sansot, then cut inside the covering defence, before beating a desperate Porta to the goalline with a bewildering burst of speed.

The Jaguars also had their moments. Porta started it with a chip which Cuesta Silva plucked out of the air to run clear. He drew Heunis before passing to Sansot who, when caught by Michael du Plessis, gave to Silva, who was stopped by Heunis, who reverse-passed to the waiting Sansot, who had nothing left to beat.

VENUE	SOUTH AFRICA	RESULT	SOUTH AFRICA				SOUTH AMERICA AND SPAIN			
			T	C	P	D	T	C	P	D
PRETORIA	WON	32–15	5	3	2	0	2	2	1	0
CAPE TOWN	WON	22–13	4	0	2	0	1	0	3	0
		54–28	9	3	4	0	3	2	4	0
SERIES: SOUTH AFRICA PLAYED 2; W2, L0, D0										

Ray Mordt and Carel du Plessis watch the forward exchanges during the Newlands test, which South Africa won 22–13.

A rare slip-up for the normally sure-footed Naas Botha. The extremely wet conditions at Newlands caused his downfall in the test between South Africa and Australia.

NAAS BOTHA

Naas Botha's exile from South African rugby lasted from June 1983 when, wearing a green jersey with a Springbok emblem on it, he bid a group of friends and fans an emotional farewell at Jan Smuts Airport, until March 1985, when he received the green light from the International Rugby Board to return to the amateur game. In between, Botha, one of the most gifted players in Springbok rugby history, had tried yet failed to make the grade as a specialist kicker in American football.

Within days, Botha played in a team of Springboks against Northern Transvaal at Loftus Versfeld and his rustiness was painfully evident. By the end of the 1985 season he was back, however, as the best flyhalf in the country and a supreme matchwinner. He reached new milestones of 379 points and 29 dropgoals in first-class rugby, and 188 points and 20 dropgoals in the Currie Cup competition, during his first season back in Northern Transvaal colours.

Naas Botha was probably the most newsworthy South African rugby player of all time. Whatever he did, it became news. He was instantly recognizable, a delight for cartoonists and satirists, but above all he was a genius of a rugby player. When he was still playing Under-20, the 1976 All Blacks made a point of going to watch him play. They even asked for him to play against them for the South African Barbarians, guaranteeing the safety of the young player – an invitation that was declined.

The boy from Pretoria, who took his rugby so seriously he would camp at Loftus Versfeld to see his heroes play, made rugby football his life and the game was kind to him. He worked remarkably hard at improving his skills, was blessed with natural talent, and was ardent enough to give the game his full attention. His was a recipe for genius – one that blossomed early.

At the age of 19, he played in the Northern Transvaal team. At the age of 22, he captained the Blue Bulls and became a Springbok. Those who accused Naas Botha of being only a kicker should have seen him when first he played for South Africa and let loose one of the fastest and best backlines South Africa has ever known. When the Springboks beat the 1980 Lions at Newlands they scored five tries and not a single conversion, not even a dropped goal, something that was to become a Naas Botha speciality.

He was one of the fastest runners in that backline. Possibly his greatest all-round performance on the world stage was against Auckland in 1981, but then he was also the player who came close to clinching the 1981 series for South Africa, demonstrators and bombers aside.

When he returned from America in 1986, he was just in time. Errol Tobias, who had played so well against England in 1984, was 36 in 1986, and the New Zealand Cavaliers arrived, regarded as the All Blacks in all but name. Naas Botha was one of the great wet-weather players of all time, and in the first test in 1986 Newlands was wet. Botha was at his best. In Pretoria he again let his back loose for four superb tries.

Naas Botha was for a long time on centre stage in South African rugby. His level of fitness made him durable. He was still captaining South Africa and playing fly-half at the age of 34. He was also playing rugby most of the year as he found Rovigo in Italy a suitably rewarding place for his talents.

At the end, he faded from active participation, a strange happening for a man whose least actions attracted headlines. But he stayed on in rugby as a coach and as a television commentator.

Who said Naas Botha never passed the ball? Naas in action at Loftus Versfeld, Pretoria.

Naas Botha kicks with his usual precision while Peter Whipp watches.

CHAPTER 41

1986

NEW ZEALAND CAVALIERS
TOUR SOUTH AFRICA

▲▲▲

Jaco Reinach on the run in a match against the New Zealand Cavaliers.

South Africa hosted the first-ever 'rebel' team when thirty All Blacks, led by Andy Dalton and managed and coached by Ian Kirkpatrick and Colin Meads, arrived for four tests against the Springboks. Called the New Zealand Cavaliers, the team was, barring John Kirwan and David Kirk, a full-strength All Blacks team. And for competition-starved South Africa they provided a season to remember.

But first there was an awful fuss at boardroom level. The New Zealand Rugby Football Union had not given the tour its blessing, the International Rugby Board demanded that it be stopped, and the South African Rugby Board, metaphorically speaking, kicked for touch by promising an enquiry. Dr Craven and Professor Fritz Eloff, the South African Rugby Board's delegates to an International Rugby Board meeting in progress at the time, had to endure severe censure but, all things considered, it was a small price to pay.

The tour was organized by the Transvaal Rugby Union, headed by Dr Louis Luyt, and the sponsors, Yellow Pages, were fully justified in labelling it the 'Battle of the Giants'. The four tests proved to be action-packed, merciless contests in the true tradition of All Blacks–Springboks rivalry. The standard of play was high, however, and there was nothing dour or dull about it.

At the outset, Meads said that the Cavaliers would have supplied more than ninety per cent of an official All Blacks team had one been selected at that point.

Carel du Plessis played in all four games against the New Zealand Cavaliers.
He scored a memorable try at Newlands.

Strong up front as always, the New Zealanders also had a better than competent set of backs. Except for three of the four tests and the match against Transvaal, when they did not field their strongest combination, they went through the tour undefeated against the toughest available competition.

There were the inevitable incidents and controversies. Andy Dalton, who made an outstanding impression as captain, had his jaw broken by Burger Geldenhuys, the Northern Transvaal Springbok flanker, at Loftus Versfeld. This led Dr Craven to declare that Geldenhuys, one of the favourites for the national team, would not be acceptable to the South African Rugby Board should he be selected for any of the tests. The match against Natal led to a general and unsightly brawl and in the third test, Uli Schmidt, the Springbok hooker, severely injured Dave Loveridge, the established All Blacks scrumhalf.

After the final test, the New Zealanders allowed their simmering dissatisfaction with Ken Rowlands, the Welsh referee who handled the series, to get out of hand. Dalton in his after-match speech made some cutting remarks about Rowlands, which prompted Naas Botha to come to the Welshman's defence, not neglecting the opportunity to point out that the Springboks, in turn, had reason to complain about Clive Norling's refereeing during the 1981 series in New Zealand.

Gert Smal stands behind the deadball line, counting the minutes of his cooling off sentence in a game against the Cavaliers.

Naas Botha captained the Springboks, who wore the emblem of their sponsors, Toyota, on their chests, in all four tests. Coached by Cecil Moss, the selectors named only 19 players, ten of them newcomers to international rugby.

There were six new caps in the team for the first test at Newlands. Jaco Reinach, a Free State right-wing with a national track record for the 400 metres, and his teammate, scrumhalf Christo Ferreira, replaced stalwarts Ray Mordt, who had joined the professional ranks, and Divan Serfontein, who had retired.

Uli Schmidt, the mobile Northern Transvaal hooker, was an obvious choice and with Burger Geldenhuys not considered, the inclusion of Transvaal's Wahl Bartmann, Gert Smal and Jannie Breedt gave the side a loose-forward trio with tremendous potential but no international experience. Breedt, who had captained his provincial team with distinction, was made Botha's understudy and the pack leader. There had been some speculation beforehand that Schalk Burger would get the captaincy but Botha's appointment could not be faulted.

With a broken jaw keeping Dalton out of the tour and Frank Shelford keeping the obvious deputy leader, flanker Jock Hobbs, out of the side, the Cavaliers settled for Andy Haden as captain. He was given a combination in which experience was the dominant feature. This, despite the fact that flyhalf Grant Fox, lock Murray Pierce and Shelford were included at the expense of players with more test experience.

Statistics show that in the history of the rivalry between the All Blacks and the Springboks the touring team has never been able to win the first test of a series. But heavy rain made the Newlands surface soft and the New Zealanders were expected to be far more at home in such conditions. In addition, the Cavaliers enjoyed an overwhelming advantage in international experience. Their line-up shared 219 tests between them compared to a rather meagre 75 for Botha's men.

A masterful performance by the Springbok captain sunk the Cavaliers in a match they seemed to have in hand when they led 15–12 midway through the second half. The Springbok forwards, who were outplayed in the first half, looked streets better after the resumption. However, a fair amount of possession was all Botha needed to guide his team to a thrilling victory.

Botha, with three penalties, two dropped goals and a conversion, totalled 17 points out of the Springbok score of 21, while Fox notched 11 of his side's 15 points, succeeding with three penalties and a conversion of the penalty try awarded near the end of the match. With the score 15-all and with no more than ten minutes left to play, the sell-out crowd, watching the game through a filter of rain, were beginning to welcome the prospect of settling for a draw. Then came a lineout deep in the Cavaliers' territory. Moolman won possession, scrumhalf Ferreira served quickly but somewhat erratically, and Botha had to reach far forward to take a difficult pass. Miraculously he managed to control his balance as well as the slippery ball. He stab-kicked for the cornerflag, the ball landing behind the goalline and rolling erratically over the soaked grass towards the deadball area as Carel du Plessis set off on one of the most exciting runs in tradition-rich Newlands history – a race to reach the ball before it could roll out of play.

The New Zealand cover defenders were really irrelevant. With the exception of fullback Kieran Crowley they were all caught on the wrong foot. Crowley was several metres in front of Du Plessis but in turning around he had lost speed and the heavy field held him back. Du Plessis sped past him with remarkable sure-footedness on such a slippery surface as the ball made its way to the neutrality of no-man's land – not more than a metre from the deadball line it spun to a stop and a fraction of a second later the wing swooped on it with a headlong dive.

Botha was left with a difficult conversion. In these conditions someone was needed to hold the ball and Danie Gerber took the job. As Botha steadied himself, eyes glued on the ball after one long look at the posts, he signalled Gerber to tilt the ball slightly to his right, then he corrected an over-compensation from the Springbok centre. The kick was true and the self-assurance of the Springbok fly-half was typical of his performance. His two dropgoals were textbook efforts under pressure from his opponents, the state of the game and the elements.

▲▲▲

Jock Hobbs took over as All Blacks captain for the second test in Durban, a match which had those experts who liked to keep an eye on history when they make their predictions, in a quandary. New Zealand had never yet won a test in Durban but, conversely, the second test of a series between the All Blacks and the Springboks almost always went to the touring team.

With Botha's kicking form deserting him in the swirling wind of King's Park, the Cavaliers squeaked home 19–18 and, scoring two tries to one, they deserved their victory. The Springboks squandered their opportunities with Botha the main culprit. He did put over four penalties and a conversion but missed half-a-dozen others and he also fluffed four attempted dropgoals. In the closing minutes Botha missed what would have been a match-winning dropgoal from point-blank range, the sort of effort he would normally put over with his eyes closed. Danie Gerber also erred once by choosing the wrong option after a brilliant run. Jaco Reinach scored the South Africans' only try after Botha had attacked from his own quarter and Gerber had split the defence before passing to the flying Free Stater.

Uli Schmidt wrestles for the ball in the loose maul, with Michael du Plessis (left) and Johan Heunis in support.

Warwick Taylor and Murray Mexted notched tries for the visitors and Grant Fox added three penalties. He also converted Mexted's try, which came when the All Black forward burst over from a scrum near the line. Taylor, an above-average centre, got his try after Ferreira had dawdled in controlling a ball near his own line and Botha, after receiving his scrumhalf's desperate pass, had also shown uncharacteristic tardiness in clearing.

▲▲▲

The Springbok selectors made three changes in the team for the third test in Pretoria a week later. Both props, Anton Barnard and the massive Flippie van der Merwe, were axed and replaced by Frans Erasmus and Piet Kruger, respectively. Erasmus had a reputation for being a powerful scrum-

Having made the tackle, Michael du Plessis scrambles for the available ball.

mager and an energetic worker, while Kruger had been on the substitutes' bench for the first two tests. The third change was at scrumhalf where Ferreira, who had not come up to expectations but who in all fairness had not enjoyed much protection from his forwards either, had to make way for the nippier Garth Wright, the first University of Port Elizabeth product to become a Springbok. He had not played with Botha before but Cecil Moss, the national coach, had no qualms about this as the flyhalf had always been able to adapt to different partners. Schmidt, Breedt and Smal had found their feet quickly and by the time of the third test their positions had been entrenched.

The Springboks went 2–1 up in the series by winning the third test 33–18, four tries to one. It was a superb performance by the South Africans, particularly the backs, whose sophisticated skill from scrumhalf Wright to fullback Heunis, made their counterparts look ordinary. The New Zealand forwards held their own, however, and for long periods seemed about to take a stranglehold on the game. But the Springbok pack, particularly in the latter part of the second half, recovered to win vital possession for their backs.

Moolman, Burger and Smal did exceptionally well in the lineouts, and Breedt, Bartmann and Smal formed an effective loose trio. Schmidt played a remarkable game. He did his work in the tight phases, and shone as an extra loose-forward. His try after Carel du Plessis had taken advantage of a shrewd, direction-changing pass from his brother Michael to tear the New Zealand defence apart, was proper reward for his fantastic performance.

The finest movement of the afternoon was rounded off by Gerber who, in the process, grabbed his fifteenth test try. Botha had just landed a penalty and the Cavaliers kicked off from the halfway line. Erasmus wrestled the ball loose and passed it on to Bartmann. He popped it to Wright who, in the solitary lapse of his debut, sent out a long but poor pass to Botha. The ball rolled and bounced along the ground but Botha took it with amazing aplomb and with a flick of his wrists he instantly passed it on to Gerber. From Gerber it went to Michael du Plessis, who drew the defence with delicate timing before putting his brother, Carel, in possession. The left-wing jinked inside, beat New Zealand's Fox with ridiculous ease and forced fullback Crowley into the tackle before giving Gerber, now running flat-out on his outside, a pass right out of a textbook. With the ball resting in the crook of his arm, Gerber turned on an incredible burst of speed to outstrip a desperate defensive effort by Craig Green and, safely over the goalline, he also evaded Taylor to give Botha the most comfortable of conversions.

Botha, who put over four conversions and three penalties, got his first test try when he chipped ahead, placing the ball perfectly and putting Mexted, who gathered, in a no-win situation. Heunis tackled his man hard, the ball popped free and Botha pounced on it to beat the cover to the line. The fourth try of the afternoon went to Reinach who outpaced everybody in a 35-metre sprint after Schmidt had picked up a loose ball and Gerber had driven the breach. Crowley went over for the Cavaliers' only try after some magnificent driving by his forwards. Fox, who kicked splendidly, converted the try and put over three penalties and a dropgoal.

▲▲▲

The Cavaliers had to win the final test to draw the series and it was no fault of their forwards that they failed. They were on top for long spells with the Whetton twins, Gary and Alan, particularly rampant. The inexplicable decision to drop the capable Fox for Wayne Smith did not pay off, however. Fullback Robbie Deans was not in the same class as a placekicker and Smith was overfond of cutting inside.

The Cavaliers also contributed handsomely to their own downfall by conducting an unproductive feud with the referee, a positively suicidal thing to do when faced with a kicker like Botha. The Springbok skipper tallied 17 points with five penalties and a conversion which gave him a total of 69 for the series, at an incredible average of 17 points a match, and only one point short of being double the previous highest aggregate by an individual against New Zealand. The Springboks' other points in their 24–10 triumph came from a try by Wright, converted by Botha, and an excellent dropgoal by Michael du Plessis. For the Cavaliers, scrumhalf Andy Donald scored a try and Deans was successful with two penalty kicks.

The South African threequarters, so dominant in the third test, failed to repeat their devastating form and it was only after Botha had reverted to tactical kicking that the Springboks, who until then had been frequently saved by the grand defensive work of their loose-forwards, Smal, Bartmann and Breedt, began to look like winners. Their only try came in the final minutes when Wright collected a shrewd kick by Helgard Müller, who had come on for the injured Reinach, and dashed over for a try which earned him a delighted hug from his captain.

The Cavaliers, who had proved themselves to be well up to international standard, and worthy representatives of their country off the field, returned home to the anticipated abuse of the anti-apartheid ranks and their prime minister, David Lange, who crudely accused them of being 'liars and mercenaries'. Their subsequent disciplining by the New Zealand Rugby Football Union did not amount to much and there was good reason to believe that most of the members of the team would have toured South Africa again if the opportunity had presented itself.

▲▲▲

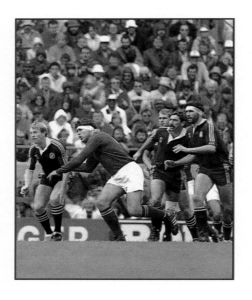

Surrounded! Schalk Burger could just be playing scrum half in the match between the New Zealand Cavaliers and the Springboks.

The Springboks were again denied international competition in 1987, but a gruelling Currie Cup season with many highlights underlining the inherent strength of local rugby, kept interest high. The South Pacific Barbarians produced some startlingly unorthodox rugby on a brief tour which was the brain-child of Craven, who saw in it an opportunity to give less prominent teams a chance to gain experience. In the two matches of the tour, the South African Barbarians beat the Islanders in entertaining encounters which provided spectacular movements but hardly the kind of opposition the Springboks, cynically ignored by the organizers of the game's first-ever, so-called World Cup tournament, had deserved.

Hopes glowed brightly early in 1988 that Northern Transvaal and Eastern Province would be officially allowed to invite an international combination to visit South Africa on the occasion of their fiftieth and one-hundredth anniversaries, respectively. But once again promises were broken, leaving players and the public frustrated and disillusioned.

Springbok scrumhalf, Garth Wright, prepares to pass the ball while Uli Schmidt (left) and Jannie Breedt (right) look on.

VENUE	SOUTH AFRICA	RESULT	SOUTH AFRICA				NEW ZEALAND CAVALIERS			
			T	C	P	D	T	C	P	D
CAPE TOWN	WON	21–15	1	1	3	2	1	1	3	0
DURBAN	LOST	18–19	1	1	4	0	2	1	3	0
PRETORIA	WON	33–18	4	4	3	0	1	1	3	1
JOHANNESBURG	WON	24–10	1	1	5	1	1	0	2	0
		96–62	7	7	15	3	5	3	11	1
SERIES: SOUTH AFRICA PLAYED 4; W3, L1, D0										

CHAPTER 42

1989

WORLD XV TOUR SOUTH AFRICA

▲▲▲

The 1989 season marked the centenary of the South African Rugby Board and although political, academic, sporting and commercial isolation was virtually complete, the International Rugby Board (IRB) sanctioned a mini-tour by an International XV to mark the occasion. The decision created bitter acrimony among the members of the IRB, with Wales eventually to sever long-standing ties with South Africa, and other countries afterwards expressing concern over rumours that the visiting players had been paid large rewards to tour.

There is no doubt that a visit to Harare the previous season by Craven and Luyt, where they met members of the African National Congress and undertook unequivocally to remove all racial discrimination from the game in South Africa, went a long way towards making it possible for the IRB to allow the tour. In the climate that prevailed in 1989, Craven and Luyt's meeting with the still-banned African National Congress angered many conservative local rugby authorities and earned censure at government level. In retrospect, it was a major step to prepare South Africa for quick readmission to international competition once political change came.

Garth Wright (Number 9) watches Jannie Breedt and Adolf Malan lose the battle for lineout possession.

At the time, however, there was a strong feeling that South Africa should leave the IRB and rely on rebel tours, regardless of the consequences. In the light of future events – which could hardly have been predicted then – it is fortunate that this desperate step was never taken. In addition to Craven's steadfast support of maintaining international relations at all costs, credit must also go to particularly sensitive liaison work done by Professor Fritz Eloff and Jan Pickard, the Northern Transvaal and Western Province presidents.

Even so, it was a critical period in South African rugby history and, with rumours abounding and political pressures almost unbearable, the centenary tour was in the balance up to the moment the manager, former Ireland skipper of the all-conquering 1974 Lions and one of the most respected players of any era, arrived at Jan Smuts Airport with three players in tow. Within days, the rest of the touring party flew in from various points of the compass.

With the exception of New Zealand, all the traditional rivals of the Springboks were represented in the squad, officially named the FNB International team. The presence of no fewer than ten Welshmen, in addition to their two IRB members among the many dignitaries to accept invitations to join the touring party, caused much dissent back home. France contributed eight representatives, Australia six, England four and Ireland and Scotland one each. Bob Templeton, from Australia, was the coach and Roland Bertranne, the distinguished former Tricolor centre, assisted McBride with the managerial duties. Pierre Berbizier, scrumhalf for France, was elected captain and Kerry FitzGerald, from Australia, was chosen to referee both test matches.

It was a side well up to international standard and with vast experience of the game at its highest level. Naas Botha was the most-capped Springbok with 21 tests; in comparison Berbizier had 48, Laurent Rodriguez, the outstanding eighth-man from France 49, and the illustrious Philippe Sella, then rated by some to be the best centre in the world, had made a total of 59 appearances for France.

To make the Springbok task tougher, they had been out of touch for so long that refereeing interpretations were inevitably strange. This fear was to be realized, specifically in the lineouts, and there was also an over-all lack of cohesion in the local team. This was also understandable. Season after season of Currie Cup rugby, one of the most relentless of domestic competitions in the world, certainly served to keep South African rugby uncompromisingly hard, but the continuous provincial rivalry was divisive and tended to stifle innovation.

The World Team, on the other hand, had little opportunity to form a unit and also had to cope with heavy off-the-field demands. They beat Natal 33–20 at King's Park, but lost 13–36 to a President's XV in Port Elizabeth, and 19–32 to Northern Transvaal at Loftus Versfeld.

▲▲▲

Jannie Breedt was appointed to lead the Springboks in the first test at Newlands. There were six new caps in the original selection, but Jan Lock, the Northern Transvaal tighthead prop, had to withdraw because of injury and was replaced by Flippie van der Merwe. Tragically, Lock was destined never to gain his Springbok colours; he died following a match for the Northern Transvaal B-team in 1991.

The newcomers who played at Newlands were Kobus Burger (right-wing), Faffa Knoetze (centre) and Niel Hugo (lock), all from Western Province; Heinrich Rodgers (loosehead prop) and Adolf Malan (lock) from Northern Transvaal.

Garth Wright, one of the quickest scrumhalves in the world, gets his line away in the match against the World XV.

Whose ball? Jannie Breedt seems to have won it for his side as Adolf Malan and Gert Smal watch.

Two notable names absent from the Springbok line-up were Gerber, at centre, and Bartmann, on the flank. Gerber was going through a period of health and injury problems, while Bartmann's form had temporarily slumped from the high standard set in 1986. The reserves were Andrew Patterson, Frans Erasmus, Wahl Bartmann, Robert du Preez, Helgard Müller and André Joubert. Long-serving Dr Cecil Moss held the coaching reins and Abie Malan was appointed manager.

A cold north-west wind drove sheets of rain across Newlands as more than 250 Springboks of the past walked onto the famous ground in a moving ceremony before the first test started.

The match failed as a spectacle but was a dramatic cliff-hanger nevertheless. The International XV dominated up front, out-scrumming the Springboks and holding territorial advantage for most of the time. The South Africans showed great grit, however, and with Naas Botha, excelling as always in wet weather, using the boot effectively, they never panicked. Heunis had to leave the field with a knee injury early on, but André Joubert substituted extremely well, bringing off at least three outstanding tackles when all seemed lost.

The International XV were the first to score. Laurent Rodriguez barged over for a try converted by Denis Charvet after seven minutes. A Botha penalty and a try by Knoetze converted by Botha gave the South Africans a 9-6 lead at half-time.

They played their best rugby of the match in the early part of the second half. First Botha flashed up from nowhere to intercept a lazy pass from his opposite number, Franck Mesnel, and with a startling burst of speed he left the defence standing for a marvellous try. Minutes later, Botha also succeeded with a penalty and when the Springbok forwards, shortly afterwards, drove with great purpose for Smal to score and Botha to convert, a runaway victory appeared to be on the cards. But the overseas team's forwards staged a mighty comeback and Denis Charvet succeeded with a penalty goal. With Botha suffering from a strained stomach muscle and off the field, the South Africans were in a desperate situation, Michael du Plessis going to flyhalf, and Müller off the bench to partner Knoetze at centre.

Charvet, combining well with his centre, created room for Sella to score. Just on fulltime, the predominantly French threequarter line moved beautifully, stretching the South African defence to breaking point and sending Ian Williams over for Charvet to convert. The Springboks were left with a one-point win (20–19) and with key players Botha and Heunis injured, a week of worries lay ahead before the second test at Ellis Park.

Most disturbing of all was the way the South African forwards had faded in the closing stages and the inability of such proven lineout experts as Hugo and Malan, Breedt and Smal to control

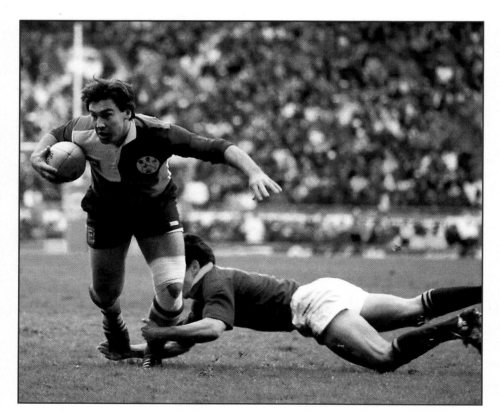

Garth Wright tackles in the match between South Africa and the World XV in 1989.

possession. The referee's interpretations, admittedly, did not always agree
with local practice but the international pack also had the better scrumming technique and often pushed their
opponents around. It was painfully
obvious that the effects of isolation
were noticeable up front.

▲▲▲

Botha and Heunis were still troubled
by injuries, but the selectors decided to
risk playing them in the second test.
The only change in the team was an
enforced one, Erasmus coming in as
tighthead prop for Van der Merwe,
who had pulled a calf muscle. Balie
Swart took his place on the bench.

The gamble to play Botha and
Heunis came off, although both were
not entirely at ease. Botha proved to be
the difference between winning and
losing. He scored 14 of his side's total of 22 points with a conversion, three penalty goals and a confident left-footed drop. Heunis, his leg heavily strapped, went
through for a splendid try after being fed on the blindside by Wright and beating
three defenders. The rest of the South African points came from a try by centre
Michael du Plessis, who had played with his usual subtlety and had much to do
with the way Knoetze settled down in midfield. Du Plessis and Burger, on wing,
did well on the defence during a critical period in the second half when the
International XV won all the quality possession going. Williams and Berbizier
scored tries for the visitors, with fullback Martin converting one. Martin also
landed a penalty, as did centre Charvet, for a final score of 16.

Although the Springbok victory wrapped up the mini-series, and making
allowances for injuries, their general performance was not satisfactory. The tight-
forwards again struggled, even after the outstanding lineout star Bob Norster
went off with a dislocated shoulder. Geldenhuys, Smal, Schmidt and Breedt did
well enough in the loose, but the pack failed to dominate. They conceded two
strikes on their own put-in and in the final minutes were pushed from a five-
metre scrum into their in-goal area to give Berbizier the easiest of tries.

*Garth Wright chooses the easiest way to
cross the advantage line.*

Venue	South Africa	Result	South Africa				World XV			
			T	C	P	D	T	C	P	D
Cape Town	won	20–19	3	1	2	0	3	2	1	0
Johannesburg	won	22–16	2	1	3	1	2	1	2	0
		42–35	5	2	5	1	5	3	3	0
Series: South Africa played 2; W2, L0, D0										

CHAPTER 43

1990-1992

SUCCESSES AND FAILURES

▲▲▲

On 2 February 1990, FW de Klerk, who had taken over the presidency a few months before, made a policy speech in parliament which was to change South Africa forever. Banned organizations, including the South African Communist Party, were legalized and Nelson Mandela, leader of the African National Congress (ANC) and arguably the best-known political prisoner in the world, was released from prison. Apartheid, which during the regime of PW Botha, De Klerk's predecessor, was in the process of being dismantled, was now consigned to history as one law after the other was repealed to remove the pillars on which the system had rested for more than forty years.

World leaders accepted that South Africa was irrevocably committed to change and the doors to international sporting competition began to open almost immediately. The ANC, mainly through their spokesman on the subject, Steve Tshwete, played a major role in this respect.

The main condition for their support was, naturally enough, that the various sports unite under non-racial controlling bodies and that development programmes among the disadvantaged communities be established.

James Small, Springbok wing for the 1992 test against New Zealand, played the greatest number of consecutive tests for South Africa in the immediate post-isolation era. The All Blacks won 27–24 .

Of all the major sports, rugby took the longest to pluck the fruits of unification, and deep into the 1992 season, there was still uncertainty. A planned tour of Romania and Italy was cancelled; a tragedy indeed as it would have given the Springboks the chance to get rid of some of the rust caused by isolation.

The formation of the South African Rugby Football Union (SARFU) to replace the Board which had served the game for a century, was established with Danie Craven and Ebrahim Patel as joint presidents. After much speculation, and often acrimonious public debate, the time-honoured symbol of South African rugby, the leaping springbok, was retained. A fair compromise was reached by adding a row of proteas to the badge and the green and gold colours remained.

Development schemes require vast sums of money and without internationals, rugby found itself in a catch-22 situation. Making the game available to all was a primary demand, but without test matches, this could not be financed and the green light for South Africa's readmission was slow in coming.

Good sense finally prevailed and, with almost indecent haste, the Springboks were brought back into international competition and given the impossible assignment of taking on New Zealand and Australia on successive Saturdays.

NEW ZEALAND vs SOUTH AFRICA

In 1986 the New Zealand Cavaliers had been the last really stiff opposition and that series had been won largely because of the presence of several outstanding players who were probably then at the peak of their careers.

Professor Daan Swiegers and his fellow selectors contemplated their enormous task of building a Springbok team virtually from scratch. Carel du Plessis and Johan Heunis had retired, and the formidable flanker Gert Smal was out of the domestic scene because of injury. Michael du Plessis, regarded good enough to captain a South African XV the previous season, was so often inactive, he really could not be considered, and the 34-year-old Gerber, who had been struggling to regain his old form for several years, was rebuilding a career in the Western Province with not many believing that he would be able to stage a proper comeback. Botha, commuting between Pretoria and Rovigo in Italy, was still a peerless matchwinner when the occasion demanded, but he was nearing the twilight of his career.

Even more unsettling than the gradual fading from the scene of the brilliant stars of the 1980s, was the sure knowledge that the game in South Africa had not evolved in tune with the rest of the world. Not only had the South African pattern and style remained stagnant, but our interpretation of the laws, in the lineouts in particular, had become hopelessly out of step, and there were valid warnings that the Springboks would be heavily penalized by neutral referees in test matches. To compound the troubles, new laws had just been introduced which all but revolutionized aspects of forward play.

The New Zealand team selected for the five-match tour of South Africa had just lost the Bledisloe Cup series against Australia but the two teams seemed to be of equal strength. The winning margins in the first two matches were one and two points respectively and the All Blacks won the third 26–23 on the eve of their departure for South Africa. Sean Fitzpatrick led the side. Known for his mobility and fiery aggression, Fitzpatrick had extensive international experience although his appointment as captain was a recent one and followed Mike Brewer's injury earlier in the season. He was given a well-balanced team who, between them, had represented New Zealand on nearly 500 occasions. Flyhalf Grant Fox, who, in 1991, had passed Don Clarke's record as the highest-scoring All Black of all time,

Adri Geldenhuys reflects the hard nature of test rugby, waiting for the ball in a lineout.

Michael Jones (with the bandaged foot), Robert du Preez and Wahl Bartmann in the heat of the battle in the test which marked South Africa's return from rugby isolation.

was with Steve McDowell, who had played with Andy Dalton's Cavaliers in 1986. Among others in the team with exceptional reputations were John Kirwan, a wing of the highest class who had scored a record number of 33 tries in his more than 50 tests for New Zealand; on the left wing, the burly Samoan-born Vaaiga Tuigamala, brilliant loose-forwards like Michael Jones and Zinzan Brooke, lock Ian Jones and Frank Bunce, a centre who played so well for Western Samoa in the 1991 World Cup Tournament, and his hard-tackling partner Walter Little. Richard Loe, a frontranker who had problems because of alleged rough play against the Australians, was labelled the 'meanie' in the side but he generally kept his cool and, all-in-all, the New Zealanders were not as physical as any of their predecessors. The new laws had taken some of the emphasis off brute strength and the Kiwis realized it.

South African observers at their first practice under the expert eye of coach Laurie Mains, got an inkling of how different the approach to the game had become. Virtually the entire two-hour session was devoted to the honing of skills South African coaches tend to leave to the backs. Not the All Blacks; even locks and frontrankers practised tactical kicking. Their fitness was breathtaking and particularly noticeable was the absence of the paunchiness too often found among South African tight-forwards.

▲▲▲

The All Blacks opened their tour with a 43–25 victory over Currie Cup finalists Natal, with the visitors establishing their dominance in the final quarter of the game. The many costly mistakes by Natal compared to the few made by the All Blacks was to be the pattern throughout the tour.

Free State, beaten 14–33, failed to stop the All Blacks with a rather ineffective display by a team which, when firing on all cylinders, can be extremely difficult on their home ground. Brendan Venter, the talented Free State centre, who was favoured to partner Natal's Pieter Müller, broke his leg in the match and his immediate dreams of playing international rugby were shattered.

The all-round skill, speed in the loose and discipline of the All Blacks sank the Junior Springboks 25–10, but the outstanding display of Northern Transvaal lock Drikus Hattingh provided compensation. Heinrich Füls, Tiaan Strauss, Kobus Wiese and his replacement after he was injured, FC Smit, also proved themselves to be players to watch. After beating a Central Unions XV 39–6 at Witbank, the All Blacks returned to Johannesburg for the one-off test against the Springboks at Ellis Park. The national trials held in Pretoria had given the South African selectors all the information they could hope for, and even in retrospect, they selected the best available talent to take on the All Blacks and later, the Wallabies.

Perhaps faster loose-forwards could have been considered, sacrificing the experience and height in the lineouts of Jannie Breedt in the process, and perhaps there should have been a keener realization that a forward like Wahl Bartmann was an expensive luxury under the new rules. Failing to recognize the appalling slump in form of scrumhalf Robert du Preez was arguably the biggest blunder, because although Garth Wright had been injured, this scrumhalf was regarded as fit enough to be on the reserve bench and therefore fit enough to be considered as Botha's partner at halfback. But hardly anyone quibbled with the selection of the players to lead the Springboks back into the international arena and to be wise with hindsight is only too easy. Naas Botha was the oldest and most experienced player in the team; an obvious choice as captain. Danie Gerber, capping a story-book return to the top, was a few months younger than his skipper and the only other survivor of the 1981 tour of New Zealand to make the national side.

There were eight newcomers to international rugby in the team, but all of them were in-form players with a touch of class. Theo van Rensburg, at fullback, and James Small and Pieter Hendriks on the wings played a big part in transforming Transvaal into an innovative and successful team. Small, in particular, was to make nonsense of fears that he was uncertain on defence. Pieter Müller, brother of Helgard and a cousin of Naas Botha, was an obvious choice from the start, at 23 an explosive attacker and a fearless tackler. Lood Müller, Adri Geldenhuys and Ian Mcdonald were the only forwards without international experience. Prop Heinrich Rogers, the versatile hooker–loose-forward–threequarter Schmidt, Malan, Hugo, Bartmann and Breedt, all had played at limited international level.

The reserves were Garth Wright, Heinrich Füls, Hennie le Roux, Harry Roberts, Drikus Hattingh and Johann Styger. A rather sad footnote: for the first time in 96 years, a Springbok team did not have a single member with present or past University of Stellenbosch connections.

The Springboks had an aggregate of 62 international caps between them, a pitiful total compared to the more than 300 the All Blacks could boast when, on the Wednesday before the test, they announced they would field exactly the same combination that had beaten Australia three weeks earlier. The referee was Sandy MacNeill of Australia, whose autocratic attitude was to contrast sharply with the firm but courteous style Dave Bishop, of New Zealand, was to show a week later in the test against the Wallabies.

▲▲▲

More than 70 000 spectators filled Ellis Park to see the Springboks officially re-enter the international arena and they were rewarded with a performance of character and flair. The final scoreline of 27–24 in favour of the All Blacks rather flattered the South Africans, but the sheer audacity and spirit of the Springbok backline when Botha decided on all-out attack, caused even neutral observers to read more into it than they should have. Pierre Berbizier, the French coach , spoke for most when he said: 'The Springboks played with such panache. They will quickly return to the highest level. They are brave.'

In the general euphoria, the fact that New Zealand at one stage held a 27–10 lead was forgotten. Final impressions are the ones that last and there is no getting away from it that the uninhibited running of the Springboks in the closing minutes of the match was exhilarating and enough to gloss over deficiencies up front and at scrumhalf.

Naas Botha prepares to convert Danie Gerber's try in the test against New Zealand in Johannesburg.

The match started on a low point when Fitzpatrick, the All Black captain, hit Botha the first time he came within punching range of his counterpart. Fortunately, although players on both sides received warnings for foul play, the match was not in the same league for warfare as some of the past encounters between the old rivals.

The All Blacks pack played with a smooth, practised efficiency the Springbok forwards, as a unit, could not equal. New Zealand's absolute control of possession and the alertness with which they grabbed every opportunity, underlined the gap between the game at international level and domestic competition.

Nothing illustrated the difference between them more than New Zealand's first try. There was a penalty near the Springbok line and eighthman Brooke, with Joseph and Jones, loose-forwards in a class of their own, tapped the ball to himself and was over the line before the Springboks could organize their defence.

The South Africans failed to establish healthy relations with Australian referee Sandy MacNeill. The Springbok captain afterwards publicly complained about the referee's 'lack of courtesy'. There is no doubt, however, that the South African forwards found it difficult to discard the old habit of lifting in lineouts and Bartmann, in particular, seemed unable to adapt to the new rules requiring the ball to be kept alive.

The All Blacks led 10–0 at half-time, with Fox placing a penalty and converting Brooke's try. Less than ten minutes into the second half Kirwan, after a good counter-attack by Tuigamala and Bunce, went over for Fox to make it 17–3, a Botha penalty having opened the Springbok score. Another Fox penalty made the score 20–3. It was at this point that Botha realized that his team's only hope was to break the All Blacks' pattern by spreading the ball wide to his backs and to risk all-out attack. Success was almost immediate. Breedt and Van Rensburg combined with a quick throw-in and Botha and Hendriks took it further. Gerber ripped through the New Zealand defence to score. Botha converted and the picture was suddenly less gloomy – despite almost immediate retaliation from the All Blacks. The try went to Timu, but it was as a result of an expertly executed drive down midfield which wiped out the cover defence and gave an object lesson in ball control before the New Zealand fullback was presented with a hard but clear run to the line.

A stroke of luck then came South Africa's way, cancelling out to some extent a questionable ruling that Gerber had lost the ball as he dived over at the corner-flag in the first half and Small's heart-breaking experience when, in an otherwise impressive test debut, he allowed the ball to pop out of his hands with the line at his mercy.

The referee missed a knock-on by Du Preez after Geldenhuys got the ball away from a lineout, and Müller burst through for his side's second try, again converted by Botha. All fears of a humiliating drubbing now dispelled,

Sean Fitzpatrick, the 1992 All Black captain, was seen to rough up opposing captain, Naas Botha, to 'welcome' him back to the international rugby arena.

Pieter Muller, one of South Africa's try scorers against the 1992 All Blacks. His more experienced centre partner, Danie Gerber, also scored a try.

the Springbok backs attacked confidently at every opportunity, with Botha switching direction frequently and Van Rensburg smoothly coming into the line. In injury time the all-or-nothing approach by the South Africans paid off again when Gerber easily cut through the defence for his seventeenth try in twenty test matches. Botha's conversion made the final score 27–24 to New Zealand, who deserved to win, but the superb second-half fight-back left the Springboks with pride justifiably intact.

Unfortunately, the result also gave South African rugby a distorted idea of its strength and in some quarters there were even delusions of grandeur – a disastrous state of mind with the Wallabies to face in a week's time.

Meanwhile, South African rugby was once again in the eye of a political hurricane. Agreement had been reached between the ANC and SARFU that a minute's silence would be observed before each test to pay respect to the victims of violent unrest in the country. There was nothing unreasonable about the request, as it applied to all who had died, regardless of political viewpoint.

Tragically, a significant section of the more than 70 000 spectators at Ellis Park behaved as provocatively as the less disciplined participants in protest marches who burned flags and held mock trials. The national flag was much in evidence, and those carrying them had every right to do so, but the singing of the anthem during what should have been a minute's silence, was insensitive and in direct violation of the agreement. Had it been sung spontaneously before or after, no one could have argued the democratic right of those who did so.

Louis Luyt, president of the Transvaal Rugby Union, ruled that both the South African and New Zealand anthems should be played over the public address system, a move which compounded the problem.

Afterwards he dismissed the criticism of his decision by pointing out that SARFU's own constitution supported his decision not to be dictated to by any political organization. In the process, he balanced Springbok rugby's future on a knife's edge and, whether any result was achieved beyond increased bitterness, requires no debate.

NYANGA SUCCESS

Skipper Botha, coach John Williams and manager Abie Malan revealed a better grasp of public relations than all but a rare few previous holders of these positions in Springbok teams. Regular press conferences were held and the overseas media, in particular, were pleasantly surprised. Some of the bad taste left by the furore over the crowd behaviour at Ellis Park was also removed when the Springboks held a practice in Nyanga, the first national rugby team to visit a black township. High-profile players like Botha and Gerber, in particular, were shown warm affection and sport's role as a bridge builder has seldom been better emphasized.

South Africa's Adri Geldenhuys, Pieter Müller and Ian MacDonald close in on David Wilson. Naas Botha (Number 10) is in the foreground.

Initially, it seemed that all attempts by cooler heads to control the damage would come to nought and the Australians, in the midst of the controversy, were reconciled to the fact that their tour would be called off. With the aid of their president, Joe French, SARFU officials got the agreement with the ANC back on track and they again sanctioned the tour.

VENUE	SOUTH AFRICA	RESULT	SOUTH AFRICA				NEW ZEALAND			
			T	C	P	D	T	C	P	D
JOHANNESBURG	LOST	24–27	3	3	1	0	3	3	2	0

AUSTRALIA vs SOUTH AFRICA

Captaining the Wallabies on their whistle-stop, one-test tour of South Africa was Nick Farr-Jones, who had led Australia in a record 33 test matches, including victory in the 1991 World Cup series.

Western Transvaal were first to fall, 46–13, at Potchefstroom, but Northern Transvaal provided such stern opposition in going down 17–24, that hopes were raised that the Australians might not be that good when they ran up against top-flight players not overawed by reputation. Eastern Province put up their usual fight but the visitors' winning score of 34–8 in the last encounter before the test could well have been higher with a bit more exertion on their part.

After the encouraging performance against the All Blacks, the selectors understandably decided to keep the combination for Newlands intact. The only change was one forced by injury. Rodgers, who had been injured and replaced by Styger early in the second half against New Zealand, lost his place to the Free Stater. Small, who had gone off with an injury in the last few minutes of the game (with Füls substituting) had recovered and automatically returned to the side.

The Springboks seemed relaxed when they gathered in Cape Town on the Wednesday before the test at Newlands. David Bishop had been selected as the referee and was regarded with some trepidation after Sandy MacNeill's autocratic attitude at Ellis Park. While not flawless, he turned out to be an excellent choice and neither team had reason to complain.

The wet and windy weather that descended on the peninsula the day before the match and which was to continue well past the weekend, did not unduly worry the Springboks, as Botha had in the past given masterful performances in the mud of Newlands. This time it was not to be. Within the first minute, the Springbok fly-half kicked for touch, lost his balance, and fell heavily. It was an omen; Botha played the most ineffective game of his career and with his forwards outclassed and the service from his scrumhalf therefore shoddy, it was hardly surprising. Everyone is entitled to the odd bad day and probably the Springbok skipper's only real mistake was in not handing over the placekicking duties to Van Rensburg once he realized how hopelessly out of touch he was.

The Springbok forwards, with the exception of Uli Schmidt, were outplayed by the highly efficient Wallabies, where Wilson, Ofahengaue and Gavin were streets ahead in the loose, ending up with a staggering 27–10 supremacy. The South African cover defence was also painfully inadequate and Schmidt (and to a surprising extent Styger) often arrived first where danger threatened. The lineouts told the same sad story, where Eales and McCall virtually did what they liked

Australian flank, David Wilson, confronts Danie Gerber and Ian MacDonald in the test held at Newlands.

The Springbok team that played against Australia at Newlands in 1992. Back: Pieter Müller, Ian MacDonald, Adolf Malan, Adri Geldenhuys. Middle: Theo van Rensburg, James Small, Peter Hendriks, Robert du Preez, Lood Muller and Johan Styger. Front: Uli Schmidt, Jannie Breedt, John Williams (coach), Naas Botha (captain), Abe Malan, Danie Gerber, Wahl Bartmann.

with Malan and Geldenhuys. There was a slight improvement when Hattingh substituted for the injured Geldenhuys, but it was his ill-considered punch which gave the Wallabies a vital breakthrough in a penalty from Lynagh when the score was still a manageable 8–3 in the sixty-eighth minute of the match.

With their forwards unable to cope with the speed, precision and sheer class of the Wallaby pack, the Springbok backs could do little more than defend as best they could. That the score remained so low for so long is testimony to how they stuck to their task.

The Australian backs, led by Nick Farr-Jones, were about as slick a line-up as any seen in South Africa. They took full advantage of the opportunities created by their magnificent pack and always seemed to have more than one option; the pace and intelligence of their forwards, whose support never failed, must have added enormously to their obvious self-confidence. The highly-rated left-wing, Paul Carozza, scored twice, once as a result of expertly retained possession by the loose-forwards, and a quick change of direction by Farr-Jones; the other an individualistic effort which again exposed the South Africans' inadequate cover defence.

David Campese became the first player to score 50 tries (in 70 tests) in international rugby after Horan, who, with Little, formed a brilliant centre combination, and the three teammates had caught Gerber, stranded without any support, on his goalline. Horan gave a textbook pass to Campese who could have walked over had he wanted to. Lynagh added a conversion and three penalties against Botha's solitary penalty, giving the Australians a 26–3 victory, the biggest margin by which the Springboks have ever been beaten.

There could be no excuses afterwards and none were offered.

Pieter Hendriks and Theo van Rensburg run towards Australia's David Campese in the test at Newlands in 1992.

VENUE	SOUTH AFRICA	RESULT	SOUTH AFRICA				AUSTRALIA			
			T	C	P	D	T	C	P	D
CAPE TOWN	LOST	3–26	0	0	1	0	3	1	3	0

CHAPTER 44

1992

STUMBLING IN EUROPE

▲▲▲

Following the less than auspicious re-emergence in the international scene in 1992, a squad was selected for the 13-match tour of France and England.

The Springboks achieved the worst possible start to the tour by going down to the French Espoirs (Youth) XV in the opening game. Perhaps that less than palatable result should have been the flashpoint for immediate change. But despite beating a strangely disjointed and seemingly disinterested France in the first of two tests, the tour was fraught with typical foreign-land tour problems, and the South Africans suffered from other frustrations they could have done without.

These included off-field difficulties brought about by language and dietary problems plus rule interpretation, refereeing misunderstandings and confusion over social appointments.

But, as Doc Craven would have said, those details should have been sorted out in advance. Fully qualified interpreters, firm requests for certain dining requirements and fair demands for specialized treatment befitting an international touring team seemed to have been overlooked.

Some wives on tour, and an alleged walkout from a banquet which went horribly wrong, did nothing to help what proved to be a form of naivety on the part of the South Africans after being out in the cold for so long. The resulting media coverage was heavily criticized by the Springbok camp and it seemed that no advances had been made.

At the end of the day, it was a sad exercise, and further underlined the on-going seriousness of South African provincialism. Where the severity of continual Currie Cup 'tests' had taken the place of conventional rugby internationals, what was left was ash and simmering tempers. The clearest message from 1992 was that there were several aspects to be addressed, without delay.

Late in the tour, one of the team members admitted that there had been an absence of on-field strategy, with the only floppy instruction being to 'give the ball to Naas and he'll win for us'.

The heavy loss to England at Twickenham showed that the South Africans had not come as far as they would have liked in terms of coming to grips with massive changes that had occurred during the 'lost' years. They were slower to react, still obsessed with old methods and not in the same class fitness-wise, even though they had stayed well in the test until the start of the second half.

A lengthy injury list and calls for replacement players further hit where it hurt most, but the perception still existed that when in doubt, the coach (Williams) would seek Northern Transvaal players before others. But the most fundamental errors were still being made, those of handling and lack of ball retention being the

Jacques Olivier scored a sensational try against England B towards the end of the tour to Europe in 1992.

chief problems. Discipline also still desperately needed attention, and the need to concentrate on correct international refereeing interpretations became paramount. It was more than apparent that the isolation years had inflicted mortal damage on South African rugby, but it was still taking an inordinate amount of time to fully accept the severity of the effects.

Turning on typically virtuoso performances on tour, captain Naas Botha was inevitably at the centre of controversy. He confounded most critics in the test against England when he drop-kicked a sensational goal - one of 18 in 312 points in his 25 tests - but the end was nigh. One of the most amazing careers in international rugby

Tony Underwood gets ahead of Keith Andrews to score England's first try in their 33–16 win over the Springboks

came to an end when Botha announced his retirement soon after the team arrived home. After 40 games for SA, in which he scored 485 points, enough was enough. Who else could match kick 27 dropped goals in 40 matches for his country?

Apart from odd appearances in invitation teams, culminating in a Craven XV vs World XV to mark the unveiling of Doc Craven's statue just before the 1995 Rugby World Cup, it was the end. And while South African rugby bade farewell to Naas, it was also time to acknowledge the end of the test career and rugby achievements of the great centre Danie Gerber. Like Botha, he was well into his 30s at the time of the tour to France and England, but in typical style, ripped in with tries in each of the internationals against the Tricolors. Gerber extended his already impressive record to 19 tries in 24 tests, a wonderful record.

But the basically divided 1992 touring party was the beginning of the end in many ways. While the departures of Botha and Gerber from the test scene were natural spin-offs, others to drop off the international pace for one reason or another included Adolf Malan, Jannie Breedt, Faffa Knoetze and Garth Wright. Coach John Williams and manager Abie Malan were also casualties as South African rugby moved tentatively towards the 1993 season.

Was it to be a new beginning with uncomplicated opinions and plans to venture out into what was still the equivalent of rugby's unknown? Changes came, often at a cost, with urgent calls for the return of the rested, retired Botha and Gerber. It was not to be. A new selection system, new coach, new captain, new players, new tours and more injuries led to more complaints from an ever-increasingly demanding public, and worse, two more series lost.

James Small scores the second try in the first test against France. The final score was 20–15 in favour of the Springboks.

VENUE	SOUTH AFRICA	RESULT	SOUTH AFRICA							
			T	C	P	D	T	C	P	D
FRANCE (LYON)	WON	20–15	2	1	0	0	2	1	0	0
FRANCE (PARIS)	LOST	16–29	1	2	1	0	2	5	0	0
ENGLAND (LONDON)	LOST	16–33	1	2	1	0	4	2	1	2

CHAPTER 45

1993

WORLD WANDERERS

▲▲▲

The new year had barely begun when rugby mourned the loss of Dr Danie Craven, who died at his home in Stellenbosch. In many ways, the sad loss of Doc set the tone for many of the things that kept going wrong in South African rugby. Ebrahim Patel became the new president of the recently unified South African Rugby Football Union, but declined to stand for re-election at the next annual meeting. Former Springbok wing, Jannie Engelbrecht, was appointed manager of the Springboks and a new selection group was named, with past Springbok number eight and scrumhalf, Gerrie Sonnekus, as coach.

But Sonnekus was forced to withdraw because of business problems associated with the Free State Union. Natal coach, Ian McIntosh, who had been appointed as the coach of South Africa 'B', was virtually an automatic choice for promotion and it was he who took the responsibility for the two forthcoming tests against the French. McIntosh was eventually appointed coach until after the 1995 Rugby World Cup, but that's another story. Engelbrecht's popularity, too, saw him appointed until after the tournament. But events of 1994 and 1995 put an end to those, albeit in distasteful circumstances.

Chester Williams' first test try was scored against the Pumas in Buenos Aires. The Springboks won both matches played against the Argentinian team.

FRANCE vs SOUTH AFRICA

A South African 'B' team comprehensively took the French apart in East London before the test in Durban. The test was drawn 20-20, offering hopes for a series win for the South Africans the following week at Ellis Park. On that occasion and for the first time, a Springbok team played under floodlights before a capacity crowd but they went down to the French by one point, with the final score 17-18.

Both locks, Rudi Visagie and Kobus Wiese, were replaced by Hannes Strydom and Nico Wegner for the second test, which could so easily have been won had fullback Theo van Rensburg landed a late penalty attempt.

The beer tasted sour for some after the second test loss, but the close nature of the series offered encouragement for most. New captain, Francois Pienaar, had put a new face on South African rugby and while his playing ability was questioned by some - once again the ugly head of provincialism reared - he had a good off-field image, was popular with the media and liked by the players. Pienaar arrived with a grand reputation from Transvaal, who were about to hit one of the best years in their history. The tour by the French was marred by a serious facial injury suffered by their captain Jean-Francois Tordo in the game against Western Province at Newlands. Western Province prop, Garry Pagel, who was to become a Springbok in 1995, was blamed for the scraping incident, but the topic was a hot one and administrators were under severe pressure to act in such instances. Television replays were not totally convincing about Pagel's part, but even with an appeal and reduction of sentence, Pagel was out of the sport for nine months.

Uli Schmidt, South Africa's skilful hooker, scores against the 1993 French side.

Robert du Preez kicks, watched by Ed Morrison, the English referee who went on to officiate the World Cup final in 1995.

Venue	South Africa	Result	South Africa				France			
			T	C	P	D	T	C	P	D
Durban	Draw	20–20	1	0	5	0	1	0	3	2
Johannesburg	Lost	17–18	1	0	4	0	0	0	4	2

James Small, Hannes Strydom, Nico Wegener and Robert du Preez halt an Australian attack.

Tiaan Strauss has his way blocked by Australian scrumhalf, Nick Farr-Jones. Farr-Jones came out of retirement to take part in this series against the Springboks

SOUTH AFRICA vs AUSTRALIA

Soon after the French tour, the Springboks left for Australia as a team looking well-balanced and containing exciting new players such as Chester Williams, Joost van der Westhuizen, Tinus Linee and Ruben Kruger. The South Africans demolished sides like Western Australia, Australian Capital Territories and a South Australian XV. But a week before the first test, they got pipped by New South Wales and stocks took a tumble.

But the day after the loss to New South Wales, McIntosh and Engelbrecht pulled the team together on a four-hour lunch cruise in Sydney Harbour. Singing and partying did wonders for team spirit and was the basis of the historic 19–12 win over the Wallabies under floodlights at the Sydney Sports Stadium the following Saturday evening.

James Small scored two of the three tries and received assistance from the enigmatic and sometimes wayward David Campese. But it was obvious the New South Wales victory had damaged the home team's test hopes, for the Wallabies were over-confident and paid the price.

The South Africans then went north and deservedly took out strong Queensland, which made the Wallabies sit up and take notice. By now, the home side, so diligently coached by the astute Bob Dwyer, knew they had a major job on their hands if they were to win the series.

Nick Farr-Jones, who had announced his retirement, came back to do battle in the series against the South Africans, and it was his class and experience which helped set up the wins in the last two tests. The battle of Ballymore, won 28-20 by the Australians, was remembered more for the sensational sending off by English referee, Ed Morrison, of right wing James Small.

It was the first time a South African player had been 'walked', and was a shattering blow to both the player and the squad. Small was suspended for one game.

His ordering-off followed a series of ten-metre penalty 'marches', and Small once too often 'chirped' Morrison and was summarily dismissed. Head down in shame, Small made the long walk while a couple of Wallabies sarcastically applauded him.

Joel Stransky intercepted a pass and streaked away for a sensational try, and added a conversion and a penalty to give the Springboks a handy and timely 10-3 lead. Try as they might, they could not keep up with the power and experience of Australia and the test was gone.

Once again, the management had to dig deep and bring the players from

near despair to being a happy, confident bunch. Yet the image on tour was otherwise excellent, and far from being on the receiving end of bitterness after the isolation years, the Australians welcomed the South Africans and the players were treated royally.

It was back to Sydney for the third test appointment. Hopes were high, but the Wallabies had done their homework, tightened up their discipline and concentration, and turned on a professional, if slightly dull, performance to win 19-12.

There was much gloating as the trophy was carried aloft around the field, while the South Africans showered, sped to an official departure dinner and rushed to the airport for a late-night departure for home.

Tiaan Strauss leaps high to catch a ball in the third test of the series between South Africa and Australia.

VENUE	SOUTH AFRICA	RESULT	SOUTH AFRICA				AUSTRALIA			
			T	C	P	D	T	C	P	D
SYDNEY	WON	19–12	3	2	0	0	0	0	4	0
BRISBANE	LOST	20–28	2	2	2	0	3	2	3	0
SYDNEY	LOST	12–19	2	1	0	0	1	1	4	0

SOUTH AFRICA vs ARGENTINA

Things began poorly, with a loss to a Buenos Aires selection. The South Africans had to pull out all the stops in the first test, but won 29-26. Through several changes in personnel and a different pattern, the second test was won handsomely 52-23. Gavin Johnson had been flown in as a replacement and repaid the decision to call him up from a Barbarians tour of Britain to début in a test with 22 points, to equal the South African record held by Naas Botha and Gerald Bosch.

In a dreadful match against the Argentine provincial champions, Tucuman, fighting and brutality was the order of the day. The locals were known for it and had had a match called off only a year before. This time, Hannes Strydom and Keith Andrews refused to stand for the nonsense and let the locals know their views in a physical manner. Their actions saw them banished for early showers, bringing to three the number of Springboks sent off in one year.

Springbok manager, Jannie Engelbrecht, poses with Ilie Tabua, the powerful Australian flank forward.

VENUE	SOUTH AFRICA	RESULT	SOUTH AFRICA				ARGENTINA			
			T	C	P	D	T	C	P	D
BUENOS AIRES	WON	29–26	4	3	1	0	2	2	4	0
BUENOS AIRES	WON	52–23	7	4	3	0	2	2	2	1

CHAPTER 46

1994

THE ROAD TO RECOVERY

▲▲▲

Adriaan Richter gets the ball away, closely followed by Brendan Venter, Hennie le Roux, James Small and Pieter Muller, and England's Rob Andrew.

The year 1994 was one that pointed the way to improved results. The South African rugby football unions held its first democratic elections during which Dr Louis Luyt of Transvaal was elected unopposed.

SOUTH AFRICA vs ENGLAND

England came to South Africa brimming with confidence. The first test looked a foregone conclusion, but a 20 minute blitz by England bombed the Springboks into submission. Rob Andrew scored 27 points, including a try, and England won 32–15, all South Africa's points coming from André Joubert. The Springboks were humiliated and the whole world knew it. The match in Port Elizabeth turned ugly when Jonathan Callard had his face ripped open, there was fighting, and Tim Rodber and Simon Tremain were sent off. Everybody knew that Newlands would suit England, but this time the tables were turned. South Africa dominated up front and scored two splendid tries through Hennie le Roux and André Joubert, and won 27–9. Rob Andrew kicked nine points for England.

Venue	South Africa	Result	South Africa				England			
			T	C	P	D	T	C	P	D
Pretoria	Lost	15–32	5	0	0	0	2	2	5	1
Cape Town	Won	27–9	2	1	5	0	0	0	3	0

SOUTH AFRICA vs NEW ZEALAND

It was a tour that might have been great. The All Blacks were ripe for defeat but the Springboks did not grasp the opportunity. Ill discipline cost them dearly and the All Blacks surprised themselves with a 22–14 victory at Carisbrook. Then the tour lost some of its direction: James Small was cited and Adri Geldenhuys was sent off and suspended for a week. It was not a good build up to the second test.

The All Black storm brought tries to John Timu and Zinzan Brooke, which was enough to win the match the Springboks could have won. Honourable defeat was soon plunged into dishonour as television highlighted Johan le Roux biting Sean Fitzpatrick's ear. For this, Le Roux was suspended until the end of 1995.

Eden Park was the venue for the final test. The Springboks were a little unlucky not to win, scoring three tries to nil, but drew 18-all, with New Zealand's six penalty goals from Shane Howarth.

South African fullback, André Joubert, kicks for touch in the test against New Zealand.

The Springboks came home but the tour did not end as public squabbling began between Luyt and manager Engelbrecht, who was first sacked and then reinstated before being given the boot for the World Cup. Ian McIntosh was replaced as coach by Kitch Christie.

VENUE	SOUTH AFRICA	RESULT	SOUTH AFRICA				NEW ZEALAND			
			T	C	P	D	T	C	P	D
DUNEDIN	LOST	14–22	1	0	3	0	1	1	5	0
WELLINGTON	LOST	9–13	0	0	3	0	2	0	1	0
AUCKLAND	DRAW	18–18	2	1	2	0	0	0	6	0

The two captains – South Africa's Francois Pienaar tackles Wales' Gareth Llewellyn. The Springboks won the match 20–12.

SOUTH AFRICA vs ARGENTINA

The Pumas' defeats were heavy ones – 42–22 at Boet Erasmus Stadium and 46–26 at Ellis Park. The visitors did well at forward, especially in the scrums, but they had no answer to the speed and skills of Van der Westhuizen and Williams. Joel Stransky scored 35 points, including a try in each test.

VENUE	SOUTH AFRICA	RESULT	SOUTH AFRICA				ARGENTINA			
			T	C	P	D	T	C	P	D
PORT ELIZABETH	WON	42–22	5	4	3	0	3	2	1	0
JOHANNESBURG	WON	46–26	7	4	1	0	2	2	4	0

SOUTH AFRICA vs SCOTLAND AND WALES

It's never easy in Wales where even scoring more points than the opposition does not ensure victory. The tour seemed on a war footing when the Springboks became yet another team to suffer from Neath's bellicose tactics. It was a miserable match. Three days later the Springboks turned on the charm. They scored sweeping tries and won 78–7, then tumbled to a drab defeat against Scotland A. At Murrayfield they were back on form and threatened to smash records against Scotland before running up a comfortable lead, running out of steam and letting the brave Scots back. As André Joubert had been the star at St Helen's in Swansea, so Joost van der Westhuizen was the star at Murrayfield.

The final outcome in Cardiff may have made it look easy for the Springboks who preserved their unbeaten record against Wales by winning 20–12. They went on to Ireland for an easy match in Belfast and against the Barbarians to run the ball 'in the Barbarian style' while the Barbarians played dour stuff, fed on Springbok errors and rejoiced in victory of sorts.

Francois Pienaar introduces Mark Andrews to Princess Anne before the test against Scotland at Murrayfield.

VENUE	SOUTH AFRICA	RESULT	SOUTH AFRICA							
			T	C	P	D	T	C	P	D
SCOTLAND (EDINBURGH)	WON	34–10	5	3	1	0	1	1	1	0
WALES (CARDIFF)	WON	20–12	3	1	1	0	0	0	4	0

CHAPTER 47

1995

ISLANDERS MAROONED

▲▲▲

Francois Pienaar grabs the ball in the air during the test against Western Samoa. Other Springboks in the picture are Balie Swart, Ruben Kruger, Rudolf Straeuli, Ian MacDonald and Joost van der Westhuizen.

This was always going to be a big year for South African rugby – with the World Cup and all the possibilities it offered.

The start to any big venture is important. At the beginning there was uncertainty about the team and Francois Pienaar's injury. But then James Small was recalled from his 1994 exclusion brought about by an unhappy experience in a Port Elizabeth nightclub and Pienaar played after all. The only man missing was André Joubert, and his replacement, Gavin Johnson, grabbed the opportunity with both hands.

The Springboks started with a blitz and, before the Samoans had had time to forget the words of their war-dance, Johnson cut past the fullback and plunged over for a try. It was the start of a record-breaking day for 'Magic' Johnson and South Africa.

The Springbok forwards rolled over the Western Samoans who managed only scraps from a scrum which was disintegrating in retreat. Behind the pack's aggression, the backs were too skilled and too fast for their opponents.

James Small counter-attacked and Chester Williams scored the first of his two tries of the day. The interplay between Williams and Small was one of the features of Springbok play when the two were chosen. Later in the match, and significant in the light of later events at the World Cup, Chester Williams left the field to be replaced by Chris Badenhorst. As he sat on the touchline tending to his sore muscle, no-one thought that the injury would have the serious repercussions that it did have.

The try of the match came late in the second half when Johnson counter-attacked from inside his twenty-two, and forwards and backs combined in a surging movement that flowed down the field until Chris Rossouw, a surprising but successful replacement for James Dalton, scored. The Springboks played at a furious pace and eventually, but not surprisingly, ran out of steam a bit into the second half. They were innovative and hardly ever kicked at goal, preferring to play at speed or tap kicks.

Hennie le Roux gets away with the ball with Balie Swart, Ruben Kruger, Os du Rand, Joost van der Westhuizen and Francois Pienaar in support.

Part of the fade in the second half was caused by injuries and a plethora of replacements, one of the match's records. Johnson was replaced by Henry Honiball, Williams by Badenhorst, Kobus Wiese by Ian MacDonald and Mark Andrews by back-up hooker, Mornay Visser.

There were other records. The Springboks scored 60 points in a test for the first time ever. Gavin Johnson became the first Springbok fullback to score a hat-trick of tries in a test. Add his tries to five conversions and a penalty goal and Johnson broke Gerald Bosch's record of 22 points for an individual score in a test match, a record which had stood since 1975.

The Western Samoans had been popular visitors to South Africa. Such a visit had first been mooted by Dr Danie Craven with support from Louis Luyt, although the suggestion had been met with derision. But after Western Samoa's performance in the 1991 World Cup when they defeated Wales in the quarter-final and became the team which most sparked the romantic imagination, they were suddenly much sought after visitors in the rugby world, and renowned for their expansive play and harsh tackling. They were led by charismatic Pita Fatialofa, a piano mover from Auckland in New Zealand and one of the great personalities of the rugby world.

It was a match which did much to give the Springboks and the country confidence for the coming World Cup.

VENUE	SOUTH AFRICA	RESULT	SOUTH AFRICA				WESTERN SAMOA			
			T	C	P	D	T	C	P	D
JOHANNESBURG	WON	60–8	9	6	1	0	1	0	1	0

CHAPTER 48

1995
WORLD CUP

▲▲▲

South African flyhalf Joel Stransky scored a try, four penalty goals, a drop goal and a conversion in the opening match against Australia at Newlands.

SOUTH AFRICA vs AUSTRALIA

This was the match that made the Rugby World Cup 1995, that showed rugby at its best and sent rugby fever soaring. The bud of the new South Africa opened its rainbow colours on 25 May 1995. And South Africa won before the whistle was blown to start the match, claiming the hearts of the nation and of the world.

The opening ceremony lasted only 45 minutes, but will never end for those who saw it. It was intended to show the diversity of the South African nation and to make it proud – and it succeeded. You will be hard pressed to find a South African who did not weep with pride.

It was a stylish, relaxed, colourful, rhythmic, good-humoured pageant, welcoming the world and especially the participating countries, while a world-wide audience in more than 125 countries looked on.

President Nelson Mandela appeared waving, and the packed crowd stood, waved their flags and chanted his name.

Sir Ewart Bell welcomed everybody, and the State President declared the 1995 Rugby World Cup open. It was time for the game to begin.

The anthems, led by the Drakensberg Boys' Choir, were sung with fervour. When referee Derek Bevan blew the whistle, its sound was drowned by the roar

The Springboks were among the best tacklers at the World Cup. Here, Francois Pienaar collars Australia's legendary David Campese, star of the 1991 World Cup.

of the crowd – and the crowd kept on roaring until the final whistle. The spectators cheered the awarding of scrums and gave equally enthusiastic applause to both sides.

The Wallabies were expected to score. Informed belief was that they would win because they were, man for man, better than the Springboks; they were better prepared, had a settled team and were believed to be better at all of rugby's skills.

At the start it looked as if this could happen, as the Springboks made a succession of elementary mistakes, like not finding touch and turning their own lineout into an unproductive shambles. Michael Lynagh goaled a penalty, but Joel Stransky lobbed an up-and-under into the air and the Wallabies were penalized. Stransky goaled and the score stood at 3–3.

Michael Lynagh goaled another penalty, then it was Stransky's turn again: 6–6. Back it went again, and

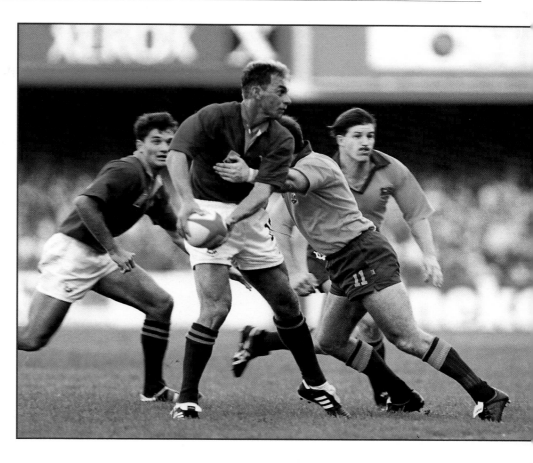

when Joost van der Westhuizen looked certain to score, the Wallabies were penalized in front of the posts. The score then stood at 9–6.

During Rugby World Cup 1995, André Joubert displayed the talent and flair that has made him one of the best attacking fullbacks the world has seen.

Willie Ofahengaue charged, and there was Lynagh slicing triumphantly through for a try which the Newlands crowd honoured in its ancient way with a double round of applause: 13–9 to Australia, and things seemed to be taking their predicted course.

Then Stransky was stopped on the Australian line after a ferocious Springbok onslaught. The Springboks moved left. Japie Mulder threw a skip pass to James Small. Small fed Pieter Hendriks who straightened up for a run at the mighty David Campese – and then the Springbok accelerated out on a curve and around Campese for a try which Hendriks celebrated with a clenched fist.

It was half-time, and the Springboks were ahead 14–13.

The second half belonged to South Africa and it was not until the end that the Wallabies managed to shake loose the grip of pressure. Stransky scored a well-rehearsed try. (During the course of the game, Stransky scored in all rugby ways: a try, a dropped goal, a conversion and four penalty goals.)

Even when Phil Kearns scored a try with three minutes left to play, the outcome remained beyond doubt. Roaring greeted the final whistle and celebrations went on long into the night.

While the Springboks were quiet in victory, the Wallabies were generous in defeat, acknowledging that the better side had won and that their mistakes were the result of Springbok pressure.

After the game Francois Pienaar presented his jersey to Nelson Mandela who, on visiting the team the day before, had called them 'my Springboks'. And they were indeed the whole nation's Springboks.

Pieter Hendriks(left) a late inclusion in the South African squad, scored one of South Africa's two first-match tries.

Ruben Kruger was, without doubt, one of the unsung heroes of the Springbok side. He played brilliantly every time he wore the Springbok jersey.

SOUTH AFRICA vs ROMANIA

The Springboks came to Newlands euphoric after the match against Australia with the full expectations of experiencing an even higher high. Instead it collapsed – not entirely, but there was a definite withdrawal.

There were those who saw it as a good thing, although how playing as badly as that could be a good thing is a mystery. There must have been a game plan to start with, but it was soon abandoned as the players rushed headlong to their own individualistic destruction.

In the end the Springboks won, but if the Romanians had had a little more faith and had run at them instead of kicking away almost every ball, they may have done better. That said, the Romanians were justifiably satisfied with their performance, which included a try from a sharp break in the centre by Andrei Guranescu. They got to the breakdown faster and in numbers. And they did remarkably well in the lineouts, especially through Sandu Ciorascu.

The Springboks started off well. Gavin Johnson goaled a penalty and they went straight back to the Romanian line for a push-over try credited to Adriaan Richter, the captain of the day. The Springboks obviously wanted to run, taking tap kicks even from under the crossbar. One, when the score was 8-0, brought blushes to hooker Chris Rossouw: Johan Roux pushed a perfect cross-kick to Rossouw where he stood unmarked, but the ball fled from his grasp over the touch line and a certain try went with it.

After that flurry the game fell away. One of the problems was the litany of injuries the Romanians produced. After each movement one would require attention – at one stage a Romanian player jumped to charge down a kick, missed the ball and crumpled to the ground. This did nothing for the game, and the crowd soon found other things to do – a Mexican wave or blow a bugle or beat a drum.

This time the Springboks went home rather grumpy. It was no way to win the World Cup. But the Romanians were pleased, after their beating from Canada. Afterwards their captain, the tall number-eight Tiberiu Brinza, said: 'It certainly was a moral victory for our team.'

Robbie Brink was convinced he scored in his début test, but the referee did not see things his way. Adriaan Richter scored his first of four World Cup tries in the match against Romania.

SOUTH AFRICA vs CANADA

This was South Africa's night of shame. After the team's exhilarating ascent to glory on the opening day of the World Cup it should all have been so different.

The precursor of the run of shame was a power failure which affected the floodlights. The match started three-quarters of an hour late, which did nothing for the crowd, the players, the officials, the good name of the World Cup or the good name of South Africa . . . Pointedly, similar power failures had happened three times the previous night, which suggested that there must have been an awareness of the problem before the 'big night', the evening on which the first-ever test between South Africa and Canada would take place, with both teams vying for a place in the quarter-finals.

In the match against Canada, aggression was evident early on – as Joost van der Westhuizen soon found out.

From the start of the match, the Springbok pack throttled their Canadian opponents – at this stage, quite properly, within the bounds of the laws and rugby's good manners. They crunched the Canadians in the scrums and beat them hands-down in the lineouts. They did not play an expansive game, content to ensure a safe victory. After 31 minutes they were 17–0 ahead, thanks to two push-over tries, credited to Adriaan Richter, and a penalty goal by Joel Stransky.

Seven minutes into the second half, Stransky made the score 20–0. That was the final score 33 minutes later – but those were particularly long minutes.

More and more the proud and combative Canadians got back into the game, hurling wave upon wave of attack against the Springbok line. The Springbok defence was magnificent, but it was an enormous physical clash.

Then there was shoving between Pieter Hendriks and Winston Stanley, in touch against the billboards. Suddenly Canadian fullback Scott Stewart came charging at Hendriks, transforming what had been juvenile petulance into brutality as other players arrived, to make not peace but war. It was uncontrolled violence.

When peace was finally restored, Hannes Strydom left the field with a lacerated eye and the referee, David McHugh from Ireland, sent James Dalton, the Springbok hooker, Rod Snow, the Canadian prop, and Gareth Rees, the Canadian captain and flyhalf, off the field – a record for a test match, but definitely not one to be admired.

The rest of the match was played out with uncontested scrums and came, mercifully, to an end.

Later, the World Cup's disciplinary committee, chaired by Ray Williams of Wales, suspended each of the three players for 30 days. The Springboks appealed against Dalton's suspension. The committee then cited two more players – Pieter Hendriks and Scott Stewart – and suspended Hendriks for 90 days, for punching and kicking, and Stewart for 60 days. Other combatants were rather lucky to avoid suspension.

James Dalton takes the long walk to the changeroom. He became the second Springbok ever to be sent off.

In the match against Western Samoa, the Springboks dominated the line-outs. Here Kobus Wiese reaches for the ball.

SOUTH AFRICA vs WESTERN SAMOA

As Nelson Mandela is to South Africa, so Chester Williams is to rugby in South Africa – the wholesome face of the new South Africa, the hope for the future, the man all the people love.

In the quarter-final, Chester Williams played his first World Cup match after replacing the suspended Pieter Hendriks. Williams raced, dived, skidded and plunged straight into the record books of South African rugby, becoming the first player to score four tries in a test match.

The foundations for a South African victory were laid by the forwards. They dominated the lineouts through Kobus Wiese and Mark Andrews. They drove powerfully with the ball in the hand, although they were less cohesive than they should have been when the ball was on the ground. In this department the Western Samoans appeared to arrive quicker and tighter. The Springboks scrummed better, but did not have the same degree of domination that they had had over the Canadians. In fact, they did not even have the ascendancy seen over Australia in the opening match. And they suffered the embarrassment of losing their own ball near their opponents' line. On the run and despite the wild tackling of the Western Samoans, however, the South Africans were better structured and faster.

Later in the game, the South Africans stopped going for the big tackle, clearly content with the certainty of their place in the semi-final.

By this stage, recklessness and bad luck had taken their toll. In two over-physical matches in a row, against desperate men who resented being outplayed, the Springboks had paid a terrible price: James Dalton and Pieter Hendriks sus-

Balie Swart is pleased that Chester Williams scored against Western Samoa – one of his record of four tries in a test.

pended, Joel Stransky and Hannes Strydom out with eye injuries, and injuries to André Joubert, Ruben Kruger, Mark Andrews and Kobus Wiese. South Africa was winning battles but at such a price that it might cost them the eventual war.

Accidents happen in rugby, but some of the Western Samoan intent was not wholesome. Two tackles by Mike Umaga were unacceptable. It's tough to imagine that the shoulder driven into Mark Andrews's ribs as he went about his legal business at a ruck was 'part of the game'.

Later there was a suggestion that Joost van der Westhuizen had been racially insulting to the Western Samoans after the match. Van der Westhuizen had suffered at their hands tackling that could have broken bones and that certainly went beyond name-calling.

But all of this detracts from some of the best tries of World Cup 1995. A quarter of an hour into the match, the Springboks attacked wide, Joost van der Westhuizen threw a long pass and André Joubert was striding elegantly ahead. He drew the fullback and passed to Williams, who was off for the corner, leaving behind a prone Joubert wasted by Umaga's tackle. Not 10 minutes later Umaga laid out Joost van der Westhuizen, and from then on, whenever Umaga touched the ball he was booed. It was all rather sad, as the Western Samoans had been popular visitors to South Africa.

Williams' third try was a beauty, as Ruben Kruger breached the line and set the backs free. Again, it was a try scored from some way out.

But the most spectacular try of the match belonged to the Western Samoans. The Springboks attacked on their right. Western Samoa got the ball and darted up the touchline. Gavin Johnson got the ball deep in Springbok territory to his left. After some interplay with Williams, Johnson lost the ball in a tackle, and suddenly Tu Nu'uali'itia was through for a great try.

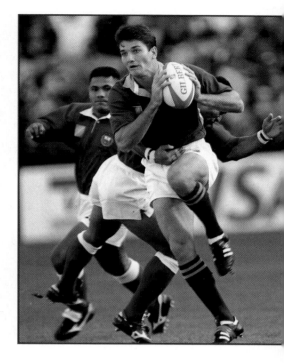

Joost van der Westhuizen risked life and limb by running at the tough Western Samoan side.

He's not going far. Francois Pienaar and Christiaan Scholtz act against a Western Samoan sortie.

SOUTH AFRICA vs FRANCE

What a match – especially considering it was a match that nearly did not even happen. It never rains in Durban in June; Cape Town is where it rains – well, that's the commonly held perception but, as it turned out, it came down in buckets in Durban in June! There was talk of postponing the match to the following day. The pitch was inspected before the stated kick-off time, and the game was put back an hour. The pitch was inspected once again at that time, and the game put back a further half hour. The extra time gave an opportunity for the excess water to be swept from the field – but it was also just enough time for the driving rain to come back.

It was Pierre Berbizier's birthday. Afterwards, he was asked what it was like to have lost on his birthday. He

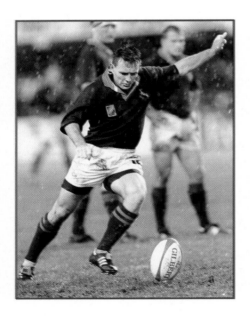

French scrumhalf, Fabien Galthie, gets his pass away, despite the wall of water.

Joel Stransky proved to be a man for all seasons and put in a solid performance against the French in the semi-final held in Durban.

said: 'I would have liked champagne. Instead I got water!' It was the sort of weather that made the result a lottery; it would have been as well to have spun a coin to decide who would go through to the final.

France won the toss and opted to play into the wind. Joel Stransky kicked off, and South Africa had an early drive as Joost van der Westhuizen turned the forwards loose. Penalty! Joel Stransky, who yet again showed the nation that he was its best flyhalf, kicked, and after two minutes the Springboks led 3–0. The French team never did get the lead.

Joel Stransky, in those ghastly conditions, missed two penalties, and then came the score that decided the match. Joost van der Westhuizen wriggled low from a lineout and the Springbok pack was on the charge. Pieter du Randt tucked in on Chris Rossouw's shoulder and they headed for the French line. Kobus Wiese and Ruben Kruger went in tandem to the left above a heap of bodies. Suddenly, Wiese changed direction and wrenched the ball to the right, and he and Ruben Kruger plunged for the line. A kneeling Derek Bevan signalled the try.

After 28 minutes South Africa led 10–0, but by half-time that lead had shrunk as Lacroix kicked two rapid penalties in succession.

The second half signalled the end of South Africa's use of the favourable wind conditions, which blew towards the grandstand side of the field where most of the action happened. The wind was not as strongly in France's favour in the second half but from time to time the rain came down like stair rods.

Stransky put South Africa further ahead but immediately Lacroix got one back, and then he slotted another, and the score was 16–12 with more than 20 minutes to play. At that stage, for the only time in the match, Lacroix missed a kick at goal.

With nine minutes to go, Stransky put the Springboks even further ahead. It was victory conceded by an inch.

With three minutes to play, victory was within the grasp of the French. Lacroix kicked a penalty to take the score to 19–15. Joel Stransky, whose kick-offs had been pinpoint-accurate, this time kicked short and France had a scrum in midfield. Christophe Deylaud lobbed one down to the Springbok '22', a long and unchallenging kick. James Small knocked on: scrum to France.

France shoved the Springboks. The Springboks held. Fabien Galthie fed Deylaud, who chopped a nasty chip. André Joubert came for it, with Ruben Kruger in attendance. Philippe Saint-André came charging in from the left wing, crashed into Kruger and the two fell to the ground – a decisive fall.

For the only time in the match, Joubert dropped a challenging kick, knocking it forward. Abdelatif Benazzi picked up and drove the short distance from the Springbok line with only Small in front of him. The big French flank stumbled – over the prone body of his captain. He went plunging for the ground with Small trying to stop him and Hennie le Roux scurrying across in desperation.

France flung their bodies in and claimed a try. Referee Derek Bevan was right on the spot. Bevan is a deliberate man, tantalizingly so at times, delaying his decision with, not necessarily for, dramatic effect. Bevan did not think it was a try, for Benazzi was short of the line – by an inch. The ref could, one presumes, have penalized Benazzi for holding onto the ball on the ground; instead he went back to the scrum for France where Joubert had knocked the ball forward.

The French were disappointed. But they had the scrum, a long one, as it fell down under the pressure of all those flashing, nightmare visions of penalty tries; then it wheeled; then it fell down again – again with the French doing marginally better than the South Africans, for whom Mark Andrews and Francois Pienaar were guarding against a Cecillon charge.

Again the scrum was set and again France had an edge of advantage. Somehow, South Africa held them back. Then Galthie fed Lacroix. Le Roux went in low on Lacroix; Joel Stransky slammed in at chest height; Mark Andrews drove his bulk in; Francois Pienaar added his power; and Kruger shunted in as well. Lacroix was quite clearly not going to score and, not surprisingly, was moved back and the determined mass of muscle fell to the ground. Scrum to South Africa! The fans were delighted.

And so, again, the nightmare visions – the lost tighthead, the snagged scrumhalf, the dropped ball. The Springboks heeled and the scrum fell; the Springboks heeled and the scrum turned – but Johan Roux passed to Stransky, who kicked the ball out.

Bevan signalled the lineout and then, after a seemingly sadistic, torturous wait, blew the final whistle. The victorious Springboks jumped for joy; the defeated French slumped in tears. And South Africa entered the record books by becoming the third country to reach the final of the Rugby World Cup on début.

André Joubert's only mistake in the Durban rain – and it nearly cost South Africa a place in the final. Philippe Saint-André challenges and Ruben Kruger supports.

Although visibility was not at its best, Springbok Kobus Wiese featured regularly in the line-outs.

No you don't! James Small and Jonah Lomu look each other in the eye.

Joost van der Westhuizen gets yet another pass away beautifully but no-one else seems to be impressed.

SOUTH AFRICA vs NEW ZEALAND

What a finish! That the World Cup was held in South Africa was in itself a dream come true. Before the political changes in the country it would have been impossible; nobody would have allowed it to happen. Before the tournament it was said that South Africa could not manage it, that the side lacked the know-how and the infrastructure. Then it happened, and we coped. In addition, the whole thing looked spectacular in our own rainbow-nation, relaxed, cheerful way.

The whole nation got behind its team – 'my boys', as Nelson Mandela called them. How the crowd cheered its leader, wearing a number-six jersey and a supporters cap, and cheered the team!

It was the dream final – South Africa vs New Zealand, for the championship of the world. Matches between the two have always been played in white heat – rugby's real test matches. This one-off match for such a prize – the William Webb Ellis Trophy – and by the end of the match it was obvious that it had indeed been between the best two teams in the world.

The day was sunny, warm and highveld still. The crowds flocked in, wearing all sorts of supporters' apparel, full of expectation, confident in their team's ability to face the awesome All Blacks, even given the threat of young Jonah Lomu who, for the week preceding the final, had had the nation in a grip of panic.

The ceremonies that preceded the game kicked off with a jet flying over the stadium; on its undercarriage were the words 'Good Luck Bokke'. The ensuing pageant continued the dream, with balloons floating into the air, tribal dancers, animal dancers, bearers carrying in a singer on a throne topped by a leopard, representatives of the 16 participating nations in traditional dress and headgear, a massive wheel of coloured cloth, the countries' emblems, helicopters bringing in national flags in order of the achievements of the countries in the pool matches,

skydivers bringing in the New Zealand flag and the South African flag, the singing of World in Union, the anthems led by a choir resplendent in the colours of the South African flag and, finally, the Haka.

New Zealand kicked off short. The ball landed short of 10 metres but a Springbok played it, a ruck ensued and the All Blacks were penalized for being offside. As soon as they had the opportunity, the All Blacks attacked, through Glen Osborne, and when the Springboks went over the ball, Mehrtens kicked the penalty goal. The All Blacks were ahead 3–0 after only four minutes of play. But six minutes later, Joel Stransky levelled the score.

It took 10 minutes of play before there was a scrum. There were lots of lineouts, and here the All Blacks triumphed, thanks to excellent lock forward, Ian Jones.

After all the hype leading up to the final, the sight of Jonah Lomu scything between the centres brought shrieks of terror to South African lips. But Joost

van der Westhuizen and Pieter du Randt stopped Lomu, to yells of relief, and throughout the game, an error by or a tackle on the big man brought cheers, first of relief and then of triumph.

Nonetheless, Mehrtens brought the score to 6–3 and then, when the Springboks attacked, he drove them back with a drop-out that landed just inside of the Springbok corner flag. But, as was the case throughout the match, the Springbok defence was calm, organized and determined.

Back came the Springboks, and they crossed the line; they were the only team to cross the line during the entire try-less match of excellent rugby. However, Ed Morrison, who refereed well, did not think it a try – to the disbelief of the Springboks involved. Instead, he awarded a scrum, and the Springboks shoved the All Blacks back. There was a penalty and Stransky made it 6–6.

Back came the Springboks and there was another penalty. This time Stransky missed. After another furious attack he slotted a drop and the game went to half-time with the Springboks 9–6 ahead.

In the second half, largely because of what Ian Jones did in the lineouts, the All Blacks grew stronger and stronger and seemed to be getting on top. But again and again the Springboks knocked them down. Kitch Christie was right when he said afterwards that the Springboks' tackling had won them the match. It was a smash-and-grab victory, and the pressure of the hard tackles forced errors, as they had done to the Wallabies in the opening match. A Mehrtens drop levelled the scores after Jones won two successive South African lineouts. Then the Springboks attacked down the right, and first Small was close, and then Joubert.

Ian Jones' astonishing dominance in the line-outs very nearly denied the Springboks their World Cup glory.

Chester Williams started a counterattack in the final which gave the Springboks the vision of victory.

Japie Mulder and James Small had few attacking opportunities in a game marked by the Springboks' committed tackling.

The end of a try-less match. South African captain, Francois Pienaar, falls to his knees amid the frenzy and chaos following Ed Morrison's final whistle.

Mehrtens missed a drop kick from a good position, and the second half ran out with the teams tied: the match would have to go into extra time.

In the event of a draw at the end of extra time, the team that had scored the most tries would be declared the winner; and in the event of no tries being scored, the team that had had fewer players sent off during the tournament would take the trophy. Given these circumstances New Zealand would win, because of what had happened during the war at Boet Erasmus when South Africa played Canada.

Extra time would be 10 minutes each way.

In the first minute, Joel Stransky jinked to avoid pressure and kicked an up-and-under. The Springbok centres had got ahead in the jinking, however, and Mehrtens kicked a penalty goal from just inside the Springbok half. The score was 12–9, with about 18 minutes left to play.

The Springboks started to come alive. They counter-attacked, the wings became active and things looked better. And Richard Loe, barely within two minutes of replacing Craig Dowd, became the only man flagged for foul play in the World Cup final.

Back came the Springboks with a Stransky penalty, and the score stood at 12–12 when the teams broke again for the crucial last ten minutes. The Springboks attacked. There was a scrum. Joost van der Westhuizen passed deep to Stransky, and he dropped high and true.

The All Blacks, noble competitors, came on the attack but the Springboks drove them back for a scrum near the All Black line. From the scrum Joost van der Westhuizen knocked, but there was no time for more play. Ed Morrison blew the final whistle. For some it was a joyous sound, for others a shattering noise. The Springboks hugged each other and then knelt in a circle of prayer. The All Blacks walked off the field, sad but dignified.

Ellis Park's big screen shows the Springboks' elation while the crowd below wave their flags and arms in jubilation.

Pienaar was asked what it had been like to have had 65 000 South Africans behind him and the team. The captain replied: 'We had 43 million South Africans behind us today,' and added, 'The All Blacks played magnificent rugby.'

Both teams, despite some administrators, had enough class to be gracious, one in victory and the other in defeat. After all, the difference had been one drop that went skew and one that went straight. Stransky, with his kick, had emulated the feat of another great player: in 1949 Okey Geffin kicked 15 points to give the Springboks a 15-11 victory over the All Blacks.

Out came the VIPs, and an elated Nelson Mandela, shaking his fists in the air in delight, presented the William Webb Ellis trophy to Francois Pienaar. As he handed it over, he said to Pienaar, 'Thank you for what you have done for South Africa,' to which Pienaar replied, 'We could never do what you have done for South Africa.'

Morné du Plessis said that about three weeks before the final, the team had begun to feel the 'surge of the nation' – and that is what carried them to victory. The country had got behind one team as it had never done in any sport in the nation's history. People danced in the streets, waved flags, sung loudly and blew hooters in cars, on trains and on tugboats. All South Africans knew that they had won more than a rugby match.

The leadership that made it all possible – President Nelson Mandela and captain Francois Pienaar – both proudly wearing a number six jersey.

Pool A	South Africa 27 / Australia 18	Newlands, Cape Town
Pool A	South Africa 21 / Romania 8	Newlands, Cape Town
Pool A	South Africa 20 / Canada 0	Boet Erasmus, Port Elizabeth
Quarter Final	South Africa 42 / Western Samoa 14	Ellis Park, Johannesburg
Semi-Final	South Africa 19 / France 15	King's Park, Durban
Final	South Africa 15 / New Zealand 12	Ellis Park, Johannesburg

COMPLETE LIST OF SPRINGBOKS 1891 TO WORLD CUP 1995

* This list of Springboks includes players who were selected for a touring team, but did not play in a test match.
* Provincial Unions in parentheses are those in which the player was resident when first obtaining his Springbok 'Colours' (either for a touring team, or in a test match in South Africa).
* International records for example: 1955 Br 2,3 means that the player played in the second and third tests against the British Isles in 1955.

Legend Br – British Isles; A – Australia; NZ – New Zealand; E – England; W – Wales; I – Ireland; S – Scotland; Fr – France; Wd – World Team; SAm – South America; USA – United States of America; SAS – South America and Spain; NZC – New Zealand Cavaliers; WC – World Cup; Arg – Argentina; WS – Western Samoa; R – Romania; C – Canada; (s) signifies substitute.

Name	International Record	Tests	Tries	Pts
ACKERMANN, DSP (WP)	1955 Br 2,3,4; 1956 A 1,2; NZ 1,3; 1958 Fr 2	8	1	3
ALBERTYN, PK (SWD)	1924 Br 1,2,3,4	4	1	3
ALEXANDER, FA (GW)	1891 Br 1,2	2	–	–
ALLAN, J (N)	1993 A 1(s); Arg 1,2(s); 1994 E 1,2; NZ 1,2,3	8	–	–
ALLEN, PB (EP)	1960 S	1	–	–
ALLPORT, PH (WP)	1910 Br 2,3	2	1	3
ANDERSON, JW (WP)	1903 Br	1	–	–
ANDERSON, JH (WP)	1896 Br 1,3,4	3	–	–
ANDREW, JB (Tvl)	1896 Br 2	1	–	–
ANDREWS, KS (WP)	1992 E; 1993 Fr 1,2; A 1(s),2,3; 1994 NZ 3	8	1	5
ANDREWS, MG (N)	1993 tour of Arg – no tests; 1994 E 2; NZ 1,2,3; Arg 1,2; S; W; 1995 WS; WC: A,WS,Fr,NZ	13	2	10
ANTELME, JGM (Tvl)	1960 NZ 1,2,3,4; 1961 Fr	5	–	–
APSEY, JT (WP)	1933 A 4,5; 1938 Br 2	3	–	–
ASHLEY, S (WP)	1903 Br 2	1	–	–
ASTON, FTD (Tvl)	1896 Br 1,2,3,4	4	–	–
ATHERTON, S (N)	1992 tour to Fr & E – no tests; 1993 tour to A – no tests; Arg 1,2; 1994 E 1,2; NZ 1,2,3	7	–	–
AUCAMP, J (WT)	1924 Br 1,2	2	1	3
BAARD, AP (WP)	1969–70 I	1	1	1
BABROW, L (WP)	1937 A 1,2; NZ 1,2,3	5	3	9
BADENHORST, C (OFS)	1994 tour of NZ – no tests; tour of S & W – no tests; Arg 2	1	2	10
BARNARD, AS (EP)	1984 SAS 1,2; 1986 NZC 1,2	4	–	–
BARNARD, JH (Tvl)	1965 S; A 1,2; NZ 3,4	5	–	–
BARNARD, RW (Tvl)	1969–70 tour of UK – no tests; 1970 NZ 2(s); 1971 tour of A – no tests	–	–	–
BARNARD, WHM (NT)	1949 NZ 4; 1951 W	2	–	–
BARRY, J (WP)	1903 Br 1,2,3	3	1	3
BARTMANN, WJ (Tvl)	1986 NZC 1,2,3,4; 1992 NZ; A; Fr 1,2; tour to E – no tests; 1993 tour to Arg – no tests	8	–	–
BASTARD, WE (N)	1937 A 1; NZ 1,2,3; 1938 Br 1,3	6	2	6
BATES, AJ (WT)	1969–70 E; 1970 NZ 1,2; 1971 tour of A – no tests; 1972 E	4	–	–
BAYVEL, PCR (Tvl)	1974 Br 2,4; Fr 1,2; 1975 Fr 1,2; 1976 NZ 1,2,3,4	10	–	–
BECK, JJ (WP)	1981 NZ 2(s),3(s); USA	3	1	4
BEDFORD, TP (N)	1963 A 1,2,3,4; 1964 W; Fr; 1965 I; A 1,2; 1968 Br 1,2,3,4; Fr 1,2; 1969 A 1,2,3,4; 1969–70 S,E,I,W; 1971 Fr 1,2; tour of A – no tests	25	1	3
BEKKER, HJ (WP)	1981 NZ 1,3; tour of USA – no tests	2	1	4
BEKKER, HPJ (NT)	1952 E,Fr; 1953 A 1,2,3,4; 1955 Br 2,3,4; 1956 A 1,2; NZ 1,2,3,4	15	1	3
BEKKER, MJ (NT)	1960 S	1	–	–
BEKKER, RP (NT)	1953 A 3,4	2	1	3
BERGH, WFvRvO (SWD)	1931–32 W,I,E,S; 1933 A 1,2,3,4,5; 1937 A 1,2; NZ 1,2,3; 1938 Br 1,2,3	17	7	21
BESTBIER, A (OFS)	1974 Fr 2(s)	1	–	–
BESTER, JLA (WP)	1937 tour of A & NZ – no tests; 1938 Br 2,3	2	2	6
BESTER, JJN (WP)	1924 Br 2,4	2	1	3
BESWICK, AM (Bor)	1896 Br 2,3,4	3	–	–
BEZUIDENHOUT, CE(NT)	1962 Br 2,3,4	3	–	–
BEZUIDENHOUT, NSE(NT)	1972 E; 1974 Br 2,3,4; Fr 1,2; 1975 Fr 1,2; 1977 Wd	9	–	–
BIERMAN, JNM (Tvl)	1931 I	1	–	–
BISSET, WM (WP)	1891 Br 1,3	2	–	–
BLAIR, R (WP)	1977 Wd	1	–	21
BOSCH, GR (Tvl)	1974 Br 2; Fr 1,2; 1975 Fr 1,2; 1976 NZ 1,2,3,4	9	–	89
BOSMAN, NJS (Tvl)	1924 Br 2,3,4	3	–	–
BOTHA,DS (NT)	1981 NZ 1; tour of USA – no tests	1	–	–
BOTHA, HE (NT)	1980 SAm (H) 1,2; Br 1,2,3,4; SAm (A) 1,2; Fr; 1981 I 1,2; NZ 1,2,3; USA; 1982 SAm 1,2; 1986 NZC 1,2,3,4; 1989 Wd 1,2; 1992 NZ; A; Fr 1,2; E	28	2	312
BOTHA, JA (Tvl)	1903 Br 3	1	–	–
BOTHA, JPF (NT)	1960–61 tour of UK – no tests; 1962 Br 2,3,4	3	–	–
BOTHA, PH (Tvl)	1965 A 1,2	2	–	–
BOYES, HC (GW)	1891 Br 1,2	2	–	–
BRAINE, JS (GW)	1912 tour of UK – no tests	–	–	–
BRAND, GH (WP)	1928 NZ 2,3; 1931–32 W, I, E, S; 1933 A 1,2,3,4,5; 1937 A 1,2; NZ 2,3; 1938 Br 1	16	–	55
BREDENKAMP, MJ (GW)	1896 Br 1,3	2	–	–
BREEDT, JC (Tvl)	1986 NZC 1,2,3,4; 1989 Wd 1,2; 1992 NZ; A	8	–	–
BREWIS, JD (NT)	1949 NZ 1,2,3,4; 1951–52 S, I, W, E, Fr; 1953 A 1	10	1	18
BRIERS, TPD (WP)	1955 Br 1,2,3,4; 1956 NZ 2,3,4	7	5	15
BRINK, DJ (WP)	1906 S,W,E	3	–	–
BRINK, R (WP)	1995 WC: R, C	2	–	–
BROODRYK, JA (Tvl)	1937 tour of A & NZ – no tests	–	–	–
BROOKS, D (Bor)	1906 S	1	–	–
BROWN, CB (WP)	1903 Br 1,2,3	3	–	–
BRYNARD, GS (WP)	1965 A 1; NZ 1,2,3,4; 1968 Br 3,4	7	2	6
BUCHLER, JU (Tvl)	1951–52 S, I, W, E, Fr; 1953 A 1,2,3,4; 1956 A 2	10	–	8
BURDETT, AF (WP)	1906 S, I	2	–	–
BURGER, JM (WP)	1989 Wd 1,2	2	–	–
BURGER, MB (NT)	1980 Br 2(s); SAm (A) 1; 1981 tour of NZ – no tests; USA (s)	3	2	8
BURGER, SWP (WP)	1984 E 1,2; 1986 NZC 1,2,3,4	6	–	–
BURGER, WAG (Bor)	1906 S, I, W; 1910 Br 2	4	–	–
BURMEISTER, ARD (WP)	1906 tour of UK – no tests	–	–	–
CARELSE, G (EP)	1964 W; Fr; 1965 I; S; 1967 Fr 1,2,3; 1968 Fr 1,2; 1969 A 1,2,3,4; S	14	–	–
CARLSON, RA (WP)	1972 E	1	–	–
CAROLIN, HW (WP)	1903 Br 3; 1906 S, I	3	–	–
CASTENS, HH (WP)	1891 Br 1	1	–	–
CHIGNELL, TW (WP)	1891 Br 3	1	–	–
CILLIERS, GD (OFS)	1963 A 1,3,4; 1965 tour of I & S – no tests	3	1	3
CLAASSEN, JT (WT)	1955 Br 1,2,3,4; 1956 A 1,2; NZ 1,2,3,4; 1958 Fr 1,2; 1960 S; NZ 1,2,3; 1960–61 W, I, E, S, Fr; 1961 I; A 1,2; 1962 Br 1,2,3,4	28	2	10
CLAASSEN, W (N)	1981 NZ 1,2; NZ 2,3; USA; 1982 SAm 1,2	7	–	–
CLAASSENS, JP (NT)	1994 tour of NZ – no tests; tour of S & W – no tests	–	–	–
CLARK, WHG (Tvl)	1933 A 3	1	–	–
CLARKSON, WA (N)	1921 NZ 1,2; 1924 Br 1	3	–	–
CLOETE, HA (WP)	1896 Br 4	1	–	–
COCKRELL, CH (WP)	1969–70 S, I, W	3	–	–
COCKRELL, RJ (WP)	1974 Fr 1,2; 1975 Fr 1,2; 1976 NZ 1,2; 1977 Wd; 1980 tour of SAm – no tests; 1981 NZ 1,2(s),3; USA	11	1	4
COCKS, TMD (N)	1980 tour of SAm – no tests	–	–	–
COETZEE, JHH (WP)	1974 Br 1; 1975 Fr 2(s); 1976 NZ 1,2,3,4	6	–	–
CONRADIE, SC (WP)	1965 tour of S & I – no tests	–	–	–
COPE, DG (Tvl)	1896 Br 2	1	–	2
COTTY, WAH (GW)	1896 Br 3	1	–	–
CRAMPTON, G (GW)	1903 Br 2	1	–	–
CRAVEN, DH	1931–32 W,I,S; 1933 A 1,2,3,4,5; 1937 A 1,2; NZ 1,2,3; 1938 Br 1,2,3	16	2	6
CRONJÉ, CJC (ET)	1965 tour of A & NZ – no tests	–	–	–
CRONJE, PA (N)	1971 Fr 1,2; A 1,2,3; 1974 Br 3,4	7	3	10
CRONJE, SN (Tvl)	1912 tour of UK – no tests	–	–	–
CROSBY, JH (Tvl)	1896 Br 2	1	–	–
CROSBY, NJ (Tvl)	1910 Br 1,3	2	–	–
CURRIE, C (GW)	1903 Br 2	1	–	–
D'ALTON, G (WP)	1933 A 1	1	–	–
DALTON, J (Tvl)	1994 tour of NZ – no tests; tour of S & W – no tests; Arg 1(s); 1995 WC: A, C	3	–	–
DANEEL, GM (WP)	1928 NZ 1,2,3,4; 1931–32 W, I, E, S	8	2	6
DANEEL, HJ (WP)	1906 S, I, W, E	4	–	–
DANNHAUSER, G (Tvl)	1951–52 tour of UK – no tests	–	–	–
DAVISON, PM (EP)	1910 Br 1	1	–	–
DE BRUYN, J (OFS)	1974 Br 3; tour of Fr – no tests	1	–	–
DE JONGH, HPK (WP)	1928 NZ 3	1	1	3
DE KLERK, IJ (Tvl)	1969–70 E, I, W	3	–	–
DE KLERK, KBH (Tvl)	1974 Br 1,2,3(s); tour of Fr – no tests; 1975 Fr 1,2; 1976 NZ 2(s),3,4; 1980 SAm (H)1,2; Br 2; 1981 I 1,2	13	–	–
DE KOCK, AN (GW)	1891 Br 1	1	–	–
DE KOCK, JS (WP)	1921 NZ 3; 1924 Br	32	–	–
DELANEY, ETA (WP)	1912 tour of UK – no tests	–	–	–
DELPORT, WH (EP)	1951–52 I, W, E, Fr; 1953 A 1,2,3,4	9	2	6
DE MELKER, SC (GW)	1903 Br 2; 1906 E	2	–	–
DENYSSCHEN, CJ (N)	1956 tour of A & NZ – no tests	–	–	–
DEVENISH, CE (GW)	1896 Br 2	1	–	–
DEVENISH, GStL (Tvl)	1896 Br 2	1	–	–
DEVENISH, MJ (Tvl)	1891 Br 1	1	–	–
DE VILLIERS, DI (Tvl)	1910 Br 1,2,3	3	1	3
DE VILLIERS, DJ (WP)	1962 Br 2,3; 1965 NZ 1,3,4; 1967 Fr 1,2,3,4; 1968 Br 1,2,3; Fr 1,2; 1969 A 1,4; 1969–70 I; W; 1970 NZ 1,2,3,4	25	3	9
DE VILLIERS, HA (WP)	1906 S, W, E	3	–	–
DE VILLIERS, HO (WP)	1967 Fr 1,2,3,4; 1968 Fr 1,2; 1969 A 1,2,3,4; 1969–70 S, E, I, W	14	–	26
DE VILLIERS, IB (WP)	1921 tour of NZ – no tests	–	–	–
DE VILLIERS, PduP (WP)	1928 NZ 1,3,4; 1931 E; 1933 A 4; 1937 A 1,2; NZ 1	8	–	–
DEVINE, D (Tvl)	1924 Br 3; 1928 NZ 2	2	–	–
DE VOS, DJJ (WP)	1965 S; 1969 A 3; 1969–70 S; 1971 tour of A – no tests	3	–	–
DE WAAL, AN (WP)	1967 Fr 1,2,3,4	4	–	–
DE WAAL, PJ (WP)	1896 Br 4	1	–	–
DE WET, AE (WP)	1969 A 3,4; 1969–70 E	3	–	–
DE WET, PJ (WP)	1938 Br 1,2,3	3	–	–
DE WILZEM, CJ (OFS)	1956 tour of A & NZ – no tests	–	–	–
DINKELMANN, EE (NT)	1951–52 S, I, E, Fr; 1953 A 1,2	6	2	5
DIRKSEN, CW (NT)	1963 A 4; 1964 W; 1965 I; 1967 Fr 1,2,3,4; 1968 Br 1,2	10	3	9
DOBBIN, FJ (GW)	1903 Br 1,2; 1906 S, W, E; 1910 Br 1; 1912 S, I, W	9	1	3
DOBIE, JAR (Tvl)	1928 NZ 2	1	–	–
DOLD, JB (EP)	1931–32 tour of UK – no tests	–	–	–
DORMEHL, PJ (WP)	1896 Br 3,4	2	–	–
DOUGLASS, FW (EP)	1896 Br 1	1	–	–
DROTSKÉ, AE (OFS)	1993 Arg 2; 1995 WC: WS(s)	2	–	–
DRYBURGH, RG (WP)	1955 Br 2,3,4; 1956 A 2; NZ 1,4; 1960 NZ 1,2	8	3	28
DUFF, BR (WP)	1891 Br 1,2,3	3	–	–
DUFFY, BAA (Bor)	1928 NZ 1	1	–	–
DU PLESSIS, CJ (WP)	1981 tour of NZ & USA – no tests; 1982 SAm 1,2; 1984 E 1,2; SAS 1,2; 1986 NZC 1,2,3,4; 1989 Wd 1,2	12	4	16
DU PLESSIS, DC (NT)	1977 Wd; 1980 SAm (A) 2; Fr	2	–	–
DU PLESSIS, F (Tvl)	1949 NZ 1,2,3	3	–	–
DU PLESSIS, M (WP)	1971 A 1,2,3; 1974 Br 1,2; Fr 1,2; 1975 Fr 1,2; 1976 NZ 1,2,3,4; 1977 Wd; 1980 SAm (H) 1,2; Br 1,2,3,4; SAm (A) 2; Fr	22	3	12
DU PLESSIS, MJ (WP)	1984 SAS 1,2; 1986 NZC 1,2,3,4; 1989 Wd 1,2	8	1	7
DU PLESSIS, NJ (WT)	1921 NZ 2; 1924 Br 1,2,3	5	–	–
DU PLESSIS, PG (NT)	1972 E	1	–	–
DU PLESSIS, TD (NT)	1980 SAm (H) 1,2; tour of SAm – no tests	–	–	–
DU PLESSIS, W (WP)	1980 SAm (H) 1,2; Br 1,2,3,4; SAm (A) 1,2; Fr; 1981 NZ 1,2,3; tour of USA – no tests; 1982 SAm 1,2	14	3	12
DU PLOOY, AJJ (EP)	1955 Br 1	1	–	–
DU PREEZ, FCH (NT)	1960–61 ES; 1961 A 1,2; 1962 Br 1,2,3,4; 1963 A 1; 1964 W, Fr; 1965 tour of I & S – no tests; A 1,2; NZ 1,2,3,4; 1967 Fr 4; 1968 Br 1,2,3,4; 1969 A 1,2; 1969–70 S, I, W; 1970 NZ 1,2,3,4; 1971 Fr 1,2; A 1,2,3	38	1	11
DU PREEZ, JGH (WP)	1956 NZ 1	1	–	–
DU PREEZ, RJ (N)	1992 NZ, A, tour to Fr & E – no tests; 1993 Fr 1,2; A 1,2,3	7	–	–
DU RAND, JA (R)	1949 NZ 2,3; 1951–52 S, I, W, E, Fr; 1953 A 1,2,3,4; 1955 Br 1,2,3,4; 1956 A 1,2; NZ 1,2,3,4	21	4	12

Name	Career			
DU RANDT, JP (OFS)	1994 Arg 1,2; S, W; 1995 WS; WC: A, WS, Fr, NZ	9	–	–
DURAND, PJ (WT)	1969–70 tour of UK – no tests	–	–	–
DU TOIT, AF (WP)	1928 NZ 3,4	2	–	–
DU TOIT, BA (Tvl)	1937 tour of A & NZ – no tests; 1938 Br 1,2,3	3	1	3
DU TOIT, PA (NT)	1949 NZ 2,3,4; 1951–52 S, I, W, E, Fr	8	2	6
DU TOIT, PG (WP)	1980 tour of SAm – no tests; 1981 NZ 1; tour of USA – no tests; 1982 SAm 1,2; 1984 E 1,2	5	–	–
DU TOIT, PS (WP)	1956 tour of A & NZ – no tests; 1958 Fr 1,2; 1960 NZ 1,2,3,4; 1960–61 W, I, E, S, Fr; 1961 A 1,2	14	–	–
DU TOIT, SR (WP)	1931–32 tour of UK – no tests	–	–	–
DUVENAGE, FP (GW)	1949 NZ 1,3	2	–	–
EDWARDS, P (NT)	1980 SAm (H) 1,2	2	–	–
ELLIS, JH (SWA)	1965 NZ 1,2,3,4; 1967 Fr 1,2,3,4; 1968 Br 1,2,3,4; Fr 1,2; 1969 A 1,2,3,4; 1969–70 S, I, W; 1970 NZ 1,2,3,4; 1971 Fr 1,2; A 1,2,3; 1972 E; 1974 Br 1,2,3,4; Fr 1,2; 1976 NZ 1	38	7	21
ELLIS, MC (Tvl)	1921 NZ 2,3; 1924 Br 1,2,3,4	6	–	–
ENGELBRECHT, JP (WP)	1960 S; 1960–61 W, I, E, S, Fr; 1961 A 1,2; 1962 Br 2,3,4; 1963 A 2,3; 1964 W, Fr; 1965 I, S; A 1,2; NZ 1,2,3,4; 1967 Fr 1,2,3	33	8	24
ERASMUS, FS (NT)	1986 NZC 3,4; 1989 Wd 2	3	–	–
ETLINGER, TE (WP)	1896 Br 4	1	–	–
FERREIRA, C (OFS)	1986 NZC,1,2	2	–	–
FERREIRA, PS (WP)	1984 SAS 1,2	2	1	4
FERRIS, HH (Tvl)	1903 Br 3	1	–	–
FORBES, HH (Tvl)	1896 Br 2	1	–	–
FORREST, HM (Tvl)	1931–32 tour of UK – no tests	–	–	–
FOURIE, C (EP)	1974 Fr 1,2; 1975 Fr 1,2	4	1	10
FOURIE, TT (SET)	1974 Br 3; tour of Fr – no tests	1	–	–
FOURIE, WL (SWA)	1958 Fr 1,2	2	1	3
FRANCIS, JAJ (Tvl)	1912–13 S, I, W, E, Fr	5	2	6
FRANCIS, MG (OFS)	1931–32 tour of UK – no tests	–	–	–
FREDERICKSON, CA (Tvl)	1974 Br 2; 1980 SAm (H) 1,2	3	–	–
FREW, A (Tvl)	1903 Br 1	1	1	3
FRONEMAN, DC (OFS)	1977 Wd	1	–	–
FRONEMAN, IL (Bor)	1933 A 1	1	–	–
FRY, DJ (WP)	1951–52 tour of UK – no tests	–	–	–
FRY, SP (WP)	1951–52 S, I, W, E, Fr; 1953 A 1,2,3,4; 1955 Br 1,2,3,4	13	–	–
FÜLS, HT (Tvl)	1992 NZ(s); tour to Fr & E – no tests; 1993 Fr 1,2; A 1,2,3; Arg 1,2	8	–	–
GAGE, JH (OFS)	1933 A 1	1	–	–
GAINSFORD, JL (WP)	1960 S; NZ,1,2,3,4; 1960–61 W, I, E, S, Fr; 1961 A 1,2; 1962 Br 1,2,3,4; 1963 A 1,2,3,4; 1964 W, Fr; 1965 I, S; A 1,2; NZ 1,2,3,4; 1967 Fr 1,2,3	33	8	24
GEEL, PJ (OFS)	1949 NZ 3	1	–	–
GEERE, V (Tvl)	1931–32 tour of UK – no tests; 1933 A 1,2,3,4,5	5	–	–
GEFFIN, AO (Tvl)	1949 NZ 1,2,3,4; 1951–52 S, I, W	7	–	48
GELDENHUYS, A (EP)	1992 NZ; A	2	–	–
GELDENHUYS, SB (NT)	1981 NZ 2,3; USA; 1982 SAm 1,2; 1989 Wd 1,2	7	1	4
GENTLES, TA (WP)	1955 Br 1,2,4; 1956 NZ 2,3; 1958 Fr 2	6	–	–
GERAGHTY, EM (Bor)	1949 NZ 4	1	–	–
GERBER, DM (EP)	1980 SAm (A) 1,2; Fr; 1981 I 1,2; NZ 1,2,3; USA; 1982 SAm 1,2; 1984 E 1,2; SAS 1,2; 1986 NZC 1,2,3,4; 1992 NZ, A, Fr 1,2; E	24	19	82
GERBER, MC (EP)	1958 Fr 1,2; 1960 S	3	–	8
GERICKE, FW (Tvl)	1960 S	1	1	3
GERMISHUYS, JS (OFS)	1974 Br 2; 1976 NZ 1,2,3,4; 1977 Wd; 1980 SAm (H) 1,2; Br 1,2,3,4; SAm (A) 1,2; Fr; 1981 I 1,2; NZ 2,3; USA	20	12	48
GIBBS, EAH (GW)	1903 Br 2	1	–	–
GOOSEN, CP (OFS)	1965 NZ 2	1	–	–
GORTON, HC (Tvl)	1896 Br 1	1	–	–
GOULD, RL (N)	1968 Br 1,2,3,4; 1968 tour of Fr – no tests	4	–	3
GRAY, BG (WP)	1931–32 W, E, S; 1933 A 5	4	–	–
GREENWOOD, CM (WP)	1961 I	1	2	6
GREYLING, PJF (OFS)	1967 Fr 1,2,3,4; 1968 Br 1; Fr 1,2; 1969 A 1,2,3,4; 1969–70 S, E, I, W; 1970 NZ 1,2,3,4; 1971 Fr 1,2; A 1,2; 1972 E	25	5	15
GROBLER, CJ (OFS)	1974 Br 4; 1974 tour of Fr – no tests; 1975 Fr 1,2	3	1	4
GROBLER, RN (NT)	1969–70 tour of UK – no tests	–	–	–
GUTHRIE, FEH (WP)	1891 Br 1,3; 1896 Br 1	3	–	–
HAHN, CHL (Tvl)	1910 Br 1,2,3	3	1	3
HAMILTON, GH (EP)	1891 Br 1	3	–	–
HANEKOM, MvdS (Bol)	1956 tour of A & NZ – no tests	–	–	–
HARRIS, TA (Tvl)	1937 NZ 2,3; 1938 Br 1,2,3	5	1	3
HARTLEY, AJ (WP)	1891 Br 3	1	–	–
HATTINGH, H (NT)	1992 A(s)	1	–	–
HATTINGH, LB (OFS)	1933 A 2	1	–	–
HATTINGH, SJ(Tvl)	1994 tour of W, S & I – no tests	–	–	–
HEATLIE, BH (WP)	1891 Br 2,3; 1896 Br 1,4; 1903 Br 1,3	6	–	6
HENDRIKS, P (Tvl)	1992 NZ; A 1; tour to Fr & E – no tests; 1994 S, W; 1995 WC: A, R, C	7	1	5
HEPBURN, TB (WP)	1896 Br 4	1	–	2
HEUNIS, JW (NT)	1981 NZ 3(s); USA; 1982 SAm 1,2; 1984 E,2; SAS 1,2; 1986 NZC 1,2,3,4; 1989 Wd 1,2	14	2	41
HILL, RA (R)	1960–61 W, I; 1961 I; A 1,2; 1962 Br 4; 1963 A 3	7	–	–
HILLS, WG (NT)	1992 Fr 1,2; E 1; 1993 Fr 1,2; A 1	6	–	–
HIRSCH, JG (EP)	1906 I; 1910 Br 1	2	–	–
HOBSON, TEC (WP)	1903 Br 3	1	–	–
HOFFMANN, RS (Bol)	1953 A 3	1	–	–
HOFMEYR, SR (WP)	1937 tour of A & NZ – no tests	–	–	–
HOLTON, DN (EP)	1960 S; 1960–61 tour of UK – no tests	1	–	–
HONIBALL, HW (N)	1993 A 3(s); Arg 2	2	–	–
HOPWOOD, DJ (WP)	1960 S; NZ 3,4; 1960–61 W, E, S, Fr; 1961 I; A 1,2; 1962 Br 1,2,3,4; 1963 A 1,2,4; 1964 W, Fr; 1965 S, NZ 3,4	22	5	15
HOWE, BF (Bor)	1956 NZ 1,4	2	1	3
HOWE-BROWNE, NRFG (WP)	1910 Br 1,2,3	3	–	–
HUGO, DP (WP)	1989 Wd 1,2	2	–	–
HURTER, MH	1995 WC: R, C	2	–	–
IMMELMAN, JH (WP)	1912–13 Fr	1	–	–
JACKSON, DC (WP)	1906 I, W, E	3	–	–
JACKSON, JS (WP)	1903 Br 2	1	–	–
JANSEN, E (OFS)	1980 tour of SAm – no tests; 1981 NZ 1; tour of UK – no tests	1	–	–
JANSEN, JS (OFS)	1970 NZ 1,2,3,4; 1971 Fr 1,2; A 1,2,3; 1972 E	10	1	3
JANSE VAN RENSBURG, MC	1969–70 – no tests	–	–	–
JANSON, A (WP)	1965 tour of A & NZ – no tests	–	–	–
JENNINGS, CB (Bor)	1937 NZ 1	1	–	–
JENNINGS, MW (Bol)	1969–70 tour of UK – no tests	–	–	–
JOHNS, RG (WP)	1960–61 tour of UK – no tests	–	–	–
JOHNSON, GK (Tvl)	1993 Arg 2; 1994 NZ 3; Arg 1; tour of W, S & I – no tests; 1995 WS; WC: R, C	6	5	63?
JOHNSTONE, PGA (WP)	1951–52 S, I, W, E, Fr; 1956 A 1; NZ 1,2,4	9	2	11
JONES, CH (Tvl)	1903 Br 1,2	2	–	–
JONES, PST (WP)	1896 Br 1,3,4	3	1	3
JORDAAN, RP (NT)	1949 NZ 1,2,3,4	4	–	–
JOUBERT, AJ (OFS)	1989 Wd 1(s); 1993 A3; Arg 1; 1994 E,2; NZ 1,2(s),3; Arg 2; S, W; 1995 WC: A, C, WS, Fr, NZ	16	3	56
JOUBERT, SJ (WP)	1906 I, W, E	3	1	8
KAHTS, WJH (NT)	1980 Br 1,2,3; SAm (A) 1,2; Fr; 1981 I 1,2; NZ 2; tour of USA – no tests; 1982 SAm 1,2	11	1	4
KAMINER, J (Tvl)	1958 Fr 2	1	–	–
KEBBLE, GR (N)	1993 Arg 1; 1994 NZ 1(s),2	4	–	–
KELLY, EW (GW)	1896 Br 3	1	–	–
KENYON, BJ (Bor)	1949 NZ 4; 1951–52 tour of UK – no tests	1	–	–
KEEVY, AC (ET)	1951–52 tour of UK – no tests	–	–	–
KIPLING, HG (GW)	1931–32 W, I, E, S; 1933 A 1,2,3,4,5	9	–	–
KIRKPATRICK, AI (GW)	1953 A 2; 1956 NZ 2; 1958 Fr 1; 1960 S; NZ 1; 1960–61 W, I, E, S, Fr	13	–	–
KNIGHT, AS (Tvl)	1912–13 S, I, W, E, Fr	5	–	–
KNOETZE, F (WP)	1989 Wd 1,2; 1992 tour of Fr & E – no tests	2	1	4
KOCH, AC (Bol)	1949 NZ 2,3,4; 1951–52 S, I, W, E, Fr; 1953 A 1,2,4; 1955 Br 1,2,3,4; 1956 A 1; NZ 2,3; 1958 Fr 1,2; 1960 NZ 1,2	22	5	15
KOCH, HV (WP)	1949 NZ 1,2,3,4	4	–	–
KOTZÉ, GJM (WP)	1967 Fr 1,2,3,4	4	–	–
KRANTZ, EFW (OFS)	1976 NZ 1; 1980 tour of SAm – no tests; 1981 I 1; tour of NZ & USA – no tests	2	1	4
KRIGE, JD (WP)	1903 Br 1,3; 1906 S, I, W	5	1	3
KRIGE, WA (WP)	1912–13 tour of UK – no tests	–	–	–
KRITZINGER, JL (Tvl)	1974 Br 3,4; Fr 1,2; 1975 Fr 1,2; 1976 NZ 4	7	1	4
KROON, CM (EP)	1955 Br 1	1	–	–
KRUGER, PE (Tvl)	1986 NZC 3,4	2	–	–
KRUGER, RJ (OFS)	1993 tour to A – no tests; Arg 1,2; 1994 tour of NZ – no tests; S, W; 1995 WS; WC: A, R, WS, Fr, NZ	10	1	5
KRÜGER, TL (Tvl)	1921 NZ 1,2; 1924 Br 1,2,3,4; 1928 NZ 1,2	8	–	–
KUHN, SP (Tvl)	1960 NZ 3,4; 1960–61 W, I, E, S, Fr; 1961 I; A 1,2; 1962 Br 1,2,3,4; 1963 A 1,2,3; 1965 I,S	19	–	–
LA GRANGE, JB (WP)	1924 Br 3,4	2	–	–
LARARD, A (Tvl)	1896 Br 2,4	2	1	3
LATEGAN, MT (WP)	1949 NZ 1,2,3,4; 1951–52 S, I, W, E, Fr; 1953 A 1,2	11	3	9
LAUBSCHER, TG (WP)	1994 Arg 1,2; S, W	4	–	–
LAWLESS, MJ (WP)	1964 Fr 1969–70 E(s) I, W	4	–	–
LAWTON, AD (WP)	1937 tour of A & NZ – no tests	–	–	–
LEDGER, SH (GW)	1912–13 S, I, E, Fr	4	1	3
LE ROUX, AH (OFS)	1993 tour to Arg – no tests; 1994 E; tour of NZ – no tests	1	–	–
LE ROUX, HP (Tvl)	1992 tour to Fr & E – no tests; 1993 Fr 1,2; tour to A – no tests; tour to Arg – no tests; 1994 E 1,2; NZ 1,2,3; Arg 2; S, W; 1995 WS; WC: A, R, C, WS, Fr, NZ	17	1	19
LE ROUX, JHS (Tvl)	1994 E 2; NZ 1,2	2	–	–
LE ROUX, JSR (WP)	1906 tour of UK – no tests	–	–	–
LE ROUX, M (OFS)	1980 Br 1,2,3,4; SAm (A) 1,2; Fr; 1981 I 1	8	–	–
LE ROUX, PA (WP)	1906 I, W, E	3	–	–
LINEE, M (WP)	1993 tour to A – no tests; tour of W, S & I – no tests	–	–	–
LITTLE, EM (GW)	1891 Br 1,3	2	–	–
LOCHNER, GP (EP)	1937 NZ 3; Br 1,2	3	1	3
LOCHNER, GP (WP) (Butch)	1955 Br 3; 1956 A 1,2; NZ 1,2,3,4; 1958 Fr 1,2	9	2	6
LOCKYEAR, RJ (GW)	1960 NZ 1,2,3,4; 1960–61 I, Fr	6	–	20
LOMBARD, AC (EP)	1910 Br	2	1	–
LÖTTER, D (Tvl)	1993 Fr 2; A 1,2	3	–	–
LOTZ, JW (Tvl)	1937 A 1,2; NZ 1,2,3; 1938 1,2,3	8	1	3
LOUBSER, JA (WP)	1903 Br 3; 1906 S, I, W, E; 1910 Br 1,2	7	3	9
LOURENS, MJ (NT)	1968 Br 2,3,4; 1968 tour of Fr – no tests; 1971 tour of A – no tests	3	1	3
LOUW, JS (Tvl)	1891 Br 1,2,3	3	–	–
LOUW, LH (WP)	1912–13 tour of UK – no tests	–	–	–
LOUW, MM (WP)	1928 NZ 3,4; 1931–32 W, I, E, S; 1933 A 1,2,3,4,5; 1937 A 1,2; NZ 2,3; 1938 Br 1,2,3	18	1	3
LOUW, MJ (Tvl)	1971 A 2,3	2	–	–
LOUW, RJ (WP)	1980 SAm (H) 1,2; Br 1,2,3,4; SAm (A) 1,2; Fr; 1981 I 1,2; NZ 1,3; tour of USA – no tests; 1982 SAm 1,2; 1984 E,2; SAS 1,2	19	5	20
LOUW, SC (WP)	1931–32 tour of UK – no tests; 1933 A 1,2,3,4,5; 1937 A 1; NZ 1,2,3; 1938 Br 1,2,3	12	2	6
LUYT, FP (WP)	1910 Br 1,2,3; 1912–13 S, I, W, E	7	2	8
LUYT, JD (EP)	1912–13 S, W, E, Fr	4	–	–
LUYT, RR (WP)	1910 Br 2,3; 1912–13 S, I, W, E, Fr	7	1	3
LYONS, DJ (EP)	1896 Br	1	1	–
LYSTER, PJ (N)	1933 A 2,5; 1937 NZ 1	3	–	–
MACDONALD, AW (R)	1965 A 1; NZ 1,2,3,4	5	–	–
MACDONALD, DA (WP)	1974 Br 2	1	–	–
MACDONALD, I (Tvl)	1992 NZ; A	2	–	–
MALAN, AS (Tvl)	1960 NZ 1,2,3,4; 1960–61 W, I, E, S, Fr; 1962 Br 1; 1963 A 1,3; 1964 W; 1965 I, S	16	–	–
MALAN, AW (NT)	1989 Wd 1,2; 1992 A; A 1; Fr 1,2; E	7	–	–
MALAN, E (NT)	1980 Br 3(s),4	2	–	–
MALAN, GF (WP) (Abie)	1958 Fr 2; 1960 NZ 1,3,4; 1960–61 E, S, Fr; 1962 Br 1,2,3; 1963 A 1,2,4; 1964 W; 1965 A 1,2; NZ 1,2	18	1	3
MALAN, P (Tvl)	1949 NZ 4	1	–	–
MALLETT, NVH (WP)	1984 SAS 1,2	2	1	4
MANS, WJ (WP)	1965 I, S; 1965 tour of A & NZ – no tests	2	1	5

Name	Career			
MARAIS, FP (Bol)	1949 NZ 1,2; 1951 S; 1953 A 1,2	5	1	10
MARAIS, JFK (WP)	1963 A 3; 1964 W; 1965 I, S; A 2; 1968 Br 1,2,3,4; Fr 1,2; 1969 A 1,2,3,4; 1969–70 S, E, I, W; 1970 NZ 1,2,3,4; 1971 Fr 1,2; A 1,2,3; 1974 Br 1,2,3,4; Fr 1,2	35	1	3
MARAIS, JH (NT)	1981 NZ – no tests	–	–	–
MARÉ, DS (Tvl)	1906 S	1	–	–
MARSBERG, AFWD (GW)	1906 S, W, E	3	–	–
MARSBERG, PA (GW)	1910 Br 1	1	–	–
MARTENS, HJ (OFS)	1993 tour to Arg – no tests	–	–	–
MARTHEZE, WC (GW)	1903 Br 2; 1906 I, W	3	–	–
MARTIN, HJ (Tvl)	1937 A 2	1	–	–
McCALLUM, ID (WP)	1970 NZ 1,2,3,4; 1971 Fr 1,2; A 1,2,3; 1974 Br 1,2	11	–	62
McCALLUM, RJ (WP)	1974 Br 1; 1974 tour of Fr – no tests	1	–	–
McCULLOCH, JD (GW)	1912–13 E, Fr	2	–	–
McDONALD, JAJ (WP)	1931–32 W, I, E, S	4	–	–
McEWAN, WMC (Tvl)	1903 Br 1,3	2	–	–
McHARDY, EE (OFS)	1912–13 S, I, W, E, Fr	5	6	18
McKENDRICK, JA (WP)	1891 Br 3	1	–	–
MEINTJES, JJ (GW)	1912–13 tour of UK – no tests	–	–	–
MEIRING, FA (NT)	1994 tour of NZ – no tests	–	–	–
MELLET, TB (GW)	1896 Br 2	1	–	–
MELLISH, FW (WP)	1921 NZ 1,3; 1924 Br 1,2,3,4	6	–	–
MENTER, MA (NT)	1968 tour of Fr – no tests	–	–	–
MERRY, GA (EP)	1891 Br 1	1	–	–
METCALF, HD (Bor)	1903 Br	2	1	–
MEYER, CduP (WP)	1921 NZ 1,2,3	3	–	–
MEYER, PJ (GW)	1896 Br 1	1	–	–
MICHAU, JM (Tvl) (Baby)	1921 NZ 1	1	–	–
MICHAU, JP (WP)	1921 NZ 1,2,3	3	–	–
MILLAR, WA (WP)	1906 E; 1910 Br 2,3; 1912–13 I, W, Fr	6	2	6
MILLS, WJ (WP)	1910 Br 2; 1912–13 tour of UK – no tests	–	–	–
MOLL, TM (Tvl)	1910 Br 2	1	–	–
MONTINI, PE (WP)	1956 A 1,2	2	–	–
MOOLMAN, LC (NT)	1977 Wd; 1980 SAm (H) 1,2; Br 1,2,3,4; SAm (A) 1,2; 1981 I 1,2; NZ 1,2,3; USA; 1982 SAm 1,2; 1984 SAS 1,2; 1986 NZC 1,2,3,4	24	–	–
MORDT, RH (Zimb–R)	1980 SAm (H) 1,2; Br 1,2,3,4; SAm (A) 1,2; Fr; 1981 I, NZ 1,2,3; USA; 1982 SAm 1,2; 1984 SAS 1,2	18	12	48
MORKEL, DJA (Tvl)	1903 Br 1; 1960 tour of UK – no tests	1	–	–
MORKEL, DFT (Tvl)	1906 E, E; 1910 Br 1,3; 1912–13 S, I, W, E, Fr	9	3	38
MORKEL, HJL (Harry) (WP)	1921 NZ 1	1	–	–
MORKEL, HW (Henry) (WP)	1921 NZ 1	2	–	–
MORKEL, JA (Royal) (WP)	1921 NZ 2,3	2	–	–
MORKEL, JWH (WP)	1912–13 S, I, W, E, Fr	5	4	16
MORKEL, PK (WP)	1928 NZ 4	1	–	–
MORKEL, PG (WP)	1912–13 S, I, W, E, Fr; 1921 NZ 1,2,3	8	–	16
MORKEL, WH (Boy) (WP)	1910 Br 3; 1912–13 S, I, W, E, Fr; 1921 NZ 1,2,3	9	2	6
MORKEL, WS (Tvl)	1906 S, I, W, E	4	–	–
MOSS, C (N)	1949 NZ 1,2,3,4	4	–	–
MOSTERT, PJ (WP)	1921 NZ 1,2,3; 1924 Br 1,2,4; 1928 NZ 1,2,3,4; 1931–32 W, I, E, S	14	1	6
MULDER, CG (ET)	1965 tour of A & NZ – no tests	–	–	–
MULDER, JC (Tvl)	1994 NZ 2,3; S, W; 1995 WS, WC: A, WS, Fr, NZ	9	1	5
MULLER, GH (WP)	1969 A 3,4; 1969–70 S, W; 1970 NZ 1,2,3,4; 1971 Fr 1,2; 1971 tour of A – no tests; 1972 E; 1974 Br 1,3,4	14	4	12
MÜLLER, HL (OFS)	1986 NZC 4(s); 1989 Wd 1(s)	2	–	–
MULLER, HSV (Tvl)	1949 NZ 1,2,3,4; 1951–52 S, I, W, E, Fr; 1953 A 1,2,3,4	13	3	16
MÜLLER, LJJ (N)	1992 NZ; A 1	2	–	–
MÜLLER, PG (N)	1992 NZ 1; A 1; Fr 1,2; E 1; 1993 Fr 1,2; A 1,2,3; Arg 1,2; 1994 E 1,2; NZ 1; S, W	17	2	10
MYBURGH, B (ET)	1951–52 tour of UK – no tests	–	–	–
MYBURGH, FR (EP)	1896 Br	1	1	–
MYBURGH, JL (NT)	1960–61 tour of UK – no tests; 1962 Br 1; 1963 A 4; 1964 W, Fr; 1968 Br 1,2,3; Fr 1,2; 1969 A 1,2,3,4; 1969–70 E, I, W; 1970 NZ 3,4	18	–	–
MYBURGH, WH (WT)	1924 Br	1	1	–
NAUDÉ, JP (WP)	1963 A 4; 1965 A 1,2; NZ 1,3,4; 1967 Fr 1,2,3,4; 1968 Br 1,2,3; 1968 tour of Fr – no tests	14	2	47
NEETHLING, JB (WP)	1965 tour of I & S – no tests; 1967 Fr 1,2,3,4; 1968 Br 4; 1968 tour of Fr – no tests; 1969–70 S; 1970 NZ 1,2	8	–	–
NEILL, WA (Bor)	1906 tour of UK – no tests	–	–	–
NEL, JJ (WP)	1956 A 1,2; NZ 1,2,3,4; 1958 Fr 1,2	8	1	3
NEL, JA (Tvl)	1960 NZ 1,2; 1963 A 1,2; 1965 A 2; NZ 1,2,3,4; 1970 NZ 3,4	11	–	–
NEL, PARO (Tvl)	1903 Br 1,2,3	3	–	–
NEL, PJ (N)	1928 NZ 1,2,3,4; 1931–32 W, I, E, S; 1933 A 1,3,4,5; 1937 A 1,2; NZ 2,3	16	1	3
NIMB, CF (WP)	1969–61 tour of UK – no tests; 1961 I	1	–	9
NOMIS, SH (Tvl)	1965 tour of A & NZ – no tests; 1967 Fr 4; 1968 Br 1,2,3,4; Fr 1,2; 1969 A 1,2,3,4; 1969–70 S, E, I, W; 1970 NZ 1,2,3,4; 1971 Fr 1,2,; A 1,2,3; 1972 E	25	6	18
NYKAMP, JL (Tvl)	1933 A 2	1	–	–
OCHSE, JK (WP)	1951–52 I, W, E, Fr; 1953 A 1,2,4	7	3	9
OELOFSE, JSA (Tvl)	1951–52 tour of UK – no tests; 1953 A 1,2,3,4	4	2	6
OLIVER, JF (Tvl)	1928 NZ 3,4	2	–	–
OLIVIER, E (WP)	1965 tour of A & NZ – no tests; 1967 Fr 1,2,3,4; 1968 Br 1,2,3,4; Fr 1,2; 1969 A 1,2,3,4; 1969–70 S, E	16	5	15
OLIVIER, J (NT)	1992 Fr 1,2; E 1993 Fr 1,2; A 1,2,3; Arg 1; 1994 tour of W, S & I – no tests	9	1	5
OLIVIER, JS (WP)	1921 tour of A & NZ – no tests	–	–	–
OLVER, E (EP)	1896 Br 1	1	–	–
OOSTHUIZEN, JJ (WP)	1976 NZ 1,2,3,4	9	2	8
OOSTHUIZEN, OW (NT)	1981 I 1(s),2; NZ 2,3; USA; 1982 SAm 1,2; 1984 E 1,2	9	1	4
OOSTHUYSEN, DE (NT)	1992 tour to Fr & E – no tests; 1993 tour to A – no tests	–	–	–
OSLER, BL (WP)	1924 Br 1,2,3,4; 1928 NZ 1,2,3,4; 1931–32 W, I, E, S; 1933 1,2,3,4,5	17	2	46
OSLER, SG (WP)	1928 NZ 1	1	–	–
OTTO, K	1994 tour of NZ – no tests; tour of W, S & I – no tests; WC: R, C(s)	2	–	–
OXLEE, K (N)	1960 NZ 1,2,3,4; 1960–61 W, I, S; 1961 A 1,2; 1962 Br 1,2,3,4; 1963 A 1,2,4; 1964 W; 1965 tour of I & S – no tests; 1965 NZ 1,2	19	5	88
PAGEL, GL (WP)	1995 WC: A(s), R, C, NZ(s)	4	–	–
PARKER, WH (EP)	1965 A 1,2	2	–	–
PARTRIDGE, JEC (Tvl)	1903 Br 1	1	–	–
PAYN, C (N)	1924 Br 1,2	2	–	–
PELSER, HJM (Tvl)	1958 Fr 1; 1960 NZ 1,2,3,4; 1960–61 W, I, Fr; 1961 I; A 1,2	11	2	6
PFAFF, BD (WP)	1956 A 1	1	–	–
PICKARD, JAJ (WP)	1951–52 tour of UK – no tests; 1953 A 3,4; 1956 NZ 2; 1958 Fr 2	4	–	–
PIENAAR, JF (Tvl)	1993 Fr 1,2; A 1,2,3; Arg 1,2; S, W; 1994 E 2; NZ 2,3; Arg 1,2; 1995 WS; WC: A, WS, Fr, NZ	21	1	5
PIENAAR, TB (WP)	1921 tour of A & NZ – no tests	–	–	–
PIENAAR, ZMJ (OFS)	1980 SAm (H) 2(s); Br 1,2,3,4; SAm (A) 1,2; 1981 I 1,2; NZ 1,2,3; tour of USA – no tests	13	2	14
PITZER, G (NT)	1967 Fr 1,2,3,4; 1968 Br 1,2,3,4; Fr 1,2; 1969 A 3,4; 1969–70 tour of UK – no tests	12	–	–
POPE, CF (WP)	1974 Br 1,2,3,4; 1974 tour of Fr – no tests; 1975 Fr 1,2; 1976 NZ 2,3,4	9	1	4
POTGIETER, HJ (OFS)	1928 NZ 1,2	2	–	–
POTGIETER, HL (OFS)	1977 Wd	1	1	4
POTGIETER, R (OFS)	1969–70 tour of UK – no tests	–	–	–
POVEY, SA (WP)	1981 tour of NZ & USA – no tests	–	–	–
POWELL, AW (GW)	1896 Br 3	1	–	–
POWELL, JM (GW)	1891 Br 2; 1896 Br 3; 1903 Br 1,2	4	–	–
PRENTIS, RB (Tvl)	1980 SAm (H) 1,2; Br 1,2,3,4; SAm (A) 1,2; Fr; 1981 I 1,2	11	–	–
PRETORIUS, NF (Tvl)	1928 NZ 1,2,3,4	4	–	–
PRETORIUS, PIL (NT)	1992 tour of Fr & E – no tests	–	–	–
PRINSLOO, J (NT) (Poens)	1963 A 3	1	–	–
PRINSLOO, JC (Tvl)	1958 Fr 1,2	2	–	–
PRINSLOO, JP (Tvl) (Boet)	1928 NZ 1	1	–	–
PUTT, KB (N)	1994 tour of W, S & I – no tests	–	–	–
PUTTER, DJ (WT)	1963 A 1,2,4	3	–	–
RAAFF, JWE (GW)	1903 Br 1,2; 1906 S, W, E; 1910 Br 1	6	1	3
RAS, WJdeW (OFS)	1976 NZ 1(s); 1980 SAm (H) 2(s); tour of SAm – no tests	2	–	–
REECE-EDWARDS, H (N)	1992 tour to Fr & E – no tests; 1993 A 2	3	–	–
REID, A (WP)	1903 Br 3	1	1	3
REID, BC (Bor)	1933 A 4	1	–	–
REID, HG (Tvl)	1906 tour of UK – no tests	–	–	–
REINACH, J (OFS)	1986 NZC 1,2,3,4	4	2	8
RENS, IJ (Tvl)	1953 A 3,4	2	–	19
RETIEF, DF (NT)	1955 BR 1,2,4; 1956 A 1,2; NZ 1,2,3,4	9	4	12
REYNEKE, HJ (WP)	1910 Br 3	1	1	3
RICHARDS, AR (WP)	1891 Br 1,2,3	3	–	–
RICHTER, AJ (NT)	1992 Fr 1,2; E; 1993 tour to A – no tests; 1994 E2; NZ 1,2,3; 1995 WC: R, C, WS	10	4	20
RILEY, NM (ET)	1963 A 3	1	–	–
RIORDAN, CA (Tvl)	1910 Br 1,2	2	–	–
ROBERTS, H (Tvl)	1992 tour to Fr & E – no tests	–	–	–
ROBERTSON, IW (R)	1974 Fr 1,2; 1976 NZ 1,2,4	5	–	3
RODGERS, PH (NT)	1989 Wd 1,2; NZ 1; Fr 1,2; tour to E – no tests; 1993 tour to A – no tests	5	–	–
ROGERS, CD (Tvl)	1984 E,2; SAS 1,2	4	–	–
ROOS, GD (WP)	1910 Br 2,3	2	1	3
ROOS, PJ (WP)	1903 Br 3; 1906 I, W, E	4	–	–
ROSENBERG, W (Tvl)	1955 Br 2,3,4; 1956 NZ 3; 1958 Fr 1	5	2	6
ROSSOUW, CLC (Tvl)	1995 WS; WC: R, WS, Fr, NZ	5	1	5
ROSSOUW, DH (WP)	1953 A 3,4	2	1	3
ROSSOUW, PB (WT)	tour to Fr & E – no tests	–	–	–
ROUSSEAU, WP (WP)	1928 NZ 3,4	2	–	–
ROUX, FduT (WP)	1960–61 W; 1961 A 1,2; 1962 Br 1,2,3,4; 1963 A 2; 1965 A 1,2; NZ 1,2,3,4; 1968 Br 3,4; Fr 1,2; 1969 A 1,2,3,4; 1969–70 I; 1970 NZ 1,2,3,4	27	6	18
ROUX, JP (Tvl)	1994 E2; NZ 1,2,3; Arg 1; WC: R, C, Fr(s)	8	2	10
ROUX, OA (NT)	1968 tour of Fr – no tests; 1969–70 S, E, W; 1971 tour of A – no tests; 1972 E; 1974 Br 3,4	7	–	–
SAMUELS, TA (GW)	1896 Br 2,3,4	3	2	6
SAUERMANN, JT (Tvl)	1971 Fr 1,2; A 1; 1972 Br 1	5	–	–
SAUNDERS, MJ (Bor)	1951–52 tour of UK – no tests	–	–	–
SCHLEBUSCH, JJJ (OFS)	1974 Br 3,4; 1975 Fr 2	3	–	–
SCHMIDT, LU (NT)	1958 Fr 2; 1962 Br 2	2	–	–
SCHMIDT, UL (NT)	1986 NZC 1,2,3,4; 1989 Wd 1,2; 1992 NZ, A; 1993 Fr 1,2; A 1,2,3; 1994 Arg 1,2; S, W	17	2	9
SCHOEMAN, J (WP)	1963 A 3,4; 1965 I, S; A 1; NZ 1,2	7	–	–
SCHOLTZ, CP (Tvl)	1994 Arg 1; 1995 WC: R, C, WS	4	–	–
SCHOLTZ, H (WP)	1921 NZ 1,2	2	–	–
SCHUTTE, PJW (NT)	1992 tour of E – no tests	–	–	–
SCOTT, PA (Tvl)	1896 Br 1,2,3,4	4	–	–
SENDIN, WD (GW)	1921 NZ 2	1	1	3
SERFONTEIN, DJ (WP)	1980 SAm 2,3,4; SAm (A) 1,2; Fr; 1981 I 1,2; NZ 1,2,3; USA; 1982 SAm 1,2; 1984 E 1,2; SAS 1,2	19	3	12
SHAND, R (GW)	1891 Br 2,3	2	–	–
SHERRELL, LG (NT)	1994 tour of NZ – no tests	–	–	–
SHERRIFF, AR (Tvl)	1937 tour of A & NZ – no tests; 1938 Br 1,2,3	3	–	–
SHUM, EH (Tvl)	1912–13 E	1	–	–
SIEDLE, LB (N)	1921 tour of A & NZ – no tests	–	–	–
SINCLAIR, DJ (Tvl)	1951–52 tour of UK – no tests; 1955 Br 1,2,3,4	4	–	–
SINCLAIR, JH (Tvl)	1903 Br 1	1	–	–
SKENE, AL (WP)	1958 Fr 2	1	–	–
SLABBER, LJ (OFS)	1965 tour of A & NZ – no tests	–	–	–
SLATER, JT (EP)	1924 Br 3,4; 1928 NZ 1	3	2	6
SMAL, GP (WP)	1986 NZC 1,2,3,4; 1989 Wd 1,2	6	1	4
SMALL, JT (Tvl)	1992 NZ; A 1; Fr 1,2; E 1; 1993 Fr 1,2; A 1,2,3; Arg 1,2; 1994 E 1,2; NZ 1,2,3(s); Arg 1; 1995 WS; WC: A, R, Fr, NZ	23	10	50
SMIT, FC (WP)	1992 tour of Fr – no tests; E	1	–	–
SMITH, CW (GW)	1891 Br 2; 1896 Br 2,3	3	–	–
SMITH, CM (OFS)	1963 A 3,4; 1964 W, Fr; 1965 A 1,2; NZ 2	7	1	12
SMITH, DW (WP)	1891 Br 2	1	–	–
SMITH, DJ (Zimb-R)	1980 Br 1,2,3,4	4	–	–
SMITH, GAC (EP)	1938 Br 3	1	–	–

SMOLLAN, FC (Tvl)	1933 A 3,4,5	3	–	–
SNEDDEN, RCD (GW)	1891 Br 2	1	–	–
SNYMAN, DSL (WP)	1971 tour of A – no tests; 1972 E; 1974 Br 1,2(s): Fr 1,2; 1975 Fr 1,2; 1976 NZ 2,3; 1977 Wd	10	1	24
SNYMAN, JCP (OFS)	1974 Br 2,3,4; 1974 tour of Fr – no tests	3	–	18
SONNEKUS, GHH (OFS)	1974 Br 3; 1984 E 1,2	3	1	4
SPIES, JJ (NT)	1970 NZ 1,2,3,4; 1974 tour of A – no tests	4	–	–
STANDER, JCJ (OFS)	1974 Br 4(s); 1974 tour of Fr – no tests; 1976 NZ 2,3,4	5	–	–
STAPELBERG, WP (NT)	1974 Fr 1,2	2	2	8
STARKE, JJ (WP)	1956	1	–	–
STARKE, KT (WP)	1924 Br 1,2,3,4	4	3	13
STEENEKAMP, J (Tvl)	1958 Fr 1	1	–	–
STEGMANN, AC (WP)	1906 S, I	2	1	3
STEGMANN, JA (Tvl)	1912–13 S, I, W, E, Fr	5	5	15
STEWART, DA (WP)	1960 S; 1960–61 E S Fr; 1961 I; 1963 A 1,3,4; 1964 W; Fr; 1965 I	11	1	9
STOFBERG, MTS (OFS)	1976 NZ 2,3; 1977 Wd; 1980 SAm (H) 1,2; Br 1,2,3,4; SAm (A) 1,2; Fr; 1981 I 1,2; NZ 1,2; USA; 1982 SAm 1,2; 1984 E 1,2	21	6	24
STRACHAN, LC (Tvl)	1931–32 E, S; 1937 A 1,2; NZ 1,2,3; 1938 Br 1,2,3	10	–	–
STRAEULI, RAW (Tvl)	1994 NZ 1; Arg 1,2; S 1, W 1; 1995 WS; WC: WS, NZ(s)	8	4	20
STRANSKY, J (N)	1993 A 1,2,3; Arg 1; 1994 Arg 1,2; tour of W, S & I – no tests; 1995 WS; WC: A, R(s), C, Fr, NZ	12	4	132
STRAUSS, CP (WP)	1992 Fr 1,2; E; 1993 Fr 1,2; A 1,2,3; Arg 1,2; 1994 E 1; NZ 1,2; tour of W, S & I – no tests	15	4	20
STRAUSS, JA (WP)	1984 SAS 1,2	2	–	–
STRAUSS, JHP (Tvl)	1976 NZ 3,4; 1980 SAm (H) 1	3	–	–
STRAUSS, SSF (GW)	1921 NZ 3	1	–	–
STRYDOM, CF (WP)	1955 Br 3; 1956 A 1,2; NZ 1,4; 1958 Fr 1	6	–	–
STRYDOM, JJ (Tvl)	1993 Fr 2; A 1,2,3; Arg 1,2; 1994 E 1; 1995 WC: A, C, Fr, NZ	11	–	–
STRYDOM, LJ (NT)	1949 NZ 1,2	2	–	–
STYGER, JJ (OFS)	1992 NZ(s); A; Fr 1,2; E; 1993 Fr 2 (s), A 3(s)	7	–	–
SUTER, MR (N)	1965 I, S	2	–	–
SWANSON, PS (Tvl)	1971 tour of A – no tests	–	–	–
SWART, ISdeV (Tvl)	1993 A 1,2,3; Arg 1; 1994 E1,2; NZ 1,3; Arg 2(s), tour of W, S & I – no tests; 1995 WS; WC: A, WS, Fr, NZ	14	–	–
SWART, JJN (SWA)	1955 Br 1	1	1	3
TABERER, WS (GW)	1896 Br 2	1	–	–
TAYLOR, OB (N)	1962 Br 1	1	–	–
TEICHMANN, GH (N)	1993 tour to Arg – no tests	–	–	–
THEUNISSEN, DJ (GW)	1896 Br 3	1	–	–
THOMPSON, G (WP)	1912–13 S, I, W	3	–	–
TINDALL, JC (N)	1921 tour of SAm – no tests; 1924 Br 1; 1928 NZ 1,2,3,4; 1931–32 tour of UK – no tests	5	–	–
TOBIAS, EG (Bol) (SARFF)	1980 tour of SAm – no tests; 1981 I 1,2; tour of NZ & USA – no tests; 1984 E 1,2; SAS 1,2	6	1	22
TOD, NS (N)	1928 NZ 2	1	–	–
TOWNSEND, WH (N)	1921 NZ 1	1	–	–
TRENERY, WE (GW)	1891 Br 2	1	–	–
TRUSCOTT, JA (NT)	1992 tour to Fr & E – no tests	–	–	–
TRUTER, DR (WP)	1924 Br 2,4	2	–	–
TRUTER, JT (N)	1963 A 1; 1964 Fr; 1965 A 2	3	1	3
TURNER, FG (EP)	1933 A 1,2,3; 1937 A 1,2; NZ 1,2,3; 1938 Br 1,2,3	11	4	29
TWIGGE, RJ (NT)	1960 S	1	–	–
ULYATE, CA (Tvl)	1955 Br 1,2,3,4; 1956 NZ 1,2,3	7	1	6
UYS, PdeW (NT)	1960–61 W, E, S; 1961 I; A 1,2; 1962 Br 1,4; 1963 A 1,2; 1968 tour of Fr – no tests; 1969 A 1(s),2	12	–	–
VAN ASWEGEN, HJ (WP)	1981 NZ 1; tour of USA – no tests; 1982 SAm 2(s)	2	–	–
VAN BROEKHUIZEN, HD (WP)	1896 Br 4	1	–	–
VAN BUUREN, MCWE (Tvl)	1891 Br 1	1	–	–
VAN DE VYVER, DF (WP)	1937 A 2	1	–	–
VAN DEN BERG, DS (N)	1974 tour of Fr – no tests; 1975 Fr 1,2; 1976 NZ 1,2	4	–	–
VAN DEN BERGH, E (EP)	1994 Arg 2(s), tour of W, S & I – no tests	1	–	–
VAN DEN BERG, MA (WP)	1937 A 1,2,3	4	–	–
VAN DER HOFF, A de la R (Tvl)	1912–13 tour of UK – no tests	–	–	–
VAN DER MERWE, AJ (Bol)	1955 Br 2,3,4; 1956 A 1,2; NZ 1,2,3,4; 1958 Fr 1; 1960 S; NZ 2	12	–	–
VAN DER MERWE, AV (WP)	1931–32 W	1	–	–
VAN DER MERWE, BS (N)	1949 NZ 1	1	–	–
VAN DER MERWE, HS (NT)	1960 NZ 4; 1960–61 tour of UK – no tests; 1963 A 2,3,4; 1964 Fr	5	–	–
VAN DER MERWE, JP (WP)	1969–70 W	1	–	–
VAN DER MERWE, PR (SWD)	1981 NZ 2,3; USA; 1986 NZC 1,2; 1989 Wd	16	–	–
VANDERPLANK, BE (N)	1924 Br 3,4	2	–	–
VAN DER RYST, FE (Tvl)	1951–52 tour of UK – no tests	–	–	–
VAN DER SCHYFF, JH (GW)	1949 NZ 1,2,3,4; 1955 Br 1	5	–	10
VAN DER SCHYFF, PJ (WT)	1969–70 tour of UK – no tests	–	–	–
VAN DER WATT, AE (WP)	1969–70 S(s); E, I; 1971 tour of A – no tests	3	–	–
VAN DER WESTHUIZEN, JC (WP)	1928 NZ 2,3,4; 1931–32 I	4	1	3
VAN DER WESTHUIZEN, JF (N)	1994 tour of NZ – no tests; tour of W, S & I – no tests	–	–	–
VAN DER WESTHUIZEN, JH (WP)	1931–32 I, E, S	3	–	–
VAN DER WESTHUIZEN, JH (NT)	1993 tour of A – no tests; Arg 1,2; 1994 E 1,2(s); tour of NZ – no tests; Arg 2; S, W; 1995 WS; WC: A, C(s), WS, Fr, NZ	13	5	25
VAN DEVENTER, PI (GW)	1969–70 tour of UK – no tests	–	–	–
VAN DRUTEN, NJV (Tvl)	1924 Br 1,2,3,4; 1928 NZ 1,2,3,4	8	2	6
VAN HEERDEN, AJ (Tvl)	1921 NZ 1,3	2	1	3
VAN HEERDEN, FJ (WP)	1994 E 1,2(s); NZ 3	3	–	–
VAN HEERDEN, JL (NT)	1974 Br 3,4; Fr 1,2; 1975 Fr 1,2; 1976 NZ 1,2,3,4; 1977 Wd; 1980 Br 1,3,4; SAm (A) 1,2; Fr	17	1	4
VAN JAARSVELD, CJ (Tvl)	1949 NZ 1	1	–	–
VAN JAARSVELDT, DC (R)	1960 S 1	1	1	3
VAN NIEKERK, BB (OFS)	1960–61 tour of UK – no tests	–	–	–
VAN NIEKERK, JA (WP)	1928 NZ 4; 1931–32 tour of UK – no tests	1	–	–
VAN REENEN, GL (WP)	1937 A 2; NZ 1	2	2	6
VAN RENEN, CG (WP)	1891 Br 3; 1896 Br 1,4	3	–	–
VAN RENEN, WA (WP)	1903 Br 1,3	2	–	–
VAN RENSBURG, JTJ (Tvl)	1992 NZ; A 1993 Fr 1,2; A 1; 1994 NZ 2	7	–	40
VAN RENSBURG, MC (N)	1969–70 tour of UK – no tests	–	–	–
VAN ROOYEN, GW (Tvl)	1921 NZ 2,3	2	–	–
VAN RYNEVELD, RCB (WP)	1910 Br 2,3	2	–	–

VAN SCHOOR, RAM (R)	1949 NZ 2,3,4; 1951–52 S, I, W, E, Fr; 1953 A 1,2,3,4	12	2	6
VAN STADEN, JA (NT)	1974 tour of Fr – no tests	–	–	–
VAN VOLLENHOVEN, KT (NT)	1955 Br 1,2,3,4; 1956 A 1,2; NZ 3	7	4	15
VAN VUUREN, TFJ (EP)	1912–13 S, I, W, E, Fr	5	–	–
VAN WYK, CJ (Tvl)	1951–52 S, I, W, E, Fr; 1953 A 1,2,3,4; 1955 Br 1; 1956 tour of A & NZ – no tests	10	6	–
VAN WYK, JFB (NT)	1970 NZ 1,2,3,4; 1971 Fr 1; A 1,2,3; 1972 E; 1974 Br 1,3,4; 1976 NZ 3,4	15	–	–
VAN WYK, SP (WP)	1928 NZ 1,2	2	–	–
VAN ZYL, BP (WP)	1960–61 tour of UK – no tests; 1961 I	4	–	–
VAN ZYL, CGP (OFS)	1965 NZ 1,2	4	–	–
VAN ZYL, GH (WP)	1958 Fr 1; 1960 S; NZ 1,2,3,4; 1960–61 W, I, E, S, Fr; 1961; A 1,2; 1962 Br 1,3,4	17	4	12
VAN ZYL, HJ (Tvl)	1960 NZ 1,2,3,4; 1960–61 I, E, S; 1961 I; A 1,2	10	6	18
VAN ZYL, PJ (Bol)	1960–61 tour of UK – no tests; 1961 I	1	–	–
VELDSMAN, PE (WP)	1977 Wd	1	–	–
VENTER, BJ (OFS)	1994 E 1,2; NZ 1,2,3; Arg 1,2; tour of W, S & I – no tests; 1995 WC: R, C, WS(s), NZ(s)	11	1	5
VENTER, FD (Tvl)	1931–32 W, S; 1933 A 3	3	–	–
VERSFELD, C (WP)	1891 Br 3	1	–	–
VERSFELD, M (WP)	1891 Br 1,2,3	3	–	–
VIGNE, JT (Tvl)	1891 Br 1,2,3	3	–	–
VILJOEN, JF (GW)	1971 Fr 1,2,3; 1972 E	6	2	6
VILJOEN, JT (N)	1971 A 1,2,3	3	2	6
VILLET, JV (WP)	1984 E 1,2	2	–	–
VISAGIE, GP (N)	1981 tour of NZ & USA – no tests	–	–	–
VISAGIE, PJ (GW)	1967 Fr 1,2,3,4; 1968 Br 1,2,3,4; Fr 1,2; 1969 A 1,2,3,4; 1969–70 S, E; 1970 NZ 1,2,3,4; 1971 Fr 1,2; A 1,2,3	25	6	130
VISAGIE, RG (OFS)	1984 E 1,2; SAS 1,2	4	–	–
VISSER, JdeV (WP)	1980 tour of SAm – no tests; 1981 NZ 2; USA	2	–	–
VISSER, M (WP)	1995 WS(s)	1	–	–
VISSER, PJ (Tvl)	1933 A 2	1	–	–
VIVIER(S), SS (OFS)	1951–52 tour of UK – no tests; 1956 A 1,2; NZ 2,3,4	5	–	11
VOGEL, ML (OFS)	1974 Br 2(s)	1	–	–
WAGENAAR, C (NT)	1977 Wd	1	–	–
WAHL, JJ (WP)	1949 NZ 1	1	–	–
WALKER, AP (N)	1921 NZ 1,2; 1924 Br 1,2,3,4	6	–	–
WALKER, HN (OFS)	1953 A 3; 1956 A 2; NZ 1,4	4	–	–
WALKER, HW (Tvl)	1910 Br 1,2,3	3	–	–
WALTON, DC (N)	1964 Fr; 1965 I, S; NZ 3,4; 1968 tour of Fr – no tests; 1969 A 1,2; 1969–70 E	8	–	–
WARING, FW (WP)	1931–32 I, E; 1933 A 1,2,3,4,5	7	2	6
WATT, HH (WP)	1937 tour of A & NZ – no tests	–	–	–
WEEPNER, JS (WP)	1921 tour of A & NZ – no tests	–	–	–
WEGNER, GN (WP)	1993 Fr 2; A 1,2,3; tour of Arg – no tests	4	–	–
WENTZEL, GJ (EP)	1960–61 tour of UK – no tests	–	–	–
WESSELS, JJ (WP)	1896 Br 1,2,3	3	–	–
WESSELS, JW (OFS)	1965 tour of I & S – no tests	–	–	–
WESSELS, PW (OFS)	1951–52 tour of UK – no tests	–	–	–
WHIPP, PJM (WP)	1974 Br 1,2; 1974 tour of Fr – no tests; 1975 Fr 1; 1976 NZ 1,3,4; 1980 SAm (H) 1,2	8	1	4
WHITE, J (Bor)	1931–32 W; 1933 A 1,2,3,4,5; 1937 A 1,2; NZ 1,2	10	2	10
WIESE, JJ (Tvl)	1993 Fr 1; tour to A – no tests; 1994 tour of NZ – no tests; tour of W, S & I – no tests; 1995 WS; WC: R, C, WS, Fr, NZ	7	–	–
WILLIAMS, AE (GW)	1910 Br 1	1	–	–
WILLIAMS, AP (WP) (SARFF)	1984 E 1,2	2	–	–
WILLIAMS, CM (WP)	1993 tour to A – no tests; Arg 2; 1994 E1,2; NZ 1,2,3; Arg 1,2; S 1, W 1; 1995 WS; WC: WS, Fr, NZ	14	9	45
WILLIAMS, DO (WP)	1931–32 tour of UK – no tests; 1937 A 1,2; NZ 1,2,3; 1938 Br 1,2,3	8	5	15
WILLIAMS, JG (NT)	1971 Fr 1,2; A 1,2,3; 1972 E; 1974 Br 1,2,4; Fr 1,2; 1976 NZ 1,2	13	–	–
WILSON, LG (WP)	1960 NZ 3,4; 1960–61 W, I, E, Fr; 1961 I; A 1,2; 1962 Br 1,2,3,4; 1963 A 1,2,3,4; 1964 Fr; W; Fr; 1965 I, S; A 1,2; 1963 A 1,2,3,4	27	–	6
WOLMARANS, BJ (OFS)	1977 Wd; 1981 tour of NZ & USA – no tests	1	1	4
WRENTMORE, GM (WP)	1912–13 tour of UK – no tests	–	–	–
WRIGHT, GD (EP)	1986 NZC 3,4; 1989 Wd 1,2	4	1	4
WYNESS, MRK (WP)	1962 Br 1,2,3,4; 1963 A 2	5	1	3
ZELLER, WC (N)	1921 NZ 2,3	2	–	–
ZIMERMAN, M (WP)	1931–32 W, I, E, S	4	1	3

SOUTH AFRICA'S OVERALL TEST RECORD (1891–1995)

Opponents	Played	Won	Lost	Drawn	For	Against
New Zealand	42	21	18	3	475	442
British Isles	40	20	14	6	471	383
Australia	33	23	10	0	510	332
France	24	14	5	5	420	263
England	12	7	4	1	175	136
Ireland	10	8	1	1	159	73
Scotland	9	6	3	0	138	48
Wales	8	7	0	1	81	27
South America	6	5	1	0	156	86
Argentina	4	4	0	0	169	97
New Zealand Cavaliers	4	3	1	0	96	62
World Team	3	3	0	0	87	59
South America & Spain	2	2	0	0	54	28
Western Samoa	2	2	0	0	102	22
USA	1	1	0	0	38	7
Romania	1	1	0	0	21	8
Canada	1	1	0	0	20	0
	202	128	57	17	3 172	2 073

ANALYSIS OF POINTS IN TESTS

	South Africa				Opponents			
	T	C	P	D	T	C	P	D
vs New Zealand	55	33	57	12*	56	26	56	11
vs British Isles	81	41	37	7	58	23	38	12*
vs Australia	90^	39	38	8	37	20	49	5
vs France	54	32	52	5	23	14	32	14
vs England	18	12	25	2	12	6	23	2
vs Ireland	32	12	8	4	10	5	10	–
vs Scotland	27	16	4	1	9	5	2	1
vs Wales	13	6	6	2	3	–	6	–
vs South America	22	16	6	6	7	5	13	3
vs Argentina	23	15	8	–	9	8	11	1
vs New Zealand Cavaliers	7	7	15	3	5^	3	11	1
vs World Team	11	5	10	1	9	7	3	–
vs South America & Spain	9	3	4	–	3	2	4	–
vs Western Samoa	15	9	3	–	3	2	1	–
vs USA	8	3	–	–	1	–	1	–
vs Romania	2	1	3	–	1	–	1	–
vs Canada	2	2	2	–	–	–	–	–
	469	252	278	51	246	126	261	50

* includes one dropped goal from a mark; ^ includes one penalty try

MOST POINTS BY A SPRINGBOK IN A TEST MATCH

Opponents	Year	Venue	Player	Points
Western Samoa	1995	Johannesburg	GK Johnson	28
France	1975	Pretoria	GR Bosch	22
Australia	1995	Cape Town	JT Stransky	22
England	1984	Port Elizabeth	JW Heunis	21
New Zealand	1981	Wellington	HE Botha	20
Western Samoa	1995	Johannesburg	CM Williams	20
British Isles	1962	Bloemfontein	K Oxlee	16
South America	1982	Pretoria	HE Botha	15
Scotland	1951	Edinburgh	AO Geffin	15
New Zealand	1995	Johannesburg	JT Stransky	15
Wales	1964	Durban	K Oxlee	12
Ireland	1981	Durban	HE Botha	12
USA	1981	New York	RH Mordt	12

* R Blair scored 21 points against the World Team in Pretoria (1977);
HE Botha scored 21 points against the New Zealand Cavaliers in Pretoria (1986).

LEADING SOUTH AFRICAN SCORERS IN TEST MATCHES

(Players who have scored a total of 20 or more points in all test matches.)

	Tests	Tries	Conv.	PG	DG	Points
1. Naas Botha (1980–92)	25	2*	46	45	15	280
2. Joel Stransky (1993–)	12	4	17	20	3	132
3. Piet Visagie (1967–71)	25	6	20	19	5	130
4. Gerald Bosch (1974–76)	9	–	7	23	2	89
5. Keith Oxlee (1960–65)	19	5	14	14	1	88
6. Danie Gerber (1980–92)	24	19^	1	–	–	82
7. Gavin Johnson (1993–)	7	5	14	11	–	76
8. Ian McCallum (1970–74)	11	–	10	14	–	62
9. André Joubert (1989–)	3	2	5	12	–	56
10. Gerry Brand (1928–38)	16	–	13	7	2*	55
11. James Small (1992–)	12	10	–	–	–	50
12. Okey Geffin (1949–51)	7	–	9	10	–	48
13. Gerrie Germishuys (1974–81)	20	12*	–	–	–	48
14. Ray Mordt (1980–84)	18	12*	–	–	–	48
15. Tiny Naudé (1963–68)	14	2	4	11	–	47
16. Bennie Osler (1924–33)	17	2	6	4	4*	46
17. Chester Williams (1994–95)	14	9	–	–	–	45
18. Johan Heunis (1981–89)	14	2*	6	7	–	41
19. Duggie Morkel (1906–13)	9	3	7	5	–	38
20. Freddy Turner (1933–38)	11	4	4	3	–	29
21. Roy Dryburgh (1955–60)	8	3	5	3	–	28
22. HO de Villiers (1967–70)	14	–	7	4	–	26
23. Jannie Engelbrecht (1960–69)	33	8	–	–	–	24
24. John Gainsford (1960–67)	33	8	–	–	–	24
25. Dawie Snyman (1972–77)	10	2*	1	4	2	24
26. Theuns Stofberg (1976–84)	21	6*	–	–	–	24
27. Errol Tobias (1980–84)	6	1*	3	4	–	22
28. Ferdie Bergh (1931–38)	17	7	–	–	–	21
29. Jan Ellis (1965–76)	38	7	–	–	–	21
30. Robbie Blair (1977)	1	–	3	5	–	21
31. Dick Lockyear (1960–61)	6	–	4	4	–	20
32. Rob Louw (1980–84)	19	5*	–	–	–	20
33. Tiaan Strauss (1992–94)	15	4	–	–	–	20
34. Adriaan Richter (1992–95)	10	4	–	–	–	20

* these tries and drop goals count 4 points each; ^ includes 15x 4-point tries and 2x 5-point tries.
NOTE: Apart from those noted * or ^ all other tries and drop goals are valued at 3 points each.

MOST TRIES BY A SPRINGBOK IN A TEST MATCH

CM Williams	4	vs Western Samoa World Cup	1995
EE McHardy	3	vs Ireland	1912
JA Stegmann	3	vs Ireland	1912
KT van Vollenhoven	3	vs British Isles	1955
HJ van Zyl	3	vs Australia	1961
RH Mordt	3	vs New Zealand	1981
RH Mordt	3	vs USA	1981
DM Gerber	3	vs South America	1982
DM Gerber	3	vs England	1984
GK Johnson	3	vs Western Samoa	1995

LEADING SOUTH AFRICAN TRY SCORERS IN TEST MATCHES

(Figures in parentheses are the number of test matches played.)

Danie Gerber	19 (24)
Gerrie Germishuys	12 (20)
Ray Mordt	12 (18)
Chester Williams	11 (14)
James Small	9 (23)
John Gainsford	8 (33)
Jannie Engelbrecht	8 (33)
Ferdie Bergh	7 (17)
Jan Ellis	7 (38)
Boetie McHardy	6 (5)
Basie van Wyk	6 (10)
Hennie van Zyl	6 (10)
Mannetjies Roux	6 (27)
Syd Nomis	6 (25)
Piet Visagie	6 (25)
Theuns Stofberg	6 (21)
Jan Stegmann	5 (5)
Dai Williams	5 (8)
Chris Koch	5 (22)
Theuns Briers	5 (7)
Keith Oxlee	5 (19)
Doug Hopwood	5 (22)
Eben Olivier	5 (16)
Piet Greyling	5 (25)
Rob Louw	5 (19)
Joost van der Westhuizen	5 (12)
Gavin Johnson	5 (7)
Jack Morkel	4 (5)
Freddy Turner	4 (11)
Tom van Vollenhoven	4 (7)
Daan Retief	4 (9)
Salty du Rand	4 (21)
Hugo van Zy	l4 (17)
Gert Muller	4 (14)
Carel du Plessis	4 (12)
Tiaan Strauss	4 (15)
Adriaan Richter	4 (10)
Bob Loubser	3 (7)
Duggie Morkel	3 (4)
Kenny Starke	3 (4)
Louis Babrow	3 (5)
Tjol Lategan	3 (11)
Hennie Muller	3 (13)
Chum Ochse	3 (7)
Roy Dryburgh	3 (8)
Corra Dirksen	3 (10)
Dawie de Villiers	3 (25)
Peter Cronje	3 (7)
Morné du Plessis	3 (22)
Willie du Plessis	3 (14)
Divan Serfontein	3 (19)

SOUTH AFRICAN CAPTAINS IN TEST MATCHES

22	DJ de Villers
21	JF Pienaar
15	M du Plessis
11	JFK Marais
10	AS (Avril) Malan
9	HSV Muller, JT Claassen
8	PJ Nel
7	W Claassen
6	HE Botha
5	WA Millar, BL Osler, SS Vivier(s)
4	PK Albertyn, PJ Mostert, DH Craven, SP Fry, GF (Abie) Malan, CM Smith, MTS Stofberg
3	FTD Aston, PJ Roos, WH (Boy) Morkel, F du Plessis, TP Bedford
2	BH Heatlie, DFT Morkel, RG Dryburgh, DJ Serfontein, JC Breedt
1	HH Castens, RCD Snedden, AR Richards, A Frew, JM Powell, HW Carolin, FJ Dobbin, BJ Kenyon, JA du Rand, DC van Jaarsveldt, PJF Greyling, CP Strauss, A Richter

* TB (Theo) Pienaar, captain of the 1921 Springbok team in Australia and New Zealand did not play in a test match.

LEADING SOUTH AFRICAN SCORERS (ALL MATCHES)

Players who have scored 50 or more points in all official matches in the Springbok jersey:

	Matches	Points
1. Naas Botha	32	411
2. Gerry Brand	46	293
3. Piet Visagie	44	240
4. Joel Stransky	26	221
5. Keith Oxlee	48	201
6. André Joubert	31	199
7. Gavin Johnson	17	173
8. Basie Vivier(s)	31	165
9. Dougie Morkel	40	140
10. Ian McCallum	17	134
11. Jannie Engelbrecht	67	132
12. Gerald Bosch	14	132
13. Freddy Turner	24	131
14. Wynand Mans	19	123
15. Okey Geffin	17	121
16. Roy Dryburgh	20	116

LEADING SOUTH AFRICAN SCORERS (ALL MATCHES) (continued)

17. Joost van der Westhuizen	34	115
18. Chester Williams	33	110
19. Bennie Osler	30	108
20. Danie Gerber	28	100
21. Dick Lockyear	20	97
22. Jan Ellis	74	97
23. John Gainsford	71	93
24. Tiny Naudé	28	90
21. Ray Mordt	25	88
22. Frik du Preez	87	87
23. Dawie Snyman	22	86
24. James Small	37	85
25. HO de Villiers	29	80
26. Gerhard Morkel	33	79
27. Gerrie Germishuys	29	76
28. Hennie le Roux	41	75
29. Paddy Carolin	18	73
30. Johan Heunis	24	72
31. De Wet Ras	5	69
32. Paul Johnstone	35	68
33. Bob Loubser	23	66
34. Errol Tobias	15	65
35. Tom von Vollenhoven	23	63
36. Boetie McHardy	17	60
37. Gysie Pienaar	21	59
38. Adriaan Richter	29	55
39. Anton Stegmann	16	54
40. Hennie van Zyl	24	54
41. Thys Burger	13	52
42. Dai Williams	18	51

LEADING SOUTH AFRICAN TRY SCORERS (ALL MATCHES)

Players who have scored 10 or more tries in all official tour matches including test matches played both away and in South Africa. Figures in parentheses are the number of matches played.

Jannie Engelbrecht	44	(67)
Jan Ellis	32	(74)
John Gainsford	31	(71)
Danie Gerber	24	(28)
Joost van der Westhuizen	23	(34)
Bob Loubser	22	(23)
Ray Mordt	22	(25)
Chester Williams	22	(33)
Boetie McHardy	20	(17)
Tom von Vollenhoven	20	(23)
Gerrie Germishuys	19	(29)
Anton Stegmann	18	(16)
Freddy Turner	18	(24)
Hennie van Zyl	18	(24)
Dai Williams	17	(18)
James Small	17	(37)
Chum Ochse	16	(22)
Hannes Viljoen	16	(10)
Ruben Kruger	16	(30)
Roy Dryburgh	15	(20)
Mike Antelme	15	(25)
Doug Hopwood	15	(53)
Syd Nomis	15	(54)
Gert Muller	15	(20)
Attie van Heerden	14	(17)
Morris Zimerman	14	(18)
Ferdie Bergh	14	(41)
Louis Babrow	14	(16)
Paul Johnstone	14	(35)
Wynand Mans	14	(19)
Gert Brynard	14	(21)
Andy van der Watt	14	(22)
Jan Stegmann	13	(16)
Bill Zeller	13	(14)
Pat Lyster	13	(11)
Mannetjies Roux	13	(56)
Thys Burger	13	(13)
Ponie van der Westhuizen	12	(16)
Daan Retief	12	(21)
Frik du Preez	12	(87)
Hannes Marais	12	(75)
Edrich Krantz	12	(11)
Tiaan Strauss	12	(37)
Jack Hirsch	11	(18)
Buks Marais	11	(18)
Martin Saunders	11	(14)
Chris Koch	11	(46)
Trix Truter	11	(16)
Keith Oxlee	11	(48)
Rob Louw	11	(28)
Jacques Olivier	11	(26)
André Joubert	11	(31)
Japie le Roux	10	(9)
Apie van der Hoff	10	(9)
Wally Mills	10	(13)
Johnny Bester	10	(14)
Eben Olivier	10	(34)
Carel du Plessis	10	(22)

287

REFERENCES

In addition to the files of the *Cape Times, Argus, Die Burger, Beeld, Vaderland, Transvaler, Citizen, Volksblad, EP Herald, Natal Mercury, Rapport, Die Huisgenoot, Sunday Times* and the *Star*, the following books were referred to:

Cape Times (compiled and edited by): *Sports and Sportsmen*, 1925.
Claassen, W & D Retief: *More Than Just Rugby*, Hans Strydom Publishers, 1987.
Clarke, D & P Booth: *The Boot*, AH & AW Reed, 1966.
Craven, D: *Oubaas Mark*, Afrikaanse Pers Bpk, 1959.
Craven, D: *Springbok Story*, R Beerman, 1954.
Craven, D: *Toetsprestasies*, Afrikaanse Pers Bpk, 1953.
Craven, D: *Ek Speel vir Suid-Afrika*, Nasionale Pers, 1949.
Difford, ID: *History of South African Rugby Football*, The Speciality Press of SA Ltd, 1933.
Gainsford, J & N Leck: *Nice Guys Come Second*, Don Nelson, 1974.
Gault, I: *The 1981 Springboks in New Zealand*, Wellington Newspapers Ltd, 1981.
Gerber, H: *Danie Craven se top-Springbokke*, Tafelberg, 1977.
Glasspool, B: *One in the Eye*, Howard Timmins, 1976.
Gouws, L: *Frik du Preez Rugbyreus*, Janssonius & Heyns, 1971.
Greyvenstein, C: *20 Great Springboks*, Don Nelson, 1987.
Greyvenstein, C: *Springbok Saga*, Don Nelson, 1992.
Greyvenstein, C: T*he Bennie Osler Story*, Howard Timmins, 1970.
Greyvenstein, C: *They Made Headlines*, Don Nelson, 1972.
Jenkins, V: *Lions Rampant*, Cassell, 1956.
Lalanne, D: *Le Grand Combat du Quinze de France*, Editions de la Table Ronde, 1959.
Louw, R (with J Cameron-Dow): *For the Love of Rugby*, Hans Strydom Publishers, 1987.
McLean, T: *Beaten by the Boks*, Howard Timmins, 1960.
McLean, T: *The Bok Busters*, Howard Timmins, 1965.
Medworth, CO: *Battle of the Giants*, Howard Timmins, 1960.
Medworth, CO (ed): *The History of Natal Rugby*, Howard Timmins, 1964.
Millar, WA: *My Recollections and Reminiscences*, Juta & Co Ltd, 1926.
Nicholls, MF: *All Blacks in Springbokland*, LT Watkins Ltd, Wellington, New Zealand, 1928.
Parker, AC: *Giants of South African Rugby*, Howard Timmins, 1955.
Parker, AC: *Now is the Hour*, Howard Timmins, 1965.
Parker, AC: *Ringside View*, Howard Timmins, 1963.
Parker, AC: *Ruffled Roosters*, Howard Timmins, 1965.
Parker, AC: *The Lion Tamers*, Howard Timmins, 1968.
Parker, AC: *WP Rugby*, WPRFU, 1983.
Platnauer, JL (ed): *Springbokken Tour in Great Britain*, GEO Wunderlich, 1907.
Price, M: *Springbok Talk*, Howard Timmins, 1955.
Price, M: *Wallabies Without Armour*, Howard Timmins, 1969.
Reason, J: *The Unbeaten Lions*, Rugby Books, 1974.
Retief, D: *Springboks Under Siege*, Now Publications, 1981.
Reyburn, W: *The Lions*, Stanley Paul, 1967.
Reyburn, W: *There Was Also Some Rugby*, Stanley Paul, 1970.
Sacks, JE: *South Africa's Greatest Springboks*, Sporting Publications, Wellington, New Zealand, 1938.
Scott, B & T McLean: *The Bob Scott Story*, Howard Timmins, 1956.
Shippey, K: *The Unbeatables*, 1971.
Starmer-Smith, N: *The Barbarians*, Macdonald & Jane's, 1977.
Sweet, R: *Pride of the Lions*, Howard Timmins, 1962.
Sweet, R: *Springbok and Silverfern*, Howard Timmins, 1960.
Thornett, J: *This World of Rugby*, Murray, 1967.
Van Rooyen (ed): *SA Rugby Annual* (several editions)
Veysey, A: *Colin Meads, All Black*, Collins, 1974.